THE 40 THOUSAND MILE MAN

ODYSSEY OF A PILGRIM

GEORGE FLORIAN WALTER

WORD ASSOCIATION PUBLISHERS
www.wordassociation.com
1.800.827.7903

ISBN: 978-1-63385-318-8

Designed and published by
Word Association Publishers
205 Fifth Avenue
Tarentum, Pennsylvania 15084

www.wordassociation.com
1.800.827.7903

CONTENTS

Chapter 6 - Pilgrimage in Bible Lands

Conclusion

ACKNOWLEDGMENTS

Kenneth F. Yossa, for editorial assistance and encouragement.

Kevin S. Patterson, for photos in "section three" and for cover photo which was taken August 27, 2011, on Three Mile Hill coming into Mount Pleasant, Pennsylvania.

Fred del Guidice, for portrait on back cover (oil on canvas) entitled: *Pilgrim George: The Fire of God's Love*, painted on June 11, 2013, in his studio in Ohio.

Thomas Walter, for storing all of my notes on "George's shelf" in his basement while I was walking to Jerusalem.

Pat, Dorothy, Peggy, and Bianca for transcribing my thirty-four cassette tapes from my 1988 walk to the Shrine of Our Lady of Guadalupe in Mexico.

Benefactors who helped me along the way all these years.

Benefactors who contributed to the publication of this book.

The Lord, to whom all glory be given.

FOREWORD

Do you know anyone who has walked 40,000 miles through forty-one countries on three continents quietly lifting up the Cross of Jesus and witnessing to the presence of Jesus in his heart? I know only one: George Florian Walter. Looking like a modern-day John the Baptist, but with a tender heart like Jesus, George embraced the life of a pilgrim/*poustinik* and sought to do the will of his Father. This all-consuming passion took him to distant places in remote parts of the world.

Early on, George was inspired to enter the seminary to study for the Catholic priesthood in the Diocese of Pittsburgh. Twelve years of spiritual formation grounded him in Scripture, in the teaching and traditions of the Church, and in the lives of the saints. But there was a void, a restlessness that could not be satisfied in the seminary. Disappointing many of his friends and family members, and upon completing his seminary studies in 1967, George put his pursuit of priesthood on hold, and drifted into a difficult time of questioning and searching.

In 1970, George embarked on a 4,000-mile pilgrimage across Europe and across the Middle East to Jerusalem. There, at last, George heard the Lord speak to his heart: *"This pilgrimage is over. But you will remain a pilgrim for the rest of your life. Now you will pilgrimage in the desert of the city of man."* That message from God was life changing!

"In May of 1970, I had come to know Jesus as my Lord and Savior walking alone through the desert in northern Spain. And I had come to know the Holy Spirit in a personal way in the community of the believers in January of 1973, in Pittsburgh, Pennsylvania. In a period of six years (1967-73) the Lord had filled in what I could not get from books, classes and sacraments. I had to set aside all of these "riches," admit my poverty, and set out on the journey of trusting in the Lord. Now I had something worthwhile to share and the next fifteen years (1973-88) would be a time of growing deeper in prayer as a hermit and as a *poustinik,* and as a time of service–especially to youths–in the power of the Holy Spirit."

Something was happening deep in George's heart that allowed him to surrender himself more fully to a loving God who would take him across unchartered waters. As a pilgrim, George would embrace a form of eremetical life and ministry practiced by the Desert Fathers of the fourth and fifth centuries in Egypt, in Syria, in Palestine (and eventually) in Russia, and elsewhere. Living as a hermit is an integral part of the Christian Gospel that cannot be jettisoned as archaic. George's vocation is unique, to say the least, but not crazy or foolish. Some think that hermits are misanthropes who dislike people. Not so. Pilgrim George traveled with a joyful heart, discovering family everywhere on his journeys, and welcoming their hospitality. He saw Jesus in the people of the world and found peace and serenity in the beauty of creation around him.

Pilgrim George traveled light with little money in his pocket so he relied upon the kindness and generosity of many people so as to arrive at his destinations. He slept in monasteries, in convents, in rectories, and in homes of believers when the opportunity presented itself. But more often, he slept under the stars or in his tent pitched alongside the road in a cluster of trees. George was most grateful when nonbelievers offered him hospitality, for it offered him a unique opportunity to tell them about Jesus. Normally bathing and washing his clothes in roadside streams, George relished an occasional shower and a chance to wash his clothing.

In some towns Pilgrim George was a celebrity who gave interviews to newspaper and television reporters, and often accepted speaking engagements. People wanted to know who was this foreigner and what was he doing in their country? In one church, people flocked to this wandering hermit to be prayed over, and the session lasted many hours. But suspicion and rejection traveled with him as well. The providence of God was evident repeatedly when George moved from country to country where armed troops patrolled the borders. There were occasional attacks by uncomprehending fringe groups who did not want the Cross of Jesus lifted up in their community. Through it all, Pilgrim George did not waver in his love for all people, and radiated God's peace and joy to them.

One of the highlights for George was at the Church of the Nativity in Bethlehem. There, on Christmas Eve of the Jubilee Year celebrating Jesus' 2000th birthday, he writes:

> I found a place to stand just a few feet from the venerated niche and, overcome with emotion, I began to thank the Lord for getting me here after eight years of walking 26,000 miles, across North America, Asia, and Europe, and to think of how He had gotten me past border guards and customs officials, over mountain passes, and across deserts. In spite of being thrown on the ground by thieves, pelted with stones by Muslim children, stolen from and lied to, deliberately misled and refused service, ousted from churches and shrines, drenched by rain and baked by the sun, lost in strange cities and cursed in a dozen languages, here I was standing on this holy night at this holy place to celebrate the Lord's 2000th birthday in Bethlehem. Was that a miracle in itself? The impact of it all was overwhelming.

I first met George Walter in the early 1970s, while active in the charismatic renewal in Pittsburgh. I did not know of his seminary background but was struck by his knowledge of Scripture and by his deep spirituality. I could see that he was the real deal, spending many hours in solitude and prayer, and walking everywhere. I did not know at the time that he would choose the life of a pilgrim/ *poustinik*. Occasionally, I would bump into George at spiritual events and would hear of his latest pilgrimage on foot. It was beautiful to listen to the stories of his encounters on the road. The enthusiasm in his voice revealed a man deeply in love with his God who transported that love to all the people he met.

What makes a man leave all that life has to offer and to seek communion with God in solitude? It is a calling rooted in a deep relationship with the Father, Son, and Holy Spirit. George's greatest desire was to "to be faithful to his call to walk in faith, lifting up the Cross of Jesus on the highways and byways of the world." In our world, very few will be called to live as a pilgrim/*poustinik*. Yet Pilgrim George reminds us that our journey in the world is brief; our stay in heaven is eternal. His life story challenges us to look at reality from God's perspective: why we are here on earth and where are we going? We all need to keep our eyes fixed on Jesus (Heb 2:12) and live out the gospel according to our state in life with honesty and integrity. "The real pilgrim is seeking the will of God – not his own will. A pilgrim has no security at all: he is a stranger in a strange land. His whole security is in the Lord and His promise to take care of those who did not worry about the things of this life (Mt 6:25-34)." We have before us an inspiring testimony of faith that can affect our outlook on life forever.

In his prologue, George shares many uplifting reasons that explain why he wrote his autobiography. I trust the reader will be inspired by the humility and conviction of this pilgrim/*poustinik* who seeks to do the will of God in all things. A closing thought from Pilgrim George, "Be at peace, all. I love you and bless you always, in Jesus,

Mary, and Joseph." Receive his blessing today and bring it to others. I am blessed to know Pilgrim George as a friend, as an intercessor, and as a servant of God. I will treasure his story and share it with others. May your pilgrim journey be strengthened by learning about this humble mystic who sought to do all for the glory of God.

Rev. Michael Salvagna, CP
St. Paul of the Cross Monastery
Pittsburgh, Pennsylvania

PROLOGUE

Why this book was written

Because I believe God told me to write it, and because He gave me the desire and provided me with the means of time, place, computer, assistance, and finances.

To glorify the Lord and to give Him credit for what He was able to do through my willingness to take His Word literally, leaving everything and radically trusting in His Divine Providence (Lk 14:23; Mt 6:25-34, 19:27-29).

As a personal testimony to the real and abiding transcendence of Jesus Christ and the Kingdom that He came to establish, which must not be reduced simply to another Social Gospel message that attempts to make a Paradise for man on earth.

To draw attention to the necessity of putting first, the First of the Two Great Commandments (love of God and love of one's neighbor) that Jesus gave us in Mt 23:34ff. If one does not "love God with one's whole heart, mind, and strength first," then they will not be able to love their neighbor properly.

To warn those who put all of their eggs in the basket of good works and social activism, that this world is passing away (2 Pt 3:10-12) and that the most perfect and just society man can form on earth, will not satisfy the deepest longings of the human heart (Jn 4:13), which is salvation in Christ (Lk 12:16-21).

To let the light of truth about God and man, as revealed in Jesus Christ, shine into the gathering darkness of a culture tearing itself loose from the wisdom and purpose instilled in it originally by the all-holy Trinity, Father, Son, and Holy Spirit.

A TIMELINE OF THE LIFE OF GEORGE FLORIAN WALTER

1941 - 2016

1941   July 25 - Born, Pittsburgh, Pennsylvania

1941   August 10 - Baptized, St. Mary of the Assumption Catholic Church, Glenshaw, Pennsylvania

1947   September 2 - Entered St. Mary Catholic Elementary School, Glenshaw, Pennsylvania

1949   May 8 - First Holy Communion at St. Mary Catholic Church, Glenshaw, Pennsylvania

1953   April 23 - Confirmed at St. Mary Catholic Church, Glenshaw, Pennsylvania

1955   June 16 - Graduated from St. Mary Catholic Elementary School, Glenshaw, Pennsylvania

1955   September 6 - Entered St. Gregory Minor Seminary, Cincinnati, Ohio

1959   June 5 - Graduated from St. Gregory High School Seminary, Cincinnati, Ohio

1961   September 5 - Entered St. Mary Seminary, Cincinnati, Ohio

1963   Graduated with BA from Athenaeum of Ohio, Cincinnati

1963   September 9 - Entered St. Vincent Seminary, Latrobe, Pennsylvania

1964   December 16 - Received Tonsure at the hands of Bishop William G. Connare, St. Vincent Basilica, Latrobe, Pennsylvania

1964   December 17 - Ordained to Porter and Lector (Minor Orders), by Bishop Connare, St. Vincent Basilica, Latrobe, Pennsylvania

1965   December 18 - Ordained to Acolyte and Exorcist (Minor Orders) by Bishop Connare, St. Vincent Basilica, Latrobe, Pennsylvania

1966   March 26 - Ordained to Subdiaconate by Bishop Vincent M. Leonard, St. Bernard Church, Pittsburgh, Pennsylvania

1966   May 29 - Received Bachelor of Divinity, magna cum laude, from St. Vincent College School of Theology

1966   June 4 - Ordained to Diaconate by Bishop John J. Wright, Epiphany Church, Pittsburgh, Pennsylvania

1966   Summer 6-week assignment to St. Mary Church, Lawrenceville, Pittsburgh, Pennsylvania

1967   May - Finished St. Vincent Seminary

1967   May 22 - Began 18-month pilgrimage in Western United States

1968   October 4 - Assigned as a deacon to Sts. Peter and Paul Church, Beaver, Pennsylvania

1969   May 31 - Applied for dispensation from Diaconate

1969   July 4 - Began as orderly, at Mercy Hospital, Pittsburgh, Pennsylvania for 7 months

1970   February 4 - Began 4,000-mile pilgrimage to Jerusalem

1971   July 8 - Signed rescript for dispensation from the Diaconate

1972   January 19 - Baptized in the Holy Spirit, Pittsburgh, Pennsylvania

1973   December - Volunteered with Children of Yahweh until 1988

1974   July - Established Hermitage of the Cross in the woods of St. Mary Catholic Church, Glenshaw, Pennsylvania

1975   Holy Week - International Youth March, Assisi to Rome

1976   July 30 - Youth Walk, Harrisburg to Philadelphia, Pennsylvania

1981   May 3 - Began 1,200-mile pilgrimage to North American Martyrs Shrines, New York and Ontario

1982   March 29 - Pilgrimage to Mt. Sinai and Jerusalem

1982   August 1 - Secretary in Rectory for St. Mary's until 1988

1984   April 15 - Youth March from Assisi to Rome

1988   May 1 - Began 2,500-mile walk to Mexico City

1988   December 15 - Began 6-month 2,500-mile walk to Carmel, California

1989   May 29 - Established Domus Patris Hermitage, Monterey, California

1992   April 1 - Began 3,200-mile pilgrimage to Anchorage, Alaska

1992 September 19 - Arrived in Anchorage, Alaska, for 7-month *poustinia*

1993 April 28 - Left Magadan, Russia, for 2,700-mile walk to Irkutsk, Siberia

1993 October 1 - Arrived in Irkutsk for 7-month *poustinia*

1994 April 18 - Left Vershina for 2,000-mile walk to Almaty, Kazakhstan

1994 September 11 - Arrived in Almaty for 7-month *poustinia*

1995 April 25 - Left Almaty for 3,500-mile walk to Cochin, India

1995 October 27 - Arrived at Mt. Tabor Retreat Center, Kerala State, India

1995 December 29 - Flew from India to Rome, Italy

1996 January 17 - Blessed by Pope John Paul II in Vatican

1996 February 13 - Left Rome for 800-mile walk to Medjugorje, Bosnia-Herzegovina

1996 May 16 - Left Medjugorje for 800-mile walk to Poland

1996 August 5 - Arrived in Warsaw, Poland, for 8-month *poustinia*

1997 April 21 - Left Laski, Poland, for 2,000-mile walk to Knock, Ireland

1997 October 1 - Arrived in Ron, Norway, for winter *poustinia*

1998 April 30 - Left Oslo, Norway, for 1,800-mile walk to Lithuania

1998 September 30 - Arrived in Lviv, Ukraine, for winter *poustinia*

1998 April 15 - Left Lviv for 1,700-mile walk to Jerusalem

1999   September 9 - Arrived in Jerusalem for 17 months in Holy Land

2001   January 18 - Left Israel for the United States

2001   April 23 - Began 1,200-mile walk to North American Martyrs, Auriesville, New York

2001   August 13 - Began winter *poustinia* at St. Mary's, Glenshaw, Pennsylvania

2002   April 23 - Began 820-mile walk to Greensburg, Pennsylvania, Toronto, Ontario, and Uniontown, Pennsylvania

2002   September 2 - Began winter *poustinia* at St. Mary's

2003   April 29 - Began 1,400-mile walk to New Hampshire and back

2003   September 1 - Began winter *poustinia* at St. Mary's

2004   April 26 - Began 1,378-mile walk to Libertyville, Illinois and back

2004   September 6 - Began winter *poustinia* at St. Mary's

2005   April 18 - Began 1,461-mile walk through British Isles

2005   September 6 - Began winter *poustinia* at St. Mary's

2006   April 24 - Began 991-mile walk to Washington, DC and back

2006   September 4 - Began winter *poustinia* at St. Mary's

2006   October 1 - Moved *poustinia* to Butler, Pennsylvania

2007   April 30 - Began 744-mile walk to Auriesville, New York and back

2007   September 3 - Began winter *poustinia* in Butler, Pennsylvania

2008 May 5 - Began 751-mile walk to St. Meinrad, Indiana

2008 September 1 - Began winter *poustinia* in Butler, Pennsylvania

2009 May 4 - Began 669-mile walk to Hanceville, Alabama

2009 September 7 - Began winter *poustinia* in Butler, Pennsylvania

2010 May 1 - Began 528-mile walk to Santa Fe, New Mexico

2010 September 6 - Began winter *poustinia* in Butler, Pennsylvania

2011 May 2 - Began 435-mile walk to Scranton, Pennsylvania, and back

2011 September 5 - Began winter *poustinia* in Butler, Pennsylvania

2012 May 21 - Began 370-mile walk to Montreal, Quebec

2012 September 3 - Began winter *poustinia* in Butler, Pennsylvania

2013 May 20 - Began 244-mile walk to Carey, Ohio

2013 September 2 - Began winter *poustinia* in Butler, Pennsylvania

2016 November 24 - Began 3-week pilgrimage in Egypt

INTRODUCTION

"No one can lay a foundation other than the one that is laid, namely, Jesus Christ" (I Cor 3:11)

The first part of my life I spent laying the foundation: the last part of my life I spent building the edifice. For thirty-two years, from my birth in 1941, to being baptized in the Holy Spirit in 1973, I was involved in digging deep and in laying the foundation of my life, as well as collecting "building materials" for the future. For the last forty-three years, from 1973 to the present–by the grace of God– the life of a pilgrim/*poustinik* has been built upon it. Jesus Himself took about thirty years (Lk 3:23) to lay the foundation of His earthly ministry, and three years to build the crowning edifice. And Jesus Himself concluded His Sermon on the Mount with the admonition to build one's house on solid rock (Mt 7:24-27).

Every thinking human being must, in some way, ask the basic questions of life: "Who am I?" "Where did I come from?" "Where am I going?" "What is the meaning and purpose of my life?" But few seemingly feel the need to dig as deep a foundation as I did. Raised as a Roman Catholic, when I got to the study of theology in the mid-1960s, I felt I had to explore, what was at the bottom of this marvelous edifice known as the Catholic Faith. So many things were changing, that I felt I could not make a lifetime commitment to it without assuring myself that it was built on something that did not change. And to do this I felt I had to step outside the normal structures of the Catholic Church (and of society in general).

It eventually took six years (from 1967 to 1973) of seeking, searching, and testing (traveling 4,000 miles on foot to Jerusalem in 1970-71), to discover that the solid rock which never changes, is God's love for me. This involved receiving the gift of a deep and abiding experience of each of the three Persons of the Blessed Trinity in a personal way. Only with that assurance, filled with "the peace that surpasses all understanding" (Ph 4:7), was I able to say yes to life and to begin to work out my eternal salvation in fear and in trembling (Ph 2:12), by walking 35,000 miles sharing the love of God through the lifting up of the Cross of Jesus through forty-one countries in forty-three years.

It is true, the pilgrim/*poustinik* way of life is not well-known in Western Christianity: it is more attested to by our brothers and sisters in the East. Although the contemplative dimension of the Christian Faith has never been completely absent from Western Christianity, it has usually been overshadowed by the active life – now often referred to as the "Social Gospel." But the full Gospel involves both the incarnational as well as the eschatological. Yes, this creation is good (incarnational dimension), but it is passing away and there is something better ahead (the eschatological dimension). The pilgrim says by his life: "You are never going to find complete happiness on this earth, no matter how just a society (in which everyone has a sufficiency of material goods) is created. You are just passing through this earthly life and you were not created to live here forever; don't get wrongly attached to the passing things of this life, as you were created for eternity."

And the *poustinik* says by his life: "Praying always" (as commanded by Jesus in Lk 18:1 and by Paul in I Th 5:17) is a very real option even for a Christian today, for our God is not only immanent, He is also all holy and transcendent. The eremetical life, as lived by the Desert Fathers of the fourth and fifth centuries in Egypt, in Palestine, in Syria (and eventually) in Russia, and elsewhere, is an essential part of the Christian Gospel that cannot be jettisoned as archaic and passé. God is worthy of a completely dedicated life in Himself; the calling to be a eunuch for the sake of the Kingdom (Mt 19:12). A life dedicated to prayer, meditation, and contemplation, is not a waste of time just because it is not performing the corporal and spiritual works of mercy. The *poustinik* points to the ultimate meaning of life, the eschatological four last things: death, judgment, heaven, and hell. Without this perspective, the incarnational aspect of the faith will not only fail to meet the deepest needs of the human heart, it will also fail to achieve God's plan for all of creation in the first place.

This humble work that you hold in your hands, dear reader, is offered to those who are seeking some light in a fragmented society that seems to be coming apart at the seams. Having cut itself loose from its moral underpinnings, post-Christian Western society has become a cultural desert. This work, however, does not attempt an exhaustive analysis of the contemporary world. It merely recounts the yearning and experiences of one soul sojourning across the decades of a life which the Creator so generously granted to him.

God has not abandoned His straying children. He is faithful: if you truly seek Him you will find Him (Mt 7:8). All of His promises are sure: when you find the precious pearl of His love, you will give up everything to attain it (Mt 13:46). He continues to offer you life-giving waters (Jn 4:13). But only those who have sought the truth of God's love for them with their whole heart, mind, and strength (Mt 22:37) will be able to find and drink of this life-giving water and be able to offer it to others in a meaningful way.

I trust that those who are inspired to pick up this testimony to what God has done in my life will be blessed by our loving Lord in every way. This is an account of the reason for the hope that is in my heart (I Pt 3:15), and a witness to some of the countless graces that He has given to me. You are cordially invited to come along and to share in this very personal journey and hopefully to receive from it a blessing from the Lord for your own life. Know that I have been praying for you to achieve the reason for which God created you in the first place.

I love you and bless you always, In Jesus, Mary, and Joseph.

Pilgrim George
Butler, Pennsylvania - 2019
pilgrimgeorge@yahoo.com

CHAPTER 1

PREPARING THE SOIL

PART ONE

MEETING THE TRINITY (1967-73)

PSALM 139

The Summer of Love (1967) was over. The Flower Children and the Diggers[1] packed up and left Hollywood. Having just spent two months there as a twenty-six-year-old Digger, I headed south to the coastal town of Laguna Beach to look up a family who had invited me to their home. One day that fall I was in the San Diego Public Library reading Karl Marx's *Das Capital* when, without much forethought, I picked up a Bible laying nearby.

I turned in the Bible to Psalm 139 and read:

> *Lord, you have probed me, you know me*
> *you know when I sit and stand;*
> *you understand my thoughts from afar.*
> *My travels and my rest you mark;*
> *with all my ways you are familiar. (vv. 1-3)*
>
> *Where can I hide from your spirit?*
> *From Your presence, where can I flee?*
> *If I ascend to the heavens, you are there;*

if I lie down in Sheol, you are there too.
If I fly with the wings of dawn
and alight beyond the sea,
Even there your hand will guide me,
your right hand hold me fast. (vv 7-10)

[New American Bible]

A WORD FROM THE LORD

It was a moment of grace for me: a deep and powerful enlightenment. It was as if the Lord threw me a life-saving buoy as I thrashed around in the deep waters offshore. He was inviting me to grab on to it while He was on the shore and holding the other end of the rope attached to the float ring. All I had to do was hang on to these words and He would pull me to safety. Of course I had read that Psalm many times before, but this time it was different. No longer was it just a bunch of words and thoughts joined together and passed down by religious societies over the ages. This was a personal word to me that spoke to my very concrete situation. It was as if I was finally open to receiving the message and benefiting from it.

A LOVING FATHER

Before, I was put off by the thought that someone–even God was observing all that I was doing and thinking: so that He could punish me. As I reflect back on this moment, it amazes me how these words from the Bible no longer threatened me, but comforted me. Now I was greatly relieved to realize that someone who could help me, saw my plight and taking pity on me, was offering a helping hand. Now my perspective had changed: I no longer wanted to run away or to escape His gaze: now I was thankful He was a loving Father who cared about me enough to pursue me and to bring me out of my distress. I still had a long way to go and it would be six more years before the basic foundation was completed. But from this point on, I was willing to admit my need for Him and to allow Him to help me.

FIRST FOUNDATION BLOCK

It would not be until the following year, August of 1968, that the first significant foundation block of a renewed life with God would be laid. I was still searching for the source and goal, and meaning and purpose of my life on earth. I found, though, that it was not going to be through relationships, books, lectures, or social institutions. After a summer of living with a temporary commune outside of Boulder, the Lord directed me to head up into the Rocky Mountains alone, so as to encounter the Creator of heaven and earth.

GOD MADE THIS

In the middle of July, I made my way on foot to Milner Pass in Rocky Mountain National Park. There, at ten thousand feet, I found a secluded place where I could camp undisturbed. I had brought along a few books by Teilhard de Chardin and Thomas Merton, as well as a basic food supply (including a sack of flour) to last a couple of weeks. One of the first things I did was to make an oven out of stones where I could bake my own bread. There, I was, for four weeks, "alone with the Alone." I was far removed from all artificial structures that usually support one's day-to-day life in society. There were no sounds from machines, from radios, or from human voices. I did not have a house or a cabin to live in: just a few sticks and a piece of plastic to keep off the rain and dew.

Then it struck me like a lightning bolt.

Man did not make all of this: he did not build these mountains, plant these trees, or paint this sky. God made this. And the God who made this and the whole universe, created me. I am not here on earth because of some accident or evolution or because of my parents or my culture. I am here because I have a loving heavenly Father who "took the time," as it were, to create me. And furthermore, if God made me, I belong to Him just like a piece of art belongs to the artist who made it. And the purpose of my life is to return home to my Father God in heaven.

The two basic questions of life: "Where did I come from?" and "Where am I going?" were answered. I came from God and I was going back to God. It was not my choice to come from Him, but I did have to cooperate if I was to return home to Him. And what made all of this so wonderful was the realization that God made me out of love. It was not an impersonal necessity or an evolutionary force: it was His free choice to make me. He truly is my Father. I am His beloved son. And this experience of perfect love drove out all fear, confusion, and doubt from my heart just as St. John says perfect love will do in his first Epistle (I Jn 4:18). Now I was free from all of the deceitful lies of Satan and false and twisted values of the world. And that is how the Lord laid the first foundation stone in my spiritual life.

THE SECOND BUILDING BLOCK

Now the next question was: "How do I get back to my true home in heaven?" Thankfully, the Lord saw to it that we would have that answer straight from His mouth. He knew that mankind, with its darkened intellect due to Original Sin, could never get it right. All of man's best guesses by philosophers, scientists, poets, teachers, statesmen, wise men, and so forth, never in a million years, could figure it out. So the Father sent His only begotten Son, Jesus Christ, to earth to be the way back to heaven. Jesus says in the Gospel of John: "I am the Way, the Truth and the Life. No one comes to the Father except through me." (Jn 14:6) So the next question to myself was: "How do I get to know Jesus?" I knew a lot about Jesus from twenty years of Catholic education. But I did not know Him in a personal way. It would be almost two more years before the Lord laid this second foundation block in my heart.

DECOMPRESSING

So, I prepared to leave Colorado and to return to Pennsylvania. I had written to the bishop who had ordained me a deacon in 1966, Bishop (later Cardinal) John J. Wright of Pittsburgh. I told him that I had found what I was looking for (or perhaps it would have been better said that the Lord had found me) and that I was ready to come back and to share my experience with him so that I could determine my next step. He wrote back and said he was eager to assist me.

Before I headed back east though, I felt I should pay a visit to St. Benedict Cistercian Monastery in Snowmass, Colorado, for a time of "decompressing," for adjusting from one world to another. My mother had written me a letter saying she was glad I was coming back.

DISCERNING THE WAY

When I sat down with my bishop in September, he suggested two possibilities for me: assignment as a deacon to a parish in Pittsburgh, in anticipation of eventual ordination to the priesthood or, if I so decided, to join a monastic community. Bishop Wright suggested I apply to Spencer Abbey (near Boston, Massachusetts) and he would recommend me.[2] An insightful comment the bishop made at this time has always stuck with me. He said: "I think you are part St. Francis and part gypsy." I interpreted this to mean that it wasn't totally spiritual nor was it completely secular. It had both a divine and human dimension. It would no doubt take the rest of my life to make the transformation from earthly to heavenly complete. After carefully weighing the alternatives and listing the pros and cons of each possibility, I chose to pursue my search for a personal relationship with Jesus in the parish setting rather than in a monastic one. So Bishop Wright assigned me to Sts. Peter and Paul Church in

Beaver, Pennsylvania, and I arrived there on October 4, the Feast of St. Francis of Assisi. I could not imagine being under a better patron.

DIACONATE AND BEYOND

I told the good monsignor who was then pastor of Sts. Peter and Paul Church, that I was willing to perform baptisms and to do house-to-house census work, but I did not want to preach or to give homilies. I did not feel I could give something (namely a deep knowledge of "the Way, the Truth, and the Life" – Jn 14:6) which I did not have myself. I also bought a used acoustic guitar and a self-instruction booklet to teach myself how to play simple chords. I found singing simple songs and hymns helped my prayer life and worship of the Lord.

This assignment went along well for seven months. Then just after Easter in 1968, I got a letter from Bishop Wright saying he had been made a Cardinal and was being called to Rome to head up the Congregation of the Clergy[3] there. I was "a loose end" as he put it, and he said I would have to make a decision before he left to either be ordained a priest or to be laicized (i.e., returned to the lay state). I could not remain a deacon because I had been ordained with the intention of eventually becoming a priest (a so-called "transitional deacon") not a permanent deacon – the latter being just revived at that time in the Western Church. I definitely knew I had to get to know Jesus. If I could not do this as a cleric, I would have to do it as a layperson. So on May 31, I went to the bishop's office in downtown Pittsburgh and signed the papers requesting Rome to give me a dispensation from diaconate. The practical effect of this was that the ecclesiastical establishment no longer had to provide me with a benefice (as a cleric they would have to provide me an assignment or with a way of making a living) and I was now on my own to seek the future the Lord would have for me.

WALKING THE TALK

As I prayed about what to do next, I decided to rent a cheap apartment (for $50 a month) in Uptown Pittsburgh–a twenty-minute walk from the famed "Golden Triangle"–to buy a New Jerusalem Bible (Study Edition) and a copy of The Jerome Biblical Commentary, and really get into the Word of God. To make some money I took a three-week course at Mercy Hospital, just up the street from my apartment, to learn how to be an orderly and worked there three days a week. This lasted just seven months. By February of 1970, the Lord had formed in my heart the idea of making a pilgrimage on foot to Jerusalem. My thought was: "Maybe by going back to the places where Jesus lived, died, and rose: the place where the Bible was written: maybe there, I could come to know Jesus as I felt I needed to know Him."

But how I got to the Holy Land was also important. (This was the age of Marshall McLuhan and his principle, "the medium is the message," was all the rage.[4]) So I decided I was not going to just fly or to take a boat there: I would walk as pilgrims had done since the Middle Ages. For, by walking, one, as it were, "earns the right to be there." One does not depend on some kind of artificial, mechanical aids that eliminate Jesus' call to "take up the cross" of suffering and sacrifice. A person engages their will each day again and again with each step, renewing the commitment to obey the Lord's command.

CROSSING THE ATLANTIC OCEAN

So on February 4, 1970, I vacated my little attic apartment on Locust Street in Uptown, Pittsburgh, and packed a small shoulder bag containing a change of clothes, a space blanket in lieu of a sleeping bag and tent, a pocket-size copy of the New Testament, a copy of Thomas a Kempis's *Imitation of Christ*, a two-volume Breviary in Latin, and a small notebook. I initially set out on foot for New Orleans and from there I hoped to be able to board a freighter headed for Europe where I would begin my walk to Jerusalem. But I first headed to Chicago, then to Dayton, Ohio, and on to Atlanta, to visit friends along the way. I felt it was also important to include my brothers and sisters in Christ in this pilgrimage project. When I got to New Orleans at the end of March, I learned I could not "deadhead" (i.e., work on a freighter one way and get off without returning back to the start) as I had hoped. I would have to work and to earn enough money to purchase a one-way ticket for First-Class passage on a freighter for $230. The quickest way for a man to earn money in New Orleans was to go to the oil fields in Plaquemines County and to hire himself out as a roustabout or as an unskilled laborer.

On May 6, 1970, I boarded the *Mar Adriatico*, a Spanish freighter hauling timber, hides, cement, and oil from the United States to Spain. I spent two weeks crossing the Atlantic Ocean and I felt like one of the Israelites crossing the Red Sea, leaving the old life of slavery behind to begin a new life of getting to know the Lord, in the freedom of the desert and eventually in the abundance of the Promised Land. I also understood it to be a renewal of my sacramental baptism which I had received twenty-nine years before, as an infant. I truly needed to be born again (Jn 3:5).

LANDING IN BARCELONA

The *Mar Adriatico* called at two ports in Spain: one on the southwest coast in the Atlantic at Cadiz and the other on the northeast coast at Barcelona in the Mediterranean. Before leaving New Orleans, I had decided the first pilgrimage destination would be Santiago de Compostela on the west coast of Spain, before heading to Paris, to Rome, to Athens, and to Jerusalem. I could have started at Cadiz and walked north (even while picking up Fatima in Portugal on the way), but I chose to go all the way to Barcelona on the east coast, and to walk The Camino de Santiago west to the Shrine of St. James. It proved to be the Lord's plan. After a few days in Barcelona being awed by the beauty of the thirteenth-century Gothic cathedral, and paying my respects to the Black Madonna on the top of Montserrat, I found my way to The Camino de Santiago. My maps told me this road ran through the desert of northern Spain and through the historic cities of Zaragoza, Logrono, Burgos, and Leon and would, after 600 miles, bring me to the historic Shrine of St. James the Apostle.

So I set up my daily routine of walking and taking rides when offered, in an attempt to end up at the eastern edge of a town or village at night so I could walk in the next morning and attend Mass. At this point of my journey, I simply appeared to be a typical traveler on foot, wearing jeans, a long-sleeved denim shirt, and a heavy, plaid overshirt. The only unusual thing about my dress was the aluminum hard hat I used in the oil fields in Louisiana; it came in handy for washing and for digging, as well as for keeping off the sun. I painted a red Chi Rho ("XP," symbolizing Christ) inside a black circle on the front of the hard hat in place of my name, "Geo," which I had originally painted on it in the United States. The weather was warm as it was June and July, so I could easily sleep outside at night along the roadside in the fields after walking my 18 miles each day.

THE SECOND FOUNDATION BLOCK

On the second week of my walk on The Camino de Santiago, the Lord favored me with the grace I had so desperately been seeking and for which this whole pilgrimage had been planned–namely to meet Jesus in a personal way. The Lord did not wait until I got to Jerusalem a year later to reveal Himself to me: He found me right here in the desert (see Hos 2:16). I had done what He had said: I renounced all of my possessions (see Lk 14:33), left my father and my mother (see Mt 19:29), denied myself, and took up my cross (see Lk 9:23). He kept His end of the bargain. This was all He needed to give me, the grace He so desired for me. It happened like this.

I had been reading the Gospel of St. Luke from my pocket New Testament, because Luke notes that Jesus proceeded "on the way

35

to Jerusalem" (ch. 9, v. 51). So it made sense to identify with Jesus' journey as I was also on my way to Jerusalem. I closed my little New Testament one day, put it back in my pocket, and all of a sudden it struck me like a ton of bricks: what Luke is writing about is true: this Jesus is not just a great historical person who lived two thousand years ago, died, rose, and went to heaven: He is alive and He is here with me in my heart! I had heard that Gospel in church many times; I had read it in the original Greek. But that day it became a living word to me. Then I knew that Jesus was with me and that I was not alone. And so the second foundation block had been laid in my spiritual life: coming to know Jesus, the second Person of the Blessed Trinity, in a personal way. The third and final foundation block (experiencing the power of the Holy Spirit) would take another two and a half years. And this would occur back in the United States.

WALK IN FAITH

So what happened in those intervening years? In one sense, everything after coming to know Jesus as my Lord and Savior would be anticlimactic. But the Lord knew what He was doing and His timing is always perfect. Now that I knew Jesus was with me in my heart, I had to learn in specific and practical ways how to "walk in faith." For now, I had come to experience a new kind of faith: I had moved from a mere creedal faith (intellectual), to a fiducial kind of faith (trusting, surrendering my heart). He wanted me to trust in Him to lead me and to guide me: to provide for me and to protect me. This is what I could not get from books, professors, programs, and Sacraments.[5] This was a unique grace and gift that came directly from the Lord. But now I had to learn how to exercise, to use, and to live by this new kind of faith. And that is what consumed the next twelve months as I made my way through Europe and the Near East to Jerusalem.

ST. JAMES THE APOSTLE

I arrived at Santiago de Compostela on June 5. For me, the significance of the shrine was twofold: (1) it was the third most important and popular destination for Western medieval pilgrims after Rome and Jerusalem and (2) it was the burial place of St. James the Greater, who is not only the patron of pilgrims but whose feast day is July 25, which is also my birthday. So I felt a very personal connection with this favored Apostle who, along with his brother John and his fishing partner Simon Peter, got to witness some of the more intimate scenes of Jesus' Public Life—the raising of Jairus' daughter (Mk 5:37ff); The Transfiguration on Mt Tabor (Lk 9:26); and Jesus' Agony in the Garden (Mt 26:37). Visiting the reputed tomb of James helped to connect me with the life of Christ and the life of His faithful pilgrim followers throughout the ages. The Apostles walked with Jesus and those who want to be disciples of Jesus today should be thankful to be able to walk in the footsteps of those who carried Jesus' message to the ends of the earth.

SERMONS IN STONE

Having completed my visit to the Shrine of St. James, I set my sights on my next destination: Paris. What drew me to this historic capital was not so much the Saints who had lived there (certainly there were plenty of them), or even the centuries-old history of the church there, but the medieval monuments in stone built by my ancestors. Especially I was interested in seeing the thirteenth-century Notre Dame Cathedral. On the way there, I spent a few hours absorbing the magnificent thirteenth-century Gothic Cathedral of Chartres. These monuments were to me, tangible, visible evidence of the power of the Christian Faith to sacrifice oneself (being that it took generations to build these huge edifices made of hand-carved stone) and to create something beautiful for the Lord. Praying in them brought me a deep appreciation for the Mystical Body of Christ.

A WRITTEN REFLECTION

While I was in Paris, I also took the time to write up a nine-page document (see appendix A) reflecting on my experience of what the Lord had been building in my heart over the past three years. I addressed it to the seminarians back at St. Vincent Seminary in Latrobe, Pennsylvania, where I had finished my theological studies in 1967. Although I never sent it to them, I kept a copy of it and I am still amazed at the clarity which the Lord had brought into my thinking at this time. Reading it today, almost fifty years later, reveals two basic points: (1) how I moved from an incarnational perspective to an eschatological emphasis and (2) how important the walking in faith and the living outside part of the pilgrimage was, in coming to know the Lord in a personal way.

CLOSE TO NATURE

By walking I became more dependent upon my immediate environment and upon the goodwill of the people who gave me food, housing, and rides. By sleeping outside, I had a more immediate sense of the earth and of the natural forces (wind, sun, and rain) of the environment. I actually felt more a part of the natural creation all around me: the warmth of the sun; the coolness of the night; the vastness of the stars; the majesty of the clouds and snow-capped mountains; the refreshment of cool springwater, fresh bread, and pure natural wine. It put me in closer contact with the Lord as my Creator and as my Giver of life.

THE FINAL REALITIES

The second insight I write about in Paris is the new eschatological perspective I had found. In my theological studies in the seminary (1963-67)–based as they were on the documents from Vatican II–the main emphasis was incarnational. That is, it focused on the goodness of creation and on the Christian's responsibility to build up "the city of man" ("Social Action" and "Social Justice" issues). This tended to blur the fact that all of the things of this earth were going to pass away in the end. And so there was no longer much talk about death, judgment, heaven, and hell (the eschatological realities of our faith) in the curriculum.

And with this realization I discovered something solid, absolute, and unchanging that I could commit my life to, namely a transcendent God who loved me unconditionally. I came to realize the importance of the First of the Two Great Commandments, "Love the Lord your God with your whole heart, mind and strength" (Mt 22:36-39). I no longer focused on the Second Great Commandment, "Love your neighbor as yourself." I went from knowing, depending upon, and fearing man and the structures of his civilization, to knowing, depending upon, and fearing only God and His will. (Mt 10:28)

On September 10, I left Paris and headed for Rome. I knew I should get across the Swiss Alps before winter if I expected to be able to sleep outside. So I packed up my little duffel bag and walked out of Paris, thanking the Lord for the restful and nourishing time He had given me on this part of my journey.

CROSSING THE ALPS

By the end of the month, I had crossed into Switzerland and made a stop at the ancient monastery of St. Meinrad at Einsiedeln, where another Black Madonna image was venerated. Thankfully, no new snow had fallen in this part of the Alps yet and I was able to climb a good way up Mount Mythen (with four- foot walls of snow on both sides of the shoveled-out path). This gave me a breathtaking view of snow-covered mountain peaks in every direction for 360 degrees. I thanked the Lord for this special gift that He had arranged for me without my asking.

Crossing Gotthard Pass (7,000 feet) on November 1, I finally arrived in Italy and began to feel more at home in a Catholic country where the culture had been saturated for two millennia by the true faith. Now it was easy to find Catholic churches for Mass, and the names of the towns and cities that evoked the rich history of the Catholic Faith. Thus I came to Bergamo which I knew was the birthplace of Pope John XXIII who set loose a spirit of change in the Catholic Church by calling an ecumenical council (Vatican II) in 1963. And when I arrived in Firenze (Florence), I checked out the famous Cathedral of St. Mary of the Flowers and Michelangelo's sculpture of David in the Academia Gallery.

THE GALILEE OF ITALY

Finally on November 21, in Central Italy, I entered the region of Umbria which has been called "the Galilee of Italy" and is said to have more canonized Saints per square mile than any other place on earth. For almost two weeks now I walked in the footsteps of St. Francis of Assisi, St. Benedict of Nursia, and St. Rita of Cascia. It was a land of lush green vegetation and gently rolling hills, much like my home area in western Pennsylvania. It had an air of quiet peace and almost tangible sense of the Lord's presence–like Eden must have been before our First Parents sinned. I drank deeply of both the natural and spiritual riches I experienced here and let them heal my soul and refresh my spirit. It was another experience of the power of the fellowship of the Saints in the Mystical Body of Christ.

THE ETERNAL CITY

On December 7, I entered The Eternal City–Rome–and headed for the Vatican. I was not so much interested in the glory that was Rome (i.e., its art, history, architecture, museums, and culture) as I was in visiting the tombs of the Apostles (Peter and Paul) and the Martyrs (especially in the Colosseum). I felt the need to experience firsthand, the visible structures that supported and communicated the faith that I had been given as an infant in my baptism and in the other Sacraments as I grew up.

My first experience of the Vatican was walking up the Via Della Conciliazione toward St. Peter's Basilica. As I came into the plaza and approached the great obelisk brought from Egypt I felt embraced by the surrounding pillars of the colonnade on both sides of the plaza. The sixteenth-century architect Bernini had achieved his stated purpose: the visitor was to experience the welcoming embrace of Holy Mother Church. That is just what I felt: welcomed home by my spiritual Mother from whose womb I had received the gift of faith.

When I entered the Basilica of St. Peter, there were tour guides leading groups around like in a museum, or like in a mausoleum because of all the tombs of so many Popes scattered around.

PRAYING IN ROME

The Lord eventually led me to a little treasure of a church off of a back alley and down some steps. The name of it was St. Praxedes and in it was venerated a pillar called "the column of the scourging of Christ." This relic had apparently been brought from the Holy Land in the thirteenth century. But what attracted me to this spot was the fact that it had perpetual adoration of the Blessed Sacrament. Therefore, the church was open twenty-four hours a day.

This also allowed me to identify with another pilgrim from the eighteenth century who greatly appealed to me, St. Benedict Joseph Labre (1748-83). Born in France, he tried in vain to enter one monastery after another and ended up sojourning all over Europe, pilgrimaging from one shrine to another. Years later, I came to figure out that I was in Assisi two hundred years to the day (November 29) that Benedict was there in 1770. He spent the last few years of his life living on the streets of Rome, sleeping in the Colosseum, eating what he found tossed out, and praying in many of the churches in Rome. He died at the age of thirty-three and was venerated as a Saint by many who knew him personally. I asked him to pray for me as I walked in his footsteps.

HELPED BY THE CARDINAL

The first day I arrived in the city, I contacted Cardinal Wright and he invited me to stay in his apartment as long as I was in Rome. Cardinal Wright saw to more than my physical needs. He also affirmed that I was in God's will by saying as soon as he had seen me: "Your eyes are bright and clear: I see you have found the peace of the Lord." It confirmed to me that I was on the right path and the Lord had been working in my life. And his parting advice on my final day in Rome, was a word that continues to this day to sound in my heart so many years later: *coraggio.* Literally it means "courage" or maybe something like the Scriptural "be not afraid" (Mt 14:27). It was definitely a powerful and much-appreciated word from the Lord for me and it has carried me far.

SAILING TO GREECE

It took me eighteen days to make the 350 miles from Rome to Brindisi and I did not stop at any of the many possible shrines a pilgrim can visit in that stretch: the Cave of St. Michael the Archangel at Mt. Gargano; Padre Pio's Friary at San Giovanni Rotundo; St. Nicholas the Wonderworker in Bari, and so forth. Anyone of these holy places could have contained great spiritual blessings for a sincerely seeking soul. But a true pilgrim is not a "religious tourist" out to collect an array of jewels for his crown just for the sake of ostentatious ornamentation. The real pilgrim is seeking the will of God.

From the port city of Brindisi on the southeastern coast of Italy, I took passage on the ferryboat *Poseidonia* for $12 and made the 150-mile journey across the Strait of Otranto in the Adriatic Sea. We first landed on the Greek island of Corfu and then proceeded on to the mainland of Greece at Igoumenitsa. After the cold weather of southern Italy in December, I was glad for a warmed space on the ferryboat where I could sit in a comfortable chair and reflect on my last few weeks of walking, and write one of my long letters back to my parents in the United states.

BIBLICAL AND CLASSICAL SITES

My plan now was to head for Athens by way of Corinth where I could pick up the journeys of St. Paul the Apostle to the Gentiles and stand literally in the Cradle of Western Civilization. I not only rejoiced to be able to stand in the ruins of the Bema (judgment platform) in Corinth where St. Paul was brought before the magistrate and accused of sedition (Acts 18:12ff), but I also was thrilled to walk around the Parthenon in the ancient Acropolis on top of the hill overlooking Athens, as well as to read the bronze plaque in the Areopagus where St. Paul tried to win the Athenian philosophers to Christ by telling them he knew "the unknown god" they were acknowledging (Acts 17:22ff).

This historic encounter reminded me that no one could enter into a genuinely personal relationship with the Lord until they were ready to leave it all. Like the Greek philosophers whose minds were filled with human wisdom ("riches"), I had been "enriched" by my studies of theology in the seminary. And like them, I had not made the necessary surrender of my will. I was reminded, as well, how the "rich" could only with great difficulty enter the narrow gate of the Kingdom of God (see Mt 19:23). The lesson of nearly two thousand years ago was still valid today; and as God's grace was available then, so it was also now.

HEADING FOR TURKEY

I headed north to visit other cities in Greece mentioned in the letters of St. Paul and in Acts: Berea, Thessalonica, and Philippi. It was in Philippi that I visited the excavated first-century city known by St. Paul and found an inscription marking the place where Paul and Silas were held in jail overnight. I then read the appropriate verses in Acts 16:25-ff. I was able to identify with the jailer who asked, "What must I do to be saved" (Acts 16:30). There was the model of humility that I needed to also imitate, if I were to receive the gift of eternal life.

A DESERT EXPERIENCE

Crossing into Turkey at Alexandroupolis, I started walking my Turkey pilgrimage at the beginning of March; it was spring and the holy season of Lent commenced. My plan was to spend Holy Week and Easter at the Catholic Church in Mersin on the Mediterranean coast: a journey of about 700 miles. There were very few Catholic churches in the area. Originally my plan was to keep along the coastline so as to benefit from the warming effect of the Mediterranean Sea. But when I left Ephesus and headed eastward toward Laodicea (because it was one of the New Testament cities [Col 4:15]), I was going into the mountainous interior. And this area was still in the grip of winter. The Lord was testing my resolve and commitment and asking me to share in His Passion in a very concrete way. By His grace I was able to endure and continue.

EASTER IN MERSIN

I visited all of the biblical sites I could: Colossae, Antioch in Pisidia, Iconium, Lystra, and Derbe, reading all of the appropriate passages in my little pocket New Testament. Only in Inconium did I find a small Catholic Church where I could attend Mass and receive Holy Communion–truly manna in the desert. In all this time I experienced nothing but hospitality from the Muslim Turks. They would offer me tea when I passed by a café and saw to it that I had a supply of bread each morning.

So it was with great relief that I arrived at the Franciscan Convent in Mersin on Wednesday of Holy Week, April 7. I did not know if Bishop Boccella, TOR, a missionary bishop from Philadelphia had notified the Franciscans of my coming or not. Nevertheless, they were most hospitable. These days of prayer and fellowship with brothers and sisters in Christ was refreshing and fortifying. When I stepped outside the Catholic compound on Easter, I was ready to complete the last leg of my journey to Jerusalem.

LAST DAYS IN TURKEY

My next goal was to walk along the northeastern shore of the Mediterranean Sea to the border of Syria: it was about a 160 miles or an eight-day walk. After much paperwork and many security clearance procedures, I was permitted to stay overnight with the chaplain of the American Airforce Base in Adana, and that enabled me to go to Mass and to receive the Lord one more time in Turkey.

One final blessing awaited me in Turkey and that was a visit to the ancient city of Antioch, or Antakya as it is now called, where the followers of Jesus were first called Christians (see Acts 11:36). It was hard to imagine this large but impoverished city as once having been the administrative capital of the Roman Empire in the East, as well as a residential patriarchal see for many centuries. It was positive proof that both political and man-made ecclesiastical structures are not permanent, and so they do not make a solid base upon which to build one's hopes.

BYPASSING SYRIA

On April 20, I arrived at the Syrian border. I passed successfully through Turkish customs but was refused entrance into Syria because

I was an American and because I was on my way to Jerusalem. Syria was at war with Israel and America was supporting Israel. I would have to find another way to reach my destination and it would obviously have to be by some other way than by walking. My first thought was perhaps that I could get a boat from Adana at least to the island of Cyprus and from there to Haifa in Israel.

When I got back to Adana, I found out I could not get a boat to Cyprus, but there were two flights a week for $21 to Nicosia on Cyprus. When I arrived on Cyprus I was only given a two-day visa, so I could not explore the Christian sites on the island but had to head right for the port city of Limasol on the southern coast of the island. There I got a ticket for a seat on one of the big Greek cruise ships that make the trip regularly from Athens to Haifa. My goal was in sight.

FIRST STEPS IN THE HOLY LAND

On April 27 (a Sunday morning) I arrived by ship in the port of Haifa in northern Israel. I had the address of a Benedictine priest-friend in Haifa and it would place me in Galilee, so I could follow the life of Christ from Nazareth to Jerusalem (100 miles to the south). But now I was on top of Mt. Carmel near the cave where Elijah had lived 800 years before Christ. From its summit, on a clear day one could see Mount Tabor to the east (60 miles away), where Elijah (along with Moses) appeared to Jesus during His Transfiguration (Lk 9:23-36). I prayed for a portion of that same Holy Spirit which enabled these Old Testament prophets to witness and to testify to Jesus as the promised Messiah.

My plan now was to walk to Nazareth, Cana, Capernaum, Caesarea Philippi, and around the east side of the Sea of Galilee to Mt. Tabor and then south to Jerusalem. The weather was warm enough that I could discard the inner lining of my overcoat and I was able to sleep outside. In Nazareth I joined the Salesians for morning Mass at the Church of Jesus the Adolescent overlooking the main part of the town. Then I visited the large cone-shaped Basilica of the Annunciation built in 1960, over Mary's house and a fifth-century Byzantine Church, now called "The Grotto."

AROUND THE LAKE OF GALILEE

From Cana I walked to the Sea of Galilee, first visiting Tiberias and then onto the western shore of the lake through Magdala to the Church of the Beatitudes on top of the mountain overlooking the lake. Next I was on to Capernaum at the northwest corner of the lake and farther north to Caesarea Philippi in the foothills of Mount Hermon. From that furthest point north–the source of the Jordan River which watered all of the land of Israel–I headed south and made my way over the Golan Heights along the western side of the Sea of Galilee.

Before heading directly south to Jerusalem from the southern end of the Sea of Galilee, I made my way back east in order to visit Mount Tabor which rose out of the plain like an offering to the Lord in heaven, 1,450 feet above the surrounding valleys. I was able to climb the serpentine switchback road to reach the top and to pray in the Basilica built in 1924, on the reputed spot of the Transfiguration. The Franciscan friars caring for the site were most hospitable. I prayed and thanked the Lord for the revelation of His glory on this spot and the testimony that the Father in heaven had given here:

"This is My beloved Son, with whom I am well pleased; listen to Him" (see Mt 17:5).

That was exactly the grace I desired: to listen to and to obey the Lord Jesus Christ.

THROUGH SAMARIA

Now I was ready to spend the next four days walking through "the hill country," called "Samaria" in Jesus' day and by modern Israelis, and called "the West Bank" today by Palestinian inhabitants. It "officially" belonged to the State of Israel, but "practically" it was occupied by Arabs (both Christian and Muslim) who considered it to be still part of the country of Jordan (once known as "Transjordan") on the east side of the Jordan River.

However, the secular history of the rise and fall of political empires was not what primarily interested me. I was more drawn to its biblical sites like Shechem, where Abraham had pitched his tent (Gn 12:7); Jacob's well where Jesus revealed Himself as the Messiah to the Samaritan woman (Jn 4); Jenin where Jesus cured the ten lepers (Lk 17:11-19); Dothan where Joseph was sold into Egypt by his brothers (Gn 37); Mt. Ebal (Sechem); and Mt. Gerazim where Joshua fulfilled God's directions (Jos 8:33-34; 24:32). All of these Scriptural associations made concrete the stories I knew from the Bible and allowed me to walk in the footsteps of the Patriarchs and Prophets. It made my faith more real and solid.

ENTERING THE HOLY CITY

On my sixteenth day in the Holy Land, I crossed the boundary between Samaria and Judea at Khan el Lubban and saw a sign indicating Jerusalem was only another 18 miles away. My expectations were coming to a climax as I thought of all the pilgrims who of old, had made a pilgrimage to Jerusalem out of religious devotion; from the Jews in the Old Testament (Ex 23:14-17) to the Holy Family of Jesus, Mary, and Joseph (Lk 2:41-43); from the medieval pilgrims in the Middle Ages, and to modern-day tourists/pilgrims. I was not the first nor would I be the last; still I was happy to be part of this long line of those who had been called and enabled to make the journey on foot in honor of the Lord of lords and King of kings.

On May 14, I arrived at the top of the Mount of Olives and saw what Jesus saw on that Sunday before His Passion as He looked out over the city of Jerusalem that was about to reject and crucify Him. As I walked through the Lion's Gate–outside of which St. Stephen had been stoned to death for proclaiming Jesus (see Acts 7:58) and through which Jesus would have passed on Palm Sunday riding a donkey–I felt like I had entered into another world. It was truly a *city of peace*: a city sanctified by the Lord in a unique way-consecrated by the Blood of the Lamb of God. Though I had been walking twelve months to get there, I felt I was not worthy to be there: this was holy ground.

THE CHURCH OF THE HOLY SEPULCHER

Many people were passing in and out of that gate and along those streets that day, going about their daily business, seemingly unaware of the holiness of the place. Although I was walking the Via Dolorosa (the Way of the Cross), I did not stop to meditate on the various stations along the way, nor did I stop to examine or purchase any of the wares being hawked by the street vendors. I felt I was here for one reason only: to honor the death and resurrection of my Lord and Savior Jesus Christ, at the Church of the Holy Sepulcher which was built over Calvary and His tomb.

Here I found a space filled with deep devotion. There were both pilgrims and tourists, but all observed a hushed silence. It was dark, as there were very few windows to let in the outside light. But it was lighted from the inside by candles, oil lamps, and a few electric lights. And most of all, it was illuminated by the devotion of believers who were in fervent prayer at the various stations around the church: the Stone of Anointing right in front of the entrance; the Hill of Calvary up the steps to the right; the Cave of Adam beneath Calvary (regarded by an ancient tradition as the resting place of the Father of Man); the Catholic Chapel where the Franciscans kept the Blessed

Sacrament and had Mass; the Chapel of St. Helen in the undercroft (where the True Cross was found); and most of all, the Edicule built over the slab on which Jesus' sacrificed Body had lain for three days until He rose on Easter Sunday morning.

TWENTY-FOUR HOURS

I spent the next twenty-four hours venerating this holy spot, although I had to wait outside in the atrium, as the church was locked up for two hours every day. Although there were numerous side chapels and devotional stations, I focused on two places: Calvary and the Tomb.

Once inside the church, I climbed the eighteen steps to the right to the top of Calvary. There I found a small chapel divided into two naves: the one on the right belonged to the Roman (Latin) Catholics and it commemorated Jesus' being nailed to the Cross and Jesus' removal from the Cross: the nave on the left was in the care of the Greek Orthodox (Jerusalem Patriarchate) and it commemorated Jesus' death on the Cross. I spent much time here contemplating the sacrifice of Jesus on this very spot, as well as attending Mass at the Latin altar. The fullness of the act of redemption accomplished here was beyond comprehension. But at least I now had a visual and physical contact with the earthly manifestation of God's love for me. Not only will my time on earth be insufficient to fully grasp this mystery; even all of eternity in heaven will not suffice.

The other place where I spent much time, was in front of the Tomb of Christ (The Edicule). There I knelt before the rock shelf on which Jesus' Body lay before the resurrection, to receive the graces the Lord was making available here. And if that wasn't enough, later a Coptic priest let me reach my hand through a hole and touch the actual rock (for a donation). My faith rested upon no cleverly concocted myth or humanly devised philosophy; it was based on a concrete historical event that happened here two thousand years ago. Thanks be to God.

DISCERNING THE FUTURE

After my twenty-four hours in the Church of the Holy Sepulcher, I looked up my Benedictine priest-friend in the new city of Jerusalem. He was there with another brother from St. Vincent's and the two of them were trying to set up a type of "Christian kibbutz" in order to initiate a dialogue with the Jews. I was invited to stay. So I began praying about what the Lord wanted me to do next. Within two weeks I heard the Lord say to my heart: **"This pilgrimage is over. But you will remain a pilgrim for the rest of your life. Now you will pilgrimage in the desert of the city of man."**

So I got the distinct sense that my vocation was not to be a member of a Christian kibbutz, nor an ordained cleric in the ecclesiastical establishment; but to be a pilgrim in the world, walking in faith and trusting Jesus, lifting Him up for the world to see how much God loves them. Religious and clerics took the "high road"; pilgrims took "the low road." Normally, priests have status and security. A pilgrim has no security at all: he is a stranger in a strange land. His whole security is in the Lord and His promise to take care of those who did not worry about the things of this life. (Mt 6:25-34)

What did the Lord mean by "the desert of the city of man?" The city basically caters to "creature comforts" (ease, comfort, pleasure, etc.). It is man made: man as fallen since Original Sin is focused on himself. (The first city in the Bible was made by Cain after he had murdered his brother Abel [Gn 4:17].) It is spiritually a desert in the sense that it is barren of God's life: it is focused mainly on our natural, physical life. The pilgrim then–just passing through–was to be an eschatological sign of something more: a goal beyond the needs of one's earthly life. His eyes and heart were set on eternity to which he was journeying.

RETURNING TO PENNSYLVANIA

The next question was: "Where was I to live out this vocation of a pilgrim?" My sense was I should return to my roots in southwestern Pennsylvania and wait for further guidance there. It was Memorial Day Weekend when I arrived back at my parents' home on Harts Run Road. I was at the end of one phase and at the beginning of another phase of my journey into the Kingdom. Now I got involved once again in St. Mary's Parish, going to daily Mass and volunteering at the religious education office, teaching children. One of the pieces of mail that was waiting for me at my parents' home required immediate attention: it was a letter from the Diocese of Pittsburgh sent in October of 1970: it said my rescript from Rome granting me a dispensation from diaconate had been approved and was waiting for me to sign.

MEETING A FRIENDLY BISHOP

So in June I wrote to the Diocese and told them I was willing to sign the rescript with two conditions: (1) I wanted to maintain my commitment to celibacy and praying the Breviary that I had made at subdiaconate in 1965 and (2) if I chose in the future I could officially resume the function of a deacon. I received back a letter from one of the auxiliary bishops, Anthony G. Bosco.

What a godsend this was. From this point on, Bishop Bosco became a personal and valued friend. By the grace of God he was able to understand my vocation and to support it in every way he could. In July of 1985, he had me on his weekly TV program, "*To Teach As Jesus Did*," as his special guest. He encouraged me to write a memoir of my pilgrimage to Jerusalem,[6] for which he wrote the foreword. Also he blessed my jean-patched robe in 1988, before I set out on foot for the shrine of Our Lady of Guadalupe in Mexico City. And he wrote about me (as I regularly sent him reports on my whereabouts) in his diocesan newspaper, *The Accent*, while he was Bishop of Greensburg,

Pennsylvania, from 1987 to 2004.[7] Until his death in 2013, I always referred to him as "my episcopal adviser."

STILL SOMETHING IS MISSING

When I came back to southwestern Pennsylvania from Jerusalem, I was moving into my last year and a half of searching and discovery that had begun in June of 1967, with my departure for California. So far, I had come to know the Father's personal love for me in the Rocky Mountains in Colorado in the summer of 1968. I had come to know Jesus in a personal way through reading the Gospel of St. Luke in the desert of northern Spain on my way to Jerusalem. But, I found there was still something missing: I had no power or ability to share my newfound faith with others.

So these next twenty months found me exploring various possibilities. I wrote a letter to Mother Theresa volunteering to help with the crisis situation of Pakistani refugees in India in October of 1971. I attended a parish discussion group that met in homes once a month. I made retreats of several days at various places: St. Vincent Seminary in Latrobe, Pennsylvania; Holy Trinity Byzantine Benedictine Monastery in Butler, Pennsylvania; and St. Paul's Passionist Monastery in Pittsburgh, Pennsylvania.

And I was practicing simple "Praise Songs" on my guitar a lot.

COME HOLY SPIRIT

Then in the spring of 1972, one of the eighth-grade teachers in St. Mary's School, invited me to a Catholic Charismatic Prayer Group at a local community college campus, led by a Franciscan priest-chaplain, and I accepted the invitation. I also began reading books about the Pentecostal and Charismatic Renewal. Part of the Charismatic Prayer Group experience was Life in the Spirit Seminars. These were seven-week sessions, taught by members of the community, based on a semi-official manual, which laid out the Gospel call to repentance, making a commitment to Jesus as Lord, and then prayer to be baptized in the Holy Spirit.[8] Around the end of 1972, I enrolled in one of these seminars.

THE THIRD BUILDING BLOCK

On January 19, 1973, at the Fifth Session of the Life in the Spirit Seminar, I prayed to be "Baptized in the Holy Spirit" (Lk 3:16; Acts 1:5). There I received the gift of tongues (glossalalia [Acts 10:44-46]), and the gift of prophecy (prophetic words and messages [1 Cor 14:1-5]). With this release of the Holy Spirit, whom I had sacramentally since my Baptism and Confirmation, I now had the power and the ability to witness and to speak about my faith in Jesus to others (Acts 1:8). Also, the Bible came alive for me as I began to read the Scriptures with a new understanding (Lk 24:45)–as enlightened by the author of the Word of God Himself, the Holy Spirit (II Pt 1:20-21). And I learned that there was a difference between "saying prayers" (coming from myself) and "praying" (coming from the Holy Spirit [I Cor 14:15]).

So now the Lord had laid the third of the three basic foundation stones in my spiritual life that I had lacked at the end of my seminary studies. I had come to know the love of the Father living alone in the mountains in Colorado in the summer of 1968. In May of 1970, I had come to know Jesus as my Lord and Savior walking alone through the desert in northern Spain. And I had come to know the Holy Spirit in a personal way in the community of the believers in January of 1973, in Pittsburgh, Pennsylvania. In a period of six years (1967-73) the Lord had filled in what I could not get from books, classes, or sacraments. I had to set aside all of these "riches," admit my poverty, and set out on the journey of trusting in the Lord. Now I had something worthwhile to share and the next fifteen years (1973-88) would be a time of growing deeper in prayer as a hermit and as a *poustinik*[9] and time of service–especially to youths–in the power of the Holy Spirit. And before relating that part of the journey, I wish to go back to my childhood and school days, for these provided more of the basic "soil" for the planting of the gift of faith in the Father, Son, and Holy Spirit.

THE PRAYER OF MY HEART

Lord, I thank You for the graces You gave me

in these years of searching and discovery.

I certainly was not worthy of them.

But You in Your infinite goodness,

chose to favor me with a deep knowledge

of Your loving kindness.

I ask that You also give those who are reading this narrative,

a deep sense of Your personal love for them also.

In Jesus' name.

ENDNOTES

1. Hippies (Flower Children) were typically teenagers who just hung out in the parks and did not work or worry about their material needs. Diggers have been defined as "hippie social workers." They were usually older (in their twenties and thirties) and were dropouts from society who took upon themselves the responsibility of providing the hippies with food, clothing, and shelter.

2. Spencer Abbey falls within the Diocese of Worcester, Massachusetts. Bishop Wright knew this community well, especially having been Worcester's first bishop (1950-59).

3. Congregation for the Clergy. This is the Vatican department which supervises the formation of priests and deacons.

4. Marshal McLuhan (1911-80) was a Canadian professor, philosopher, and public intellectual who did groundbreaking work in media theory, advertising, and television, predicting the World Wide Web almost thirty years before it was invented.

5. Sacraments. As Bl. Sister Miriam Teresa Demjanovich explains in *Greater Perfection*: "The sacraments are the channels of grace par excellence. Though they are efficaciously operative in themselves

by virtue of the dispensive (sic) power of Our Lord, still, He has ordained that their effects be proportionate to the dispositions of the recipient (p. 1)."

6. *A Pilgrim Finds the Way.*

7. As far as I can determine, Bishop Bosco wrote fourteen articles about me in his weekly commentary called: "A View From The Bridge." They appeared under the following dates: June 23, 1988; January 19, 1989; February 6, 1992; May 6, 1993; January 13, 1994; February 1, 1996; August 15, 1996; February 13, 1997; February 12, 1998; February 19, 1998; April 15, 1999; August 17, 2000; October 19, 2000; and January 22, 2004.

8. "Baptized in the Holy Spirit" refers specifically to praying for a renewal, release, or actualization of the Holy Spirit that a Catholic receives in the Sacraments of Baptism and Confirmation. As a result one experiences an often sudden but always noticeable "current of grace" (Cardinal Suenens) or "rediscovery of Pentecost" (St. John Paul II) by which one receives a new awareness of the presence of Jesus, a hunger for the Word of God, a desire to witness to God's working in one's life, and many more gifts of the Holy Spirit mentioned in Scripture (I Cor 12:1-11).

9. A *poustinik* is one who lives in a *poustinia*. *Poustinia (pustynja)* is a Russian word for "desert." In a religious context, it means a place to be alone with the Lord in prayer, whether in a desert, in a wilderness, or in the marketplace. The concept was introduced into Western spirituality in 1975, when Catherine de Hueck Doherty published the book, *Poustinia.*

PART TWO

GROWING UP
(1941-55)

A BLESSED BAPTISM

I was born on Friday, July 25, 1941, at 9:22 p.m. at St. Francis Catholic Hospital in Pittsburgh. My birthday was significant for several reasons. It was the twenty-fifth wedding anniversary of my father's parents, Alphonse and Eugenia Walter. Liturgically, July 25, was the feast day of two saints who would be important for me in later life: St. James the Apostle, patron of pilgrims, and St. Christopher, patron of travelers. My physical birth was followed sixteen days later by my spiritual rebirth through baptism.

On August 10, 1941, I was baptized George Florian Walter at St. Mary's of the Assumption in Glenshaw, Pennsylvania. My patron, Saint George, was the Roman soldier martyred in AD 304, under Emperor Diocletian who had braved torment after torment, before he was finally beheaded for his faith. The name George itself comes from the Greek words for "worker of the earth" (or "farmer") and is one of the Scriptural names for God Himself (see Jn 15:1, "Vinedresser"). Florian is my father's first name, which he received from my grandmother in honor of a popular Central European martyr who, like St. George, was a military officer and died in the same year under Diocletian's persecution. He is the patron of firefighters.

So, at the age of sixteen days, I received the graces of holy Baptism: immersed into the death and resurrection of Jesus Christ, cleansed of Original Sin and filled with Sanctifying Grace. I came under the early protection of the Virgin Mother of God under the title of her Assumption into Heaven (which was proclaimed a dogma of the Catholic Church in 1950, when I was nine years old). I had special intercessors in heaven in the persons of St. George St. Florian, St. Christopher, and St. James the Apostle, as well as St. Francis of Assisi.

SECURE ENCLAVE

My first fourteen years were happy with no great trauma. I felt secure in a very Catholic enclave. The neighborhood where I lived in the North Hills of suburban Pittsburgh, was mostly Catholic. Years later, however, I came to realize just how much God's hand was upon me from the very first moments of my existence in this world.

I had a reserved or more introverted and reflective side. I enjoyed being alone, hiking (or trapping), tramping through the woods with my Collie dog "Cookie," and building my cabins in the woods. I also spent time alone in my father's workshop making things. My father taught me how to use all of the hand tools and eventually the power tools. I spent hours putting together model airplanes of wood and tissue paper, as well as plastic models of ships and airplanes that came in kits with small pieces that one had to glue together. Reading was also a way I enjoyed being alone. I read the *Hardy Boys Mystery Stories* and adventure books as well as magazines like *Boys Life, Popular Mechanics, Life,* and *Look.*

ALTAR SERVER

It was also around this time (1951) that I began serving Mass. I attended Mass with my family every Sunday, but I also went to Mass every weekday morning at 8:00 a.m. with all of the other students in the school. So I had plenty of opportunities to serve at Mass once I was trained. I remember bringing the server's Latin prayer card home to my mother so I could learn the prayers. But this was one task with which my mother could not help me. She said: "You will have to ask your father how to pronounce the Latin." My father had been an altar server when he was younger, so he knew the prayers by heart and he helped me get the pronunciation right.

GREAT RESPONSIBILITY

Besides answering the prayers, as a server I had a number of other things to do around the altar. During the Mass the servers were responsible for moving the large, thick, heavy, Missal (with its stand) from one side of the altar to the other side at the proper time. At the Offertory we had to bring the priest water and wine in glass cruets and to present him with a towel and basin so he could wash his fingers. And during the Consecration of the bread and wine, the server not only had to hold the end of priest's chasuble (so it would not touch his shoes), but he also had to ring the bells. At St. Mary's, however, instead of hand bells we had a type of chime with metal bars that were struck with a leather hammer according to six different set patterns. To be able to play that was a coveted and even fought over position among us servers.

Then there was the distribution of Holy Communion. One of the servers got to hold the paten under the chin of each person who knelt at the Communion rail to receive Christ on their tongue. What a privilege it was to be part of this intimate moment when the Creator met the creature–the Redeemer met the redeemed. Only once, fifty years later, at a Polish Catholic Church in Belarus, did I see Communion accompanied by a more elaborate ritual: there was not only the server with the paten, but two servers with lit candles accompanied the priest as well as a server with a hand bell who rang it every time someone received the Body and Blood of Christ.

THE SACRAMENT OF CONFIRMATION

Once I reached the age of twelve, I was old enough to be confirmed. But it would be another twenty years (1973) before I came to experience in a personal manner, the presence and power of the Third Person of the Most Holy Trinity through the Catholic Charismatic Renewal.

The Bishop of Pittsburgh came to St. Mary's to confirm all fifth-, sixth-, seventh-, and eighth-graders on April 23, 1953. This date was special to me because it was the Feast Day of St. George, my special patron since baptism. I do not know if I was given the grace of martyrdom (like St. George), but we were taught that this Sacrament made us "a soldier for Christ" and the bishop gave us a slight slap on the cheek to remind us we had to be prepared for persecution. In the years to come on my pilgrimages throughout the world, I would certainly experience my share of misunderstanding, scoffing, and rejection.

Though I did not feel different after receiving the Sacrament, I remember the Confirmation ceremony very clearly to this day. My uncle Jerry was my sponsor and stood to my left as I was in the center aisle seat on the left side of the church. During the singing of the hymn, "Come Holy Ghost," I looked up at my uncle and saw him singing with all his heart, mind, and strength. It left on me a permanent impression of faith, solemnity, and devotion.

CHOOSING A HIGH SCHOOL

Actually, as I was nearing the end of my last year of elementary school, I was thinking of applying to the local Catholic high school,

North Catholic, taught by the Marianist brothers. But before I put in my application, my teacher said to me one day, "You know, if you are thinking of entering the seminary, you ought to start doing something about it." That was what it took to nudge me in the right direction. It was almost as if I did not dare to think I could aspire to such a lofty vocation on my own. I needed an external sign from the Lord that it was His desire and His invitation.

Deciding to enter the seminary–which was one of the most important decisions of my life–really was not that difficult, considering the times and circumstance of my life as well as the surrounding culture in which I had grown up. I had the physical health, the academic ability, the moral virtues, and the religious practices that were expected of a candidate for high school seminaries.

WANTING TO BE A PRIEST

After a few days of thinking about it, I told my parents: "I think I would like to be a priest." They said: "That's fine with us: do you want to be a Franciscan like your uncle Fr. Mathias, or a diocesan priest like Fr. Schneider?" I said: "I want to be a diocesan priest." So my father said: "I'll call the vocation director for the Diocese and see what he says."

So one day soon after that, with me present in the room, my father rang up the diocesan office and made known my request. The good monsignor on the other end of the line said to my father: "Why does he want to be a priest?" So my father asked me: "Why do you want to be a priest?" And my answer was: "I think that is how God wants me to save my soul." That was how we were taught to think in those days about a vocation–in terms of eternity. And that was good enough for the monsignor!

Entering a seminary in those days was very simple. There was no long discernment process: no battery of psychological tests; no face-to-face interviews. A transcript of my grades from St. Mary's School, copies of the Sacraments I had received from the Parish record books, a health certificate from my doctor; and a letter of recommendation from my pastor were all the documents necessary.

It seemed to me like the most natural of transitions imaginable. It did not faze me in the least that I was about to embark on a twelve-year journey. With God's grace, I hoped to be up to the challenge and to make it over the long haul.

Little did I realize how intense a formation I was about to experience.

THE PRAYER OF MY HEART

Lord Jesus,

You said that You are the Way,

the Truth and the Life.

I thank You for the call

to follow You closely,

as Your disciple.

You did not explain much

to Andrew, Peter, James and John;

You just said: "Come, follow Me"

and they obeyed.

I, too, will "come and see,"

trusting in Your goodness and wisdom

as to what is best for my life,

and how I can best serve You,

glorify the Father

and fulfill Your perfect plan
for my life.

All glory, honor and praise to You,
Father, Son and Holy Spirit,
now and forever. Amen.

PART THREE

SEMINARY TRAINING (1955-67)

INTRODUCTION

Just as the Catholic Church went through an identity crisis in the 1960s, so did I. For a time everything was calm and predictable, but storms began to rock the Barque of Peter. The old certainties were being challenged and I began to feel like I myself was in danger of capsizing. We went from a "closed" Church to an "open" Church; one in which everything was settled to one where just about everything was open to questioning; from a God-centered theology and spirituality, to a man-centered approach. In these years, the roots of Western society were being shaken by a revolt against tradition and authority. And the Church was greatly affected by all of this. I will reflect on how I too, was assailed by this revolution and how, with the Lord's grace, I survived the storm and found my true identity in Christ Jesus, the Lord.

HIGH SCHOOL SEMINARY

"You entered the seminary at the age of fourteen?"

People ask me this question in disbelief. Nowadays, when students enter (and even finish) college not knowing what they want to be, people think: "How could you choose your life vocation at such a young age?" Actually, it was not choosing the priesthood at the age of fourteen: it was rather saying: "I am willing to walk toward that goal. If all goes well (if it is God's will) I will arrive there safely."

On September 6, 1955, my mother and father drove me to downtown Pittsburgh, to the Diocesan Building, to join other young men who were on their way to St. Gregory's Minor Seminary in Cincinnati. Altogether, we were a large enough group to charter our own bus that could take us right to the door of the seminary I did not know a single other person on the bus, though I had met some of them a few weeks before at a gathering sponsored by the Serra Club of Pittsburgh.[10]

ST. GREGORY THE GREAT MINOR SEMINARY

At the end of my almost nine-hour bus ride, we encountered a beautiful campus of seventy-five mostly wooded acres in a rather exclusive residential suburb at the far eastern edge of Cincinnati called "Mount Washington." Soon after arriving at my new home, I learned that I would not be leaving this campus for the next three and a half months–until I went home for Christmas vacation in December. If I stepped off the grounds without written permission, I was subject to immediate expulsion; no recourse; no questions asked. But there was no need to go off-campus for food, clothing, shelter, shopping, medical attention, or recreation. Everything we needed was provided for us within the boundaries of the seminary confines. Some would say it was like a jail or a hothouse. But I did not see it that way. I figured the seminary authorities knew what was best for me and I had no problem with conforming to their wishes.

The rationale for this arrangement was that we were separated from the world around us, not because it was evil, but because it would have been an unnecessary distraction from the serious business of study and prayer that was necessary if we were going to eventually be good priests. St. John Neumann, Fourth Bishop of Philadelphia, expressed well the thinking behind this type of institution:

> ... If Christian youth are to be educated for the service of the Almighty, all contact with what would withdraw them from their holy vocation must be avoided.... It is true, the hearts of these young men are still innocent, yet they are susceptible of good and bad and the unfortunate striving after and imitation of whatever they foolishly admire in others, can very easily tarnish the purity of soul, sadden the Holy Ghost, and deprive them of the grace of their vocation. It is a great boon which the Church grants to her future servant if she opportunely snatches him from the noxious influences of the world, shelters and fosters him in the salutary atmosphere of her secluded sanctuary till his character has developed and he has grown up in the wisdom of God."[11]

LIFE IN THE SEMINARY

The seminary in 1955, was run pretty much like a monastery. There was a daily schedule that accounted for every minute of the day from rising at 6:00 a.m. to retiring at 10:00 p.m. A bell (actually electric buzzers positioned throughout the building) rang five minutes before each exercise as a warning, and it rang again when the exercise was to begin. Each day included Mass and times of prayer together in the chapel, classes, study halls, meals, and recreation times. Tuesday and Thursday afternoons were free for more extended recreation like team sports (volleyball, football, softball, basketball, handball, tennis, and bowling). Also popular were groupwalks of two to three hours off-campus led by an "upper-classman." The Sunday schedule was different: there were two Masses; no classes, and Solemn Vespers sung in the evening.

During my first two years at St. Greg's, I slept in a large dormitory with about forty other classmates. I personally had no problem adapting to the new regime at all. I liked things in order. I enjoyed the all-male environment and the sporting opportunities and I never complained about the food. As a matter-of-fact, I got so completely caught up in all of the various activities, I forgot to write home (there was no telephone available for students to use to call outside the seminary in those days) to let my parents know how things were going. After three weeks of anxiously awaiting a letter from me, my mother finally called the seminary office and asked the secretary if I got there okay. Needless to say, after I got that message I wrote faithfully every week to let my parents know how I was doing.

CHALLENGING STUDIES

The main subjects we studied included Latin, algebra, English, chant, physics, and religion. Then as we went along other subjects were added: geometry, Greek, and a modern language. For a foreign language we were given two choices: French and German. They said these were the most useful languages once we got to theology and had to read European theologians in their original languages. I chose German because of my ancestry; all four of my grandparents spoke German. It was not conversational German but reading and writing, and was taught by a Dominican priest.

Our instructors were very demanding and knew how to challenge us with two to three hours of homework. I suspect it was one way they were able to test our mettle and to weed out some of the students who were unable or unwilling to put forth the extra effort required to succeed. The priests tapped by the Archbishop of Cincinnati to fulfill the all-important task of forming young candidates for a possible future priestly ministry in the Catholic Church gave me the impression that they loved being a priest, were highly qualified, and were glad to be assigned to seminary formation. I thought of them as excellent models and I looked up to them, even if at times they made it difficult for me by requiring mental skills I had never needed before as, for example, in Latin and algebra.

One priest in particular, Fr. Lawrence Mick–took me under his wing. He became a close friend, a mentor, and a father figure for me. He taught us how to chant; directed the Schola Cantorum (small choir) group, and led the Gregorian Chant practice for Sunday High Mass each week. But he also mixed well with the students on an informal basis, playing handball with us regularly. When I got back a few days early from Christmas vacation in my sophomore year, Fr. Mick took me to my first live symphony at the Cincinnati Music Hall. He continued my piano lessons that I had taken my last few years in grade school, and introduced me to the electric organ. And he chose me at the end of my senior year to be a college infirmarian come the next year when I returned to begin my first year of college. I thanked the Lord for such a caring priest-director in my life at this young age.

A CLASSICAL CURRICULUM

My other high school instructors were also men who were very dedicated to our total welfare. My Latin teacher Fr. McCarthy, was also the disciplinarian and patrolled the hallways during study periods to make sure we were studying and not breaking any rules. My algebra teacher Fr. Caserta, was very devout and it was said he regularly had mystical experiences of oneness with the Lord when he was at prayer. Fr. Reardon, our English teacher was easygoing, very knowledgeable, and used the Socratic method of teaching.[12] I remember him showing us how to open a new book (folding a few pages at a time down in front and back) so as not to break the binding, and gave us the rule: "You don't have enough time in life to read all the good books, so only read the best books."

Our high school education could be considered "classical." Thus, we did not study Ecclesiastical Latin (which was considered easier and "decadent"), but the Latin of Cicero, Virgil, and Caesar, and read their works in the original. In Greek we did not study New Testament Koine Greek (the vernacular of the ancient Christian world), but the Greek of Homer's *Iliad and the Odyssey*. In English we began with Geoffrey Chaucer and worked our way through Elizabethan Shakespeare, the Romantics like Lord Byron, Perse Bysshe Shelley, and Keats to the nineteenth-century novelists like Charles Dickens, George Orwell, and G. K. Chesterton. We were exposed to the best of American writers, too, but the standard most used was that of the British Isles. In German we learned standard High German although at one point we did translate the twentieth-century classic, *The Diary of Anne Frank*.

SEMINARY MENTALITY

I could not speak about the priests who formed me these four years without a word about our rector, Msgr. Robert J. Sherry. It was said he was a retired army chaplain. And he ran the seminary like a military school. Once a week he gave a fifteen-minute pep talk for all of us high school students, to present the philosophy of seminary education, so that we would know what was expected of us. Basically the idea was: if you keep all the rules and keep up in your studies, you are a good student and you will make a good priest: if you break the rules and do not measure up, you will be asked to leave. One of his favorite sayings was the old bromide, "You cannot make a silk purse out of a sow's ear." In other words, if you are not good raw material, there is no possibility of forming you into a worthy priest.

On the outside I basically accepted this. And even internally I did not rebel. The years of radical questioning and even opposition did not come until another four years had passed. I would need more models of possibilities outside the institutional Church before

I could imagine any alternatives. In the late 1950s, the Catholic Church was still operating out of a "siege mentality," a remnant from the days of the Protestant Reformation four centuries earlier, when she had to defend herself against the Reformers. As a protective mother, she had her guard up; the line separating the Kingdom of God from the Kingdom of the World was carefully drawn and maintained. Our life in the minor seminary was lived pretty much inside the fortress walls.

Thus, for example, no magazines, radio, or TV were permitted except at certain times and only under strict supervision. Our mail was censored and one could only write to parents and to immediate family members. The Vatican's Index of Forbidden Books was still in effect, so one could only read what was provided in the seminary library. It was definitely a controlled environment–deliberately so. It had been that way for the past four hundred years, since the Council of Trent had decreed seminaries into existence in the sixteenth century. It worked in the past, so why should it not still work now? But there was the rumbling of distant thunder. The storm would eventually break and the floodwaters would eventually rage. Then the Lord would have to send a few lifeboats.

MY SPIRITUAL LIFE

And what was my spiritual life like at this time? I attended all of the public prayers said in the chapel: Lauds (Morning Prayer); Mass; Vespers (Evening Prayer); and Compline (Night Prayer). Once or twice a day when I passed by the chapel, I would stop and "make a visit" to the Lord who was present in the Blessed Sacrament. At that time I would just say some spontaneous or memorized prayers or ejaculations: one-line indulgenced prayers like, "Lord, have mercy" or "Jesus I love you."

There was a pamphlet rack available to us in the seminary basement that carried a fair selection of paperback religious books

70

that we could purchase. One of these books that I bought was Thomas Merton's *Seeds of Contemplation*, which I bought for 35 cents. This became one of my favorite books for meditation and for spiritual reading which I kept going back to throughout the rest of my life. I also regularly used Thomas á Kempis's *Imitation of Christ*, published by the Confraternity of the Precious Blood and illustrated by the Armenian artist and papal knight Ariel Agemian, KSG. It too, has been a faithful companion on my journey with the Lord over the years.

JESUS IS THE VINE

But there was one significant moment in my high school days where I felt the Lord speaking to me personally. Toward the end of my freshman year, my favorite priest, Fr. Mick, casually mentioned in one of his chant classes that we would do well to purchase a pocket-size New Testament in Latin and read it regularly. He said it would be helpful in our ministry if we became familiar with the Word of God in the official language of the church. I decided to follow through on his suggestion.

When my copy arrived and I picked it up at the Seminary Book Store, the first thing I did was go to the chapel alone. There I was led to check out what Gospel was assigned for the Feast of St. James the Apostle on July 25, for that was my birthday. It was John 15:1-8: the Vine and the Branches. It began, *"Ego sum vitis vera"* (I am the true vine). It was more than just reading words from the pages of a book. It was like a personal word from the Lord meant especially for me.

It was as though the Lord was laying out a program for my future.

Once I learned Greek and many years later reflecting back on this same passage, I saw that God the Father and I had the same name–George. The second half of verse one says: "... and my Father is the Vine-dresser." The word for "vine-dresser" in Greek is γεοργος (*georgos*), which is the root word for my name George. So I had another personal connection with this passage in Jesus' Last Discourse to His Apostles at the Last Supper in the Cenacle in Jerusalem. Both the Father and the Son therefore had key roles in my spiritual growth and it was only through them that I would be able to produce the fruit of the Holy Spirit, thereby glorifying the Holy Trinity and accomplishing their plan for my life. It would be a lifetime task, but already the Lord was showing me the way. Praise His Holy Name.

SUNDAY HIGH MASS

The peak experience for us seminarians was the Sunday morning Solemn High Mass. Since Vatican II in 1965, this is seldom experienced by most Roman Catholics. Only those who attend the Extraordinary Form of the Mass (the Latin Tridentine Mass) or Roman Catholics over the age of sixty, know experientially what I am referring to. It was actually the second Mass for us on Sunday morning and was at 9:00 a.m. We had already attended a Low Mass at 6:30 a.m., at which time we had all received Holy Communion. So the High Mass was not so much a time of private prayer and communing with the Lord, as it was pure public worship of the Lord for whom He is in His majesty and splendor.

On the altar were often three priests in full Gothic vestments: one was the main celebrant; another was "the deacon," and the third was "the subdeacon," all with their own specific parts. They were assisted by four or six seminarians wearing black cassocks and plain white surplices. There was plenty of incense and bells were rung to announce the more solemn parts. One got the impression from this ritual, that something important was taking place: that one was privileged to get a little glimpse of heaven: that this was the "worship in Spirit and Truth" that Jesus had spoken about to the Samaritan woman (Jn 4:23).

VACATION TIMES

Before I close this high school chapter of my life and go on to the college years, I should briefly mention how I spent the times each year when I was on vacation. At home we did not have the detailed schedule or a bell to signal what was expected of us. But we were expected to live "the spirit of the rule" at home, just as we had lived it in the seminary under the watchful eye of our priest formators. On vacations, people treated me as now belonging to a special group, as one set apart, a seminarian—one on his way to priesthood. So it was tacitly understood that I would not be interested in the same things my previous peers who were not seminarians would be interested in: parties, movies, and dating.

JANITOR'S ASSISTANT

Each morning in the summer I would attend daily Mass at 8:00 a.m. at my home parish, St. Mary's. But I did not keep up the other daily prayers we said in the seminary. I would get some type of summer job for minimum pay. Usually my pastor would hire me to work around the church cutting grass in the cemetery with a large self-propelled rotary mower. I would also help the janitor. We took down all the florescent lights in the school and cleaned them, as well as scrubbed all the floors with an industrial-size scrubber. Then we would wax and buff them until they had a brilliant shine.

HIGH SCHOOL GRADUATION

On June 5, 1959, my class received their diplomas from the Archdiocese of Cincinnati. For the occasion our class published a mimeographed booklet with a one-page profile of each graduate (with a pen and ink sketch). In the introductory "Greetings from the Rector" Msgr. Sherry said: "May the training which you received in virtue and scholarship and character formation in St. Gregory's produce abundant fruits for good in your lives. No matter what the future may have in store for you, your Alma Mater will always be concerned for your true welfare .... If you are always faithful to the principles which you have imbibed here, your life will be a success in the best sense of the word. God grant it." This type of formation for diocesan priests would eventually be judged antiquated and ineffective in providing priests for the American dioceses of the late twentieth century. Eventually it was thought better to mainstream high school students who thought they might be called to the priesthood. Potential candidates would be encouraged to even complete their college studies and get some experience of working in the world before withdrawing to a seminary campus for study and formation.

THE SPICE OF HUMOR

Reading through this graduation booklet, it becomes abundantly clear that humor was a very big part of the life of a high school seminarian in those days. One article is entitled, "Russia Converted, May 31, 1984," and has one of our top classmates whose first name was Paul, cast as "Pope Paul VI" debating with Russia and winning the argument. The one-page profile for me calls me "Reddy Kilowatt" (the cartoon mascot of a local power company) as a way to describe me being really handy when it came to "fixing anything electrical or rigging up electronic devices for picking up the sound of cracking ankles" (i.e., made by the priest-disciplinarian walking the halls checking on his charges). It also notes, regarding some of my extracurricular activities in the seminary: "He is a very good barber—if you like a burr. In sports George has run up quite a bill for breaking windows with his wicked bat." And this offering: "He has kept a diary of our four years here which he plans to publish after his death." And in another article they wrote: "George Walter terrified the dormitory with his sleep-walking antics. He just couldn't seem to get into the right bed in the dark."

Perhaps humor was a defense or survival mechanism for the students. We knew we were not here to have fun; we were engaged in the ultimately serious task of preparing–for the vocation to be an *alter Christus* (another Christ). How do young high school boys get a handle on the fact that someday they would be asked to represent the Lord of heaven and earth to God's people? Perhaps it was so mind-boggling to think that one might one day have the responsibility of making Jesus, the Savior of the world, present through the Sacraments, that it was better to distract oneself from that thought with jokes and antics that kept one's feet on the ground and anchored them to this earthly reality. Whatever the explanation, humor was definitely a characteristic of the written record of our years in the high school seminary.

FIRST AND SECOND COLLEGE

The twelve-year seminary system of that day was divided in half: the first six years were called Minor Seminary and the last six years were called Major Seminary. In the whole picture, we were one-third of the way to ordination in 1967: four years down, eight to go. In the immediate context we were two-thirds of the way through the six years of Minor Seminary: four down, two to go. When we came back to St. Greg's in September, we merely reported to the other complex of buildings across the way, to take up our first two years of college. It would not be all that much of an adjustment: just different classrooms and different sleeping rooms. Yes, we changed blazers, from high school gray to college blue to show we were different, but it was more a smooth transition than a radical break. We would step into our new pair of shoes and walk with our heads a little higher as we made our way up the ladder toward the ultimate goal of priestly service in God's holy Church.

Now that we were upperclassmen, we felt we were preparing to enter the most important stage of our seminary training in two years: philosophy and theology. But for now, our next two years still consisted of a liberal arts curriculum. In the language department, besides Latin, Greek, and German, I decided to add French to my class load. I had always admired the sound of French and it piqued my interest as how to pronounce this mysterious language. My first semester in college, the introductory conversational French course, was taught by a priest who went to France every summer to hone his skills.

AN UNFORTUNATE BIOLOGY CLASS

The biology class was taught by a priest who had worked on the Manhattan Project which developed the atomic bomb that was dropped on Japan at the end of World War II. So he was certainly qualified in terms of academic experience; his spiritual discernment, however, left something to be desired. It was he who introduced his students to Teilhard de Chardin (1881-1955), the Jesuit priest-anthropologist whose writings were becoming very popular at this time.

Our professor suggested we get a three-volume set by de Chardin which included *The Phenomenon of Man, The Divine Milieu,* and *The Future of Man.* Because de Chardin was a paleontologist and I was an avid collector of fossils, I felt a kinship with him. His books were filled with terms like *hominization, noosphere, cosmogenesis, Omega Point,* and *Cosmic Christ.* His basic thrust was to cast the Christian Faith in evolutionary terminology. It was a noble effort but had serious drawbacks, especially with regard to theological notions like Original Sin, creation from nothing, salvation history, divine providence, and human freedom. In June 1962, the Holy Office[13] issued a *monitum* or "warning" saying that seminary authorities needed to guard their students against exposure to these potentially dangerous books. In my case, the warning came two years after I had ingested the poison.

It would not be until 1968, in the Rocky Mountains, that I was able to be cured of its harmful influence.

INFIRMARIAN

One of the more defining elements of my two years of college at St. Greg's, was in being chosen to be a student infirmarian. There were two of us. The other infirmarian and I shared a small dormitory room between the dispensary and the sick dorm. Anyone who had a cold, ache, or pain, lined up outside the dispensary door to see us each night after Compline (the final hour of the Divine Office), before they went to bed.

Beyond this health service to the college seminarians, however, the infirmarian inherited another responsibility that was quite unrelated to health–and somewhat devious. A large cardboard box full of very valuable (and irreplaceable) papers eagerly sought after and pored over by the students, was passed onto each successive infirmarian. They were copies of the exams given by the professor of English literature, that went back many years. Thus, when exam time came, students would ask to borrow this box so they could see what kind of questions they might expect to find on the upcoming exam.

Did the professor know about this secret stash? I do not see how he could not have known. But why did he not take steps to confiscate it? It would have been easy for him to just ask us to hand it over to him. Perhaps he was satisfied that at least it got his students to put in time preparing for his test. Nevertheless, he carefully guarded the number of copies of the exam he had printed. (Remember, this was before the day when a cell phone or ipad could easily photograph a set of exam papers. Nothing even like a copy machine was available for our use!) The exam was typed out on wax stencils and mimeographed in the seminary print shop. Were the students in the print shop bold enough to make an extra copy (against his strict orders) of each exam and privately hand it over to the secret file? Whatever was happening here, students and teacher had played this cat-and-mouse game for ages.

SPORTS, MOVIES AND SPEAKERS

Outside of classwork and study, we had more than ample diversionary and recreational activities. First of all, there were sports to play. Outside in the fall and spring we could play softball, football, tennis, and handball. In the winter we were confined to the inside and could bowl, and play basketball, handball, and Ping-Pong. For the less athletic there was a card room where one could play Canasta, Pinochle, Five Hundred, and Bridge. Once in awhile I would join in with these games since I came from a card-playing family.

Practically every Saturday night, we had a full-length feature movie. We rented these on acetate film, wound on large metal reels that came by mail. We saw just-released movies like *Bridge on the River Kwai*, *Ivanhoe*, *The Keys of the Kingdom*, *Treasure Island*, *Madam Curie*, *Deep in My Heart*, and *The Student Prince*. For the most part we were not allowed to watch movies on TV. So what we saw was able to be carefully screened—and had the advantage of no commercials.

We also had guest speakers visiting the seminary regularly to broaden our perspective and to augment our education. A number of times the well-known Irish Bard, Seamus MacManus, came by to give us a talk and to read us his poetry. Dr. Tom Dooley (1927-61), the American physician and one-time candidate for beatification, came by regularly to give us inspiring accounts of his humanitarian work in Vietnam and in Laos, combating disease and communism. We would also have visiting lectures on church history or the Shrine of Lourdes. Everything possible was done to equip us for a well-rounded future service to the church.

SUMMER CAMP

My first summer as a collegian took on a new and exciting development. I was a camp counselor for the diocesan Catholic Youth Council boys' session of Camp Fatima in Renfrew, Pennsylvania, in rural Butler County north of Pittsburgh. The staff was mostly seminarians. That made for a nice fellowship among the counselors and excellent role models for the five hundred or more young Catholic boys ages nine to fourteen who attended camp each summer. We were paid a small stipend and of course received our room and board free. As seminarians we also got $100 taken off of our seminary education bill for every year we worked there as a further incentive to make this a part of our summer activities.

ENTERING MAJOR SEMINARY

In September of 1961, coming to the end of our six years of training in the minor seminary, my classmates[14] and I in "second-year college" (equivalent to sophomore year) from Pittsburgh attending St. Greg's, began to think more about where we would be assigned for the major seminary the following year. There were a few possibilities. One was in Rome. That was really only for the very best students and none of us from Pittsburgh considered that a possibility. We could also be sent to Catholic University in Washington, D.C., but that did not appeal to any of us either. The most likely assignment would be St. Vincent Seminary in Latrobe, Pennsylvania, and that was our hope, as it would be closer to home and was reportedly easier scholastically than the other possibilities.

It was a great disappointment for us therefore when, on May 18, 1961, we each received a letter from the vocation director of the Diocese of Pittsburgh saying it was Bishop Wright's wish that we take our two years of philosophy and receive our BA degree from Mount St. Mary's of the West in Norwood, Ohio; thus we would not be going to St. Vincent's until we started theology in two more years. His reasoning was that in the past those students who transferred from St. Greg's to St. Vincent's had to attend summer sessions at Duquesne University in Pittsburgh to meet the requirements for the BA degree from St. Vincent's. Of course it made sense logically and was ultimately for our good, but it was a bitter pill for us (and our families) to swallow as we looked forward to being closer to our families and not having to make that long eight-hour bus trip six times a year.

TWO YEARS ON THE ROCK

Mount St. Mary's of the West (dating back to 1851) would now be my "dear mother" for the next two years. Affectionately referred to as "The Rock," it was built on the highest piece of ground in a business district on the outskirts of Cincinnati. It was quite a change physically from the spacious wooded campus we had at St. Greg's. When I entered the first year of philosophy on September 5, 1961, my class was comprised of six years of major seminary: two years of philosophy and four years of theology.[15] We were all in one building but in two separate wings joined in the middle by the chapel which could easily handle the whole student body.

We were here primarily, of course, to study and hopefully in two years, to receive our bachelor's degree in philosophy, which in those days was called "the handmaid of theology." The theory was that one needed to know the scholastic (Aristotelian/Thomistic) way of thinking in order to understand theology which was couched in those terms. To the State of Ohio Department of Education, St. Mary's Seminary was known as "The Athenaeum of Ohio, College of Liberal Arts, Upper Division." My class load for these two years was twenty credit hours in philosophy (logic, cosmology, ethics, politics, and metaphysics), the history of philosophy, history, speech, German, education (for accreditation), sociology, psychology, and even one semester of Hebrew to prepare us for eventual studies in the Old Testament. (At the coaching of one of my professors, I tried trigonometry, but I could not get past the first couple of weeks so I dropped out of it; math was never my forte.)

In early 1962, a decree had come from Rome saying that our philosophy courses had to be taught in Latin. We all groaned! Philosophy was hard enough; now it had to be in a foreign language. But our professor made a gallant effort to comply and made it as easy for us as he could. He would ask us true and false questions in class and on the exam, so all we had to do was answer *verum* (true) or *falsum* (false). At least that way we had a 50/50 chance of getting it right. That only lasted one semester and word came down "from on high" that we could go back to having the professor teach us in English (but still from the Latin textbooks).

MY BACHELOR'S THESIS

To get our Bachelor of Arts degree, we had to pick a subject and write a thesis. I was overjoyed when my philosophy professor said I could write my thesis in the field of paleontology, because science/physics was part of philosophy in the classical Greek scheme of Aristotle. I had been collecting fossils in Ohio and in Pennsylvania for the past seven years, so I could use them as the basis of my thesis. The title ended up being, "The Pennsylvanian and Mississippian Periods in Pennsylvania and Ohio." It dealt with the geological formations and fossil records for the periods when coal was forming 325 million years ago. The plates of photographs of fossils I attached to my thesis included not only ferns and petrified wood, but also brachiopods, crinoids, corals, and even some trilobites. I know there is a copy of my thesis at the Athenaeum of Ohio in Cincinnati, if anyone ever has an interest in reading it.

SPIRITUAL FORMATION

And what was our spiritual formation during these first two years of the major seminary? First of all, it was impressed upon us, by the way we dressed, that we were now entering upon a more immediate preparation for priesthood. When outside the seminary, we wore a black suit, white long-sleeved shirt, black tie, black shoes, and black hat. Inside the seminary walls, we dressed like priests. That is, we wore a black cassock and Roman collar to classes and to meals. On Sundays in chapel we added a white linen surplice and biretta (a clerical three-cornered hat). We could substitute khaki shirts and trousers for work and play.

Our daily schedule included Holy Mass, Prime and Compline, meditation, "particular examination of conscience," Scripture reading, and Benediction of the Blessed Sacrament. At night in chapel, after all of the public prayers were said, before going to our rooms in silence to retire, we read over the following day's topic of meditation. I also remember buying a paperback book by St. Teresa of Avila, *Way of Perfection*. So we were encouraged to get into the daily habit of making mental prayer (meditation).

VATICAN COUNCIL II

One of the most defining moments of my life, however, occurred just after I got back to St. Mary's Seminary for my second year of philosophy: the opening of Vatican Council II by Pope John XXIII on October 11. We knew it was coming of course for the Pope had announced it already back in 1959, and every Catholic was praying for its success. I remember some seminarian got thirty-five-millimeter slides of the opening session in St. Peter's Basilica in Rome, with all of the thousands of bishops gathered there, and made them available to anyone who wanted copies of them. It was such an historic moment and such pageantry.

During our second semester, in the fall of 1963, Hans Kung, the well-know theologian from Europe, was making the rounds on a speaking tour of the United States. The whole seminary body went to hear him speak. The title of his talk, I believe, was the same as his 1961 book: "The Council: Reform and Reunion." His basic thesis was that the aggiornamento (updating) called for by Pope John XXIII, was the reform of the Church that Protestant reformers had called for, four hundred years ago. He even quoted the Latin adage: "Ecclesia semper reformanda est" (The Church is always reforming itself). It would take another sixteen years for the full implication of this theologian's numerous heterodox ideas to develop to the point where the Vatican had to strip him of his license to teach as a Roman Catholic theologian, especially because of his notions of papal infallibility and the admissibility of euthanasia.

The other part of the title of Kung's talk, "Reunion," implied that it was Pope John's intention to get the Catholic Church onboard with the Ecumenical Movement and make it possible for all of the various denominations to be reunited with the Catholic Church. It was heady stuff and there were scholars in the wings ready to run with these ideas according to their own agendas. What did we young seminarians in their early twenties understand about all of this? Change sounded good to us. I remember reading a poster about this time saying: "All living things change and to be alive means to have changed much." What was not pointed out, was that change of itself is ambiguous: both growing and decaying things are changing: one for the better–the other for the worse. The full force of the principle of change introduced into the Church would not break for a few years yet. But the seeds were being sown now: it would take awhile for their fruits (both good and bad) to become evident.

SAINT VINCENT SEMINARY

I was happy to receive a letter at home from the bishop's office dated June 20, 1963, saying: "Having successfully completed the course of philosophy and about to enter the study of theology in preparation for the Priesthood in the Diocese of Pittsburgh, Bishop Wright assigns you to St. Vincent Seminary, Latrobe, Pennsylvania." Finally it looked like I was headed down the home stretch: eight years down, four to go.

Little did I suspect at the time how tumultuous those last four years would be.

Saint Vincent Seminary, in Latrobe, Pennsylvania, located in the heart of southwestern Pennsylvania's Laurel Highlands, has a long and venerable history. Many Irish and German Catholics had settled on the rich farmland in this area all through the eighteenth century. St. Vincent's was founded in 1790, in a building called "Sportsman's Hall" as the region's first diocesan parish to serve the faithful in this "cradle of Catholicism in western Pennsylvania." In 1846, it began to be served by Benedictine monks from Bavaria, who proceeded to establish a monastery, a college, and America's fourth oldest major seminary on the property, besides the parish church which is now a minor basilica. So when I arrived on the beautiful sprawling rural campus of St. Vincent Archabbey on September 8, 1963, I became part of a well-established Catholic tradition.

At the time I did not realize it, but what I had been looking forward to here on this campus for over two years had, seven months before, almost all gone up in smoke. On January 28, 1963, a devastating $2-million fire had raged through classrooms, living quarters, chapel, and offices and had nearly consumed all that the Benedictines had carefully built up over so many years. Over four hundred firefighters from thirty-one fire companies battled those blazes all day long in temperatures that hovered around minus 10 degrees. They barely managed to save the basilica church, parts of the monastery, and the seminary building where I would be spending my next four years. By the time I arrived in September, all of the debris had been cleared away, new grass had been planted, and the Benedictine life continued on without skipping scarcely a beat. But there was still a scar, both on the physical plant and in the hearts of those who had lived through that nightmare. But God's hand was upon them

84

and Divine Providence provided: by the marvelous grace of God, a new semester could begin and I, with the other students and faculty, would be able to work our way through another year of formation in preparation for serving God's people.

THE PHYSICAL FACILITIES

When I entered Wimmer Hall, the brick building at the edge of the campus just to the south of the basilica that housed the seminarians in those days, I found everything I needed for my physical maintenance and intellectual growth. I was assigned a small, private room with a bed, a desk, and a chair where I could sleep and do most of my studying. The toilets and showers were down the hallway and shared by the other students on the floor. The dining hall was on the lowest level and the meals were prepared by German-speaking Benedictine nuns from nearby St. Emma's Monastery. The chapel we used was in the crypt of the basilica. The building that connected our dormitory to the basilica contained our classrooms, and on the lowest level, our recreation room. We had access to Sportsman's Hall which had a gym where we could play basketball and bowl, as well as an auditorium where we could attend plays and lectures. Also available were outside playing fields for softball games and an area for volleyball. The seminarians had a special area called "The Cherry Path" for taking walks on the property and finally there was a large lake where we could ice-skate in the winter when it froze over.

THE SCHOLASTIC PROGRAM

I found myself part of a class of thirty-three students who made up our first year of theology. Fifteen of us were studying for the Diocese of Pittsburgh; four were with the local Diocese of Greensburg; four were Benedictines; and the rest were from the Dioceses of Harrisburg, Washington, D.C., Brooklyn, and Camden. We were not given a choice as to what classes we would take but were handed a weekly schedule that included five hours of Dogmatic Theology; four hours of Moral Theology; three hours of Patrology (Church Fathers); three hours of Sacred Scripture; two hours of Catechetics; and one hour each for Sacred Eloquence (homiletics); and Chant. Two hours of Canon Law were added in the second semester.

All of our professors were Benedictine priests and the youngest of them was our Scripture professor, Fr. Demetrius Dumm OSB. Fr. Demetrius had succeeded as rector that same year, having been vice-rector from 1955 to 1963. A far-reaching decision had apparently been made by the theological faculty the summer before I entered to put aside the theological manuals of dogma and moral theology that had been standard for the past four hundred years in seminary training, and to take the documents of Vatican Council II as the basic texts for our classes. This in my opinion now was a disastrous step. It meant that the accumulated wisdom of saints like Thomas Aquinas, Alphonsus Ligouri, honed by centuries of systematic arranging and presentation of the teaching of the Church, were jettisoned and replaced by documents written by a handful of modern scholars. In addition to that, all that we received in the classroom then, was one Benedictine's take on these documents. What did we know? We were not scholars and were hardly familiar with the theological traditions of our past. We docilely followed along and tried our best to make our way through the forest of unexplored and often far out contradictory theological opinions.

SHAKING THE FOUNDATIONS

This was the time of what was called, "The Death of God" theologies. The cover of *Time* magazine, in its April 6, 1966 issue, asked, "Is God Dead?" And this was not questioning whether Jesus–the Second Person of the Holy Trinity–died on Calvary on Good Friday, suffering death for our sins or not. It was asking whether the God proclaimed by Christians for two thousand years was no longer

A facsimile of my seminary schedule from St. Vincent's

St. Vincent Seminary
Latrobe, Pennsylvania
SEMINARY DAILY SCHEDULE
[1964-65]

A.M.

6:25	Rise
6:45	Angelus, Meditation (Basilica)
7:15	Breakfast, Recreation til 8:00
8:15	Class or study
11:20	Mass (Basilica)

P.M.

12:15	Lunch (No visit to Chapel after lunch)
	Recreation
3:15	Class or study
4:15	Study
5:15	Rosary (Chapel)
5:30	Supper (No visit to Chapel after supper)
	Recreation
7:15	Compline (Crypt)
	Study
10:15	Recess
10:45	Prepare to retire
11:00	Lights-out.

SUNDAY SCHEDULE

A.M.

6:40	Rise
7:00	Solemn High Mass (Crypt)
	Breakfast, recreation
	10:30 Study

P.M.

12:15	Lunch, Recreation
5:00	Vespers (Basilica)
5:30	Supper (etc. as on daily schedule)

needed, understood, or relevant to modern men and women. Thrown into this mix was Existentialism which was a philosophical system that began with man and centered on human experience rather than on God and who He is: the primacy of the subjective rather than the objective. So we studied "Situation Ethics" in which individual circumstances could make what was objectively wrong, right. Secularism came on the scene and overthrew the sense of the sacred and the importance of the transcendent. Liberation theology took the Gospel and reduced it to economics, politics, and a worldly kind of freedom. Demythologization of the Scripture denied the miraculous in the Bible and set up a false dichotomy between "the historical Christ" and "the Christ of faith." This went on and on; we were being hit from all sides by waves of dissent-based theologies and philosophies crashing all around us.

As one might imagine, this all caused a good bit of unrest and anxiety among us students. How were we to sort all of this out? What should we take seriously and what should we slough off as irrelevant? If all of the old certainties were being called into question, how could we preach the Gospel to the People of God with any conviction or authority? Once the principle of change had been introduced into the church through "the new liturgy" (the "Novus Ordo"), what was to stop change from being applied in the areas of morality, dogma (doctrine), and Scriptures? A Latin adage, lex orandi, lex credendi, lex vivendi (The law of praying is the law of believing, [which] is the law of living) implies that the way in which we pray dictates the way in which we believe, which further dictates the way in which we live. If the Mass becomes more casual, more secularized (worldly), more Protestantized (hymn singing), more feminized (female lectors, eucharistic ministers, and servers) and more laicized (non-ordained people in the sanctuary), then what is to stop our way of believing and living from following suit? Would this not lead to a crisis of faith?

LIVING THE CHANGES

All of this was also reflected in our seminary community–how we lived among ourselves on a day-to-day basis. We, as a student body, were asking for (perhaps demanding) more freedom and opportunities for self-expression. For example, we did not want to have to wear cassocks during the day, but only at liturgical functions (secularization). We wanted to be able to go off-campus without getting permission from the seminary authorities (freedom from authority). We wanted to be able to relate more and mix with the students in the college division (diversity/dialogue). We wanted our own student publication without censorship (self-expression). We did not want to live under a set of rules handed down from seminary authorities–we just wanted them to issue us "directives" (autonomy). We wanted our own student government (community/responsibility) and we actually did draw up a document which we called a "Seminary Constitution" with elected officers and regular student body meetings. As Fr. Demetrius remarked to me decades later (2002) about those years, "Those were difficult times."

Much of this was due to the prevailing culture around us that was itself going through its own seismic convulsions, and these were influencing us seminarians. This was the time of the civil rights movement, Martin Luther King, and the race riots across the country. Some of my classmates went to the South in the summer of 1965, to help out with voter registration in the black community. This was the era of the unpopular Vietnam War and student unrest on college campuses. Some of those in the seminary questioned our exempt status as students for the priesthood and eventually burned their draft cards. This was also the era of the pill and debates about the morality of artificial contraception and we were reading authors (e.g., Noonan and Curran) who said the Church should change its ancient teaching on the matter. The Holocaust in the Second World War was being revisited and we actually put on Rolf Hochhuth's play, *The Deputy*, which maliciously and falsely maligned Pope Pius XII regarding his role in dealing with the Nazi menace. This was also the time of the hippy phenomenon in California. These were the young people who were disillusioned with the materialism of their Greatest Generation parents, and who wanted to make love, not war. They dropped out of the Straight Culture and went to work every day, paid taxes, and so contributed to the gross national product. Rather, this new breed just wanted to spend all of their time grooving, or as they said, turning on.

Since we were being given basic courses in psychology and in sociology, we were being encouraged to look at life not only with the eyes of faith, but also through these lenses of the human sciences. So I got involved with what was called, "The Chardin Center" and participated in taking surveys in specific areas around Pittsburgh with the goal of eventually doing some community organizing. Even Saul Alinsky, the thinly veiled Socialist radical from Chicago, was invited to the campus to give a talk. Many of my fellow seminarian classmates and I attended. It was one more blow inflicted upon the identity of the priest, as radical secularizing forces in the church were moving the priest away from the altar and out into the role of "community organizer." I did not part ways with this direction which embraced man's earthly life, for another five years when I set out on my first walking pilgrimage to Jerusalem in 1970, and set my sights on heaven.

SEVEN STEPS TO PRIESTHOOD

While all of this intellectual and emotional turmoil was fermenting, we were being moved toward priesthood by the reception of Minor and Major Orders. In those days we spoke of "The Seven Steps toward Priesthood." They were divided into four Minor Orders (Porter, Lector, Exorcist, and Acolyte) and three Major Orders (Subdeacon, Deacon, and Priest). All of these were proceeded by Tonsure (a ceremonial snipping of a lock of hair) which made one a cleric (as distinct from a layperson). Thus in my first semester of the Second Year of Theology on December 16, 1964, I received Tonsure at the hands of Bishop William Connare of the Diocese of Greensburg. The following day he conferred on all of the members of my class the Minor Orders of Porter and Lector. One year later he conferred on us the higher Minor Orders of Acolyte and Exorcist. These Orders were pretty much just ceremonial offices in modern times, although they did go back to the third-century church in Rome where they were true clerical ministries. After receiving them, we truly did not have any new duties or responsibilities or privileges. They were merely canonical requirements for receiving Major Orders.

Receiving Subdiaconate, however, on March 26, 1966, from the hands of Bishop Vincent M. Leonard at St. Bernard Church in the Pittsburgh suburb of Mount Lebanon, was another matter. This Order brought with it the obligation of perpetual celibacy and recitation of the Breviary. This required more reflection and deeper awareness of the seriousness of what we were approaching. Several months before the ceremony, each candidate was given a one-page printout entitled, "Declaration of Freedom and Knowledge of Obligations Assumed" (by receiving Subdiaconate, Diaconate, or Priesthood). We were to copy out each of the four paragraphs in longhand. Then in the presence of the rector, with a hand on a Bible, we signed the document under oath. The four paragraphs attested to our full freedom (without coercion) in asking for this Order; our full knowledge of its obligations and our intention to observe them; the meaning of the law of celibacy; and our intention to obediently observe all of the commands of our ecclesiastical superiors. For those of us from the Diocese of Pittsburgh, this was followed up by a personal one-on-one meeting with Bishop Wright who came to the seminary so he could talk to each of us individually. We were very glad for this opportunity to speak directly to our bishop about matters that deeply concerned us.

MOVING FORWARD

In all of this, of course, I was praying for God to guide and to enlighten me to make the right decision. I distinctly remember how the Lord answered my prayer during the ceremony for ordination to subdiaconate. I was sitting in the sanctuary of St. Bernard's Church after having been prayed over and clothed with the tunicle, the outer garment proper to the Order. It was no longer just words now, or thinking and talking: here was a concrete action which brought it all home to me with great clarity. It said: "This is what you are getting yourself into." But instead of a great sense of peace and "rightness" about what was happening to me, my general sense was, "I do not belong here; this role as a cultic minister, is not my calling. The Lord is asking me for something else." Subdiaconate was followed up in just over two months with diaconate on June 4, 1966, by Bishop Wright at Epiphany Church in Pittsburgh's Uptown neighborhood. Then came a six-week summer pastoral assignment to an inner-city parish, St. Mary's in Lawrenceville, adjacent to downtown Pittsburgh. Here I dressed in a black suit and Roman collar, with the title, "the Reverend Mr. George Walter." I spent most of each day that summer pounding the pavement, walking from house to house, filling out census cards. I did get to baptize a few babies and so exercised this sacramental aspect of the diaconate.

SAND ON THE TRACK

Then, in returning to the seminary for my fourth and final year of theology, I experienced more and more clearly a discomfort with living out the ordained ministry. I felt like I was loosing traction on the direct track taking me toward ordained priesthood. I wondered if there were not another track that would shunt me off to the side for a bit. Finally, on December 10 of 1966, during my personal interview concerning ordination to the priesthood with Bishop Wright, I agreed I would not petition for ordination with my class of 1967, which was slated for June. Nevertheless, I would finish out my second semester of theology with my classmates. (I had already received my Bachelor of Divinity with high honors on May 29, 1966.) Then I would take a year's leave of absence, without requesting a dispensation from the diaconate. Now the question was: "What would I do at the end of the second semester if I was not going to be ordained with the rest of my classmates?"

I toyed with the idea of joining VISTA or the Peace Corps. I even wrote to the Catholic research organization, the Center for Applied Research in the Apostolate based in Washington, D.C. But somehow the thought of traveling alone west to California formed in my mind and I eventually decided to head out into the desert of the secular world. Thus I thought, with no particular commitments, I could better give my restless heart the opportunity to seek the ultimate meaning of my life. Without my clearly realizing it at the time, I was becoming "a pilgrim of the absolute." And this is how I made it to California in the summer of love in 1967.

A poem by Louis Evely (1910-85) seemed to fit my situation at this time:

From the first step

those who've followed Jesus

have had to revise their concept of God

and therefore break with everything

that imbued them with it:

friends, connections, social milieu

and the entire conventional framework of ideas and practices

that Jesus came to turn inside out.

We have to abandon the whole worm-eaten structure

that Christ came to blow up—

abandon it immediately, utterly—

when we follow Jesus,

when we start believing in God,

in the true God,

in the living God.

When someone starts believing for good,

when he starts taking God seriously once for all,

he usually begins by scandalizing everybody;

all those "good Christians" who are too "humble"

to depart from the accepted pattern:

all those who feel they have the right religion -

a time honored one that jolts nobody.[16]

THE PRAYER OF MY HEART

Lord, I trust myself into Your hands.

Protect me on my journey.

I surrender to Your guiding Holy Spirit,

as I seek Your plan for my life.

I am willing to go wherever You send me

to do whatever You choose for me to do.

With Your help nothing will be impossible.

And with Your blessing

my life will glorify Your holy name,

and bring Your light

into the darkness of our world.

Now and forever.

Amen

ENDNOTES

10. The first Serra Club was formed in 1935, to promote vocations to the ministerial priesthood and to the consecrated religious life in the Catholic Church. Currently it has 500 clubs with 15,000 members in forty-six countries. For more information, see <serrans.org>.

11. Bishop John Neumann, CSSR, Pastoral Letter, October 2, 1859.

12. The Greek philosopher Socrates (399 BC) taught his students by asking and answering questions to stimulate critical thinking and to draw out ideas and underlying presumptions.

13. Holy Office. This was the Vatican Congregation (now known as the "Congregation for the Doctrine of the Faith") entrusted with guarding Catholic Faith and morals, judging heresy, applying canonical sanctions, examining books, and prohibiting books held to be dangerous to faith and morals.

14. Classmates. Only three of us five were left from the original twenty-six who had entered the first year of high school from the Diocese of Pittsburgh in 1955; the other two joined us in our first year of college in 1959. Of these five, only one would eventually be ordained to the priesthood in 1967.

15. Enrollment. Nineteen years later, in 1980, with enrollment down to seventy, the seminary building in Norwood was sold and St. Mary's of the West moved to the Mt. Washington facility. By 1998, only twenty-seven students were enrolled at St. Mary's.

16. Louis Evely, *That Man Is You* (New York: Paulist Press, 1963), 11-12.

CHAPTER 2

HOME MISSIONARY

PART ONE

THE CALL DEEPENS (1973-81)

EVANGELIZING FROM ST. MARY'S

After I was "baptized in the Holy Spirit" in January of 1973, I became involved in both Catholic Charismatic and Protestant Evangelical programs. Thus, in May of 1973, I attended a "Lay Witness Retreat" at a local Protestant Church where I learned how to share Bill Bright's "Four Spiritual Laws"[17] and went house to house with a partner, taking a religious survey and offering people a chance to make a commitment to Christ. At that time, I counseled at seventeen showings of the Rev. Billy Graham's movie, *Time to Run*. Three weeks later, I witnessed with the Pocket Testament League out of the North Side Assembly of God in a poor area of Pittsburgh. I also attended large rallies like the outdoor camping event, "Jesus '73" in Morgantown, Pennsylvania and the annual ecumenical Pittsburgh Charismatic Conference at Duquesne University in Pittsburgh.

At St. Mary's, I was involved in a small home-based ecumenical prayer group with Catholics and Episcopalians. Each week from 2:30 p.m. to 3:00 p.m. I prayed with one of the teachers at St. Mary's Elementary School. Three days a week, six hours a day, I worked as a maintenance man at a local industrial complex in Indianola,

Pennsylvania, a fifteen-minute ride from St. Mary's. During the school year, I taught eight ninth-grade boys religious education every Monday night in the church vestibule–in essence, it was a Bible study. I also weekly typed the parish bulletin.

A CHARISMATIC PRIEST

Then on April 1, 1973 (April Fools' Day), a "fool for Christ," a young priest by the name of Fr. Gus Milon, OFM, came to St. Mary's to speak to the youths and my life took a new direction. Fr. Gus was a Spirit-filled Franciscan assigned to the Ben Avon friary in Pittsburgh from 1970 to 1981. He preached retreats, worked with the poor, and was very active with the Charismatic Renewal (in both Catholic and Protestant segments) in the Pittsburgh area and beyond. When I met him, he felt that the Lord was calling him into youth ministry in the Pittsburgh area. He was joined in this work by a dynamic and unconventional Glenmary sister by the name of Sr. Gus Taurish[18] (yes, her name was Gus, too) who lived in nearby Greensburg, Pennsylvania. She had been presenting teen retreats in various parts of the country, especially in Cincinnati, Ohio, with the Franciscan retreat master and popular speaker Fr. Richard Rohr, OFM. In December of 1973, Fr. Gus invited me to join an adult leadership team he was putting together to minister to teens in monthly weekend retreat settings.

This youth ministry was eventually called "Children of Yahweh"[19] (COY) from Jeremiah 15:16 which says, "God's People will be called by His name." God's name in the Old Testament (Ex 3:14) in The Jerusalem Bible was translated as "Yahweh." We began by giving "Jesus Weekends" for teens, mostly to the children of parents involved in the Catholic Charismatic Renewal. Fr. Gus would have Mass each day and he and the lay leaders would give talks on what it meant to be a Christian. Saturday night always included "a candlelight service" in which each teen was given an unlit candle and had the opportunity to come forward on their own to pray out loud in their own words and to commit or recommit their lives to Christ. It was always a powerful and life-changing experience for all involved.

TEEN MINISTRY

To follow up with the teens who found new life in Christ on these weekends, we began establishing weekly prayer meetings for teens in different parts of the city of Pittsburgh, and sponsored annual, one-day, "Jesus Rallies" at the South Park Fairgrounds in Allegheny County. There, hundreds of young people and adults could attend workshops for spiritual growth as well as hear evangelistic messages and listen to Christian music groups on stage. Several times a year we would organize walking pilgrimages to a shrine or church, carrying a large wooden cross and banners proclaiming the Lordship of Jesus Christ. We would sleep in school or in church basements or pitch tents in a campground. Thus the teens had a taste of leaving the conveniences of home and sacrificing themselves to follow Jesus. The walking pilgrimages were great public witness events as well as a powerful means of forming disciples for Christ.

CALLED TO POUSTINIA

In the summer of 1974, while living with my parents and working with the teens, the Lord called me to *poustinia* (the Old Slavonic word for hermitage). I was walking through the woods one day behind St. Mary's Church and cemetery, and came across an old, abandoned pump house. It was made of glazed ceramic blocks plastered over with cement and had a poured concrete slab for a roof. It was a perfect six foot cube, like the Holy of Holies in the Temple in Jerusalem (2 Chr 3:1-8). There was no door on it and inside it housed an old broken pump, which had at one time supplied the well water for the church and the school on top of the hill. As I looked at this tumbled down structure, I began to remember how over the centuries God had called some of His disciples to abandon the world and to take up life in a cave or in a hermitage. I wondered if perhaps the Lord was showing me this pump house in order to call me to a similar way of life. It would fit into the life of poverty and prayer that I had already embraced. When I prayed about the possibility, I had peace in my heart.

So one day I asked my pastor, Msgr. Jacob C. Shinar (1915-81), if he would allow me to fix up the pump house and use it as a place of prayer. I would spend three days a week there in prayer and the other four days continuing my work as a volunteer at the parish doing the bulletin, helping at the religious education office, and working with the teens. Having received his permission, I cleaned it out, put a door on it, and inside built a wooden bunk and a kneeler, paneled the walls with cardboard, and put in a small wood stove for heat in the winter. I could not do much with the floor, since a trickle of water continually ran through the middle of the tiny building. Now that I no longer lived at my parent's home, I would visit them once a week for dinner on Tuesdays. Otherwise, I spent my nights in my "cell" which I called "Hermitage of the Cross of Jesus."

A SIXTEEN-DAY FAST

To inaugurate my life as a semi-hermit, I began a water-only fast on July 1. I had been reading books on fasting and looking at Jesus' words about fasting in the Gospels (Mt 4:2; 6:16-18; 9:14-15; 17:21)). I also learned that the apostles and disciples in the early church fasted (Acts 13:2-3; 27:33; 1 Cor 7:5) and that the early hermits like St. Paul of Thebes and St. Anthony the Great, who went out into the Egyptian desert to pray, fasted as well. Fasting was too closely connected with prayer in the Christian tradition to be ignored by anyone setting out on a more rigorous life of prayer.

I did not know how long this fast would go. From my reading about people who fasted, I learned that a person in normal health could fast for forty days before their body started consuming itself. I was willing to go that long if the Lord desired this for me.

During this time of fasting I carried on my normal activities, even to shoveling dirt and cutting a large field of tall grass with a hand scythe. My brothers and sisters in Christ were keeping an anxious eye on me, especially those with nurse's training. Finally, on July 16, I was with a group of our youth ministry in Cincinnati, and one of the readings for the day was from Acts 27:33, where St. Paul is on a storm-tossed ship on his way to Rome. He says: "Today is the fourteenth day that you have been waiting, going hungry, and eating nothing. I urge you, therefore, to take some food." I took this as a word from the Lord for me personally and broke my fast by eating an orange and a piece of bread.

What did I learn from this fast? First to my great surprise, after five days I had no more desire for food at all. Next I became totally grateful to my heavenly Father for every single thing of my day. I got physically weak and had to move more slowly and carefully. And I noticed the cold more. By the end of the fast I had lost twenty pounds. But I felt like I never had to eat again. I learned that joy is not dependent upon satisfying my physical desires, but upon doing God's will with a pure heart, and that although love (mercy) is more important than sacrifice (as Jesus says in Mt 9:16), without sacrifice there is no true love (Jn 15:13).

ANOTHER WALK TO ROME

A great event of my life occurred in 1975, the "International March of Christian Reconciliation" from Assisi to Rome, March 21-30. In it, 155 young people from fourteen nations walked the 110 miles between the two cities in eight days, beginning on Palm Sunday in Assisi and ending in Rome for Easter Mass with Pope Paul VI, in the piazza of St. Peter's Basilica. It was just one of the events planned for Holy Year 1975, proclaimed by the Pope, having as its theme, reconciliation. It was not widely publicized so as not to attract unwieldy thousands of participants. But our indefatigable Sister Gus had received word of it and managed to get COY declared the march's official representatives from the United States.

Our COY group from the States walked, prayed, and fasted as we raised the money necessary to finance our trip over to Italy and back. Six weeks before we left we organized a one-day, 20-mile walk to St. Paul's Cathedral in the Oakland section of Pittsburgh. We carried banners, sang praise and worship songs, and visited churches along the way. We made this pilgrimage of faith and got a little taste of what the eight days of walking through the Italian countryside might be like.

TAKING THE PLUNGE

The actual walk in Italy of course was something of a culture shock for most of our group who had never been out of the country. Trying to communicate in a foreign language, not knowing how to pay for things in Italian lira, being separated from family, home, and friends, and having to carry all of your possessions on your back for a week was a real challenge and called for a deeper faith and trust. Like most youths, ours were readily adaptable and up for a challenge. And it gave everyone a sense of being part of a larger–even worldwide–faith community. Although it was an ecumenical walk and different faith groups were represented, it was a Catholic event, so there was Mass every day. It also helped broaden the teens' horizons by experiencing the town and spirituality of St. Francis of Assisi, the Catholic culture of Italy, and the Church of Rome.

HOLY WEEK

Since the march took place during Holy Week, it probably was one of the most spiritually, physically, and emotionally intense identifications with Jesus' suffering, death, and resurrection, that these pilgrims would ever experience. Not everyone got the opportunity to carry the cross at the front of the procession, but everyone had to shoulder their own backpack and be of assistance to their fellow pilgrims. It was not only a test of physical endurance, but also an exercise of faith and of maturing discipleship.

The culmination of the walk was celebrating Easter Sunday Mass at St. Peter's Square with Pope Paul VI and with 400,000 people from all over the world. The offertory procession was composed of youths from the march from Assisi. One of the offertory gifts was a bundle of olive branches gathered from the walkers that had been given to them on Palm Sunday by the Bishop of Assisi and that had been carried every day of the walk.

CATHERINE DOHERTY

During the next several years (1976-81) the Lord continued to develop my life as a pilgrim/*poustinik*: three days a week of prayer in my hermitage and four days a week of volunteer ministry at St. Mary's Parish and with the teen ministry Children of Yahweh. One day in 1976, Fr. Gus handed me a book to read. I rejoiced in reading it, as it confirmed my way of life as pilgrim/*poustinik*. The name of the book was simply *Poustinia*, but subtitled *Christian Spirituality of the East for Western Man*. The author was Catherine de Hueck Doherty,[20] the Russian baroness who entered into Catholic communion from Orthodoxy in 1919, and founded the Catholic lay apostolate in Canada by the name of "Madonna House" in 1947.

Born in 1896, Catherine grew up in Russia. Her father was Russian Orthodox and her mother was a Roman Catholic, of Polish descent.[21] She had to leave Russia during the Bolshevik Revolution and she eventually came to the United States where the Lord called her to live the Gospel of radical poverty and faith, especially among the urban and rural poor of both the United States and Canada. She and her husband Eddie moved to Combermere, Ontario, and began forming lay apostles to staff houses of prayer in various cities around the world.

The name Catherine Doherty seemed familiar to me, but it took me awhile to place it. Then I remembered. While I attended St. Gregory's Seminary in Cincinnati, in 1956, for many months a book by the title of *Dear Seminarian* was read to us in the refectory while we were eating our meals. This book was by none other than Catherine herself. Now, twenty years later, I found Catherine speaking to me on a whole new level–the level of prayer and of the desert spirituality of solitude and silence. She wrote other books along the same line, like *Strannik, and Urodivoi,* and *Molchanie,* that spoke directly to my new way of life. As a matter-of-fact, in *Poustinia,* she relates that the *poustinik* in Russia divided his weekly routine between contemplative prayer alone with the Lord in his *poustinia*, and volunteer service to the nearby village–just as I had been doing for the past two years at St. Mary's.

WALK TO PHILADELPHIA

A significant portion of my volunteer work each week continued to be with the Children of Yahweh youth ministry. The year 1976, was the bicentennial celebration of the American Revolution. That year, the 41st International Eucharistic Congress was also being held in Philadelphia from July 30 to August 7. Our youth ministry believed the Lord was inviting us to make a pilgrimage there on foot. Since walking from Pittsburgh to Philadelphia–a distance of 300 miles–would take two weeks (at 13 miles a day) we decided to walk to the congress from Harrisburg. This route reduced our distance by more than half. I was chosen as the one who would lay out the route ahead of time and make the arrangements for nightly stops along the way.

So one day in June I left my *poustinia* and hitchhiked to Harrisburg, not having a car. It was a leap of faith, for I only had one week to traverse the 112 miles from start to finish, to find churches along the way to put us up each of the five nights we would be on the road, and then to get back to Pittsburgh. I had the name and address of a woman in Harrisburg who was the leader of a Charismatic prayer group there, so once I arrived in Harrisburg, I got in touch with her. By the grace of God she had an extra car in her garage. She said I could borrow it for the week, drive the route to Philadelphia, and then bring the car back to her. What a gift from the Lord and from this woman of faith!

By arranging to walk at least 19 miles a day (which is a hard push with a group!) I figured we could make the trip in six days. I was able to find a church to host us each night, except one. So the day we got to that particular town on our pilgrimage, Fr. Gus went ahead and found a convent of sisters who were willing to house us. It was on this walk that our group was walking through a town one day behind the old rugged cross. A man later told us that when he looked out of the window of the restaurant where he was eating at the time and he saw us passing by, he knew for certain that God loved him. It showed us that if we obey the Lord and do what He tells us, His Holy Spirit can touch hearts and draw them to Himself without any special effort on our part.

THE ARMOR OF GOD

It was in these years that the Lord began to equip me with six physical, visible signs of the "spiritual armor" to be worn by every Christian soldier (Eph 6:11-17). I already gave a public witness to my faith by having stenciled on the back of my jacket, "Children of Yahweh, Jesus loves you" and I wore a large button with this same logo on it. First, I had a jean cap that had embroidered on it, "Jesus is Lord" (helmet of salvation). Then during my sixteen-day fast, the Lord inspired me to carve a wooden crucifix and after the fast to wear a missionary crucifix in my belt (shield of faith). Next, at a Jesus Rally, I heard a talk by the Catholic evangelist Larry Tomczak who mentioned in his teaching, that we should not be embarrassed to carry the Bible (our spiritual "school book"—the sword of the Spirit) around in our hand. From that moment on, I carried my Bible wherever I went and continue to do so until the present day. Over the next five years the Lord would add to my ensemble, "the belt of truth," "the shoes of the Gospel," and the "breastplate of righteousness."

BUILDING THE BODY

During this time of being a "home missionary," I was involved with the Charismatic Movement in the Pittsburgh area. I prayed with a team supporting two priests who did deliverance ministry at St. Paul's Monastery. I volunteered my time at the downtown office for the CCC (Charismatic Communications Center) and helped publish their monthly newsletter, *The Body Builder*. I traveled on foot to Kane Hospital in the South Hills of Allegheny County each Sunday morning to help wheel patients to Mass; represented COY at the Fellowship of Youth Ministers (FYM) in a monthly meeting; conducted a biweekly adult Bible study Prayer Group at St. Mary's; taught ninth-grade CCD three times a month; and helped with Confirmation retreats at the Gateway House located on St. Mary's property. Through all of these activities as well as through daily prayer, private retreats, and spiritual direction, the Lord was teaching me how to use the gifts of the Holy Spirit for the building up of His mystical Body, the Church.

Then the Lord literally knocked me off of my feet for a period of six weeks. At the beginning of January 1977, I broke my ankle and had to stay at my parents' home to recuperate. Nevertheless, this was a time of many graces as it provided me with an opportunity for quiet prayer and for reading. It was during this time that I read the whole Old Testament from cover to cover, outloud (as John advises in Rv 1:3). I also read David Wilkerson's, *Cross and the Switchblade*. Thankfully, the doctor who set the bones in my ankle did a good job and I was able to walk another 35,000 miles on pilgrimages around the world in the following years, with only occasional, painful flare-ups.

"BEHIND THE INN" COFFEEHOUSE

It was also at this time that COY began to sense the Holy Spirit moving us in a new direction. Instead of focusing on the youths of Spirit-filled Catholics spread over the whole Diocese of Pittsburgh, we heard the call to rent a building and to open a youth center in an impoverished area of Pittsburgh. In those days, Evangelical Protestant youth ministries were developing the idea of "coffeehouses" for young people. Fr. Gus was most familiar with McKees Rocks, Pennsylvania, where he had been active in ministry to the poor for the past seven years. So by June of 1977, we had put a down payment on a three-story building on Island Avenue. We remodeled the downstairs to include a large room with a half dozen rustic round tables, a small chapel that would accommodate ten to fifteen people for Mass or prayer, an office area with desks and file cabinets, plus a restroom. The second floor had our kitchen, living room, dining room, an additional restroom, and two bedrooms. The third floor had three small bedrooms.

Why did the Lord give us so many bedrooms? It soon became clear that He wanted us to set up a "school of evangelization" for young men and women over the age of eighteen in which they could come for one year and be trained to share the Gospel with youths. This school we called "YEAST" (Youth Evangelism and Apostleship Training). We gave classes in Scripture, public speaking, counseling, discipleship, youth, and cults. They also had the opportunity to work with the teens who came to the center, go out on street ministry, help in teen retreats, assist the poor in the neighborhood, participate in youth pilgrimages, and grow spiritually.

A LEARNING EXPERIENCE

In July of 1981, Fr. Gus departed for reasons of health. During the eight years I had known Fr. Gus, he had a very formative influence on me. From him I learned to point everything to Jesus as the beginning and end of all. He demonstrated how to proclaim the Gospel from the heart rather than from the head, from a book, or from a written text. His love for those who were suffering led him regularly to ask the Lord to give him the burden and to take it away from those who came to him in need. From him I learned that real ministry to the poor must involve more than caring for their physical needs–it had to bring them to life in Christ. In his life witness, I saw how the Gifts of the Holy Spirit could be exercised in practical ways. In the end, I was thankful for the opportunity to be a close collaborator with him for those spiritually fruitful years.

THREE-MONTH WALK

I took off from the youth ministry from July 14, 1980 to August 14, 1980, to be in my *poustinia* to pray about my future involvement in COY. During this time I read about the Jesuit missionary North American Martyrs and about Kateri Tekakwitha, the Lilly of the Mohawks, who had just been beatified by Pope John Paul II on June 22, of the same year. I began to feel strongly that the Lord wanted me to take three months to make a pilgrimage–alone and on foot–to their shrines in Auriesville and in Fonda, New York. So I began preparations for it in the summer of 1981. It seemed like it was time to renew the literal "walking in faith" aspect of my calling as a pilgrim for the Lord. By the end of February of 1981, I felt the Lord inviting me to go forth without a penny and to trust Him completely to care for me. I also felt directed to walk to Combermere, Ontario, and to visit Madonna House, because their spirituality greatly appealed to me. I not only listed every single road in the forty-two counties I would be walking through during the 1,300-mile journey, but looked up all of the Catholic churches along the way, sending a letter to the bishops of each of the fifteen Catholic dioceses where I would be traveling and telling them when I planned to be walking in their area.

OUR LADY OF AMERICA

During this time of preparation the Lord equipped me with another of the external signs of the spiritual armor of God that St. Paul talks about in Ephesian 6:11-17: namely "the breastplate of righteousness." It took the form of a small icon of the Mother of God, Mary, the sinless one, which I would suspend on a rope and wear around my neck. The tradition of the pilgrim wearing an icon of the Mother of God over their breast, came to my attention from reading the book *Strannik,* by Doherty. And what image of Mary did the Lord choose for me? None other than "Our Lady of America,[22] produced in the style called *eleousa* or "loving tenderness." This was a rather new icon and it came from our Byzantine brothers and sisters in West Patterson, New Jersey. I had first encountered it at the Lay Congress on Evangelization in Washington, D.C., August 21-23, 1980. What impressed me was not only that it was done in the iconographic style of Eastern Christians, but also that it was called a "pilgrim icon" – one that would tour various churches. When I wrote to the Prayer League of Our Lady of America, in New Jersey, I received a very enthusiastic response and they asked me to write to them and to keep them informed about my journey. They sent me gratis a print of the original to which I was able to attach a string so I could wear it around my neck as a "breastplate." That's how the Lord equipped me with "the breastplate of righteousness" of the Christian soldier described in Ephesians 6:14.

THE WALK TO AURIESVILLE

On Sunday, May 3, after receiving the blessing of my pastor Msgr. Shinar, I left St. Mary's, Glenshaw, and headed east toward

Monroeville, Pennsylvania. There, I was to go to Mass at North American Martyrs Roman Catholic Church. Since this newly built church honored the three Jesuit missionaries, Fr. Isaac Jogues, Rene Goupil, and John Lalande, who were martyred on the Mohawk River near present-day Auriesville, New York, it seemed most appropriate for me to be sent off from this particular location.

I made it in plenty of time for the 10:00 a.m. Mass on May 4. Fr. Gus was the main celebrant and another priest-friend, Fr. Clarke, concelebrated. After Mass, each person present came up one by one to pray over me for the anointing of the Holy Spirit. Thus, fortified with heavenly graces and assured of the prayer support of my brothers and sisters in Christ, I was sent off on this new adventure for the Lord to walk in faith along the highways and byways of North America.

THE PEACE OF JESUS

I was now headed toward Loretto, State College, and Scranton (all in Pennsylvania) and then up to Auriesville (in New York State) where I hoped to finally arrive on May 30, after covering a distance of about 450 miles. Very early in this walk, I learned an important lesson for the rest of my years of pilgrimaging, defining what my particular ministry was to be: to lift up Jesus Christ (Jn 12:32) by my way of life and by the sign of the Cross (symbolized by the crucifix on my staff) to all who passedby in their vehicles. Since I walked facing traffic, the drivers were only a few feet from my staff. If only unconsciously and if only for a fraction of a second, they were getting a glimpse of the sign and proof of how much God loved them—so much that He sent Jesus into the world to die for their sins (Jn 3:16). Also, the Lord impressed upon me that even though I had to be attentive to where I was placing each footstep, I was to look each driver in the eye, to smile at them, to offer a prayer for them, to wish them the peace of Jesus, and to call down God's mercy upon them.

DAILY ROUTINE

On this walk I tried to get to Mass daily if possible and to go to Confession weekly. If I ended up for the day at a Catholic Church, I would ask the pastor if I could sleep in the church hall or in the school basement and they would usually permit me to do so. I did not buy food but only ate what was offered to me or what I could find alongside the road—edible wild plants, scallions, and cattail shoots. I did not have a tent, so when I slept outside I just used the new blue three-quarter length Canadian army coat that I had bought just for the trip, plus a piece of plastic. It got down to the forties the first few weeks and my feet got pretty cold by morning, until I got walking and warmed them up.

CARMELITE HOSPITALITY

One of the early surprise gifts of hospitality on this walk came from two Carmelite hermits in New Florence, Pennsylvania. I did not know about this hermitage before I started my pilgrimage, but I was told about them on the way. I gave them a telephone call a few hours before I arrived and spoke with Fr. Bede, the prior and co-founder of the community. He said: "You are most welcome." I am glad I did, for in meeting Fr. Bede and Fr. Simeon, I came into direct contact with an authentic, modern-day expression of the charism of a life of prayer, silence, and solitude.

Their hospitality was overwhelming. The first thing they did when I arrived about 7:30 p.m. on May 6, was to make me a big meal of rice, asparagus, and an egg omelet. I ended up staying the next day, and joined into their simple life of prayer, reading, work, and silence. It was a beautiful gift from the "Lord of surprises."

FRIENDLY NURSING HOME

In light of the spiritual warfare that all the followers of Christ are called to wage, the Lord arranged a very interesting and enlightening situation for me on May 16. I had already climbed over Bald Eagle Mountain, and was on my way to Lewistown, Pennsylvania, for an evening Mass. Now, after about two hours of walking on the level valley floor, I was looking for a rest stop. Then I spotted on my left a large building with the sign, "The Friendly Nursing Home–Visitors Welcome." I said to myself: "I am a visitor; I wonder if they would welcome me." So I asked the Lord for a sign indicating that I should stop there. I said to the Lord: "If you want me to pay those old folks a visit, let me see one of them at a window."

I walked past one window after another and got to the very end of the building without seeing anyone looking out. Then at the east end of the building there was a sign: National Nursing Home Week–May 10-17. I said to myself: "OK, Lord, that is Your sign: not the one I chose but the one You chose. So I will go in." Walking in the front door, I found nurses providing morning care to the patients, housekeeping people cleaning, and patients sitting or walking around. The first nurse to come up to me was Ms. Evans; I asked her if I could visit with some of the patients. She was agreeable and so she began to search for some with whom I might talk.

She eventually managed to gather some of the more ambulatory patients in the parlor on the second level and invited me to go up and speak with them. In all, about twelve elderly men and women in various states of wakefulness were sitting around. I had not taken off my pack, canteen, or icon and still had my staff and Bible with me. So I shared with them about "The Armor of God" (Eph 6:11-17) and demonstrated each piece with what the Lord had equipped me.

I ended with "the shield of faith" (the cross on my staff) which we must put up to "quench the fiery darts of the enemy" (Eph 6:16) who lies to us saying, "no one loves you," "you are a failure," and so forth, to which we must respond in faith with the truth: "No, God loves me. Jesus thinks I am worth dying for. If I make it to heaven, my life will have been worth it." I am not sure what effect this brief show-and-tell had on them. But I was blessed and strengthened in my resolve to live out these inspired words of Scripture. After a little snack of cheese, crackers, cake, butter, and peaches, I continued on my pilgrimage refreshed physically and spiritually. Praise be to God.

THE MARTYR'S SHRINE IN AURIESVILLE

Finally on Friday, May 29, I arrived at the Shrine of the North American Martyrs—the place where in 1642, Rene Goupil, and in 1646, Fr. Isaac Jogues and John Lalande, met their violent deaths at the hands of the Mohawk warriors. This was also the birthplace of Saint Kateri Tekakwitha, in 1656. Fr. Egan, the Jesuit shrine director, put me up in the guesthouse called "Jogues Manor." There I could sleep, take a shower, wash my clothes, use the kitchen, rest, write, and pray. Also, of course, I was able to pray and to go to Mass in the Colosseum as well as walk "The Ravine" where Rene Goupil was buried by Fr. Isaac after he was tomahawked for making the Sign of the Cross over a young child. This was an awesome natural sanctuary most fit for meditation and reflection, without a single tourist or commercial kind of addition. The other unique feature I discovered at the shrine was a Rosary made of stones laid out in the grass in memory of Teresa, another Indian girl who was martyred for her faith. A sign there said it was her custom to pray this Rosary on her knees as she moved from stone to stone, so I tried it myself.[23]

ON TO FONDA

On Sunday, May 31, I was ready to leave Auriesville and to head to Midland, Ontario, where the other Jesuit missionary martyrs are honored. It was a distance of about 450 miles and I had allotted for it thirty-four days, hoping to arrive there on July 4. On the way I planned to visit Madonna House in Combermere and to stay with this dynamic lay apostolate community for two weeks. Little did I realize at the time how the Lord was planning to use these days to set my course for the coming decade.

My next travel goal was Fonda, New York, just 5 miles up the Mohawk River. I had written ahead to the local superior, the Father Guardian. He had responded quite positively on January 17, to my letter, saying, "Yes, we have accommodations here for a pilgrim on foot." So I was hoping for one more night inside out of the mosquitoes before possibly facing a long stretch of nights outside.

But it was not to be.

THE PERFECT JOY

It was about 7:30 p.m. when I got to the shrine and the guardian was just backing his car out of its parking space. He honked his horn and motioned me over. I introduced myself and he said very curtly: "Oh, no. You cannot stay here looking like that. Another fellow like you was here a couple of days ago and ripped off two tires from my garage." I said: "That is OK. God will provide."

As I started walking I shook my head and said to myself: "Lord, what was that all about?" Then He reminded me of the story about "The Perfect Joy" in *The Little Flowers of St. Francis,* about St. Francis of Assisi. In it St. Francis is walking from Perugia to Assisi in Italy on one cold winter day with Brother Leo. During a 2-mile stretch Francis explains the meaning of true joy–innocently suffering with love. He tells Brother Leo that even if all of the brothers become saints, worked miracles, raised the dead, had all wisdom, exercised the gift of prophecy, and converted all infidels to faith in Christ, that would still not be the perfect joy. Rather, he says that if they arrive at their friary tonight all drenched with rain, frozen with cold, exhausted from hunger, and the doorkeeper does not recognize them and three time comes out to beat them with a club, calls them imposters, rolls them in the mud, and slams the door in their faces, and they bear all of this with patience, humility, charity, and joy, overcoming themselves, thinking all the time of the sufferings of the Lord, and happy to be counted worthy to be rejected like the Lord and suffer (when they should have been accepted and welcomed), then that is perfect joy.

Of course I did not suffer anything near this extreme. Still it was an opportunity to be wrongly judged and to be rejected for no particular fault of my own, and a chance to not react, protest, or condemn, but to accept it graciously in the name of the Lord As St. Paul says: "I will not glory save in the cross of our Savior Jesus Christ" (Gal 6:14). To be fair to the Father Guardian though, I must mention that I did get a letter of apology from him dated June 1–the very next day–which was waiting for me when I got back to Glenshaw at the end of July.

GETTING TO THE BORDER

My next big hurdle would be crossing into Canada at Cape Vincent, New York, in one week's time. On the way there, the Lord let me meet one of His special angels in human guise. He was a priest by the name of Fr. Charlie. I was sitting on the steps of his little white-framed church–St. Mary's in Glenfield, New York–at 6:30 a.m., waiting for someone to open the door. Then I heard this voice call out: "Oh, you are the fellow from Pennsylvania. The chancery office sent a letter saying you were coming this way." I thought to myself: "Praise God for Bishop Brzana of the Ogdenburg Diocese. He had followed up on my letter to him and prepared the way by notifying his pastors along my way of walking: how thoughtful of him."

After Mass, Fr. Charlie took me to the rectory and blessed me with a dozen different first-class relics. He gave me a list of people I could call upon on my way north and he called ahead to prepare my way. On the following day, Pentecost Sunday, I walked most of the way to

Cape Vincent where I would be poised to take the ferry across the St. Lawrence River into Canada on Monday.

CROSSING THE RIVER

This point of entry into Canada to which the Lord had directed me was quite unique. One went by ferry from the State of New York to Wolfe Island and then by another ferry from the other side of the island to the mainland of Canada. The ferries were very small. This was obviously not a highly traveled crossing. Fr. Paul at St. Vincent's was concerned that I might be required to have a sufficient sum of money to get into Canada.

(Indeed, a few years later, another pilgrim-friend of mine on his way by foot to St. Anne de Beaupre at another crossing was refused entry three times for lack of sufficient funds.) I only had $25 on me but I said to Fr. Paul: "Let us trust the Lord will open the way for me; but if they will not let me pass I will come back and see you."

Well, by the grace of God, I was not forced to return. When I got off the ferryboat with the other passengers, a Canadian customs official was standing on the shore. I gave him my passport and told him I was going to Combermere, Ontario. He could not figure out my name from the passport (he thought that I was my brother Tom, as I had his name penciled into the front of the passport as my emergency contact) and he did not know where Combermere was. He asked the purpose of my visit and if I had enough money. I said I was on pilgrimage and had $25, which was more than enough, as I would be fasting a lot. He looked at me once more and said, "OK. Go ahead," and returned my passport. I tucked it away in my Bible and with a sign of relief thanked the Lord for opening one more door and speeding me on His way.

ARRIVING AT MADONNA HOUSE

Now that I was in Canada, I had passed the halfway mark of my overall summer pilgrimage and had six days to walk the approximately 120 miles to Madonna House where I planned to spend two weeks. I hoped to arrive there on Saturday, June 13, so as to be there for the Feast of the Most Holy Trinity on June 14. With my best efforts, plus the help of brothers and sisters in the Lord, I was able to fulfill my original plans. What I was not prepared for was the reception I would get from Catherine Doherty herself.

About 2:30 p.m. on June 13, I started down Defoe Road with St. Joseph House on the corner. Within a half mile I came to the Madonna House complex of buildings. I then had my first run-in with Catherine.

She was walking with a group of Madonna House staff. Her first words (in typical Russian style) were a put-down. She said: "Do not think your walking is so great: in Russia we do it all the time." Then as if she did not understand I had just walked forty days from near Pittsburgh without any problem she said: "Besides you cannot walk on pilgrimage in North America today: you will be picked up for vagrancy." I thought to myself: "Catherine, you write so beautifully about pilgrimage in theory: you should be able to rejoice in its practice."

But this was just the first tangle: there was more to come.

MEETING A PRIEST IN POUSTINIA

Guests were blended into the normal schedule and life of the community. So I was scheduled to join them for tea at 3:30 p.m. (how British, I thought), manual labor from 4:00 p.m. to 5:00 p.m. (cutting wood), and Vespers at 5:30 p.m. in the rustic log chapel on the island that had both a Roman cross and an Eastern-style onion dome to signify the union of Western and Eastern Christianity. After a dinner of soup and salad with the staff and guests, I was introduced to Fr. Bob Wild, a Madonna House priest who lived in one of the *poustinias* on the island.

After briefly sharing my testimony and a period of prayerful silence before the icon and open Bible in his poustinia, Fr. Bob shared with me the charism of Nazareth–Jesus' hidden life-the call to the desert and silence, before being sent out to preach and to evangelize. We decided I would just follow the daily schedule of the "family" for a few days and then determine if I needed to make any special adjustments. In the meantime, I was free to come see him or any of the other Madonna House priests as I chose. After a shared spontaneous prayer, I left his *poustinia* and went to the island chapel for quiet prayer until 9:00 p.m. Then after the 9:00 p.m. to 10:00 p.m. tea in the main house and after singing the *Salve Mater* in Latin, and receiving the blessing of all of the priests present, everyone dispersed to the dormitories.

SUNDAY MASS

Mass on Sunday was celebrated at 9:00 a.m. in the island chapel. Fr. Wild was the main celebrant and nine other Madonna House priests concelebrated. Archbishop Joesph Raya, the prolific author and flamboyant retired Melkite Greek Catholic Archbishop Emeritus of "Galilee and all the Holy Land," had a seat of his own near the altar. It was the Feast of the Most Holy Trinity on the Roman Catholic calendar and I was so thankful to the Lord that He had gotten me to this holy place to celebrate the feast with such fervent Catholic brothers and sisters in Christ. Actually, I was here for some of the greatest summer feasts: Corpus Christi (the Body and Blood of Christ) the following Sunday, June 21; St. John the Baptist, June 24; the Sacred Heart of Jesus, June 26; the Immaculate Heart of Mary, June 27; and finally the Feast of Saints Peter and Paul the day I left, June 29.

WORK ON THE FARM

Sunday was a free day but Monday began the workweek, which went through Saturday; I was assigned to "the farm" each of those days. The farm–or more properly "St. Benedict's Acres"–was a 200-acre plot of ground 5 miles south of the main complex of buildings on Defoe Road. It provided fertile enough soil, in the alluvial deposit area full of big boulders left over from the last ice age, to raise all of the food to sustain this large community, plus enough surplus to give some away to the poor. I was assigned to the task of weeding the carrots or lettuce. But one day, Larry, who was in charge of the farm, asked me to help him till the potatoes and corn with a horse and hand tiller. I was to control the horse with the reigns as he guided the tiller between the rows of young plants. Since I felt very close to the earth myself, I was very thankful to be assigned to the farm to learn about "apostolic farming" (the title of one of Catherine's books) and experience firsthand, the simple life of all of our ancestors through most of human history. It was good to experience the spiritual principles involved (not just ecology), thus better appreciating Catherine's perspective in this area.

CATHERINE DEPARTS

Since my initial encounter with Catherine, it seemed that I had been rubbing her in the wrong way; she kept challenging me. She could not accept my wearing the icon of Our Lady of America from the Byzantine Melkite Church in New Jersey. She said: "There is only one 'Our Lady of America' and that is Our Lady of Guadalupe." It was as if she was trying to defend one title of Our Lady's and objecting to any other expression of devotion to our Heavenly Mother by her devoted children. Finally, she came up to me one evening and said, "I cannot even pray for you because you are wearing that icon." I was devastated. I thought, "Catherine, if God commands His followers to love both their neighbors and their enemies, where does that put me? A nothing!" So I thought maybe I should leave before my two weeks were up, so as not to disturb her. The priests there said, "Do not take it personally. It is 'The Bee's' Russian way. Even we don't always understand her actions." Others on the staff attributed some of her actions and words to her physical condition: "She is very hard of hearing." "She is getting old." "She is tired." "It's the Russian way [i.e., the put-downs, kidding, teasing, poking fun, the challenging to see what the other was made of]." Thankfully, it was announced on Tuesday morning, June 23, that Catherine was leaving for a few days. Now I could finish out my plan to stay for the two full weeks.

MY NEXT PILGRIMAGE

In spite of Catherine's unpleasant behavior toward me, the Lord used her to speak to me very clearly. First of all, her "word of the Lord" that she spoke to me within minutes of our first encounter, "A pilgrim needs to have a very pure heart" (or else the journeying will be a cop-out and do nothing but build up one's own ego), spoke volumes to me. Then her focus on Our Lady of Guadalupe turned my eyes again toward Mexico City. This confirmed an unpremeditated response on my part to a reporter's question in Watertown, New York, several weeks previously. The reporter had asked: "Where will your next pilgrimage take you?" And I had said, "Maybe to Our Lady of Guadalupe." By the time I finished my pilgrimage 1981, I was almost certain the Lord wanted my next pilgrimage to be to her shrine in Mexico City in seven more years.

HONORING MARY

Mary the Mother of God was becoming more and more real to me on this pilgrimage. During my time at Madonna House, I was reading Fr. Stephano Gobbi's *Mary Speaks to Her Beloved Priests* and St. Louis de Montfort's *True Devotion to Mary.* Then I was led to make a public consecration to the Immaculate Heart of Mary in the Island Chapel, on June 28, the Feast of the Immaculate Heart of Mary (1981). And finally, years later, when news of the so-called apparitions in Medjugorje, Bosnia-Herzegovina (be they true or false) became known in the West, I noted that on the day of the first "apparition" June 24, 1981, I was in *poustinia* at "Marian Meadows." I had also been graced the previous few months by being able to say the fifteen decades of the Rosary many a day on my pilgrimage. So I was drawing closer and closer to my Heavenly Mother and more appreciative of her formative influence in my life. Thank you, Lord Jesus, for this wonderful gift.

ON TO MIDLAND

On Monday, June 29, it was time to say goodbye to my Madonna House family and hit the road. The Madonna House kitchen staff packed me a lunch that, with rationing, plus adding the edible wild plants from along the side of the road, plus gifts from people I met, would carry me all the way to the Shrine of the Canadian Martyrs in Midland, Ontario. That was a distance of about 150 miles and I had allowed six days to walk it by averaging 25 miles a day. That proved to be a little too ambitious. I ended up averaging about 20 miles a day, so it took me almost eight days. But it was a blessed time: more like a wilderness walk with lots of lakes and woods and no big towns. (But it was mosquito country.)

A NAZARETH EXPERIENCE

The first of many gifts of hospitality I encountered in these eight days occurred just a few miles from Combermere on the first day out. I was on the third sorrowful mystery of the Rosary, slowly climbing a long, gradual hill, when I looked up and saw a young man with a short trimmed beard, approaching me on my side of the road, along with his wife and four young children, all on foot. As they drew near, the man held out a cup of cold water and a slice of bread saying, "Hello, pilgrim! Welcome! This is not Russian bread, but it is all we have." I thought in amazement, "Is this a staged shot reenacting a scene from nineteenth-century Eastern Europe? Who in this day and age would know, understand, and practice such an ancient ritual?" This devout family, Mark and Patti and their four children, said they lived on a farm just up the road and I was welcome to stop by for a visit. Sensing that the Lord had arranged this encounter for His glory, I took them up on the offer, even though I was not hungry and had just had a rest stop.

I felt it was like visiting the Holy Family in Nazareth, when Jesus was a boy there. The atmosphere exuded simple human warmth plus a deep faith commitment to God. Truly things were not all neat, sterile, and clean. But it was a home where true life was nourished, where God was a very real part of every aspect of their lives. I began to imagine Mary and Joseph's home in Nazareth as something like this. Joseph was not miles away earning money working for someone else; he was a constant part of the family. Jesus was not the only child to be found in the kitchen. His cousins and some of the village children his age, attracted by the love and generosity of Mary, were to be found visiting the Holy Family, too. No doubt they, too, offered hospitality to poor and needy wayfarers.

VACATION LAND

The area I was passing through had towns with names like Maple Leaf, Maynooth, Bancroft, Cardiff, Head Lake, Sebright, and Orillia. It was vacation land; many cars were pulling trailers with boats and signs were posted along the roads indicating "boat access." People from "The City" (Toronto) owned summer homes in this area or drove up here to get away from the congestion and in order to breathe a freer, less polluted air. Although I was given hospitality in several rectories, most nights I slept outside. And not having a tent with a zippered netting over it, I got eaten alive by mosquitoes. I was determined not to buy any repellent (as a voluntary sacrifice), but would have used some if it had been given to me. I did find a First Communion veil I could use to put over my face, but my hands were still exposed. I just tried to remember my Lord suffered much more than that for me.

A NIGHT IN TOWN

On Saturday, July 4, I came into the largest town in the area, Orillia. It was apparently the hub of this boating and vacationing land. The pastor of Guardian Angels Catholic Church had the St. Vincent de Paul Society arrange a room for me in the Champlain Hotel. I prayed and asked the Lord if I should take the room for the night or just head out-of-town and let Him provide a simpler place alongside the road. I ended up going to the hotel, and finding it far from modern and luxurious, I decided it would be alright to take it for a night, to possibly get a decent sleep away from the mosquitoes.

After a shower and after washing my clothes, I felt the Lord directing me to ask for a meal at one of the restaurants in town. It was not my usual procedure. I came to a Chinese restaurant and going around the back, I asked at the kitchen door. They shooed me away. I tried at a second restaurant and the owner came out and served me. He prepared me a dish of ham slices, French fries, and cooked vegetables, plus buttered French bread. He brought it out to me himself and set up a milk crate, but would not let me sit on it until he got some newspaper to put down first. Then he turned another crate over for a table. He asked if I wanted soup, crackers, and tea. He was back and forth as if I were an honored guest. He said he had seen me walking earlier in the day.

I asked the Lord to bless him abundantly for being kind to a pilgrim.

MARTYRS SHRINE

With one more night of sleeping outside, I was able to make it to the North American Martyrs Shrine in Midland the next day, Monday, July 6, about 1:00 p.m. After seven weeks of walking and praying, my goal came into sight. I remembered how, traditionally–as, for example, in Poland even today–when walking pilgrims get the first sighting of their destination, they prostrated or knelt on the ground and uttered a heartfelt prayer of gratitude to the Lord.

It ended up, unfortunately, that I received no hospitality from the Jesuits who staffed the shrine. It was such a privilege to be moving about on this holy ground where five of the martyrs had walked and lived back in the middle of the seventeenth century. I felt specially blessed to be able to venerate the bones of the martyrs kept in St. Joseph Church. But also spiritually powerful was the grave of St. John de Brebeuf in St. Marie, the reconstructed Christian Indian Village down by the Wye River. There the martyr's body lay interred for several months before his fellow Jesuits retrieved his bones. With the arrival of marauding Iroquois in 1649, the Jesuits abandoned the site and took the holy remains with them. This was holy ground and thankfully it was cordoned off for prayer. It was even accessible to those who only wanted to pay their respects at the gravesite, and not pay the fee to tour the rest of the village.[24]

BACK TO THE STATES

When I left the Martyrs Shrine I was heading back toward Pittsburgh. My plan was to walk for the next eleven days, cross back into New York at Niagara Falls, and visit Our Lady of Victory Shrine in Lackawanna, New York, just south of Buffalo. From there, I would hitchhike and accept rides to get back to Sewickley, Pennsylvania, for my birthday on July 25. There, I would celebrate with the Children of Yahweh Youth Ministry. From Sewickley, I would make my way back to my *poustinia* in Glenshaw. With that my pilgrimage would be completed and I would have fulfilled my vow to walk and to pray and to lift up the Cross of Jesus on the highways and byways of North America.

The biggest challenge that lay ahead of me was navigating the sprawling metropolis of Toronto and the congestion of cities situated along the western side of Lake Ontario. I did find a route that kept me out of Toronto, but I had to pass through the larger cities of Oakville, Burlington, and Hamilton, on the lake. Thankfully, the Lord led me to a few Catholic churches where the pastors were open to my mission and left me sleep inside three of the eleven nights. Probably the most memorable encounter with priests was on July 17, in Buffalo at St. Jude's Church. I got there in time for the 5:30 p.m. Mass.

After Mass, I venerated a relic of St. Jude with the other parishioners and then I introduced myself to the young priest, Fr. Larry, who had just said the Mass. He invited me to join with him and the pastor for a steak dinner they fixed themselves on an outdoor grill. I wanted to make the 4 more miles to the Shrine of Our Lady of Victory before dark, so I did not want to stay with them for the night. But the pastor, Fr. Ed, said before I left at 7:30 p.m., "You are welcome to stay here; it was a pleasure having you, as we do not have many visitors like you come by." So in a short two hours I passed from initial suspicion which was his first impression of me when he saw me in church, to warm acceptance. I marveled at the power of the Lord to change hearts so quickly and thanked Him for this firsthand experience of the power of His grace.

"HERE'S A PILLOW"

The most memorable night I spent outside in this eleven-day stretch was on July 16, my last night in Canada, before I walked over the Peace Bridge into New York. I had left the highly congested and tourist-packed area around Niagara Falls and the Panasonic Tower, and was walking along the scenic, tree-lined Niagara Parkway with the fast-flowing river on my left and a park area with grass and picnic tables on my right. As it began getting dark I prayed and asked the Lord what place He had prepared for me (from all eternity) for sleeping that night. It would have been easy to choose any number of spots in the wooded area of the park but I felt the Lord saying, "No. Keep going."

Then I came upon a sign on my right saying, Redemptoristine Nuns. I was told about this convent of cloistered women earlier in the day and felt the Lord urging me to ask them if I could sleep on their grounds. After all, it was holy ground and maybe I could go to Mass with them in the morning. So I went to the door of the convent and rang the bell. Sr. Mary came to the door and I made my request known to her. Without any hesitation or further ado, she said, "Okay." I could sleep in the grass near the fence by the Sacred Heart statue.

But I was hardly set up there and settled down when I heard this voice out of the dark: "Walter, here is a blanket and a pillow. I do not want you to get cold." Can you believe it? I knew I would fall in love with these dear sisters the next morning when I met them for Mass at 7:30 a.m. And so it was as they invited me in at 6:00 a.m. to join them in praying the Office of Readings and Morning Prayer followed by holy Mass with them and then breakfast with their chaplain, Fr. Pat.[25]

OUR LADY OF VICTORY

My visit to Our Lady of Victory Shrine –the most beautiful Catholic Church in America in my estimation–was rather brief. I arrived on Friday evening, July 17, just as it was getting dark. The pastor rather reluctantly agreed to let me sleep on the floor in the basement of the basilica. The next morning, I was able to attend two Masses at 7:30 a.m. and at 8:30 a.m. I appreciated being able to read how Fr. Baker had built this beautiful tribute to the Mother of God, as well as to get a sense of his spirit of compassion for orphans and for people in need of spiritual care. I prayed the prayer for his eventual beatification.

FRIENDS ALONG THE WAY

With this visit to the shrine over, I felt my pilgrimage for the summer, in a sense, was complete. This was the last holy site on my list to visit. Now I had one week to get back to Pittsburgh. My cousin Jerry lived in nearby Rochester and he picked me up to stay with him for the weekend. On Monday, Jerry left me off at St. Theodore Catholic Church on the west side of Rochester where I could attend the 8:30 a.m. Mass and meet the local prayer group leader Ellie, who was a good friend of mine. I shared at her prayer meeting that evening and stayed with her, her husband and their five sons that night. Then I was back on the road Tuesday morning, July 21, and now I was willing to take rides to cover the remaining150 miles to Pittsburgh. During those rides, the Lord gave me plenty of opportunities to witness verbally and to share my faith with fellow travelers on the journey. Each one was loved infinitely and the Lord was offering them special graces to reveal His plan for their lives. Finally, on July 22, the Feast of St. Mary Magdalene, I got to Zelienople, Pennsylvania, and St. Gregory Catholic Church around 5:30 p.m.. After making a Holy Hour there, I set out to walk to the home of friends of mine who lived just 4 miles down the road, but along the way I had a most interesting encounter with a police officer.

HOW DOES ONE PRAY?

About 6:30 p.m. I was walking in the very exclusive residential area of Sewickley Heights when a police officer pulled up in his cruiser and got out to question me. After checking my identification and having satisfied himself that I was no threat to the neighborhood, he got back into his car and drove away--but not too far-off. Five minutes later I saw his car backed off the highway and he was sitting on the hood waiting for me to come by. As I came alongside him, he introduced himself.

"Hi. My name is Tom. Back there was official. This is personal. Can you tell me how to pray and contact God?"

I thought to myself, "God, how wonderful that you set up such a meeting. It truly is a blessing to be in Your will; to be where You want us when You want us there. Here is a hungry and thirsty soul just waiting to be nourished by Your Holy Spirit and You choose me to be an instrument of Your work. Please guide my thoughts and words to further Your Kingdom on earth."

After explaining how he had been raised Catholic but was now seeking to know and to experience the Lord in a personal way, he said he could not find anyone who could make much sense to him. But when he saw me, he felt I would understand and be able to answer his questions. So for the next half hour I explained about faith in God being a free gift and what we have to do is open our hearts to receive it. I reminded him of what Jesus said, "Seek and you will find" (Mt 7:7-11) and that prayer is simply lifting up your mind and heart to God. My prayer was: Thank you Lord for arranging all things well, and please hear the cry of Tom's heart.

SEWICKLEY TO GLENSHAW

The next day, Saturday, July 25, was my fortieth birthday. I began it by attending Mass at Sts. Cyril and Methodius Catholic Church across the street from our coffeehouse in McKees Rocks. There, I was welcomed by the pastor, Fr. Ken, a Spirit-filled priest and good friend. Then I began my 12-mile walk back to Glenshaw, where I had started my pilgrimage on May 3. I arrived at my parents' home on Harts Run Road around 3:00 p.m. After an enjoyable evening with them, I walked the last mile up to my pump house hermitage at 11:00 p.m. and laid myself down to rest at the foot of the Cross. I thanked the Lord for His protection over so many miles of unknown territory. It was His grace enabling me to accomplish His will beyond what is naturally possible and normal. I now had to be faithful to what God had done in me and said to me.

ENDNOTES

17. The Four Spiritual Laws. The Protestant evangelist and Campus Crusade for Christ founder Bill Bright (1921-2003), wrote a tract in 1952, entitled, "The Four Spiritual Laws." In basic outline these laws can be understood in a Catholic sense. They provide a shorthand way of laying out God's plan for salvation through Jesus Christ. Briefly, they are (1) God loves you; (2) sin prevents you from experiencing God's love; (3) Jesus came to take away your sins; and (4) trusting in Jesus will enable you to experience this forgiveness personally.

18. Sister Gus Taurish (1924-80) was born in Greensburg, Pennsylvania, and was baptized Barbara. She gave up a commission as a U.S. Navy flight nurse to become a cloistered Carmelite nun. In 1958, she transferred to the Glenmary Missionary Sisters, and worked in Appalachia. As a religious sister she received the name Augustine, but she was known simply as "Sister Gus." She published two books covering her work in youth ministry, *The New Children* (Monroeville, Pennsylvania: Whitaker House, 1975) and *Watch Children,* (New Wilmington, Pennsylvania: Son-Rise, 1980).

19. YHWH was an ancient Hebrew name of the One True God, generally believed by modern scholars to have been pronounced "Yahweh" and meaning something like, I am who am. Eventually, use of the Sacred Name was never enunciated out of reverence. Hebrew texts substituted for it the word Adonai (Lord), both in Scripture and in spoken word. This custom continued to be observed by Christians as well, until the mid-twentieth century. Then the first editions of the Jerusalem Bible, initially published in French (1956) and later in English (1966), restored "Yahweh" to Old Testament texts. However, since 2004, use of the Sacred Name in liturgical texts (mostly hymns) and in translations of the Old Testament, has been forbidden by the Holy See out of respect for the unbroken custom among Christians who have always avoided its use, but undoubtedly as well as out of reverence for ancient Judaic practice.

20. Catherine Doherty. Baroness Ekatarina (Catherine) Fedorovna Kolyškina (1896-1985) was born in Nizhny Novgorod, Russia, about 200 miles east of Moscow along the Volga River. She was the one-time wife of Baron Boris de Hueck (from whom she eventually received an ecclesiastical annulment following their divorce) and later remarried the American journalist Eddie Doherty, who would be ordained a Melkite Greek-Catholic priest. Her cause for eventual canonization is currently underway under sponsorship of the Diocese of Pembroke, Ontario.

21. Orthodox. There was a "family story" that Catherine's father was secretly baptized a Catholic, which at the time was illegal, he being a Russian Imperial subject. See Robert Wild, *Catherine Doherty: Servant of God* (Combermere, Ontario: Madonna House, 2005), 18.

22. Icon. The original icon of Our Lady of America (probably measuring around two feet by three feet) was commissioned in 1972, by Fr. Albert Gorayeb of St. Ann Melkite Catholic Church in West Patterson, New Jersey, and took three years to complete. It was completely covered with a silver risa (only the faces and hands were visible) plus 2,300 large and small gems including a 76-point star sapphire. It was solemnly blessed on June 27, 1976, to commemorate the bicentennial of America in 1776.

23. Auriesville Shrine. In 2015, the Jesuit order withdrew from supervising the shrine, citing "a lack of Jesuit priests." A team of volunteers and benefactors, working with the Roman Catholic Bishop of Albany and the Jesuits, have formed a nonprofit group called, "Friends of Our Lady of Martyrs Shrine" to keep the shrine open and to have weekend Masses said there. See <www.auriesvilleshrine.com> for more information.

24. Shrine in Midland. On another visit to the shrine, twenty years later, the curator of the museum would give me some of the soil from this grave with the Saint's decomposed flesh in it.

25. Redemptoristines. This was the beginning of a relationship with these dear nuns that lasted many decades. Sadly, they had to eventually close their convent for lack of vocations and the remaining two elderly nuns went to a nursing home in Toronto. But I kept in touch with them by mail and even visited them in 2012. The last one died in 2016.

PART TWO

SEVEN MORE YEARS (1981-88)

THE NEXT SABBATICAL

As I prayed and meditated in the following days and weeks about the fruits of this pilgrimage, two things became clear to me. First, I was to continue in the youth ministry and in the *poustinia*, but in seven years (1988) I was to leave all of this and to take up the life of a pilgrim full time, like a sabbatical year (Ex 23:10-11) of more total trust in the Lord. Secondly, the first goal of my year of pilgrimage was to visit the Shrine of Our Lady of Guadalupe in Mexico City. From there I was to walk on toward California. It was like the Lord was saying: "If you want to have the title of pilgrim, then hit the road." Otherwise calling myself a pilgrim (as in "pilgrim/*poustinik*") was just an empty word: it did not have any teeth in it.

ON HOLD

From August of 1981, when I returned from the North American Martyrs Shrines, to May of 1988, when I set out for Mexico, the Lord had me in a holding pattern. It was as if I was in a countdown to blast off for distant shores. During this time the Lord was preparing me for a new stage of trust and surrender, when He would take away all material and visible supports and sustain me purely on faith and on the spiritual principals of His Kingdom. But in reflecting back on these seven years, I can see God's loving hand gently guiding me.[26]

During these seven years, I led a number of pilgrimages for small groups both locally, in Italy, and in the Holy Land. I gave talks to various groups, churches, and retreat centers. But I also had to deal with a significant lack of comprehension from people around me, including priests, pastors, and spiritual directors. (It would not be until 2001 that the Lord sent me a priest of the Byzantine rite who was well acquainted with the early Desert Fathers, as a spiritual director who could understand and affirm my vocation as a pilgrim/ *poustinik*.) In the meantime, the Lord comforted and strengthened me in many ways. One of these was through the correspondence of a Capuchin missionary from Papua, New Guinea, who had met me many years before. He wrote the following to me, in 1985:

> I felt deeply that despite the misgivings of so many people about your life-style and externals at the time, the Lord had something special and different in mind for you .... While your form of spirituality and life-style will not be acceptable or even understood by most people and most Catholics either, those who know Church History and more the spirituality common to the Eastern Church would immediately see the validity and the value of it.[27]

PARISH SECRETARY

One of the most significant changes in my life from 1981 to 1988, happened in January of 1983, when the new pastor Fr. Hrico, asked me to take over the duties of parish secretary. This involved having me in the rectory office from 9:00 a.m. to 4:00 p.m., answering the telephone, taking down messages for the priests, typing up letters for the pastor, answering the doorbell, and typing up and laying out the weekly parish bulletin. I agreed to do it four days a week; that allowed me to continue my teaching responsibilities in McKees Rocks with the Charismatic teen ministry the other three days of the week. It also gave me a regular income by which I was able to pay off my seminary bill for the six years of my philosophical and theological education provided by the Diocese of Pittsburgh.[28]

Being concerned with appearances and with making a good first impression, the pastor asked if he could take me shopping to buy me some new black slacks and collared shirts to wear when I was in the rectory office. I accepted. Also, I kept my beard trimmed. He arranged that I get a general physical exam from a parish physician. I felt these were minor adjustments that I could put up with as I knew it would all come to an end in 1988. My special patron during these years was the fourth-century ascetic St. Jerome, who was secretary to Pope Damascus in Rome before he headed to Bethlehem to live in a cave and to translate the Scriptures from the original languages into spoken Latin—the Vulgate.

PILGRIMAGE TO THE HOLY LAND

It had been discerned early in 1981, by our Children of Yahweh leadership, that the Lord was calling us as a ministry to pilgrimage in the Holy Land and specifically to visit Mt. Sinai where the Lord revealed His name to Moses as Yahweh (Ex 3:14). So on March 30, 1982, eleven of us flew from New York to Rome. It was a leap of faith, as we had no reservations anywhere and we planned to be on pilgrimage for twenty-one days. All we had were our airplane tickets from New York to Cairo and back. We trusted that the Lord would provide transportation, food, and lodging for us each night, even if it meant there might be days of fasting and we might be sleeping outside on the ground in our sleeping bags. There were many last-minute, down-to-the-wire arrangements, but with the

Lord's help we made it. Our faith was strengthened and other people were blessed to meet us.

PROVISION IN CAIRO

One of our first "divine interventions" occurred in Leonardo da Vinci Airport in Rome. As we waited to board our flight to Cairo, a man came up to us and said, "Are you Children of Yahweh?" Amazed beyond belief we said, "Yes! How do you know us?" He said his name was Frere Boulard, the director of the College de la Salle in Cairo, and he had gotten a telegram from us telling him of our arrival in Cairo, although the telegram did not say from what country we were originating. He had a bus waiting for us at the Cairo Airport to take us to the college where we were welcome to stay that night. All we could do was praise the Lord and thank Him for taking care of His needy children.

The next "arrangement" we needed was a way to get from Cairo to St. Catherine's Monastery at Mt. Sinai, a trip of about 250 miles. The next day, April 1, eleven "Fools for Christ" (or maybe just naive, gullible American tourists) decided to spend a day in Cairo and to inquire about transportation to the Holy Mountain which, at this time, still belonged to the State of Israel. Cairo, of course is an Arab city full of talented businesspeople (including young boys) who are very clever at helping tourists (for a fee). We were led by three eager, young Egyptian boys to a wood shack that they called a "bus station." There they sold us "tickets" (i.e., three tiny pieces of paper with Arabic script on them stapled together) for $7 a person, which they assured us would get us to St. Catherine's the next day and back two days later. When we told Frere Boulard what we had done, he was flabbergasted and was certain we had been scammed. So he took our "tickets" with him to check out our story. He came back later shaking his head saying, "I cannot believe it. This is apparently legitimate. I never knew one could make such a long trip so cheaply."

He had apparently momentarily forgot Who was arranging things for us behind-the-scenes.

INTO THE SINAI

Our ten-hour trip to St. Catherine's the next day was no less miraculous. A brand-new, air-conditioned, Peugeot bus took us the 80 miles from Cairo to Suez in two and half hours. There we had to disembark and to take a ferry across the Suez Canal; in that process we left Egypt and entered Israel. The only problem was the bus that was waiting on the other side to take us to St. Catherine's was already almost full and it did not have enough seats for all of us. It seems that a private tour bus had broken down coming off the ferry. Not expecting such a large group as ours from Cairo, the ticket agent had overbooked the seating. We were willing to stand in the aisle, but the Egyptians said that was not fair and after a heated discussion, they unloaded the bus of the special tour people and asked us to take our seats. We of course thanked the Lord that His guardian angels were with us. Actually, one of the Lord's "angels" rode with us from this point on. He was a Spirit-filled Coptic Christian who spoke English and who became our defender, interpreter, tour guide, and animator. While on the bus, he said to us: "Sing some songs to Jesus and I will explain in Arabic to the Muslims that you are praising Allah." So for the next hour I led praise songs in the bus with my guitar and all seemed to enjoy it.

ARRIVING AT ST. CATHERINE'S

Once we got to St. Catherine's, our "angel" helped us find a place to sleep for $1 per person a night in a "hotel" without a roof; it only rains one inch a year in this part of the Sinai Peninsula. There we slept in our sleeping bags on foam mats laid on a "floor" of fine crushed stones. The second night we slept on the ground on top of 6,500- foot Mount Sinai after a four-hour climb up a serpentine foot path and rough stone steps the final 1,000 feet. And on the third night our "angel in Arabic disguise" helped us get rooms in the monastery guesthouse after pulling strings to get me a personal interview with the Greek Orthodox archbishop Damianos, the abbot of St. Catherine's Monastery.

The following day, before we parted from our "angel" back in Suez, Egypt, he praised our bold witness to our Christian faith, as he pointed to the crucifixes we had affixed to our staffs. He said as an Egyptian he was not allowed to witness to his faith because of the pressure of the majority Muslim culture in which he lived. That is why he and his wife were so greatly blessed by our constant singing of praise songs and our joyful living of our faith in Our Lord and Savior Jesus Christ. He asked us to light a candle and to pray for him and his family "at the grave of Jesus" in Jerusalem; as an Egyptian Christian he was not permitted by his government or by his church leaders to visit those holy sites.

ENTERING ISRAEL

Before we got to the Church of the Holy Sepulcher in Jerusalem in three days (by way of Galilee) to fulfill our promise, we had to go through many adventures. The first was crossing the border of Egypt into Israel at El Arish near the Mediterranean Sea. At El Qantara on the Suez Canal, we missed the last bus to the border and had to take two taxis. By the time they drove us the 100 miles to the border, it was dark and the border station was closed until 8:00 a.m. the next morning. Since there were no hotels or accommodations there, in the desert, our drivers wanted to take us back to civilization to sleep; but we insisted we could spread out our sleeping bags right there on the sand under a palm tree.

The next morning it took two hours to pass through Egyptian and Israeli customs. Then we had to take two taxis to Gaza and two more to Tel Aviv, where we got a regular bus to Nazareth. We arrived at the town where Jesus grew up and to the Church of the Annunciation where the angel Gabriel came to Mary, at 4:00 p.m., just in time for a Mass in English at which we could all receive Holy Communion after five days in the desert without the Eucharist. What a blessing to receive the Bread of Life in the very spot where the Eternal Word of God became flesh for the life of our souls.

A NIGHT IN NAZARETH

Now we had to see where the Lord would have us stay for the night. This time He did not immediately open the first door at which we knocked. As a matter-of-fact we knocked on door after door, from the Sisters of Nazareth right across from the Church of the Annunciation to the Salesians on top of the hill. Everywhere we got the same greeting, "No room." So the Lord allowed us to experience what the Holy Family faced in Bethlehem on the first Christmas: "No room in the inn." One religious sister said, "We are booked two years ahead for Holy Week. No one comes to the Holy Land at this time of year with such a large group without reservations." Yet the Lord sent us another "angel," a young Catholic Palestinian named Faheed. He offered to go with us until we found a place.

After two hours of tramping all over Nazareth with full packs and darkness setting in, we figured we had tried just about every possibility for lodging there was. Then the Lord sent Acam, a relative of Faheed, who had a large apartment building in town he was remodeling to rent and said that if we were willing to sleep on the floor we could stay there for $2.50 a person. That was the answer to our prayer. Also, it gave our local friends a chance to join in with us in our songs of praise and worship.

AROUND THE SEA OF GALILEE

The next day we took a bus to Tiberias and had a fish dinner right on the Sea of Galilee close to the youth hostel where we stayed that night. On Holy Thursday we got up at 2:30 a.m. to walk the 9 miles to the Mount of Beatitudes where Jesus had given the Sermon on the Mount (Mt 5-7). Since the shrine church was closed for repairs, we had to sit outside in the grass just like Jesus' audience did when He multiplied the loaves and the fish (Jn 6:1-15). Then we walked down to Capernaum where Jesus had taken up residence in Peter's house, and there we found the Lord provided an empty double decker diesel-powered boat at 9:00 a.m. which was willing to take us back to Tiberias for $3 each. So we got to experience a boat ride on the Sea of Galilee where Jesus and His apostles had sailed and fished back in the days of His public ministry. That got us back to our youth hostel in time to check out before the 10:00 a.m. deadline. The Lord was certainly taking care of all of the details of our journey of faith.

JERUSALEM

That night we got to Jerusalem and the Lord provided bamboo bungalows reminiscent of the booths in which the Israelites lived during the Feast of Tabernacles (Lv 23:39-43) each year. It was a kibbutz called "Ramat Rachel" (Rachel Weeping) and commemorated Jacob's wife, Rachel, weeping for her children (Gn 35:19; Jr 31:15). As a teen ministry we felt this location was chosen by the Lord to remind us to pray with tears for the youths of the Western world who are perishing spiritually for the lack of stable families and for being denied access to the truth of God's love for them in Christ.

On Good Friday at noontime our own small group walked and prayed the Way of the Cross on the Via Dolorosa in the Old City of Jerusalem. We walked on the stones Jesus probably walked on in Roman times and jostled the crowds today shopping in the markets along the busy streets of Jerusalem. Sometimes we could find a quiet chapel at one of the stations where we could pray with less distractions and of course once we got inside the Church of the Holy

Sepulcher for the twelfth to the fourteenth stations, we were cut off from the whole world of business around us.

Pilgrims joined us along the Via Dolorosa as they were attracted to us by the Holy Spirit. This was how we met Elaine, a Russian Jewish convert to Christ, who said she was drawn to our group by the joy of the Holy Spirit she saw. She shared with us the persecution she and her Christian mother received from the local rabbi who comes to their home in Tel Aviv to destroy crucifixes and religious objects. Neither she nor her mother can now get jobs because they became Christian. We prayed with Elaine before she left us at the end of the day as her life was a vivid reminder that the disciple of Christ can expect both rejection and persecution as well as special graces to remain steadfast.

EASTER SUNDAY

Holy Saturday, being the Sabbath day of rest in Israel, was "a free day" for us. That is, everyone was able to do what they wanted. Of course if one did not want to venture off alone, one could buddy up with one or two other pilgrims and let the Holy Spirit guide their group for an adventure in the Lord. But it was Easter Sunday that became the day to remember.

All began well enough Easter morning with the day dawning bright and clear. Our plan was to attend the 11:00 a.m. English Mass of the Resurrection at St. Anne's Church near St. Stephen's Gate inside the walls of the Old City of Jerusalem. After breakfast and Morning Prayer at the kibbutz we set out at 9:00 a.m. singing songs of praise on an hour and a half walk (a real "entrance procession") to the Old City. We entered the walled city at New Gate and proceeded down St. Francis Street. But it soon became obvious all was not well up ahead. People were running around shouting. Some were rubbing their eyes from the effects of tear gas. Then we heard gunshots in the distance.

CHANGED PLANS

Since we could not get to St. Anne's as planned, we passed through Damascus Gate and got outside the city walls, and headed for the Church of All Nations at the foot of the Mount of Olives. There we found an 11:30 a.m. Mass in English just about to start. We were able to sing out songs of praise. After Mass we decided to head to our tour office to confirm our travel arrangements for the next day. To get there we climbed the Mount of Olives to head for the New City of Jerusalem.

But on the top of the Mount of Olives the streets were deserted: rocks lay all about, car windows were smashed, and sirens were blowing as ambulances raced back and forth carrying the wounded. Some Palestinian bystanders shouted at us: "How can you be carrying a guitar when our people are dying?" Apparently an American soldier had gone crazy and shot a Muslim in a mosque in Jerusalem and this event was the source of all the ruckus. Thankfully the Lord had me wearing my *keffiyeh* (the head scarf typically worn by the Middle Eastern men, like the black-and-white checkered one worn by Yasser Arafat when he was the leader of the PLO) so it appeared that we were not altogether unsympathetic to the Palestinian cause. After about a forty-five-minute walk we got out of the troubled area and into the Jewish section of the New City where we found the travel agents.

The Lord taught me an important life lesson from this experience. Namely, you cannot lead people when they refuse to follow. No matter how loyal or obedient and submissive one's followers have been in the past, if the leader attempts to guide his flock through a situation that strikes fear or terror into their hearts, they will balk and refuse to go on. One has to work within their current situation, "where they are," and try to reach the ultimate goal by another, perhaps longer way around. Leaders, in other words, have to take account of people's free will, and need to exercise sensitivity, realism, and flexibility. It spoke to me of how the Lord God has to work with each of His children to get them to their final destination in heaven.

BACK TO EGYPT

Once again it became evident that the Lord was working on our behalf. When we got to the tour agent, he said Galilee Tours and VIP Tours (both of which took people to the border) were filled up for Monday from weeks before, and the border would be closed Tuesday and Wednesday. We could fly there for $100 each. The Lord, however, led us to another agency, Egged Tours, which agreed to put on an extra bus to take all of us to the border on Monday for $25 each. Leaving Jerusalem at 6:45 a.m. on Monday, we arrived at the temporary border between Israel and Egypt at El Arish roughly four hours later.

There we had another five-hour-wait while our passports were taken from us for processing. And at El Qantara on the Suez Canal, we had another hour wait until the ferry–which could only hold 125 people–made four crossings to get this whole group of "refugees" across the water, to where ten new empty buses took us to Cairo. It was almost midnight when the bus left us off at the street going to the College de la Salle in Cairo, and the Arab guard opened the gate for us to leave us into the compound. Marie Therese showed us to a dormitory where we could sleep for the night and brought us some cheese and Egyptian pocket bread.

ROME AND ASSISI

Arriving in Rome, our group split in two as four were flying back to the States that day and seven of us were staying another six days to take in Assisi, the city of St. Francis–and my most favorite city in the whole world. Again we had no reservations in Assisi and arrived unannounced on Thursday, April 15. When we pulled into the train station at the foot of Assisi at 3:30 p.m., it was rainy and chilly. By the time we got to the Basilica of St. Francis on foot, the rain had stopped. But we were not able to locate my priest-friend Fr. Max Mizzi, OFM. So yet again the Lord sent us one of His angels, this time in the form of a twenty-nine-year-old, unchurched Italian fellow by the name of Giovanni. He was very concerned about our needing a place to sleep.

He took us around looking for rooms but none could be found. Not wanting to let us sleep outside in the porch of the Temple Minerva where the homeless congregate, he said: "If you are willing to be up and on your way by 6:00 a.m. before my landlord comes, we could try and get all of you in my tiny attic apartment." We agreed to give it a try. When we arrived at his second-floor room he showed us a storeroom off to the side, filled with empty boxes. These we had to stack one on top of another to make a clear area in the center of the room. Then we swept the brick floor, laid down thick comforters, pads, and blankets and spread out our sleeping bags one against the other like a mosaic.

We rejoiced to experience just a small taste of the gift of poverty for which St. Francis was called "Il Poverello" (the Poor Little Man). For bathroom facilities the next morning at 5:30 a.m. the Lord sent a little German nun along the street who took us to the hotel where she was staying with a group of forty girls from Switzerland. And so began three full days in the blessed area which 800 years ago witnessed the grace-filled life of a worldly troubadour turned ascetic. This was the man who preached and who lived the Gospel of Jesus in such a powerful way that he has inspired both believers and unbelievers to the present day.

A SUCCESSFUL CONCLUSION

For three days we feasted our spirits by attending Masses in the Basilica of St Francis, the Portiuncula, and San Damiano, as well as by visiting the *carcere* (hermitages, literally "cells"), the Rocco, and Rivo Torto—all places sanctified by Brother Francis and by the early

Franciscans. My Maltese Franciscan priest-friend, Fr. Max, had found us rooms in a private home so we were able to leave our packs there and to explore and to pray in all of these hallowed places. However, by Monday morning, April 19, we were ready to shoulder our packs once again and catch our train back to Rome. Then on Tuesday we made a flight back to New York, and a ride in a rented car back to Pittsburgh. It was 4:30 a.m. when we arrived at the Behind the Inn Coffeehouse in McKees Rocks. Instead of going to sleep, we spent two hours singing and praising the Lord in our chapel. Then we all went over to St. Cyril and Methodius Church across the street for the 8:00 a.m. Mass. For now all we could do was thank the Lord for a safe journey of 17,000 miles and countless blessings.

THE SHOES OF THE GOSPEL

As I continue along on this reflection of my "home missionary" years from 1973 to 1988, and before reflecting on my next pilgrimage from Assisi to Rome in 1984, I would like to briefly recount how the Lord added the final touch to the "The Armor of God" that would ready me for the walk to Mexico and beyond in 1988. It concerns the third of the six pieces of the soldier's armor, "the shoes of the Gospel" (Eph 6:15). Actually the verse in the New American translation reads: "Your feet (will be) shod in readiness for the Gospel of peace." I always knew one had to have "sturdy hiking boots with good ankle support for rough terrain." But what does Jesus advise when He sends out His Apostles? He says in Mark, "wear sandals" (Mk 6:9). And in Matthew and Luke he says, "take no sandals" (Mt 10:10; Lk 10:4) which in the context could mean, "take no second pair of sandals for emergencies because God will provide."

Practically speaking, if one would try walking barefooted long distances, daily, for months and years on-end, they would wear off their feet! That is why working horses and mules are given metal shoes on the bottom of their feet. So putting on sandals signifies one is setting out on a mission and in terms of the Kingdom, the purpose is "to proclaim peace" (Lk 10:5) or in the words of the prophet Isaiah: "How beautiful upon the mountains are the feet of him who brings glad tidings, announcing peace, bearing good news, announcing salvation, and saying to Zion, Your God is King" (Is 52:7). Jesus sends out His Apostles, evangelists, and missionaries (and pilgrims) to proclaim: "Repent for the Kingdom of God is at hand" (Mt 3:21). The meaning of this is: "The King–the Lord–who can forgive your sins and thus set your hearts at peace is on His way (Is 61:1-3)." So St. Paul reminds the Lord's heralds to have their "feet shod in readiness for the Gospel of peace."

So how did the Lord get me to give up the wisdom of the world (hiking boots) and accept the foolishness of the Gospel (sandals; see 1 Cor 3:19-20)? One Sunday afternoon in the summer of 1983 as I–in my hiking boots–was making my 13-mile walk from McKees Rocks back to my *poustinia* at St. Mary's, I saw a large piece of retread laying alongside the road. I felt the Lord saying: "Pick it up and make sandals of it for yourself." So I reached down, grabbed it with my free hand, and stuffed it into my pack. In the next few days I cut two soles out of it to match my feet, and tied them on with ropes. I found I also had to put extra rubber on the back as heels for balance and to keep the ends of the ropes from wearing off. I also needed to wear socks to keep the ropes from digging into my feet. And these sandals would be redesigned over the next ten years until I made my final pair in Anchorage in 1993. These would last twenty years and eventually had 30,000 miles on them when I finally hung them up in 2013. New heels had to be put on every 3,000 miles.

THE CALL TO PILGRIMAGE

While I was happily witnessing the Lord's love to youths in McKees Rocks and to the children at St. Mary's, as well as speaking at various prayer groups and Bible studies, the call came from the Lord to join a weeklong international pilgrimage from Assisi to Rome in 1984. It came via a letter from my friend Fr. Max Mizzi, OFM in Assisi. On March 22, I received a letter from him inviting me to bring a group of youths to walk with a group of young people from Assisi to Rome from April 15 to April 22, to celebrate the conclusion of the special Holy Year of Redemption called by Pope John Paul II to commemorate 1,950 years since Jesus' death and resurrection.

I ended up taking two boys with me: my nephew Michael and the son of a couple involved in COY leadership by the name of Edward. This was a pilgrimage that I believe was planned and executed not by man but by the Lord. We had ten days to get tickets (every airline we checked said they were booked), passports (normally taking four to six weeks), and absentee permissions. Yet the Lord pulled it off by putting us in touch with a ticket agent who sent us the tickets even before we sent him the money and providing us with one-day "walkthrough" passports for the teens. Indeed it became obvious that we serve "the Lord of the impossible" (Mt 19:26).

MORE DIFFICULTIES

Actually this was only the beginning of the excitement that lay ahead. When we arrived in New York, we found out that our flight to Rome was canceled because the airport workers at Leonardo da Vinci Airport in Rome were on strike. So we had to spend twenty-four hours in New York. In Rome we had the challenge of making the train connections to Assisi without knowing how to communicate in Italian. Nevertheless, we did make it to Assisi for the first gathering of pilgrims the Saturday before Palm Sunday. At 6:00 p.m. in the inner courtyard of the Convento (the main Franciscan monastery in Assisi), we were given a brief orientation and shown the huge dormitory where we would be sleeping that first night.

BEGINNING THE WALK

The Lord was not slow in putting His pilgrims to the test. The first two days of the walk it rained. We had to walk 17 miles the first day and 18 miles the second day. There were many blistered and sore feet and the emergency medical technicians accompanying us had their work cut out for them as they patched feet, gave rides, and even took some to the hospital for treatment. Wetness, weakness, and fatigue attacked even the most seasoned walkers like Fr. Max. My own feet felt like they were on fire, as they "complained" about having to walk so many miles in the new rubber tire sandals.

Being alone and available to meet and to share with other walkers who might need a listening ear was one of the particular gifts the Lord gave me on this pilgrimage. One of the most memorable gifts was meeting a group of new Franciscan friars, called in Italian Frati Minori Rinnovati (Friars Minor of the Renewal).[29] They felt called to live the charism of St. Francis in all of its radical poverty. They had no money and possessed nothing. They went barefooted (not even wearing sandals on the walk) and their habits were made of coarse, natural woolen gray cloth with patches sewed on (although apparently by a machine) wherever a hole appeared. They lived in empty steel containers on a garbage dump near Naples. They ate only what people gave them and lived like the birds of the air as the Lord had invited His first disciples to do (see Mt 6:25-34). And most importantly, they exuded the joy of the Lord in this simple way of life. I thanked the Lord for this example of living the Gospel of divine Providence in a literal way in our day and age.

TAKE UP THE CROSS

A traditional part of these youth pilgrimages is the carrying of a large rugged wooden cross in front of the line of marchers. That is the sign behind which the pilgrims rally and in whose honor they walk. It was beautiful to see how the young Italian fellows fought for the honor of carrying the cross. Of course there were plenty of other ways in which one could share in Christ's Passion on this walk and identify with the call to the disciple: "Deny yourself, take up your cross and follow Me" (Lk 9:23). Just being attentive to the needs of brothers and sisters on this walk was sharing in the sacrifice of the Cross of Jesus.

Another great blessing for me from the Lord was meeting young men who had made the walk in 1975, that I also was on and who now were in the seminary studying to be priests. I had heard that many vocations to priesthood and religious life came from these youth walks and now I was seeing the truth of it firsthand. It made perfect sense, for these kinds of total immersion pilgrimages, led by priests and by vowed religious, were like furnaces that refined the spirit. They were living experiences of discipleship: of putting everything else aside (at least for a week) and focusing on nothing else but walking, praying, and following the Cross of Jesus. It was better than many a weekend retreat that could be mainly in one's head and yet hardly engage the will and the body. The pilgrimage experience involved sacrifice and total commitment of body and soul. It was little wonder that the Lord was able to use these "spiritual exercises" to speak deeply to his searching and open children. Thanks be to God for the organizers of such marches who were willing to invest so much–including themselves–in these powerful tools of evangelization.

IN AND AROUND ROME

The last few days of the walk were not so difficult: the Lord gave us a break. The rain stopped: the sun came out and the mileage we had to make each day was cut almost in half. Also during the Triduum of Holy Thursday, Good Friday, and Holy Saturday, there were more church services to attend. And so the mood lightened up, the guitars were brought out, and songs of praise again filled the air. There was one song that I had contributed to the walk that became a favorite and I was asked to lead it over and over again. It was a catchy tune called, *I Will Sing. I Will Sing*. As a matter-of-fact after the final Mass in the piazza of St. Peter with Pope John Paul II on Easter Sunday as we said our goodbyes and headed back to our home countries, the group asked me to lead the song one more time. Since I did not have my guitar with me I led it a cappella. Singing "Alleluia, glory to the Lord" (the refrain) was how we parted. It was how we also hoped to meet again in the New Jerusalem, the Kingdom of God come down from heaven (Rv 19:5-7; 21:2).

TRIP HOME

We got the flight to Milan and then were back in the air to New York where we landed on schedule at 3:00 p.m. Finally we arrived back in Pittsburgh to be greeted by family and friends at the same spot where we had said goodbye to them eleven days before. We thanked the Lord for all He had done for us both physically and spiritually. Now we were more than just seasoned travelers: we hopefully were wiser in the ways of the Lord, and more certain of His loving Providence. Now we were responsible to make good use of the gifts and graces He had so generously given to us.

WRITING THE NARRATIVE

When I returned from pilgrimage in Italy to my *poustinia* in Glenshaw, I had just four more years before I would hit the road as a more permanent walking pilgrim. That would begin the period of being a "foreign missionary," which lasted almost thirteen years. Naturally in the coming four years I would be trying to tie up loose ends and to have all my bills paid (I still owed the Diocese of Pittsburgh several thousand dollars for my seminary education). In 1985, I felt the Lord urging me to print up my detailed journal from my 1981 walk in honor of the North American Martyrs. With the help of a friend and a mimeograph, I made 100 spiral-bound copies, 220 pages each, and gave them to friends.

The Lord then put it on my heart to write about my first year-long pilgrim walk that took me from Barcelona to Jerusalem (1970-71). This resulted in a 187-page book entitled: *A Pilgrim Finds the Way* (a turn of phrase recalling Jesus' being "the Way" in John 14:6, and the book composed by an anonymous nineteenth-century Russian pilgrim who learned to use the Jesus Prayer from a monastic elder.[30]) As resource material for this work I had fourteen lengthy, detailed letters that I had written to my parents during that walk, and which my mother had kept. I also had a little pocket notebook in which I had recorded thoughts, insights, poems, quotations, and dreams. I felt inspired to write this memoir in the third person so I would not have to be always saying, "I" as if I did it in my own strength and thereby rob the Lord of the credit for what He did. As part of his tithe to the Lord, a friend who owned a printing company volunteered to publish 6,000 copies free of charge as a trade paperback, along with a few hundred hardback copies. I never secured a distributor for the book but gave copies to people whom I thought would enjoy or benefit from reading it.

A PILGRIM FINDS THE WAY

There was one particular copy of this book, though, that meant the most to me. It appeared in the hands of a middle-aged woman from my neighborhood who stopped at my *poustinia* on Trinity Lane, Butler, Pennsylvania, in the winter of 2015.[31]

She held the paperback copy of *A Pilgrim Finds the Way* that I had given her a year earlier. It was well-worn, faded, dog-eared, and had lots of book-marking strips sticking out of it: it had obviously been through a lot.

She held the book up and said, "This book saved my life."

"Praise the Lord," I said. "How is that?"

"Do you remember a year ago my car broke down on Trinity Lane and I stopped here for some water for my radiator?"

"Yes. After talking with you briefly, I handed you a copy of my book."

She said, "Well at that time I was on my way to score some drugs. But I began reading your book and I never made it to my destination. I have not touched drugs since that day. I carry the book with me everywhere I go and share its contents with anyone who will listen to me. Now I am helping others get free of drugs."

I thought, "Thank You Lord. Seeing this fruit makes all the effort worthwhile. Obedience to Your will and inspiration is certainly the best way to live one's life. Now another pilgrim had found the Way, also."

A CONTEMPORARY PILGRIM

At this point, I wish to introduce my readers to a pilgrim-friend of mine, Fr. Arcadius Smolinski, OFM (1921-2005).[32] I first came to know about him in 1975, from my friend Fr. Gus Milon, OFM (1944-2007). Fr. Gus gave me a copy of the Assumption Province *Newsletter* (#15) which contained an article entitled, "Who Is This Pilgrim Arcadius?" by one of the Franciscan friars Dacian Bluma, OFM. I was greatly encouraged to know that a fellow American living in the twentieth century had felt the call to the life of a permanently wandering pilgrim. And he was a priest at that, so he had a solid theological background and had a superior who gave him such an obedience–even if only on a year-to-year basis.

I wrote to Fr. Arcadius in the fall of 1984, and got my first letter from him dated December 10, 1984, posted in Medjugorje, Yugoslavia. Before he died in 2005 (after walking on pilgrimage for thirty-two years), I had received a total of nine letters from him; not bad for a pilgrim and one who wrote to me in his first letter and said, "I feel urgency to prayer and penance. Have no time for correspondence."

MEETING IN JERUSALEM

Nevertheless, just knowing that such a man existed today, was a great encouragement to my own life as a pilgrim. After thirty-two years of faithfully serving his American Franciscan Province as a librarian, director of novices and guardian, as well as a confessor, preacher, and retreat master (along with a five-year span of living directly with the poor in Chicago), he answered the Lord's call to become a pilgrim and stranger as an itinerant friar. Without money (or even a passport, I had been told) he would walk each year from Rome to Lourdes to Cracow and back to Rome. He also at one time walked through the Balkans and to Jerusalem. He had a great devotion to Mary, the Mother of God, and often encouraged me in his letters to make the total consecration of St. Louis de Montfort to her. And whenever he came to a shrine and stayed for a few weeks or months, he spent much of his time in the confessional.

I was finally able to meet up with Fr. Arcadius in the Holy Land during the Jubilee Year 2000, and we were able to share a few hours walking and praying together on the Mount of Olives opposite the Old City of Jerusalem. I can still picture him sitting in a chair behind a screen in the back of the right aisle in the Church of All Nations, hearing the confessions of pilgrims (in English, Polish, and Italian) all during the Jubilee Year 2000. This is what he loved to do best—exercise his priesthood, bringing God's mercy and forgiveness to poor sinners on earth. Fr. Arcadius's Franciscan brothers have, since his death, collected documentary information on his life, should the Lord choose to use him to further His Kingdom on earth by miracles. Even if he is never beatified or canonized, I pray a full biography of his life will eventually be written for the benefit of the Church Militant on earth.

THE JESUS PRAYER

Part of the Lord preparing me for the coming years of pilgrimaging was learning the Jesus Prayer–"Lord Jesus Christ, Son of the living God, have mercy on me a sinner." I had first come across this prayer when I read *The Way of the Pilgrim* in California in 1967. At the age of ninety-two, my grandmother Eugenia Walter (1888-1980) was in a nursing home in Pittsburgh. I received word that she was not doing well so I borrowed a car on February 13, 1980, and drove from St. Mary's to the Morningside section of Pittsburgh about 8 miles away. My aunt Loretta was beside her bed when I entered the room.

She greeted me and said: "Grandma has not opened her eyes since I have been here, but she is still alive. Maybe you can pray for her."

I took up a position opposite my aunt on the other side of the bed, laid my hand on her hand, and began praying very slowly: "Lord Jesus Christ, Son of the living God, have mercy on me a sinner," over and over. After about ten minutes she opened her eyes, looked at me, smiled, closed her eyes, and breathed her last. With the comfort of prayer and the name of Jesus (whom she loved as the Good Shepherd) she gently slipped from this life to the next.

TWO MORE MOMENTS

On July 17, 1980, I got the distinct impression that the Lord wanted me to visit my aunt Josepha (1911-80) who was in the isolation ward at St. Margaret Hospital in Aspinwall, Pennsylvania. Josepha had refused treatment for breast cancer; it had now metastasized. It was just a matter of time before the cancer would claim her life. When I arrived at the unit the nurse on duty said, "She is in a coma and cannot respond but if you put on a gown and gloves you can visit her." Noticing her labored breathing, I just laid my hand on her right arm and began saying the Jesus Prayer according to the rhythm of her breathing. When she breathed in I said: "Lord Jesus

Christ" and when she breathed out I said: "have mercy." After a few minutes her breathing became slower and slower, so that the prayer became simpler and simpler until eventually she took her last breath on earth. It was as though she just needed the gentle presence of the Lord she had served her whole life, present in the prayer of faith and repentance, to make the final transition.

On my forty-fifth birthday, July 25, 1986, my mother was in Pittsburgh's Allegheny General Hospital recovering from an unsuccessful hernia operation. I received a call at the McKees Rocks Youth Center; it said she was not doing well and had not been able to sleep for days. I took the next bus into Pittsburgh and walked across the Sixth Street Bridge over the Allegheny River to the hospital. I found her in the intensive care unit and after anointing her with blessed oil, began praying the Jesus Prayer with her. Within five minutes she was sound asleep for the first time in several days.

AUTO ACCIDENT

There was one event in August of 1987, that could have ended my plans to walk to Mexico the following year. Six of us from St. Mary's had made a two-day pilgrimage to Our Lady of Consolation Shrine in Carey, Ohio, and we were returning in two cars back to St. Mary's. I was in the front passenger seat of the lead car, a little Chevrolet Chevette and two other pilgrims were in the back seats. We pulled up to a stop sign, but our driver could not see a van pulling a trailer and boat coming southbound in our direction on an intersecting road. She pulled out right in front of it. Just before the impact, I looked to my left and saw what was about to happen and cried out, "Jesus, have mercy."

Our driver took the full impact on her side and our car was propelled across the road into an empty lawn. We all were taken to the local hospital. I was thankful that the Lord had me put my seat belt on in such a way that it prevented my neck from getting whiplash. I

155

thanked my guardian angel, whom I have named Steadfast, for his unseen help and protection.

PILGRIM GARB

As time drew closer for my departure, I felt the Lord asking me to wear a jean-patched, full-length robe, on the pilgrimage. Up to this time I had just sewed denim patches on my blue navy peacoat when it got a hole in it. So I collected lots of used jeans, cut them up into rectangles, and gave them to a seamstress-friend of mine who measured me up and made of them a full-length robe with a hood on it. One part of my inspiration came from seeing St. Francis's patched robe in Assisi, another from considering denim material as modern "sackcloth" (a biblical sign of repentance – [Is 58:5]). A few weeks before I left, I took the robe to Bishop Bosco (who had now been installed as the Bishop of Greensburg, Pennsylvania) to be blessed. The final addition to the pilgrimage was a donkey.

A SURPRISE CALL

Most of my friends knew that I believed the Lord wanted me to take along a donkey on this trip, but the Lord had told me I was not to do anything to acquire it myself–He would arrange it all Himself. A week before I was to leave a good friend of mine, Chuck, was inspired to take $200 and go to an animal auction. When he got to the auction he asked if there were any donkeys for sale. It just happened there were a couple of little mules that were for sale at $180 each. Chuck bought one: but how was he to get it home?

A man then stepped up and said: "I have a trailer. I will haul your mule to your house for $20."

So that made up the rest of the $200 the Lord had Chuck put in his wallet that morning. When Chuck got home he gave me a telephone call and said: "George. I have your little mule for you."

I had begun to sigh with relief when I saw the days were drawing near for my departure and I had no donkey. I could not imagine taking care of a large animal for six months of walking along the roads of America. But here she was: just as the Lord promised.

I walked Unita (the name the Lord had given me for her) over to some local stables and Robert, the owner, began to teach me how to lead her, to give her commands, and to care for my new sidekick. One priest-friend I shared with previously (Fr. Mike Salvagna, CP, who wrote the foreward to this book), had suggested, "Maybe your donkey is to carry sandwich boards glorifying the Lord." One of his hired hands cut out two pieces of plywood. Another painted them light blue and printed Jesus Is Lord on one, and God Loves You on the other. That was the Gospel in its simplest form. Robert himself proceeded to make a twisted rope harness for Unita to carry the signs on.

Now we were ready to depart the next morning. And that began the next chapter in my life, "A Missionary to Other Lands."

THE PRAYER OF MY HEART

Lord, I thank You for these fifteen years
of ministry in the power of the Holy Spirit,
among family and friends in the land of my birth.

I place all of them beneath Your Cross
and ask that You care for them with Your merciful love.
Bring to completion in each of their lives,
the good work You have begun in them.

I am grateful for each and every one of them,

for being a part of my life,

and I consider each of them a gift from You

and a sign of Your everlasting love,

I now place myself in Your hands

for the next stage of my journey home to You.

In the name of the Father and of the Son

and of the Holy Spirit. Amen.

ENDNOTES

26. These seven years are contained in five volumes (numbers eleven through fifteen) of the forty, three-ring binders that now document my life from birth to age seventy-five. Perusing these many letters, notes, writings, reflections, events, and people involved, one can see how carefully and thoroughly the Lord worked in my life: much better than I could ever have done on my own.

27. From a letter by Fr. Dunstan Jones, OFM Cap (a member of St. Augustine Province, Pittsburgh). It was written February 1, 1985, while he was stationed in Papua, New Guinea.

28. Seminary bill. In July of 1969, the remaining charge for my seminary education stood at $5,700. At $950 a year for tuition, room, and board (on the college and graduate levels), this was a tremendous bargain.

29. "Frati Minori Rinnovati." This branch of the Franciscan Family (FMR) was established in Sicily by a group of Capuchin friars in 1972, and it was recognized as an Institute of the Consecrated Life–in effect, a diocesan-level religious order–in 1983. The members seek to live out the rule of St. Francis in a more literal and radical fashion. This order is not to be confused with the separate Community of Franciscans of the Renewal (CFR), which also originated within the Capuchins and for similar reasons, but within the United States, in 1987.

30. *The Way of a Pilgrim and The Pilgrim Continues his Way*. Translated from the Russian by R. M. French (New York: Seabury Press, 1965).

31. *Poustinia* on Trinity Lane. This was on the former grounds of Holy Trinity Monastery, the first Byzantine-Benedictine monastic foundation in the Western Hemisphere, established in the years following World War II. Initially it was under the jurisdiction of the American-Cassinese Benedictine Congregation. On October, 1, 2006, it transferred to the (Ruthenian) Archeparchy of Pittsburgh. Due to a paucity of members, Holy Trinity was dissolved as a monastic community in November of 2014.

32. Fr. Aracadius Smolinsky, OFM (1921-2005), born in Cleveland, made his first profession of vows with the Franciscan Friars (Polish) of Assumption Province in Pulaski, Wisconsin, in 1940. He

earned a master's degree in library science, was assistant director and then director of novices, and lived with the poor on the streets of Chicago. In 1975, he requested to live as a pilgrim in Europe and spent the next thirty years walking throughout Europe and the Near East. I first heard about him in 1975, and began writing to him in 1984. In the twenty years I corresponded with him, I was privileged to receive nine handwritten letters from him.

1   Boyhood home - 3137 Harts Run Road Allison Park, PA

2   First 17 days of my life: daily diary written by my maternal grandfather or grandmother in 1941

3   St. Mary's Pine Creek Church (built in 1867) where I was baptized August 10, 1941

4   Mom and Dad (Florian and Mary Rita Walter): My First Easter, 1942.

5   At 11 months: June 1942.

1   "Budding carpenter" two years old: July 1943.

2   First Day of School - Six years old: 1947.

3   St. Mary's Grade School where I attended grades 1-8.

4   The F.J. Walter family complete (mom, dad and 3 boys): May 1949.

5   I am dressed as a server with my Uncle Father Mathias Gallenz, OFM Cap. June, 1951

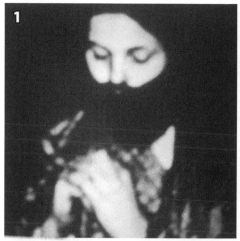

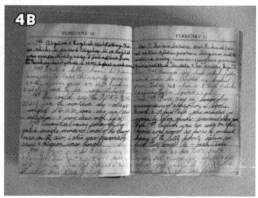

1   Playing St. Joseph in Christmas Pageant, 1953.

2   Leaving for seminary: September 1955.

3   St. Gregory Seminary High School, Cincinnati, Ohio

4   High School diary (4A closed: 4B open)

5   Nineteen years old - April, 1960 - with cassock and collar.

1   St.Vincent Benedictine Seminary (Wimmer Hall), Latrobe, PA.

2   Vatican Council II - St. Peter's Basilica, Rome, Italy.

3   Me at Trappist Monastery, Snowmass, Colorado, August 1968.

4   Silk screened card announcing my walk to Jerusalem, February, 1970.

5   Wearing aluminum hard hat on walk to Jerusalem.

6   Returning from Jerusalem, 3137 Harts Run Rd, May 29, 1971.

7   Items from my pilgrimage: 1) Diary, 2) New Testament 3) Scallop shell from Santiago.

CHAPTER 3

POISED FOR RUSSIA

NORTH AMERICA

Glenshaw, Pennsylvania to Anchorage, Alaska

May 1, 1988 to April 21, 1993

Five Years - 8,200 miles

PART ONE

OUR LADY OF GUADALUPE (1988)

DAY OF DEPARTURE

After the 7:30 a.m. Mass at St. Mary's, Glenshaw, on Sunday, May 1, 1988, I was ready to "step out of the boat" (the safety of my daily routine) and "walk on the water" (unknown territory ahead) toward Jesus and His Mother in Mexico City, 2,500-miles away (cf. Mt 14:22-33). I felt secure under the mantle of our Lady, the Mother of God, my heavenly Mother and intercessor, as I was beginning in her month of May, which this year had a blue moon (two full moons in one month). It was also a Marian Year as declared by Pope John Paul II. I took no money with me; when money was given to me along the way, I sent it back to Pittsburgh for other pilgrims. It was to be a "sabbatical year" of not working or sowing but rather completely trusting in Divine Providence in a literal way (Lv 25:1-7). I planned to survive on the charity of well-wishers along the way.

I took no tent to sleep in, but carried a large piece of clear plastic which I could lay down on the ground first, if I needed to bed down outside at night or to throw it over me for protection from rain or dew. My guitar was in a vinyl case with a strap slung over my left shoulder. Over my other shoulder was a bag with a change of clothes in it, along with maps, extra patches, a pocket tape cassette recorder, and personal items. Also, I carried a small woolen blanket upon which I had sewn a large cloth image of Our Lady of Guadalupe that I could drape over my shoulder, like Juan Diego's *tilma* (cloak).

For the first time I put on my "new" blessed, hooded, full-length robe made of denim patches. Around my neck was hung the image of Our Lady of America from the Melkite Church in West Paterson, New Jersey. For my head I started out with the "Jesus jean cap" I had worn and patched for years, but on the second day I replaced that with a large Mexican sombrero which was replaced by new sombreros until 1995, when I finally put them aside in Islamabad, Pakistan, and switched over to the Middle Eastern *keffiyeh* (head scarf). In my left hand was a copy of the Four Gospels, the essential core of divine revelation. And in my right hand was my staff (Ex 4:17) in the form of a Tau ("T"). It was made from the branch of a dogwood tree and had mounted on it a missionary crucifix with a relic of the true cross embedded in it. On my feet were the rubber tire sandals tied on with ropes. I was fully equipped with "the armor of God," as listed in St. Paul's letter to the Ephesians.

My little mule Unita, which I was mistakenly calling a *burro* or "donkey" for the first four months, was standing by. Her rope harness made from hand-twisted hay ropes, was carrying the two signs like sandwich boards, but the harness ropes still needed the fleece I was carrying sewed around them, so that they would not irritate Unita's skin. This sewing project took many weeks and was not completed till my mother, father, and Chuck met up with me in Centerville, Ohio, on May 21. Unita would eventually carry a two-gallon plastic bucket and twenty-five feet of rope so I could lower the bucket over the railing of a bridge we were crossing to get her water to drink. I did not intend to ride her so she could be ready for the Lord's entry into the New Jerusalem (Lk 19:30). And my guardian angel had a lot of work to do helping me manage her along the roads, around the bends, and over the bridges along the way.

FIRST STAGE

After a final blessing from the pastor of St. Mary's, Fr. Harcarik, as well as the taking of pictures and videos and receiving of hugs and good wishes from family and friends in St. Mary's parking lot, we were off on the first leg our journey for the Lord. Dividing up my eight-month pilgrimage into four stages, I was now beginning stage one–Glenshaw, Pennsylvania, to Belleville, Illinois. It was approximately 600 miles and averaging 13 miles a day, it took us two months, May and June. This was a time of getting used to traveling with a mule for a companion, which included the physical logistics of adjusting her harness, learning her habits, and caring for her needs in general.

But it soon became obvious that having her along made me much more approachable. When I walk alone on pilgrimage in Western countries (Eastern European countries are a whole different story) only two or three people a day will stop to talk, to offer help, or to take a picture. With the little mule along it was ten to fifteen people a day. Often mothers (or fathers) would bring their little children "to see the donkey." Grandmothers would stop to examine the donkey and to entertain me with stories. Others would bring food and water (sometimes just for her, sometimes just for me, and sometimes for both of us). Some would inquire about our mission, thank us for our witness, or ask us for prayers. And others would simply want to take a picture. So I did much more verbal sharing each day than if I had been walking alone in quiet contemplation and prayer. It was an adjustment I willingly made for the furthering of the Kingdom.

TAPE RECORDINGS

The Lord had me take along a pocket tape recorder and I often turned it on to record actual conversations as they occurred spontaneously along the way. Every week or so I would send the full tapes back to my friends and family in Glenshaw; they would duplicate them and pass them around. One good friend of mine, Donna, wrote to me on June 4, 1988 saying:

> Your mother very generously shared the first three tapes, days 1-3. I listened to all of them and the immediacy of this walk was startling. It felt as though we were walking too, and I was (and am) moved by what you shared. I smiled, chuckled, outright laughed at one point, and wept at others. Something very beautiful was happening in Ohio this spring!

The effects of these tapes–which were often of very poor quality due to road noise in the background, and low batteries–was amazing. My friend Chuck took it upon himself to condense all thirty-three tapes into five and duplicated these for those interested in listening to them. Other friends decided to transcribe all thirty-four of these tapes as best they could, to type them up, and to make three copies. The total project was 830 pages. Many newspaper reporters, radio talk show hosts, and TV newscasters would report on my walk along the way, but this raw data recorded on-the-spot probably provides the most intimate sharing in any pilgrimage walk I have ever made.

UNPLANNED ENCOUNTERS

In this first 600-mile stretch, I had two stops planned ahead where people were waiting for me: Centerville, Ohio, and Belleville, Illinois, at the Shrine of Our Lady of the Snows. But the Lord also kindly arranged a number of other interesting stops. For example, on May 3, I had the opportunity to talk for forty-five minutes with a young woman in her mid-twenties. She was alone, severely depressed, and on foot for 10 miles. She said she had tried to commit suicide five times in the past month, but was hoping for a sign from God. Meeting me was that sign.

Then there was the overnight stop at Franciscan University of Steubenville, where Fr. Michael Scanlon, TOR–then president of the university–gave me his priestly blessing. At Holy Family Camaldolese Hermitage in Bloomingdale, Ohio, my good friend Father Abbot Charles Kubsz, Er. Cam. (1913-96), had me sign the guest book and paste in it a Polaroid picture of Unita and me, on May 6. On Sunday, May 15, I made it to St. Mary of the Assumption Church in Lancaster. It was First Communion Sunday, so after Mass the children—in their finest apparel—all wanted to have their picture taken with Jesus' donkey, tied up to the tree in front of their church that Sunday.

CENTERVILLE, OHIO

On Saturday, May 21, I arrived in Centerville, Ohio, just south of Dayton and met my friend Bob and his wife Bev. Bob had withdrawn from the seminary in the first year of college in 1960, but after marrying and raising four children, he became a permanent deacon and was deeply involved in his parish church, Incarnation.

Bob had arranged to put up Unita in an empty barn that was about a half-mile from his house. Being the clever mule that she was, however, she figured out how to open one of the gates and began to make her way back to Bob's house. The police found her trying to cross the highway and brought her back. So Bob and I had to walk her back to the barn and to secure the gate.

My mother, father, and Chuck had come down from Glenshaw to visit for the weekend with me. They spent much of their time sewing the fleece onto the hay ropes that made up Unita's harness, so I was thankful the Lord provided a way to accomplish a task I had put off far too long. Of course they were all glad to see that I had fared so well the first few weeks of my summer pilgrimaging, and they enjoyed hearing the stories of how the Lord had provided for both me and Unita.

CHILDREN'S LETTERS

My mother had brought personal greetings from a number of people in Glenshaw, including notes from the fourth-grade class at St. Mary's School. The students wrote questions, such as, "How are you doing?" Are you tired?" Are your feet sore from walking?" Are you hungry?" What made you want to visit Mary (in Mexico) and why did you walk?" How is your mule?" Are people nice to you?"

And there were words of encouragement, such as in this letter: "I found your picture in the newspaper and we put it on the board in school. I hope you make it safely. I think you are very brave: I might want to be like you. I cannot wait until you come back and tell us everything. We are praying for you (night and day). May God descend the Holy Spirit on you." I wrote a general letter answering their questions so that their teacher could read it to the whole class. As it turned out I returned in 2001, thirteen years later. By that time, these students would be out of college and probably dispersed to the four corners of the earth. They may have forgotten about the pilgrim with the mule by that time, but for this moment in our lives, we shared the journey of life together.

SLEEPING INDOORS

When I left Centerville on Monday morning, May 23, it was raining. I had only two more days of walking in Ohio, then I crossed over to the State of Indiana and spent fourteen days walking through Hoosier[34] territory. I then crossed into Illinois and walked ten more days to get to Our Lady of the Snows Shrine in Belleville, on the western side of Illinois. Of those twenty-six days, I slept outside only eleven times: the other fifteen I was invited to sleep indoors by people who saw me walking and opened their hearts and homes to me on-the-spot.

A few nights I was invited to sleep in people's campers or in motorhomes. One night I even slept in a child's tree house in the family's backyard. When I slept outside in the fields I had to deal with ticks and mosquitoes, so to protect myself, I used a discarded child's First Communion veil as a screen over my face and hands— the only parts of my body not covered by my jean-patched robe and hood. I noted that the hem on the bottom of my robe was wearing through and that the toes of my socks had holes in them from hitting the grass at the open tops of my sandals.

AN INSTRUMENT OF PEACE

I was beginning to experience the wear and tear of the journey. Nevertheless, it was all worth it, for I began to see how God was using the pilgrimage to build up the Body of Christ. One woman in eastern Indiana came up to me and said: "You sure warm the hearts of a lot of people in Fayette County." Another young mother with two small children stopped to share how seeing me walking and seeing the sign on Unita saying, "God loves you" gave her the strength she needed at this moment to forgive and to bear the pain of her husband's recent infidelity. Another day a woman came up to me and said, "Seeing you is like getting my spiritual vitamin B12 shot today."

Then there was the truck driver in western Indiana, near Linton, who, after a serious accident, came up to me to ask for a prayer. Late on Saturday afternoon, June 4, I was walking south of Worthington. At this point the land flattened out and the cornfields stretched as far as the eye could see. I was just coming into Switz City and ready to cross a little bridge, when I heard two toots of a horn from a tractor-trailer that was slowing down as it passed me on my side of the road. Then I heard the squeal of brakes behind me. Turning around I saw the rig fishtail, go off the road, and go over on its side. The berm was narrow and obviously too soft to support such a heavy load.

Unharmed, the driver climbed out of his cab as people stopped and began to gather around his overturned vehicle. He was perfectly calm and started witnessing about trusting in the Lord, saying, "Those who trust in God find unity in brothers and sisters," and "The Lord is part of every situation; nothing is by accident." Then he came back to where I was and said, "As soon as I saw you walking I felt the Lord say in my heart, 'Get that man to pray for you and you will be delivered from your depression and from your smoking habit.' I do not care if I lose my insurance or driver's license–the Lord works in mysterious ways and I praise Him in all circumstances."

Thanking the Lord for this very dramatic proof of the power of the Cross of Jesus and the power which comes from trusting in Him, I laid my hand on him and prayed for the Holy Spirit to come and to anoint him completely and to bring him healing, deliverance, and protection in every way. The Lord was testing the faith of His child (see Heb 12:7) and He was receiving glory from this servant of His who sought to walk in faith and hope. Glory be to God.

LEARNING ABOUT UNITA

These three weeks of walking enabled me to better understand Unita. She displayed a number of interesting characteristics. For instance, at every opportunity she loved to lie down and roll in the dust. She was sensitive enough to be bothered more by the sound of turning bicycle wheels than by loud motorcycles or semitrailers. She would not drink chlorinated tap water and often tried to drink from stagnant puddles.

Perhaps one of the most serious issues with Unita was my need to be continuously aware of her whereabouts, as her rope could break in the middle of the night or she could pull out her stake if not tied to a tree and be off on her own. One of Unita's more amusing escapes happened early Friday morning on June 3. I had been invited to have supper and spend the night with a very hospitable family in Spencer, Indiana. They allowed me to sleep in their fully equipped motor home and I tied Unita to the front bumper. During the night she regularly scratched herself on the bumper and rocked the whole camper.

When I no longer felt the rocking, about 4:00 a.m., I began to be suspicious; looking out the window, I saw that her rope had become undone and she was gone. I called the police. The officer receiving the call said, "The paper boy found her headed up the road this morning." So I walked down to the police station to retrieve the little recalcitrant mule and made a mental note to be more careful about securing her during the night.

MORE ENCOUNTERS

There were a number of other memorable people and events on this leg of the pilgrimage also: There was Dan, the reporter for the *Indianapolis Star* who came to do an extensive interview and who wrote later to my parents (he also kept in touch with them for many years); Karen, the "Spirit-filled" wife and mom who prayed a long and beautiful prayer of protection over me and Unita; an unaccepted invitation to preach at a local revival; the people who stopped with bags of tin cans asking if I was out recycling; as well as the many friendly police who made sure I did not need anything and who helped me find the right roads.

OUR LADY OF THE SNOWS

Finally on Saturday morning, June 18, I began to draw near to the Shrine of Our Lady of the Snows staffed by the Missionary Oblates of Mary Immaculate.[35] My introduction to the shrine came in a very personal way through Father Jim Malley, OMI who came out to meet me on the road. His first words to me were, "Your reputation has proceeded you. You have been in the paper and half of the shrine staff says they have driven by you in the past two days. We have accommodations for you and your friend. We have a little maintenance shack where we keep animals during Christmas so we have water, buckets, hay, and so forth for your little mule."

When I arrived at the shrine, the priests and staff came out to greet me. They put me up in the oblate house, so now I could shower, use the washer and dryer, and even help myself to food in the kitchen. For the next two days, I went through my stack of mail that had been waiting for me and made myself available to people at the Visitor Center if they wanted to talk or to receive prayer. I got to Mass both days and had plenty of time to rest. So it was a time of physical and spiritual renewal.

BACK ON THE ROAD

On Monday, June 20, I left the shrine after Mass and after sharing with the priests and staff, as well as signing some autographs. My next planned stop was John Michael Talbot's "Little Portion Hermitage" in Eureka Springs, Arkansas.[36] I had been reading about John Michael since his conversion from playing guitar in a rock band, to becoming an Evangelical Protestant, to becoming a Roman Catholic, and ultimately a Secular Franciscan. I found his music inspirational. His following of St. Francis of Assisi, along with having a vision for an itinerant ministry, spoke to my own calling.

Eureka Springs lay about 350 miles away and it would take me twenty-seven days to walk it with Unita. My immediate goal, however, was to cross the Mississippi River into Missouri and start heading south. But my maps showed only interstate highways crossed the river near St. Louis, so I had to walk south in Illinois for five days until I came to Chester; there I hoped I could walk with Unita across a bridge into Missouri. The Lord had it all planned: He just left me in the dark about it until the last minute; it was to be a walk of faith and not of sight (2 Cor 5:7).

OPENING A PATHWAY

On Friday, June 24, on the Feast of St. John the Baptist, after walking for five days in blistering heat, I headed down the long hill in Chester toward the bridge over the Mississippi River. Coming up to the checkpoint of the bridge on the Illinois side, the attendant leaned out of his booth and said in a most friendly way, "The mayor welcomes you to Chester; waives your toll fee, and provides a police escort across the bridge."

So I turned around to look behind me and sure enough, I saw a flashing light on a police car as he pulled out onto the highway. He waved me and Unita on in front of him, so I stepped out on the road and headed for the old rusty, narrow, two-lane bridge in front of us. We then proceeded to walk down the middle of the single lane going west (there was no sidewalk on either side of the bridge) with the patrol car, his lights flashing, slowly following us with all the cars going west at this time inching their way along behind him. It must have been quite a sight. For fifteen minutes that day the Lord had a long line of followers, some perhaps rather unwilling. Hopefully, some received the grace of God's loving presence into their hearts as a result of this unexpected delay.

Thank you Jesus!

WELCOME TO MISSOURI

On the other side of the bridge I tied up Unita in the shade, and went inside the air-conditioned restaurant to eat, drink, and watch a video that had been taken of us a few days before. It was a wonderful welcome to "The Show Me State" and I rejoiced in the publicity that the Lord was receiving and how the Gospel was being proclaimed.

Unexpectedly, the next day I came upon another shrine, this time in Perryville, Missouri. It was called, "The National Shrine of the Miraculous Medal," and it was staffed by French-national Vincentian priests. Then I was on my way toward Silver Lake, Missouri, where I wanted to attend the 8:00 a.m. Sunday morning Mass at the tiny St. Rose of Lima Catholic Church.

COUNTRY ROADS

For the next week or so, I walked through backcountry roads and parts of the Mark Twain National Forest. There was very little traffic and people could stop in their cars or trucks and talk to me without pulling off the road and still not be in the way of any other traffic. It rained a few times and one night all my effects got soaked, but it was a welcome relief from the heat which had me regularly taking off my headband and wringing out the perspiration.

The ticks were especially bad in this area and one night I pulled twenty-four of them off of me. I learned to hang my pants up at night because ticks typically crawl upward, so by morning they had all gathered around the waist area where it was easy to pick them off. I also saw my first "microscopic tick" that can only be pulled out with tweezers. I had to continually check Unita for ticks, as well.

UNITA'S NEEDS

Unita was very popular in this part of Missouri because many of the farmers here had mules themselves. In Mountain View, Missouri, I found a veterinarian to check Unita over. Her coat of hair was shiny, her hoofs were doing fine and she did not need shoes, and her weight was normal. One problem was a back molar that was growing sideways and was irritating the side of her cheek.

It needed to be "floated" (filed off) every few weeks.

Then I began to notice that Unita was backing up to telephone poles when she could find one and scratched herself on them. I was told this was a sign she needed deworming. Because of the heat Unita liked to stop in the shade of a tree when we came to one along the side of the road. And she was showing the first signs of becoming tenderfooted.

A TRAPPIST MONASTESRY

On July 1, I met a priest in Piedmont, Missouri, by the name of Fr. Dan. When I told him the way I was walking, he suggested I pay a visit to Assumption Trappist Monastery 20 miles east of Ava, Missouri. So for the next few days I directed my steps toward Eureka Springs, Arkansas, by way of this remote monastery that lay nestled in the rugged, wooded, Ozark Mountains. I arrived at the monastery on Friday evening, July 8, and I was in time for Vespers at 6:00 p.m. They put me up in the guesthouse and I stayed two nights, leaving after Sunday morning Mass which was at 9:00 a.m. in the monastery chapel. Before I left one of the monks, Fr. Theodore, gave me a piece of paper with detailed, rough handwritten directions that they had on file showing how to travel by roads from their monastery to Little Portion Hermitage in Arkansas. It was a gift from the Lord, for without it I would probably have gone too far, forcing me to have doubled-back if I was on my own.

ON TO ARKANSAS

When I left the Trappist Monastery, a six-day walk lay ahead of me so as to arrive at the Hermitage which was just over the Missouri/Arkansas border. It was another hot 103-degree day but it rained just about every day so that cooled it off somewhat. This part of the Ozark Mountains was full of lakes and it was very touristy. There were many vacation homes, motels, resorts, and golf courses. The local people (who called themselves "hillbillies") were very hospitable and went out of their way to provide for all of my needs.

An incident happened just before I arrived at Little Portion that reminded me how the Lord works outside of human efforts and expectations. I had tried my best to get to the Hermitage by Saturday night so that I could get to Mass on Sunday. But with the rain, the heat, the number of visitors, and with Unita's lameness, Saturday night, July 16, I ended up just over the state line, when it got dark and I camped outside.

A PROVIDENTIAL MEETING

I was looking for a dirt road as I headed south. It was supposed to be about two and a half miles from the state line. At this point, I discovered that I misread the directions given to me by the Trappists. The next morning, Sunday, I started walking at 5:30 a.m., still hoping to get to Mass at the Hermitage. I must have missed my turnoff and I then backtracked toward Missouri.

About 8:30 a.m. a pickup truck stopped and a man about sixty-five years of age named Charlie got out and said, "I came back because I need a blessing." He also mentioned that his wife really wanted to meet me; as they only lived fifteen minutes away by foot he asked if I would come for breakfast. Realizing I was not going to make it in time for Mass, I figured the Lord had something else in mind for me this Sunday morning.

Did He ever?

As they prepared me some scrambled eggs, bread, and gravy, Frankie (the wife) said she prayed that I would come by. She needed to talk to someone about her recent decision to follow the Lord. She was being tempted with discouragement and financial problems. Tears came to her eyes several times when I shared with her how the Lord uses trials and difficulties to strengthen our love and to mature our faith in Him. I marveled at how the Lord worked through my error in reading the directions, my going out of the way, and backtracking so that I ended up right where He could get us together. How blessed it is to walk in the Holy Spirit!

ARRIVING AT LITTLE PORTION

It was near noontime before I left Frankie and Charlie's, but I only had one hour of walking left to get to "Little Portion." People who had attended the 10:30 a.m. Mass there were passing me on their way out. So I saw that the Lord had apparently asked me to sacrifice going to Mass that weekend for the sake of ministering to two of His precious sheep. It proved to me once again that He knows what is best for each of us and our personal plans and desires—and sometimes even certain requirements made of us—have to be submitted to and rearranged according to His higher wisdom. "Lord, Your will be done."

When I arrived at the hermitage, I found out that people there were expecting me and everything was prepared for my arrival. One of the children showed me which hermitage (his father called them "condominiums") had been set aside for me. It was a well-constructed, modern type edifice with big windows, painted dry wall, and carpeting . It had running water and there was electricity to power the lights, a ceiling fan, a hot water heater, and an air conditioner.

A wood stove stood ready for heating in the winter. A self-composting toilet was installed in the bathroom which was cordoned off from the single large room making up the interior. A loft overhead with an access ladder provided a sleeping area. Of course there was a large stack of mail waiting for me.

THREE DAYS

The Evening Prayer was at 5:30 p.m. in the chapel and supper was in the dining hall at 6:00 p.m. I got to spend time with Ray, a young father with five young children, because he took an interest in trying to help Unita's tender hooves. At first he tried cutting shoes out of rubber tires but he could not get the glue to hold and he was not in favor of nailing them. So he ended up making her booties out of carpet that were tied on with rope.

On Monday night I was able to share with John Michael Talbot, himself, at suppertime. He said he had read my book, A *Pilgrim Finds the Way*, several months before, and enjoyed it immensely. He noted that it confirmed how the Lord had called him to itinerant pilgrimage, in which members of his community would walk from church to church and evangelize. They had done that in Arkansas from Eureka Springs to Little Rock and were invited to continue it in California for six months. So the spirit of St. Francis of Assisi, poverty, and the charisms of the mendicant friars of the thirteenth century, really united our hearts and vocations. Before I left on Wednesday he said to me, "You are welcome to stay as long as you want. Just talk to Sister Viola and she'll arrange everything."

I was not tempted to take him up on his generous offer, but I did appreciate his kindness. In fact, I have never felt drawn to community life; I too much valued my solitude and silence, even though while on the road it was quite often interrupted. I have observed that, at least for my spiritual needs, it would be difficult to live a contemplative life in a community, especially one with such an active evangelistic outreach as Little Portion had. I appreciated their living a Gospel lifestyle and I would keep them in my prayers, but I did not feel led to give up the way of life to which I felt the Lord had called me as a pilgrim/*poustinik*.

ON TO TEXAS

When I left Little Portion community on Wednesday morning, my next destination was San Antonio, Texas. From Eureka Springs to San Antonio was about 600 miles and it would take me fifty-five days. All of those days were not spent walking. Occasionally I would stay two nights in the same place, as, for example, on July 26-27, when a man offered me the use of a small, empty cabin while he found someone to put iron shoes on Unita who was tender-footed from walking on sharp and broken igneous rocks; she desperately needed more protection on her hooves.

Still, it was blistering hot with the temperatures up in the nineties and hundreds. But there was also plenty of rain in this area. So the Lord found a way to keep us cool enough to walk. The first twenty of the fifty-five days to San Antonio we walked in western Arkansas. It was so close to the State of Oklahoma that at one point a man told me it was only 4 miles west to the state line. The people were friendly; they loved the Lord (and mules) and because of the heat, they were always bringing Unita and me ice and water–and so much food that I had to refuse much of it. The peaches and home-grown tomatoes were coming into season, so many people shared their harvest with me. And numerous times people invited me right into their homes for dinner.

PEOPLE'S RESPONSES

Every little town that had a newspaper sent out a reporter and photographer, to interview me, so many people knew about our walk from reading about it in their local newspapers. Several radio stations sent people out to do a taped interview with me, so many others heard about us on the airwaves and stopped to tell us they appreciated our mission.

Near Eureka Springs people thought I was advertising for the annual passion play. Of course there were also some mocking comments like, "Hey, Moses!" and "He is crazy–even wears a dress–don't bother about him."

Some particularly memorable occurrences took place in this stretch. I met a man who left the Trappists and the Catholic faith, but asked me to sing the Latin Marian hymn, *Salve Regina* for him. Unita brayed her disapproval when I handed back to the man offering it, a long loaf of bread I did not have room for (so I took out a few slices for her). I also lost my portable Book of Gospels somewhere along the way. One family came out four days in a row bringing me food, water, and even a tarp and poles for shelter from the rain at night. And poor Unita was hit by two little boys who threw stones at us; and when one stone hit her, she bolted and pulled me along until she wore herself out.

INTO THE LONE STAR STATE

On August 10, I crossed from Arkansas into Texas and headed for San Antonio by way of Tyler and Palestine. Within a few days, Unita had lost her left front shoe and so I was praying about finding another farrier. The Lord provided one on August 14, in Daingerfield, Texas, the weekend I stayed at Assumption Catholic Church. But by August 17, I needed another farrier in Big Sandy to put new shoes on her other three feet. I was beginning to wonder if having Unita along was more trouble than she was worth. A number of people offered to buy her from me, but the Lord did not give me peace about that, so we kept trudging on together.

Once we crossed into Texas we lost the ticks, but the fire ants took their place. And for those who have never experienced these insects, they attack in massive numbers. When Unita would step on a nest of them they would swarm up her leg and she would stamp on the ground, trying to shake them off. I was told if a cow dropped her newborn on a hill of them, they would kill it immediately with their combined, ferocious bites.

The fire ants were attracted to food like bees are to honey. I had to hang my food bag up on a tree at night and put oil on the string so they would not climb down it into the food. The same with sleeping; I would lay my plastic down on the ground and run a bead of oil all around the edges so they would not cross it and attack me. One night I woke up with them all over me and looking around I saw they had climbed up a tall piece of grass and bent it over the oil barrier onto my plastic like a bridge and marched across it in a steady stream.

I was having trouble with my tape recorder at this point. Probably the dampness affected it because sometimes we would get soaking wet in the downpours that frequented this part of our trip. Also the batteries at times were too low for the recorder to function at its normal speed. I found out that a new set of batteries only lasted two weeks when I used the recorder many times every day. So I had to ask people for new batteries and new tapes. Then sometimes the tape recorder clicked on accidentally and there would be many minutes on the tapes where there was nothing but background sounds. It certainly was a challenge for my four intrepid volunteer transcribers back in Glenshaw to make sense of these poor quality recordings back in 1988. But I thank the Lord now for their valiant efforts.

CHANGE OF SCENERY

The scenery now changed as I headed straight south. I began seeing large cotton fields, even though this part of Texas got lots of rain and everything was green. Normally, cotton is grown in the "dry farming" areas of Texas that only get ten to twelve inches of rain a year. As expected, I also began seeing oil wells or at least the little pumpers above them that were dotting the landscape.

I had a few more losses during this phase of my pilgrimage. In Tyler, Texas, I was inside Immaculate Conception Church for a few hours but when I came outside discovered that my guitar had been stolen. Whoever took it did not get much because it was warped from the rain, the strings were rusty, and it had a hole in the back of it. Also, my staff was accidentally broken one day by a pickup truck that ran over it, as I had laid it in the grass and it was hard to see. After having walked about 1,300 miles, the heels on my sandals had worn down to the point where I needed to add a new piece of rubber tire that I found alongside the road.

LOCAL LORE

An interesting piece of local lore I was given in this area was about how the town of Dime Box got its name. Supposedly, back in pioneer days, there was a store in this area that sold everything for a dime. One could even buy a box of snuff for a dime. So if someone could not get to the store and wanted a box of snuff, they just left a dime in their mailbox and the mailman knew to take it and to leave them a box of snuff.

Fall was setting in and the leaves were turning. It was going down into the fifties at night and there was heavy dew in the morning. Sometimes I walked for days on end without breaking a sweat. Here most of the fields were fenced to keep in the cattle, but the right of ways were spacious; sometimes I could camp in them when clumps of trees were left to stand between the fence and the road. Thankfully a number of people took me in at night and one evening the owner of a motel gave me a room gratis.

A TV station in Bryan, Texas, did a short interview along the highway that was shown on the evening news. A few days later a grandmother stopped and told me her three-year-old granddaughter kept pestering her. "Let us turn on the TV; maybe we will see the man and his donkey." Several visitors also kindly commented, "You are an inspiration for all of us."

One request I definitely refused was the woman who asked me for three numbers so she could go play the lottery.

SAN ANTONIO

On September 11, I finally arrived at Therese's house on Cincinnati Avenue in the middle of San Antonio. Thankfully, it was a Sunday and so there were not so many cars on the roads and no police told me I could not walk a mule through the city (maybe St. Anthony of Padua–after whom the city was name–was interceding for me).

Therese was out-of-town attending a wedding in Pittsburgh, but she had given her neighbor her key and told her that I was expected. She had left a two-page note for me, saying I was to make myself at home, which I did the four days I was there.

Though I used the time to wash, to sew, and to repair everything, my main project was to make two new signs to hang on Unita. The ones that came from Pennsylvania were all but destroyed by being bumped up against guardrails, trees, and bushes. Therese had kindly provided me with two new pieces of plywood the exact dimensions I had sent her by letter with two holes drilled in the top for fastening them with rope. All I had to do was paint them blue and put on the lettering. I put God Loves You on one sign, and Jesus Is Lord on the other. I also put the same phrases in Spanish–Amo te Dio and Jesus el Senor–on the reverse sides for when I crossed into Mexico.

TORNADO WARNINGS

Therese arrived back at her house on Tuesday, so we had time to share, to pray, to go to Mass, and to visit with friends she had over. By Thursday, I was all put back together and ready to head southeast down Mission Boulevard along the San Antonio River. Then after taking two days to visit the five mission complexes restored from Spanish days, I reached the border with Mexico.

Before I left the last mission (Mission Espada) Hurricane Gilbert was kicking up in the Gulf to the east of us and severe weather warnings were going out for our area. The park rangers were concerned for my safety on the road, but I felt the Lord directing me to continue on the journey without fear. That night the Lord provided me with a "concrete bunker" under an overpass to be safe from the winds and rain. But the next night, September 17, the Salazar family invited me in for two nights as tornadoes were expected to go through the area. When I finally did set out again on September 19, I came upon large swaths of uprooted trees and roofless buildings. But the Lord had

His protecting hand over us and we were back on schedule. Thanks be to God.

THE BORDER IN SIGHT

Therese did drive out and find us a couple of times, delivering more mail and food supplies. Now I was being given tortillas and beans more often. The scenery changed to desert and the only trees were scattered mesquite, cactus, and live oak. Usually, there was a paved berm for us to walk on and then a grassy right-of-way between that and the fence marking the boundary with private property. Actually it was as if the Lord had prepared this "highway of grass" –green from the recent rains–right through this dry desert area, making a verdant pathway for Unita and me these last two weeks in the United States.

On this approach to the Mexican border, I learned one day from a veterinarian that I would need papers to get Unita across into Mexico. I would have to prove that she was disease free and had her proper vaccinations. At 3:00 p.m. on Monday, September 26, the Lord got me to a vet clinic between Premont and La Gloria, Texas, ten days before I planned to enter Mexico. There, I met a veterinarian by the name of Glen who was eager to help me in every way possible. He not only vaccinated Unita, he also collected serum from her for the tests, provided me with deworming medicine, and gave me salve for the thrush Unita had developed in her hooves. When I told Glen that she needed her shoes attended to, he called the best farrier in the area. He took off all four shoes, trimmed Unita's hooves, and remounted two new stainless shoes and two good, old ones he had taken off.

OUR LADY PROVIDES

As usual, the Lord provided for food and water in this stretch through kind passing motorists. Even a few semitrailers stopped to care for our needs. The most amazing servant was a man named Leonard who came seven different times in a stretch of six days, bringing us supplies and visitors to whom he wanted to introduce us. One day, his wife stopped by herself and said, "Leonard's life has been changing for the better since he met you, more than in all the years I have known him."

Thank you, Jesus.

When I arrived at the shrine near McAllen, Texas, I thought that I was in a tropical country with orange and palm trees. Here, they could grow crops all-year-round and just now they were harvesting cantaloupes and watermelons. I was told Texans came from all over the north to vacation here and to enjoy this mild climate. The priest, Fr. Pete, who put me up in the Pilgrim Hostel free for four days, was most hospitable. Here I could attend Mass, prayer meetings, and Bible studies. And here I experienced my first of many Mariachi bands playing lively Spanish-language songs with guitars, trumpets, violins, and bass.

CROSSING THE RIO GRANDE

On Thursday, October 6, I was up early for the 6:30 a.m. Mass and then headed out on the road. At 5:00 p.m. I walked across the bridge spanning the Rio Grande, which at this time was flowing fully–about the size of the Allegheny River in Pittsburgh. At the American side they charged me 10 cents and they charged Unita 10 cents. But there was no checkpoint on the Mexican side. I came right down into the city of Reynosa on the Mexican side and camped on its eastern outskirts under an empty building. I could not believe there were no police or customs officials. Who was going to check my passport and Unita's papers?

The mystery was never solved completely, but on Sunday, my friend Leonard came by, and he told me the local authorities knew all about me at the border from a friend of his and they were expecting me. My second night in Mexico I camped in the right-of-way just past what I took to be a service station at which every bus stopped. I had bypassed the first one and gone down the other side of the road to check out a block building with a tin roof that was actually a shrine with statues, candles, prayer cards, and flowers. And I camped in the right-of-way within sight of the police checkpoint. But there was no investigation and no questions; the Lord's angels had prepared the way for us to pass.

CALCULATING DISTANCES

Mexico City lay approximately 600 miles south of the border. If I averaged 10 miles a day, it would take me two months of walking and I would arrive on December 6. That would be perfect because my mother had put together a pilgrimage from St. Mary's in Glenshaw and thirteen people who knew me were coming to meet me at the shrine. They planned to arrive in Mexico City on December 7. The road signs indicated San Fernando was 140 kilometers (87 miles) away. So I had eight days of walking to my first intermediate goal.

My first Sunday in Mexico was coming up and I was looking for a Catholic Church where I could attend Mass. This seemed to be an agricultural area with large farms but very few villages. So I was not too hopeful that I would be successful. I walked all day Sunday and found no village or church. But around 6:00 p.m., I came into the little village of Alfredo V. Bonfil. There I found a very humble church by the name of Our Lady of Guadalupe. It was just a concrete block structure with a low ceiling. There was no Mass but they had all-night adoration from 4:00 p.m. to 6:30 a.m. A special group called the Eucharistic Adorers made up the bulk of those present and they prayed and sang beautifully. They were glad to have me spend the night in the church with them and they made sure I had everything I needed. So although I did not get to Mass that weekend, I was able to keep watch before the Eucharistic presence of the Lord with this group of devout worshipers.

LIFE IN THE SLOW LANE

Unita and I pretty much lived our lives in the slow lane, which could be another name for the right-of-way (the paved highway being the fast lane). And in Mexico the right-of-way is often a rather busy place. At times there is actually a dirt road through it, parallel to the highway for cars or for donkey carts to use. Unita and I were almost run over one night when a big tractor came zooming down the right-of-way in the dark with no headlights on it, not expecting there would be campers there.

In places where the grass in the right-of-way was high, men were cutting it and loading it onto wagons to feed their livestock. Also, we came across goats and donkeys tethered in the right-of-way so that they could graze. Since there were no public facilities along the roads, cars would stop, everyone would get out, and men headed one way and women the other way into the bushes to relieve themselves. So we had to be careful about where we chose to rest and to camp at night.

THE SIERRA MADRE ORIENTAL

Thankfully, I got to Mass on October 16, at St. Martin dePorres Catholic Church in San Fernando, but the following Sunday I was far from all human habitation and could not find a church. The land was flat until we arrived at the foothills of the Sierra Madre Oriental Mountains which we could see off to the west where there were peaks well over 10,000 feet. But the mountains generously provided us with rivers like the Purificatio and the Corona, with clear running waters on their way to the Gulf of Mexico. So Unita had plenty of good drinking water and I had bathing and washing water.

CIUDAD VICTORIA

Just before we arrived in Ciudad Victoria (the capital of the State of Tamaulipas) on October 26, a middle-aged couple, Maggie and Ashley, who owned a lot of property in this area and who managed a hunting ranch for guests nearby, befriended us. They ended up providing for all of our needs the next few days, sending out food and water and providing places to sleep at night. Providentially we were able to be of service to them when Ashley ended up in the hospital with an asthma attack and I was able to go and to pray with him.

Another man, Lazaro–a widower with three small children–spent many hours walking with me and helping me find the streets and roads I was looking for, in and around Ciudad Victoria. It was his nine-year-old daughter who had come home the night before and told him, "Daddy, when I saw that man walking, I felt God's love in my heart."

Surely this was a family filled with the Holy Spirit of God.

RENEWAL COMMUNITY

My steps at this time were being directed toward a Charismatic Renewal community by the name of La Communidad del Amor de Dios (Community of God's Love) in Xilitla, in the State of San Luis Potosi. They were about a twenty-day walk from the Shrine in Mexico City, so I wanted to get to Xilitla around November 15. That meant that in Ciudad Victoria, I had to walk straight south for seventeen days until I got to the turnoff to Xilitla. To keep with this plan, I had to up my daily distance from 10 miles to 12 miles (15 to 20 kilometers) a day. Theoretically, that should not have been a problem, but practically it became a challenge because so many people began stopping me, asking for prayers, bringing me food, inviting me in to eat and sleep, and walking with me, that I had a hard time making any progress.

They must have been picking the oranges and bananas from their orchards because everyone was offering them to me. They were tying bags unto Unita's saddle behind my back and she was carrying a heavy load. Eventually, I had to give bags of food away whenever I could. Unita was also carrying two gallons of drinking water for me. She threw her back right shoe again (the next farrier pointed out it was because that hoof was not growing out evenly). So the Lord had to provide another farrier, which He did in Ciudad Monte on November 2. But she was being well fed with treats of corn and alfalfa.

SURROUNDED WITH LOVE

In this area I started climbing up into the mountains. I was warned to be on the lookout for bandits in these hills, but there were usually so many people surrounding us, bandits would not have a chance to get even close to us. At one point a Charismatic group of teenagers accompanied me with songs I had taught them like *Yo Tengo* (I Have the Joy) and *He Decidio* (I Have Decided).

After I arrived at Xilitla on November 16, I no longer belonged to myself. I was at the mercy of the crowds. Now I was always surrounded by dozens, sometimes hundreds, of people singing songs, carrying banners, and rejoicing in the Lord–all in honor of Our Lady of Guadalupe. They walked with me for hours, took me into their churches, asked me to write *bendictiones* (blessings) on little pieces of paper, and knelt in the road so I could pray over them. When I went into the churches I had to lead them in the Rosary which I was able to do in Spanish. Fortunately, I had memorized the Hail Mary and the Our Father in Spanish and had with me a meditation of each mystery in Spanish. At times this got me in trouble with the local priest if he did not know who I was, and so he might have feared that I was misleading his people.

ON TO QUERETARO

After spending two days with the renewal community in Rioverdito, made up of a priest, a religious sister, and a layperson from Rutherford, New Jersey, I was heading southwest into the State of Queretaro. It was a very mountainous area with thick vegetation and lots of rain. With so many brothers and sisters around me, I had a place indoors to sleep every night and often could get a hot shower. Truly this was the place where Mi casa es su casa (My House Is Your House) was being said to me constantly.

The road was hilly and full of bends, and Unita became very tired. Nevertheless, somehow the people all around her made her pick up her pace, which I did not mind because now I had to make 15 miles (24 kilometers) a day to get to Mexico City on time. The next big town was Jalpan de Serra, which commemorated Fr. Junipero Serra (1713-84), who served as a missionary in this area between 1750 and 1758. I arrived there on November 23, but I passed through and went on to Pinal de Amoles on top of the mountain, near the highest mountain pass in the state.

DOWN TO THE DESERT

After leaving Pinal de Amolis, we continued to climb to the pass called "the Gate of Heaven." Then we started down toward the desert plain on a series of long switchbacks. The main city that we were aiming for was San Juan del Rio, 83 miles (139 kilometers) distant. During this descent Unita started going very slow. One day she just went over to the side and laid down with all of her packs on. I began to wonder if she was going to make this last stretch of fifteen days.

Still many people were walking with us. As a matter-of-fact as we neared the bottom of the mountains, a bus stopped and an elderly couple got off. When the bus pulled away, the couple told me, "We are from Zimapan, a town 100 miles from here. We read about you in our newspaper. We feel you should not walk through the desert alone. So we are going to accompany you for the next week." And so they did. The husband, Aurelio, was seventy-two years old and his wife (who could not have been much younger) noted that he was "a real pilgrim." But they both hung in there, eating what I ate, resting and sleeping where I slept. And whereas others came and went, they stuck it out. Our Lady can certainly inspire great sacrifices.

ARRIVING AT THE BASILICA

After four days of walking with us, the elderly couple took a bus back home. But Aurelio came back alone on November 30, and guided us over the last seven days right to the Basilica of Our Lady of Guadalupe in Mexico City. He was my guardian angel. He could explain to people what I was doing. He could ask directions and find the right roads. He often went and bought some refreshments for us. And most of all, when we arrived at the shrine on Tuesday, December 6, he went to the priest (Fr. Jose) in charge of welcoming pilgrims and told him about my coming.

So when our little group of pilgrims arrived at the steps of the new basilica, Fr. Jose came out in cassock and surplice and with a bucket of holy water. He said a prayer over us and then he sprinkled Unita and me and all of the pilgrims. Aurelio must have told him I had been ordained a deacon because he motioned for me to follow him into the sanctuary and to stand just a few feet from the original, 450-year-old *tilma*/icon of our Lady, which hung on the back wall. All of the other pilgrims had to go below and pass beneath the image on the moving walkway.

I was overwhelmed by the experience. I thought to myself, "After all these years of seeing photographs and artist's copies, here I am now in the actual presence of the original." It was a little foretaste of heaven, for there we will no longer see copies or imaginative representations of Mary, Jesus, and all of the Saints: we will behold the originals, face-to-face. We will behold them as they are. What a day of rejoicing that will be: the fulfillment of all of our desires and the completion of all our journeying. Praise be to God.

INVITATION FROM JUAN

When I came back out of the Basilica, Fr. Jose said I was welcome to stay in the guesthouse and a place could be found for Unita. But before I could give him an answer, a young man by the name of Juan with his two-year-old daughter Sami on his shoulders, and wife Nicolasa beside him, invited me to stay at their house.

The Feast of Our Lady of Guadalupe was on Monday, December 12, giving us five days before the great celebration. The pilgrims from Pittsburgh arrived on Wednesday, December 7, and I visited with them at their hotel several times. One night we even had a two-hour prayer meeting in one of the conference rooms in the Romana Hotel. Juan's mother was in the hospital at this time for surgery so we went to pray with her. On Sunday night, December 11, Juan sent a stretch limousine to the hotel to pick up my mother and father and the other pilgrims for a "last supper" at his house.

FEAST DAY

Then there was the grand finale–the Feast of Our Lady of Guadalupe on December 12. Already at 1:00 a.m. the streets leading to the shrine were crowded with pilgrims–mostly young people, walking toward the shrine with blankets, backpacks, statues, and other images of Mary, and baskets of flowers and fruits. Firecrackers were going off, processions were forming, outdoor altars were lit up, and Mariachi bands were playing. By 11:00 a.m. I was part of this rejoicing crowd going up to the Temple of the Lord. People were dressed in costumes, dancing, singing, playing drums, and sounding trumpets, all praising the Lord. To an outsider it might have appeared like sheer cacophony, but to those with the eyes of faith, it was a wholehearted celebration of personal devotion to the Mother of God who was also the special heavenly patroness of the Mexican people.

Amazingly our little group, caught up in the movement of the densely packed crowd, kept moving closer and closer to the entrance of the basilica. The question was, would there be room for us inside or would the church be packed to capacity before we got inside? By the grace of God we made it inside and were present for the solemn "Stational Mass" celebrated by four bishops. As can be imagined, it was nearly impossible to go anywhere inside the church. For Communion, groups of priests fanned out and tried to get to those who raised their hands, indicating they wanted to receive the Body and Blood of the Lord Jesus, but they could not get to everyone. Our group did not receive Holy Communion this day, because the priests never found us with our hands raised. Still, we were wonderfully uplifted by this joyful celebration of the faith in a culture that was transformed by the sacraments of holy mother Church over hundreds of years. It was vastly different from the normal Sunday Mass in the United States, but I thanked the Lord for the great privilege of being able to experience this member of the Mystical Body of Christ, as they so enthusiastically expressed the faith they nourished deep in their hearts.

ENDNOTES

34. Hoosier. One day a local fellow told me a humorous folk etymology of Hoosier. He said in frontier days, when travelers came upon a cabin, they called out their approach at a distance and those inside shouted, "Who's there?" In Appalachian English this got slurred into "who'shere?" and that eventually was shortened into "Hoosier."

35. The title of this shrine is connected to the legend of a marvelous snowfall on the Esquiline Hill in Rome, in August of AD 352. This snow indicated the site of a church that Mary, the Mother of God, wanted to be built there. That church is now known as the "Basilica of St. Mary Major," and is one of the four main pilgrimage churches in Rome. The present shrine in Belleville was built in 1958, to foster devotion to Our Lady of the Snows, whose devotion was first introduced to the Midwest in 1941, by Fr. Paul Schutte, OMI, "The Flying Priest of the Arctic," who had a strong personal devotion to Mary under this title. Presently, the 200-acre shrine draws over one million pilgrims and tourists each year.

36. John Michael Talbot. The website, <johnmichaeltalbot.com> describes John Michael as a singer, guitarist, prolific songwriter (55 albums to date), best-selling author (29 books), motivational minister, television presenter, and founder and general minister of The Brothers and Sisters of Charity. He has also won a Grammy.

PART TWO

ON TO CALIFORNIA (1989)

SETTING OUT AGAIN

Before I left Juan's I wrote a report of my walk, had it duplicated, and sent it to two hundred people who wanted to hear from me. On December 15, Juan got a truck for Unita and transported us 16 kilometers to the west of the city, to where he thought we could start our walk. My goal was now to walk toward California to complete my sabbatical year (May 1, 1988 to May 1, 1989).

I had been told that if I tried to take Unita back to the States, I would have to quarantine her at the border for six months and to pay for her room and board. But on my way to Mexico, I had been given the address of an orphanage in Ario de Rosales that I was told would probably welcome a little mule to add to the other animals they were acquiring for the sake of the children. Without contacting the orphanage beforehand, I made my way toward the State of Michoachan west of Mexico City to find Ario de Rosales. It was about 180 miles (300 kilometers) from Mexico City and it would take until the end of December to get there.

This area of Mexico was still mountainous and I crossed the Continental Divide on December 20. It was cold at night (there was even some ice on my plastic in the morning) but warm during the day. Thankfully there were many pine forests along the way and they made excellent camping places at night.

CHRISTMAS 1988

On Christmas Eve and Christmas Day I got no offers of hospitality, even though I attended midnight Mass at the Catholic Church in Guerenando. So the Lord allowed me a very real identification with His reception in Bethlehem the first Christmas. But the memorable gift from the Lord to me on Christmas Day was meeting one of His little servants–a woman who was a pilgrim.

Her name was Elena. She was a native Mexican, about fifty years of age, and said she had been walking alone for fifteen years in South America, throughout the whole continent. She was quite intrepid, mentioning to me that she walked through the jungle alone and had to light fires at night to keep the wild animals away. When she got to a Catholic Church, she would stock up on old church bulletins and free religious objects to pass out on her journey. I thanked the Lord for this example of His call to one of the least likely persons to witness to the truth of His divine providence and to the grace He gives to those who answer the call to radical discipleship. I considered this meeting with Elena as the Lord's special 1988 Christmas gift to me.

ARIO DE ROSALES

At 2:00 p.m. on December 30, I came into the outskirts of the town of Ario de Rosales, and at the moment of my arrival, I heard a man's voice in English, hailing me from the top of a cliff beside the road to my right. His name was Ed and he was from the States but had moved his wife and two children to Mexico. They were now living in Ario de Rosales. He said the orphanage I was looking for, Mano de

Ayuda, was another 20 kilometers south, but I was welcome to stay in his home.

On January 1, I walked Unita to the orphanage and arrived at 7:30 p.m. John, the director of the orphanage, was not there, and they would not let me in. So I slept outside the gate that night. John had not returned by 9:00 a.m. the next day, so I left him a note (no one there spoke English) with Unita, and I started off on my own to walk toward California. I never heard from John after that but Ed later received secondhand information that he was not pleased with Unita and sold her to a Mexican. So I do not know how Unita ended her days. She had served the Lord well (insofar as an irrational animal could be said to serve) for seven months, but I was glad to not have responsibility for her day and night anymore. Now I was more free to focus totally on pleasing the Lord and following the lead of the Holy Spirit, somewhat now perhaps as "the Lord's donkey" myself.

THE GULF OF MEXICO

I was now heading north again all the way to Santa Ana in northern Sonora near the U.S. border. I hoped to take advantage of the warming effect of the large body of water (the Gulf of California) to the west of me. It worked fairly well but there were still some cold nights sleeping outdoors and I needed two blankets for a few weeks.

I survived during this time by being offered food by the locals and by finding edible food alongside the highway. This included potatoes, tomatoes, hot peppers, oranges, tangerines, papayas, bananas, watermelon, cabbage, and corn on the cob. Popular in this part of Mexico was roasted (really, often more charred) ears of corn (*elote*). I could find fresh ears of corn lying alongside the highways, so I would gather a few of them into my bag and then at night I would make a fire and roast them for myself. Early in this walk someone gave me a bottle gourd (*bule*) for holding my drinking water. It was like a canteen, but since it was organic it was also porous; the water could evaporate through the sides, thus cooling the water inside–something both practical and culturally appropriate.

STEADFAST TO THE RESCUE

On January 27, my guardian angel, Steadfast, rescued me from drowning. I was bathing at the edge of a swift-flowing river. While rinsing off I lost my footing and got swept out into deep water. I went under and began swallowing water. Natural skills were not enough in this situation. I was in need of supernatural help. And the Lord sent it swiftly, as it must not have been time for me to end my earthly sojourn. Praise be to God.

Another close call occurred one day as I was walking along the road. One of the first things I did after dropping off Unita, was to find a piece of wood to use as a staff–the one I started with in Pennsylvania had been broken–and mount a crucifix on it. The piece of wood I chose was not all that strong (it actually was dry rotted) but was light and had a comfortable diameter for grasping. I cut off a piece to make a crossbar at the top and I mounted the black, ebony inlaid, missionary cross that I had rescued from my broken staff.

On this day I was walking in a heavy traffic area. I was facing the traffic southbound as usual and on the other side the road was a solid line of cars, trucks, and buses, moving very slowly northbound. All of a sudden a pickup truck from the northbound lane, seeing no cars on my side coming toward me, decided to break rank, pulled out from his lane, and came zooming up from behind me, attempting to pass the long line of traffic ahead of him. The mirror on the driver's side hit the crosspiece on my staff, shattering both the wood and his mirror, and giving me quite a scare. He had to be just inches away from my right hand and shoulder. I do not know if he was deliberately trying to scare me or if he just got too close in his haste to be on his way. My guardian angel was again protecting me from harm.

ASKING FOR PRAYER

Lent started on February 8 this year, so I was able to relate my sojourn through this desert with Jesus' forty-day fast (Mk 1:12-13) that began His public ministry. Only in my desert, people were able to see me, to stop, and to ask for prayer. On the evening of February 11, it was already dark and I was at my camping place when this family pulled up in their car. As they approached me I saw that the wife was carrying a bundle in front of her all covered up. She asked if I would pray for her two little babies named Guadalupe and Jesus. When she uncovered them so that I could see them, I was taken aback to see that they were attached to each other at the hip; they were conjoined twins. The parents did not speak English so I did not know if an operation to separate them was going to be possible or not, but I certainly felt privileged to be able to intercede for them and to call upon the Holy Spirit to pour out an abundance of His grace on them now and in the coming days.

Another amazing request for prayer came from a young fellow by the name of Joseph on March 17. He and three young men stopped and were excited to see me walking. They spoke good English, gave me water, and asked me to sign all their Bibles. They said they were from Palos Verdes, California, and were praying about opening a Christian restaurant. Amazingly, Joseph was a paraplegic, from the waist down–physically deformed but spiritually reformed. Glory be to God.

Through my walking, the Lord reminded me of a most important lesson through a young man in an old, painted pickup truck, who stopped to talk with me on February 15. He came up to me and said, "I just had to turn around and come back and tell you this. When I passed you and saw you walking just now, I felt like I no longer wanted to smoke." I don't know what he was smoking, but I thanked the Lord for His sovereign power that delivered him from his addiction. So it was not anything I said or did to him, it was just the work of the Holy Spirit. I was merely the instrument or contact point for His working, even without my being consciously aware of it. I was just being obedient to His call to walk and to pray and to trust in Him. If I was in His will - where He wanted me to be - He could do His work of building the Kingdom on earth.

MORE PURIFICATION

The Lord put me through a number of trials during this Lenten season. First, there were the chiggers, tiny, nearly invisible mites which infect the skin and produce itching and oozing welts that last for weeks. My right ankle (the one I broke in 1977) began hurting me, causing me to slowly limp along especially during the first few miles in the mornings. When I realized it was probably arthritis flaring up from sleeping on the cold sand of the desert, I began to look for discarded cardboard to put under the plastic that I slept on at night. I began wrapping that ankle in Styrofoam, before bedding down at night. That helped considerably.

The final testing and stripping came on Holy Thursday, March 23. By this time I had stopped my movement north and began going west toward Tijuana. I had reached San Luis Rio Colorado, just before the Colorado River flowed out into the Gulf of California. A little after 6:00 p.m. I arrived at Immaculate Conception Catholic Church. Mass for the Lord's Supper had already started, but I stayed for all-night adoration which followed and which did not conclude until 7:00 a.m. the next morning. This included a Charismatic Prayer Meeting and from 2:00 a.m. to 4:00 a.m. praying with a group of teens. It was manna from heaven after the spiritual fast of the weeks in the desert.

THIEF IN THE NIGHT

When I came into the church, I unpacked all of my gear in the back of the church and made my way up near the front on the left side. After the Blessed Sacrament was reposed at 7:00 a.m. in the morning of Good Friday and people began exiting the church, I went back to retrieve my equipment. However, as I looked around at where I had left everything, I saw that my pack, Mexican blanket, and *bule* (water bottle) had been stolen. All that was left was my sombrero, staff, and food bag. The notebook with all of my names, addresses, and telephone numbers was in that pack. I wondered if my friends in the States would be soon receiving desperate letters from "me" in Mexico asking for money. As far as I know, none did.

MISSIONARIES IN TIJUANA

My days in Mexico were now drawing to a close. On April 1, I was approaching Tijuana and was headed for the port of entry to the United States at Otay Messa. As I started walking up a long hill, two young fellows met me and said I should stop at Mother Theresa's new seminary that was being built nearby. It seemed to be the Lord's arrangement, so I agreed to their proposal. There I experienced a warm welcome from the priests and from the seminarians and spent three delightful hours eating, showering, praying, and sharing. Before I left, one of the priests there carefully wrote out a list of names of all of the priests and seminarians there, so I could pray for them by name as I walked. Little did I realize I would meet up with one of them seven years later on the steps of St. Peter's Basilica in Rome in December of 1995.

SAINT JUNIPERO SERRA

As I crossed the border into southern California, I wondered what lay ahead for me. It was April 1, and as a "Fool for Christ" I just trusted in Him to lead me as He chose. I had one more month until May 1, when my sabbatical year of walking would be up. By that time I should have been able to walk up the coast to the Monterey Bay area. I knew there was a Camaldolese Hermitage in Big Sur, and thought maybe there the monks would allow me to live on their property as a *poustinik* until the Lord sent me on to Canada and to Russia. In the meantime, I would walk in the footsteps of the great eighteenth-century Spanish Franciscan missionary to this area, Junipero Serra y Ferrer, OFM (1713-84). It was he who began building a string of mission compounds up along the Pacific Coast from San Diego to San Francisco.

Actually, I was walking in Fr. Junipero's footsteps, as he had walked from Mexico City to San Diego where he founded the first mission, San Diego de Alcala on July 16, 1769. He had walked this distance in spite of an ulcerous leg, which caused him much pain and even brushes with death. But his motto was *siempre adelante, nunca atras* (always forward, never back). I felt like I knew that kind of determination in my bones and so took his motto for my own.

My next intermediate goal was St. Andrew Russian Byzantine Catholic Church in El Segundo, a suburb of Los Angeles. I had been given this address by Ruthenian-Byzantine Catholic friends back East and Fr. Alexei, the pastor, knew that I was coming. I had given this address to friends who wanted to write to me, so when I arrived there on April 8, I had forty-five pieces of mail waiting for me. It was obvious I was not alone on this missionary journey: I had a whole cadre of brothers and sisters praying and rooting for me in the background.

NAVIGATING THE BASE

As I looked at my map of southern California, I saw one great obstacle that might block my walk to El Segundo: a large tract of land north of San Diego, listed as a restricted military area. It was Camp Pendleton, the Marine Corps Base. I wondered if I could get through it or would I have to walk around it. All was in the Lord's hands.

On April 4, around noontime, after walking through Oceanside, I came to the south gate of Camp Pendleton. I asked at the gate about the possibility of walking through the camp on my way north to San Clemente. "There is only one person on base who can give you that permission and she just happens to be right now standing over there." Thanking the Lord for such providence, I approached the commanding officer and explained my request. She said I could walk the bike trail, but I had to be out of the other end by dark: I could not camp overnight on the property.

I agreed to her terms and set out immediately to fulfill them. But I knew I would need the Lord's help to complete the project, for it was approximately a 20-mile walk and I had only six hours till dark. I would have to average over 3 miles an hour (my normal average was 2 miles an hour) including rest stops. By the grace of God I did it as I came out of the base on the other end just as it was getting dark. The Lord enabled me to walk a record 25 miles that day.

RUSSIAN BYZANTINE CATHOLIC CHURCH

Now I was on the historic El Camino Real, named in the period of history when the king of Spain claimed this territory, in the early eighteenth century. After spending a wonderful hour with the paraplegic Joseph and his family in Palos Verdes, I arrived at St. Andrew's Church in El Segundo at 6:00 p.m., Saturday evening. Fr. Alexei and his whole church community were eagerly expecting me. I was their honored guest for the next two days. It was good to be with Byzantine Catholic friends again in my home country.

CATHOLIC CULTURE

When I left the warm fellowship of St. Andrew's on Tuesday, April 11, I was now headed north up the coast toward the Camaldolese Hermitage near Big Sur that I wanted to visit. But I was not in a hurry, so I took the time to enjoy walking in an area rich in Catholic tradition. Just reflecting on the names of the places I was passing through, nourished my faith.

San Diego, which was named after St. Diego de Alcala, and reminded me of Juan Diego, the visionary of Our Lady of Guadalupe.

San Juan Capistrano, named for the great fifteenth-century Italian Franciscan preacher, and hosting the amazing 6,000 mile journey of the cliff swallows who fly every year from this mission to Argentina and back, arriving punctually here each March 19, the Feast of St. Joseph, and departing again on October 23, the Feast of San Juan de Capistrano.

Los Angeles, short for El Pueblo de Nuestra Senora de los Angeles de la Porciuncula (The Town of Our Lady of the Angels, of the Portiuncula)–my choice of a dozen possible titles–reminiscent of the Little Portion (Portiuncula) hermitage on the plain below Assisi where St. Francis lived with his first disciples.

The bigger than life-size statue of St. Monica still standing in the public square of Santa Monica, reminded me of her son, the great Saint Augustine, Bishop of Hippo and Father of the Church.

How wonderful to be able to walk, and to pray in such an atmosphere of our ancient Catholic Faith.

A HUMOROUS STORY

I did not get to visit all twenty-one California missions in the three years I spent on the West Coast, but eventually I visited most of them. When I was in Poland in 1996-97, one of the frequently asked questions was: "What was the funniest thing that ever happened to you on your travels?" One of the most humorous occurred at Mission San Bonaventura on April 15, in Ventura, California.

This mission had a bookshop and a museum that I found quite fascinating. After buying a book on the California missions and a little pamphlet on the life of Fr. Junipero Serra, I took some time to look over the articles in the glass cases. To read some Latin texts from the Mission time period, I had to kneel down on the floor to get a closer look at them as they were on the bottom shelf. While I was bent over on one knee, a middle-aged couple came into the store. Each went their own ways as their curiosity led them. The woman turned into the aisle I was in, down at the other end. When she saw me kneeling in the aisle, she stopped dead in her tracks. I never moved but kept on reading, hardly distracted by her presence.

She slowly backed up and retraced her steps to find her husband. I overheard her say to him, "Dear. You ought to see this life-size statue over here in the aisle (referring to me). You would almost think it was real. I wonder why they have it right there in the aisle like that?" She turned white–as if seeing a ghost–when I eventually got up and greeted her briefly on my way out of the store. This incident was part of how I eventually learned that, if at all possible, I had to give people fair warning and not let them be caught by surprise when they met me for the first time.

IMMACULATE HEART HERMITAGE

Now I was on the Pacific Coast Highway, which ran closely along the Pacific Ocean and wound around the foothills of the Santa Lucia Range of mountains. This little-populated, uncommercialized, 90-mile stretch of rugged coastline south of Carmel, California, was called "Big Sur," and it retained all of its pristine beauty. The views of the ocean and the mountains were breathtaking. On April 29, even before I reached the little village of Big Sur, I happened to glance to my right and caught sight of a tall white wooden cross. Just beyond it was a sign, Immaculate Heart Hermitage of the Camaldolese Monks. There it was, the goal of my walk since Mexico City, which I had commenced four months before. I took off my sandals and socks and began the 2-mile climb up the narrow, paved, switchback road to the top of the mountain.

On top I found a large flat area overlooking the Pacific Ocean. On it were the numerous buildings of "New Camaldoli," where the present community of monks had been living out their daily routine of *ora et labora* (prayer and work) since their founding in 1958. I was familiar with their way of life from reading and visiting various Benedictine and Camaldolese[37] monasteries around the country. I wondered if they would understand and be open to the way of life of a pilgrim/*poustinik*.

WELCOME BUT SORRY

I was welcomed by the guest master, Brother Isaiah, who gave me a room in the retreat house where I was able to bathe and to eat. The second day–a Sunday–I attended Vigils (the nighttime/predawn office once known as "Matins") at 5:45 a.m. with the monks, Lauds (Morning Prayer) and then Mass at 11:00 a.m. It was a spiritual feast after coming in from the desert of the highway. After lunch in the common refectory, I briefly met the prior Fr. Robert, and we set up an appointment for Monday. Brother Isaiah moved me from the Retreat Center to hermitage number twenty-two in the cloister, which was named after my biblical hero, St. John the Baptist. (In some contemplative orders, it is the custom to name the rooms or "cells" after various saints.) I trusted that through his intercession I would end up exactly where the Lord wanted me.

But the next day it became clear I had not yet arrived at the place the Lord had chosen for my *poustinia*. Fr. Robert explained to me they would not be able to accommodate me there because they were at the moment trying to return to their particular calling which involved stability whereas my calling involved just the opposite, itineracy. He suggested I contact the bishop in Monterey to see if he could help me. So I called the diocesan offices from the monastery and got an appointment for Friday morning. After lunch I left the Camaldolese monastery and walked another 10 miles north toward Carmel and

Monterey. Arriving at the House of Prayer next to the Carmelite Nuns' Monastery in Carmel on the third night, Sister Sharon let me sleep in the enclosed garden.

ASCENSION THURSDAY

On Ascension Thursday, I walked into Carmel proper and went to the 12:30 noonday Mass in the Mission Church, where Fr. Junipero Serra's body was buried. From there, I made my way into Monterey about 4 miles away to meet my friend Annie who was from Glenshaw, Pennsylvania, but who was now finishing her two-year stint at the Military Defense Language Institute in Monterey. She introduced me to Fr. Matthew, a priest of the Oratory of St. Philip Neri, who was the chaplain for the institute and who had Mass in the base chapel at 6:00 p.m. Fr. Matthew and I connected in the Holy Spirit immediately and after Mass he invited me to sleep on the floor of his office for the night. That was the way in which the Lord led me to where I would eventually set up my *posutinia* for the next three years.

It was only, in hindsight, a few months later, that I was able to see how the Lord had put all of the pieces together. And the key was Ascension Thursday. Every day of my walk from Mexico City, I said the full Rosary–all fifteen decades. And every time I came to the second glorious mystery, the Ascension of Jesus into heaven, I felt this exultation in my heart. I had never experienced anything like this before, and was not sure what it meant. But every day it was the same thing: invariably I felt a wave of grace in my heart when I came to pray the decade of Jesus' Ascension. It never happened on any other mystery. Then when I saw how the Lord brought me to the Carmelite nuns' monastery, the Carmel Mission and the Oratory of St. Philip through positioning my friend from Glenshaw there, I realized all of this happened on Ascension Thursday! I believe it was the Lord's way of confirming His holy will for me at this time.

A PRUDENT BISHOP

On Friday, May 5, at 10:30 a.m., I went to my appointment with Bishop Thaddeus Shubsda (1925-91). I shared with him my calling as a pilgrim/*poustinik* and how I felt the Lord wanted me to be in *poustinia* here in Monterey for three years before heading for Alaska and on into Russia. He was completely at a loss as what to make of me. He wanted to know who would support me. He pointed out that it would not be prudent for him to approve of my staying in his diocese. He might as well have said, "Why don't you just keep walking out of my diocese?"

Since a pilgrim knows an apparently closed door does not necessarily mean a permanently locked door (for it might just need a strong push), I got the good bishop to agree that if, by the end of the month, I had found a spiritual director and a place to stay, it would be a sign the Lord wanted me to remain in this area. Little did I realize at the moment all that the Lord had in store for each of us in the immediate future.

THE LORD COMES THROUGH

On my part, I began asking around about possible places where I might set up my *poustinia*. I contacted the local Catholic Charismatic community, wrote to the congressman of the district, talked to local priests and pastors, as well as people on the streets. Finally on the last day of the month, Fr. Matthew notified me that the founding priest of the Oratory, Fr. Doman,[38] was interested in meeting me.

What a joy it was to meet this wise and holy, long-suffering servant of the Lord, though he was nearing the end of his earthly journey himself—he died June 5, 1990. As a matter-of-fact, he asked me if I would be willing to sort through his books and papers to put them in some order before his passing. Most pertinent to my immediate needs, he agreed to be my spiritual director and offered me the use of a spare room in a house the Oratory owned as well as a fenced-in lot next door to that which I could fix up for my *poustinia*.

ENDNOTES

37. Immaculate Heart Hermitage (also called "New Camaldoli Hermitage") was founded in 1958, at the direction of the superior of the Camaldolese hermits in Europe, where St. Romuald (AD 950-1025), based his living out of the eremetical tradition of living in separate hermitages (the whole complex being called a "lavra"), on the Rule of St. Benedict (AD 480-547).

38. Fr. Emeric Doman, Orat. (1918-90) was born in Miskolc, Hungary. He received his doctorate in Sacred Theology from the University of Vienna. His formation years with the Oratorians took place in Rome. He was a longtime resident of the Monterey Peninsula.

PART THREE

HOLDING
(1989-92)

DOMUS PATRIS POUSTINIA

So, although I had been seeking a remote place off in the mountains to become a hermit, the Lord provided a *poustinia* near to people in a residential neighborhood. It overlooked the Monterey Bay. I felt the Lord saying, "Stay here three years, then head for Alaska and Siberia." For now, all I knew was that the Lord had me in a holding pattern.

And how did I spend these three years "on the launchpad?" Each week I spent four days in my *poustinia* in Monterey and three days in Carmel, the neighboring town. While in my *poustinia* (I named it Domus Patris–House of the Father) I set up a routine of prayer five times a day in my prayer room, a tiny plywood building known to the Oratorian priests as "the telephone booth." It was completely carpeted inside–floor, walls, and ceiling. The lot I had been given was almost the exact size of the Tabernacle which Moses constructed in the desert (Ex 27:9-13) to house the Ark of the Covenant. It had a high wood fence on all four sides. I fixed up a former rabbit hutch with a roof and sides and put in a sleeping bunk, workshop, and food prep area. Also, I spent a few hours each day caring for the grounds, planting flowers and vegetables, and setting up Stations of the Cross.

My largest project was making an outdoor, adobe brick oven for baking fresh ground, whole wheat bread. There was water and electricity on the lot. I had access to bathroom facilities in a building next door that belonged to the Oratory. There I could also keep my papers, books, and typewriter out of the dampness. Sunday morning, I went to Mass at the Catholic chapel on base; Monday evening, I attended the Charismatic prayer meeting at the San Carlos Mission Church in Monterey; and Wednesday night, I participated in a Bible Study at the institute's Catholic chapel.

THE CROSSROADS MARKETPLACE

Each Thursday morning I would walk from my *poustinia* in Monterey, over to the Crossroads Mall in Carmel, to be available to anyone who wanted to stop and to talk or to receive prayer. Thursday nights I attended an ecumenical/Evangelical Bible Study at Peyton's Place (a restaurant) in the mall for locals, street people, and the homeless. On Friday and Saturday mornings I attended Mass at the Carmelite Nuns Monastery in Carmel and spent the rest of the mornings in private prayer and in meditation in their front garden that overlooked the Pacific Ocean. Then in the afternoons I would walk back to the Crossroads Mall for unstructured sharing and visiting. At night I slept in a little lean-to I had constructed alongside the road, not far from the Carmelite monastery.

THE HEART OF CALIFORNIA

In all of my travels around the world I have not yet found a more beautiful place than the Monterey Peninsula. The climate is ideal—warm in the winter, cool in the summer. It is as if this is the point where the North meets the South; there are giant pines as in Canada and tall palm trees as in Mexico. Of course there is the Pacific Ocean–

my favorite among all of the creatures the Lord has made. And best of all, there was the Monterey Bay. Every time I came over the hill from Carmel and caught a glimpse of that bay, my heart skipped a beat and I would think, "Thank You, Lord, for this jewel of Your handiwork." I used to say to people, "Adam and Eve no doubt had a beautiful garden in Eden before the Fall, but one thing they were missing was the Monterey Bay."

No wonder the Carmelite priests named this area Carmel on the first Spanish exploration of this area in the early seventeenth century. It reminded them of Mt. Carmel in the Holy Land. Apparently it so reminded Padre Junipero Serra of his native Majorca in Spain, that in the eighteenth century he chose this as his headquarters for all of his missions on the California coast. I could see why Pope John Paul II, on his 1987 visit to this area, called Carmel "the historical and spiritual heart of California." God had sent me to the heart of California to pray and to intercede for all of the people of this area, past, present, and to come. California was heavily into New Age spirituality and people were openly dabbling into everything from holistic healing to the occult. A tremendous spiritual battle was going on for the souls of the American people, both in its majority in the clutches of consumerism and materialism as well as in the minorities in the grips of poverty and marginalization. I often prayed to St. Junipero Serra for the evangelization of this area which he so loved and for which he labored. I often went to the Carmel Mission where his body lay buried in the sanctuary and even got the custodian to let me spend a night in prayer in his cell.

St. Junipero Serra, Pray for us!

SPECIAL LENTEN FASTS

One of the unique gifts the Lord gave me during this three years in *poustinia* was the ability to observe two forty-day Lenten fasts (in 1990 and in 1991) in a more rigorous way than is usually possible when one is part of the average Catholic community. Here I did not have the pressure from close brothers and sisters who might try and temper my ascetical practices. So, in the Lent of 1990, I observed a mostly water-only fast. And in the Lent of 1991, I kept a twelve-ounce water fast, and six-ounce fast of Ezechiel Bread, which had grains and legumes (Ez 4:9-11). I did not go to Carmel during this time and I changed my normal Sunday Mass, so as to not be among familiar faces. I wanted to keep it a desert experience as much as possible.

These fasts made me much more attentive to the Word of the Lord speaking to my heart and open to the glory of all creation surrounding me. Focusing on just fellowship with the Lord and reducing fellowship with brothers and sisters, eliminated normal distractions, routine bodily concerns, and brought me face-to-face with the meaning of the Cross. This led to deeper awareness of sin in my life and an experience of my own poverty, all of which in turn launched me out into deeper repentance and unalloyed joy. This was all concretized in a symbolic way by bringing my hands together, folding them palm to palm, as a most proper and significant posture before the all holy God. This sign of folded hands has remained with me to the present day.

JOHN'S REVELATION

My second Lent (1991) I did an in-depth study of the Book of Revelation. Preparation began right after the 1990 Lenten retreat and culminated in a line-by-line commentary, recorded on twenty, one-hour cassette tapes, covering all twenty-two chapters of Revelation. I had an average of two hundred Scripture references for each of the twenty-two chapters. I was not trying to come up with the definitive interpretation of the Apocalypse. Rather, I compared the role of a commentator on John's revelation, to guides leading tour groups down the Amazon River. The sights and sounds were so rich and abundant that each individual guide would be able to point out certain things, relate certain parts of its history, and give a particular interpretation. No guide's presentation was definitive or true to the exclusion of the others. Just so did I consider my guided journey through the last book of the Bible.

My overall perspective, however, was this: John was describing what a Christian should see when they look at the world around them in faith (in the power of the Holy Spirit). It is about God's judgment on mankind, past, present, and future. And it involves these four Judgments: (1) judgment on the Christian churches (chaps. 1-3); (2) judgment on the historic Israel (chaps. 4-11); (3) judgment on the pagan nations (chaps. 12-19); and (4) judgment on all mankind together at the end (chaps. 20-22). To me it was an amazing journey of faith and I was willing to share it with whoever was open to traveling with me.

SPIRITUAL WARFARE

If one is engaged in spiritual warfare "in the heart of a people," one can expect opposition from the enemy. For me, on the Monterey Peninsula it was not long in coming, and just eight months after my arrival. On December 18, 1989, around 10:00 p.m., walking back to my *poustinia* from the Monday night Prayer Meeting at the cathedral in downtown Monterey, I was attacked from behind. I was coming up the hill on Franklin Street and had just passed a cross street, noting in my peripheral vision, a car parked at the stop sign off to my right. Next thing I knew, someone came up from behind me, grabbed my staff out of my hand, and started beating me over the head with it. Providentially, the staff was made out of a brittle piece of a dry-rotted limb of a dead tree branch, and it broke immediately into three pieces, so it soon became almost useless as an attack weapon. Nevertheless, I fell to the ground stunned, though not unconscious.

Thankfully, the Lord had His angels handy and they rushed to my assistance. One twenty-eight-year-old man had just parked his car a few houses behind me. He told police later that he saw a seventeen-year-old African-American male get out of the car parked at the stop sign, run across the street, and attack me without cause. Then another man ran from the same parked car in an attempt to stop his buddy from hitting me and pulled him back into their car. There was another eyewitness to the scene of the crime, a man thirty-three years of age standing on the porch of his home, which stood next to the street on which the attack happened. He rushed to the scene and got the license number of the car as it speeded away.

Within minutes the Monterey police arrived and made a full report of the attack. Five minutes later the police stopped the car with the young men in it who had been out drinking and the witnesses identified my attacker. When the mother of my attacker was contacted, she said her seventeen-year-old son had been going downhill since his father passed away a year ago, and he did crazy things when he drank. The courts assigned him to three months in Juvenile Hall and made him pay off my $450 emergency room bill where I had to get nine stitches on my head.

In the weeks that followed, I obtained a copy of the police report and it contained the address of my attacker. When I went to visit him and to tell him I forgave him, he was all meek and scarcely remembered what he had done. He was not out to rob me; he was just out of control when under the influence of alcohol. Satan was able to take over control of his will at that point and have him try to do me harm. But the Lord had more in store for me. I had only walked 10,000 of my destined 40,000 miles. He did not want to lose this pair of willing feet at this early stage of His plan.

SAVED AGAIN

There was one other serious roadblock Satan tried to throw into my path. I was visiting a friend's home in Carmel Valley with a few brothers and sisters in Christ. At one point we were taking turns swinging out from a high cliff on a car tire swing suspended at the end of a long rope whose other end was attached to an overhanging tree branch. Instead of sitting inside the tire, I decided to stand in it with my rubber tire sandals, not realizing they might be difficult to extricate on the way back.

Sure enough, my foot got stuck and I could not get it out of the tire. I was dragged out over the ravine and fell off, landing squarely on my back on top of a protruding rock. A friend of mine standing nearby said she heard my back crack and she immediately uttered a prayer for God's help. I tried getting up and could not move. I turned over on my hands and knees, stood up, and never felt any pain then or any time thereafter. That could only have been the Lord, either healing a broken back on the spot or sending an angel to catch me and to gently lower me to the ground (Ps 91:1-3). Apparently, He still wanted me to lift up the Cross of Jesus in Asia, in Europe, and in the Middle East, and He was willing to do His part in getting me there on schedule.

HIS EYES WERE OPENED

In September of 1990, Bishop Shubsda was diagnosed with melanoma and given less than a year to live. Squarely faced with the "ultimate realities" (death, judgment, heaven, and hell) his perspective on life (and on me) did a 180-degree turnabout. He wrote to me on January 9, 1991, saying, "Thank you for your example of prayer and for your great confidence in God." After the First Friday Mass at the Carmel Mission in March, he greeted me on my way out of church: "We appreciate your prayerfulness, your devotion, and the witness of your life." I thanked the Lord that the good bishop had a change of heart through the grace of spiritual insight. I have no doubt that the trial he was undergoing was purifying his heart.

Two weeks before he died on April 21, 1991, I felt the Lord urging me to go to the hospital and to pray over him. A nurse who was sitting in the room keeping watch, said to me, "He has been in a coma and is not responding, but he probably can hear you." So I went over to his bedside, laid my hand on him, and prayed out loud spontaneously for a few minutes. Before I left the room the bishop sat up in bed, raised his right hand, and making the sign of the cross, gave me his episcopal-priestly blessing. What a grace. He had heard and responded. I thanked the Lord for allowing me to be part of His working in the bishop's final ascent to Calvary. Glory be to God.

MORE MISSIONS TO VISIT

As the summer of 1991, began to draw near and realizing it would be my last one in California, I decided to take a month and go on a walking pilgrimage–just to keep in shape as well as to pray at three more of the twenty-one missions founded by the Franciscans in the late eighteenth century. I decided to first head north around the Monterey Bay as far as Boulder Creek, then swing east out into the Salinas Valley where the highway carried heavy traffic north and south and then walk south until I got to the head of Carmel Valley where I would walk west and come back into Carmel on the coast. That way I could pick up the Missions of Santa Cruz, San Jan Bautista, and Soledad. It was a circular journey of 275 miles and I set aside the whole month of June for its accomplishment.

On this walk a few friends joined me at various points to walk and to pray along with me. Occasionally I stayed with friends I knew, but mostly I slept outside. I did not yet have a tent, so I just put up a piece of plastic as a protection from the rain and dew. The coastal part of the trip was through mountains and redwood trees. The Salinas Valley had flat farmland and desert. Of course numerous people stopped to ask for personal prayer and had questions about the Faith. As can be expected, in the agricultural San Joaquin Valley, I encountered a lot of Mexicans and I was blessed by their expressive faith and wholehearted devotion. And from Catholic priests I got the whole range of responses from the cold shoulder to "I envy your way of life." It felt good to be back on the road and trusting in the Lord more completely for my daily bread.

IMMEDIATE PREPARATIONS

With the turn of the calendar year from 1991 to 1992, I was making plans to wrap up my three years of holding pattern on the Monterey Peninsula and head north to Alaska. I decided to leave on April 1. That meant I had three more months to tie up loose ends and to make final preparations. One thing I did–having learned a lesson about walking into a diocese without forewarning–I wrote ahead to the Most Reverend Francis T. Hurley, at the time Archbishop of Anchorage and introduced myself to him. I sent ahead of my arrival a packet of material describing my vocation as a pilgrim/*poustinik*, plus a copy of my book, *A Pilgrim Finds the Way*. As it turned out, Bishop Hurley had a missionary spirit himself; he had slipped into Siberia disguised as a geologist in the early 1990s, to establish a clandestine Catholic Church at Magadan, in the Soviet Far East. So he had a deep and personal awareness of this aspect of my calling.

But there was one more project the Lord had laid on my heart before departure: to spend a week alone camping at the foot of Mount Carmel in the Los Padres National Forest 25 miles south of Monterey. I had scouted out the area in the summer of 1991, and found a remote spot called "Apple Creek Camp Site" at a 2,920-foot elevation where there was a spring of water. I planned to fast on bread and water so I did not have to bother with carrying food or cooking utensils. All I took was my Bible, my Latin Breviary, a copy of *Ascent of Mount Carmel* by St. John of the Cross, two loaves of Ezekiel Bread, and a piece of plastic to set up as a kind of shelter.

APPLE CREEK CAMPSITE

On Ash Wednesday, March 4, 1992, I left my *poustinia* in Monterey and headed to Apple Creek Camp Site, arriving there at 1:30 p.m. the following day. It rained all that day and through the next, so I came down with a sore throat, cough, and laryngitis. But it was worth the sacrifice. The plastic that I tied up to a bay tree provided enough covering so that I could read the Breviary and do some writing, but I had to keep wiping off the condensation from my breath, forming on the inside of the plastic.

The unique gift the Lord gave me here that made the time worthwhile was what I can only describe as "the singing of the angels" and I never experienced it at any other time in my life. I heard it just "above" the gurgling water of the brook that ran right beside my tent. It did not take a great effort to hear it, but it did take a slight attentiveness to it. It was barely perceptible, like a delicate perfume; a still, small voice; or perhaps like a "sounding silence" (or "silent singing"). I could also describe it as a choir of monks very softly chanting the Psalms in Latin on a recitative note, with inflections at the beginning and at the end; it sounded like one, blended voice. But it also had the richness of an Italian tenor or a choir of young boy singers as one can hear in the Vatican. Was it similar to what John heard in Revelation, "His voice was like the sound of rushing water" (Rev 1:15)? To date I have not found anyone who could testify to it or explain it to me.

RETURNING TO THE CITY

On Thursday, March 12, I climbed another 1,400 feet (2.2 miles) to the top of Mt. Carmel and camped there that night. The following day, I walked back to Carmel on the coast and Saturday back to my *poustinia* in Monterey. After a full ten days of silence on the mountain,

I was able to pay very close attention to every word of Scripture and every prayer at Mass that I heard. The experience I had cleared out the "mental cobwebs." I was off to a good start for Lent 1992.

Now I was preparing for my departure on April 1, in earnest, and plans were made to see everyone for a final time. The leader of the Monday night prayer group at the cathedral had a gathering in my honor in his home. I was invited to give farewell talks at various churches in the area and to several different renewal groups. I made myself a new six-foot-high staff out of a piece of eucalyptus tree and mounted on it my bronze missionary crucifix. A friend bought me a lightweight nylon tube tent, weighing under three pounds (Eureka/Gossamer), like bicyclists carry as protection from the rain and especially from the mosquitoes in Canada. And finally, I came up with a map of the North American northwest coast that showed my 3,000-plus mile walk from Monterey to Anchorage. I had marked where I hoped to be each of the twenty-four Sundays I planned to be on the road from April 1 to September 19. I gave copies of this map to over sixty brothers and sisters in Christ who promised to keep me in their prayers.

And so I was on the move once again, homing in on my goal of pilgrimaging in Russia, like the anonymous nineteenth-century pilgrim in *The Way of the Pilgrim*. My three years in a holding pattern in Monterey awaited the dissolving of the USSR in 1990, for that opened the doors to foreigners to once again more freely enter and to travel in that country. I would proclaim in a simple way by walking in faith with the Cross of Jesus, the triumph of the Immaculate Heart of Mary (as promised at Fatima) over the Red Dragon (cf. Gn 3:14; Rv 12). The people had been starved spiritually for seventy years. They were ready to receive a fresh proclamation of God's love for them. I prayed the Lord would be able to make me a small part of this new move of His grace.

THE PRAYER OF MY HEART

Father in heaven:

I thank You for the call to pilgrimage

in Holy Russia.

You have faithfully led me the past five years

on the North American continent.

Provide now for my launch into that land of death,

the gulags of the Soviet prison camps.

Help me to lift up the Cross of Jesus

and proclaim the victory of His resurrection.

Send the power of Your Holy Spirit,

of Your love and mercy,

to accompany me and all those I meet,

now and forever.

Amen.

CHAPTER 4

PILGRIMAGE IN ASIA

ASIA

Magadan, Russia to Cochin, India

April 21, 1993 to December 29, 1995

Thirty-two months - 8,200 miles

PART ONE

MONTEREY TO ANCHORAGE (1993)

GETTING STARTED

On Wednesday, April 1, 1992, in Monterey, it dawned clear and bright. I was up at 4:00 a.m. to take care of last minute details. After Mass at the Holy Spirit Chapel at the Defense Language Institute at 6:30 a.m., half a dozen people accompanied me the first few miles of this projected six-month walk to Alaska. There were tears and hugs, prayers offered, and pictures taken, as I headed north through Seaside and Castroville. I had walked this way in June of the previous year, so many people knew me along the way.

At this point, I planned to arrive at the Ukrainian Byzantine Catholic Monastery, Holy Transfiguration, in Redwood Valley near Ukiah, California, during Holy Week. It was a good 300 miles away. To make it in fifteen days, I had to average 20 miles a day. Such a distance is not all that much, but after a winter of not walking, my feet were very tender. Also, my left ankle started giving me trouble, so sometimes I could only walk a mile or two and had to rest. Eventually, I learned that if I soaked it in ice-cold water from alongside the road, I was able to walk on it. The new tent came in handy for the rain at night and especially for keeping away the mosquitoes.

HOLY TRANSFIGURATION MONASTERY

On April 6, I walked over the Golden Gate Bridge in San Francisco. It had a wide walkway and there were lots of walkers and joggers on it, both locals out for their morning exercise and tourists taking pictures. I crossed the bridge in about an hour with a group from Germany, so I said my Rosary in German that day. On April 13, I left the coast, and headed for the interior to pick up Ukiah and the monastery. At 3:45 p.m. on Wednesday, April 15, I arrived at Mount Tabor Monastery and joined Archimandrite Boniface[39] and his twenty monks for Liturgy of the Presanctified.[40] The monks gave me a private hermitage with no electricity, heat, or running water, but it was dry and clean and that was a luxury for a pilgrim just off the road.

I spent four wonderful, spiritually rich days, celebrating Jesus' Last Supper, death, and resurrection with this fervent, removed from the world, close to angelic, heavenly liturgical community. The reverent, harmonized a cappella, Eastern chants, combined with the candles and incense were all a feast for the senses as it lifted my spirit to the invisible world of the transcendent, all-holy Lord God Almighty. And then there was the triumphant antiphon on Easter, "Christ is risen from the dead; trampling death by death; and on those in the graves bestowing life!" sung over and over dozens of times. I truly felt like I was in touch with the depth of the contemplative Russian spirit I hoped had survived the Communist era and that I might still encounter in my pilgrimage through Siberia.

One of the outstanding memories I had of these days, however, was a comment by Archimandrite Boniface early in the services of Holy Week. Seeing that there were visitors present of all ages, from toddlers to grandmothers, he counseled, "Just participate in the liturgy to the extent that you are able." In other words, if you are eighty years old and you have been doing this all your life, God expects more from you than if you are five years old and all of this is new to you. How gentle, understanding, and compassionate, I thought. Just like one would expect from an elderly father full of joy and sensitive to the needs of his children.[41]

HEADING FOR CANADA

When I left the holy Mount Tabor on Monday, April 20 (the Second Day of Easter in the Byzantine calendar) I was now looking at forty-two days of walking until I hoped to cross into Canada on June 6, from Sumas, Washington. In this area I had many beautiful encounters with previously unknown members of the Body of Christ. One was Fr. Vladimir, a Russian Orthodox priest who fed me a bowl of fasting soup and sent me on my way with a paperback copy of *Fifty Spiritual Homilies* by St. Macarius the Great, which is now very well-worn, but still read and deeply treasured.

And there were some unique events along the way, like walking through a giant sequoia forest during an earthquake on April 25, and having my name put into a time capsule in Gold Beach, Oregon, on May 2, to be opened in 2,000 years. But there was a brief encounter I had with a young mother on May 27, near Olympia, Washington, that deserves a more detailed account because of its testimony to the awesomeness of Christian hospitality.

IN OBEDIENCE TO JESUS

On Wednesday, May 27, about 9:00 a.m., I was walking along the road saying my Rosary when this beat-up old car stopped across the road from me, and the woman driving shouted over to me, "Are you hungry?" When I said yes, she continued, "I live up this road on the right here; follow me and I will cook you breakfast." So I headed up her driveway on foot behind her car.

Her name was Carolyn and she was home alone; her husband was at work and she had just taken her three children to school. Now she had a half hour to get ready for work and at the same time make me some bacon and eggs. As she went about her work with joy and enthusiasm, she explained to me how it came that I was receiving this gift of hospitality in her home.

She said she saw me earlier in the morning on her way to school with her three children. When she passed me, she had the biggest smile on her face. Her children, seeing her, asked, "Mommy, why are you smiling?" She said to them, "Do you see that man? He has nothing. But he is probably the happiest person on two feet." "Why, Mommy?" they asked. "Because he has Jesus in his heart," she answered.

With that, she felt the Lord telling her to stop and to offer me breakfast. She said she often felt the need to reach out and to help strangers, but she always prayed and asked the Lord about it before she acted. So she said prayerfully, "Lord, if you want me to stop, let me see that man on my way back home." Well, as she approached her driveway she saw me walking right across the road from it. She took that as a sign that her thought was from the Lord.

As I enjoyed a delicious hot meal, her husband called on the telephone. When she told him she had a guest for breakfast he panicked. She was able to calm him down. She explained to me that no one else in her family could understand how she could minister to total strangers and to take such risks. Her family perhaps did not have the gift of hospitality nor the power of the Holy Spirit that she had been given. For her it was the most natural, loving thing and it always worked out well. I thanked the Lord for this precious spiritual fruit He let me find and gather for His table this day.

CROSSING THE BORDER

On Saturday, June 6, Pentecost weekend, I arrived at the border station at Huntingdon, British Columbia, across from Sumas, Washington, at 9:00 a.m. The Canadian immigration official on duty said I could not enter because I did not have a credit card. When I came back at 7:00 p.m. (hoping to find a different official on duty) I was told that even though I had the required minimum in cash ($600) I had no job or permanent address, so I was not allowed in. When I said I wanted to talk with the senior official, they said that he was not here on the weekends. I would have to come back on Monday.

When I arrived on Monday at 8:45 a.m., I was ushered into the office of the senior official, Russ, who was most cordial and helpful. He said he could let me in "as a lay helper to the Catholic Church in its work of evangelization" if I got a letter of recommendation from my bishop. So I returned to Sumas, called Bishop Bosco, my episcopal adviser in Greensburg, Pennsylvania, and explained my situation. He immediately composed a letter saying that "he would be willing to assume some responsibility toward this mission" and faxed that letter to Russ at immigration. (During that call, he mentioned that he also needed to protect himself and the diocese from possibly being sued if I got in trouble.)

When I arrived back at Canadian immigration the fax from Bishop Bosco had arrived. Russ was so excited about the letter, he not only gave me a five-month visa for Canada, he also handed me several copies of the letter saying, "Here, these may come in handy for you sometime later." (Indeed four years later in Rome I enclosed a copy with my application for a private meeting with the Holy Father, John Paul II.) With that I stepped onto Canadian soil, thanking the Lord for getting me over one more giant hurdle, and set my sights on the city of Prince George 400 miles to the north.

FRONTIER TERRITORY

The only other address beside Anchorage that I carried with me this summer was in Whitehorse, Yukon Territory. I had written ahead to the Madonna House mission there and received back a warm welcome. They were also willing to hold mail for me until I arrived.

But that lay 1,400 miles away–nearly half of the total summer's walk. I hoped to be with them for the Feast of the Assumption of Mary into heaven on August 15. But between then and my entry into Canada, I had eighty days of walking 20-25 miles a day. "Lord, come to my assistance."

Now I was in frontier territory. This was the land of hunters, trappers, fishermen, prospectors, lumberjacks, forest rangers, mountain climbers, cross-country cyclists, and lovers of the wilderness in general. And I met them all, day after day, in heat and mosquitoes, and in cold and rain. There was certainly lots of wildlife. People warned me about meeting bears along the way and equipped me with a whistle and pepper spray. Thankfully, I never even came close to needing them.

GOLD NUGGETS

And yes, this was a "gold rush" area, where back in the 1850s, men risked their fortunes and their lives to get rich quick. As a pilgrim I saw myself looking for a different kind of "gold nugget"– the kind that pleases the Lord; the human heart that is growing in His love. These I would collect each day and offer them up to Him. Here is a sampling of some of these spiritual treasures I found:

> Sixty-five-year-old Jerry, who shared stories of his travels to thirty-two states; how he built his own house from scraps he found at mills and dumps; how he cared for a disabled man for ten years; how he took in an unwed mother until she had her child; how he currently feeds three people supper every night; and how he grows his own food. Even with all of this, he lives on $322 a month.

> Bishop Fergus O'Grady, OMI (1908-98), missionary bishop in Prince George for thirty years, whose infectious enthusiasm for the faith, for Mary, for teens, for people, and for life in

general, swept up all around him into the mighty current of the Catholic Faith. He half seriously offered to ordain me a priest for his diocese.

Sandy, a middle-aged truck driver stopped and said: "I use to be worried about the transmission in this old dump truck I am driving, but after talking with you yesterday, I could not get you out of my mind all night, and now I have great peace like never before."

SHORTCUT TO ALASKA

On July 13, after walking 300 miles west, I turned north onto a mostly dirt highway that went all the way up to the Alaska Canadian Highway in the Yukon Territories. This 400-mile long road was called the "Stewart-Cassiar Highway," but it was also known as "the shortcut to Alaska." I was told if I had walked this road the previous year, I would have had to face semitractor trailers specially built to haul raw asbestos from the nearby mine that pounded this highway nonstop, day and night. I thanked the Lord the mine had been closed and I was delivered from such a defilement of the natural beauty of the land. Many people knew about me in this area from reading an article on my journey that appeared in the Houston, British Columbia, local newspaper on July 15.[42]

ALCAN HIGHWAY

When I crossed from British Columbia into Yukon Territory on August 3, I was back on a paved road and one more traveled. I had eleven days to make it to Maryhouse (the Madonna House) in Whitehorse. This highway had been constructed in 1942, as part of the World War II effort, and so this year, 1992, the highway was celebrating its fiftieth anniversary (and it was my fifty-first birthday). One day a photographer for *National Geographic* took my picture as part of his documentation of the anniversary year.

By averaging 25 miles (40 kilometers) a day I was able to arrive in Whitehorse on August 14, in time for noon Mass at Sacred Heart Cathedral. I spent three days at Maryhouse, getting to know the staff and sharing in their prayer and ministry to the poor. I learned how Catherine Doherty came to found this house after seeing what she took to be an "Eskimo mother with child," as a sign from the Lord. Also a staff member named Trudy, who had a keen interest in the Russian apostolate, began briefing me on what I could expect to experience once I got to Siberia. I began to feel the excitement of the coming adventure of the Russian Far East.

ENTERING ALASKA

When I left Whitehorse on August 17, I began the last month of the summer's pilgrimage. From Whitehorse to Anchorage it was approximately 600 miles. This far north the days were noticeably shorter on light, the weather was already turning cold, and the leaves were changing color. I was given mittens, a hat, a $300 down sleeping bag, and as I got closer to Anchorage, boots for the slush and snow. One priest gave me this excellent advice: "Remember sweat turns to ice when the temperature goes below freezing." Before I left the Yukon Territory, I enjoyed the thought that the mountain range to my left was called "St. Elias Mountains" as it reminded me of my favorite Old Testament prophet (I Kg 17-19).

On August 29, I entered Alaska and began walking again on "home ground." I was meeting people who had, for one reason or another, succumbed to the attraction of this frontier wilderness. I met several young people from the States who were attracted to the opportunity to homestead (160 acres were free if one cleared 3 acres the first year). People were picking red raspberries, blueberries, and cranberries. In this area it is understood that if one has no place to go and one comes upon an unoccupied cabin, one may enter and use whatever they need. If the cabin is locked, often the key is hung outside in plain view for an emergency. I availed myself of this unwritten agreement several times.

END OF THE HIGHWAY

I successfully passed through the larger towns of Tok, Glennallen, and Palmer, finally arriving in Eagle River on September 18. There I found the Antiochian Orthodox community of St. John the Evangelist. It was a richly rewarding time. They told me their main house was a former Precious Blood Sister's convent and that Thomas Merton gave his last retreat here on September 18 (twenty-four years to that very day), 1968, before his fatal trip to Bangkok. My hosts handed me a transcript of his talks to the sisters on that occasion. In reading the text I was amazed at how traditionally Catholic his talks were; nothing like the speculations of his later *Asian Journal.*[43]

On Saturday, September 19, at 5:00 p.m., I walked up the steps of Holy Family Cathedral in downtown Anchorage. By the grace of God and with the help of hundreds of caring people along the way, I had completed my proposed 3,000-mile, 5 1/2 month journey for the Lord. Now I was ready to see what the Lord had in mind for me in my winter layover at the edge of the North American continent. In the spring I trusted He would be getting me across the North Atlantic onto the Asian continent.

POUSTINIA PROVIDED

My first night in Anchorage I slept in my tent, in an empty lot downtown. On Sunday, September 20, Archbishop Francis T. Hurley welcomed me to Anchorage and invited me to move into his house until we found a suitable place for my winter *poustinia*.

It turned out that the pastor of the Cathedral, Fr. Bede, and the Dominican staff there, were most supportive and helpful. The pastor agreed to let me use a small room in the Cathedral Center designated as "the library" for my winter *poustinia*. I could lay my sleeping bag out on the rugged floor at night to sleep and use the restroom facilities in the center. So after three weeks of living with the Archbishop, I left his house and moved into the Cathedral Center.

That became my base of operation for the next seven months.

LOOKING AHEAD

Now I began to pray, "How do I get to Russia and how do I prepare for this journey in Siberia?" The first thing the Lord provided was access to "The Russian Desk" at the Chancery Office of the Archdiocese of Anchorage. They would help me get the necessary visa. That, along with my passport, would allow me to enter Russia at the border. The next questions were, "Where do I start my walk in Siberia?" and "Is it possible to connect the holy places of North America with those in Asia by foot?"

I knew from my study of geography that Russia was only 51 miles from the United States at the Bearing Strait, and that these waters often froze solidly in winter. Did the Lord want me to go that way? I started asking around about the possibility. I was told, first of all there are no roads the last 1,000 miles from Anchorage to the strait. One could do it in February when they clear a path over frozen lakes from Anchorage to Nome for the Iditarod Trail sled dog race. But there were very few settlements out there and one would have to prearrange food drops along the way. Also, there were stories of men who had walked across the strait and were turned back on the Russian side because they, also, have no roads for the first 1,000 miles on their side. The logistics seemed to be against my walking it. Besides, one of my purposes was to lift up the Cross of Jesus. Who would see it out there? I needed to look for an alternative.

THE CHURCH IN SIBERIA

Of course the Lord had been preparing the way ahead of me. In 1991, Archbishop Hurley had already established Nativity of Jesus, a fledgling Catholic community, in Magadan, located in the Russian Far East. Magadan was a port city and staging area for the prisoners who, during the Communist era, had been sent to the work camps (gulags) in the interior of Siberia. I was told that it was in Magadan that a road started that would connect with other roads traversing all of Siberia (eventually leading all the way to Moscow, 9,000 miles away). Magadan then seemed to me like the logical place to start my walk across Asia.

And where should I stop for the winter? I also learned from the Russian Desk, that the next closest Catholic Church in Siberia was in Irkutsk–Our Lady of the Assumption–near the southeastern end of Lake Baikal, 3,000 miles west of Magadan. That looked possible if I started on May 1, from Magadan, as the snow would be mostly melted by then. If I could make 20 miles a day, I would arrive in Irkutsk by October 1. So I tucked away the address of Our Lady of the Assumption in Irkutsk, believing my heavenly Mother, under her title of my home parish in Glenshaw, would be looking out for me. This time, the Holy Spirit did not urge me to write ahead to them. He knew it would not do much good because the Catholic priests, sisters, and lay missionaries there were from Poland and they did not know English. I would have to show up on their doorstep and in whatever Russian I had acquired by that time, make known to them my need for a winter *poustinia*.

LEARNING RUSSIAN

So what was I going to do about language? I realized early that I would have to acquire at least an elementary knowledge of Russian just to be able to read the road signs, for they would not be in the Roman alphabet (like English) but in the Cyrillic alphabet. At the same time,

I could not expect people in the remote interior to know English as a second language. Thankfully, the Lord provided a middle-aged couple who were known as "the translator's translators" (i.e., people who understood the finest points of translation) who offered to help me while I was in Anchorage. Since Saints Cyril and Methodius, back in the ninth century, had based their transcription of the Slavonic language into a written form on the Greek alphabet (with which I was already familiar from seminary studies), I was one step ahead. I came up with a list of phrases like, "Where is the post office?" and "Do you have any drinking water?" I had the Russian couple write out and record these phrases on a tape recorder so that I could memorize them and begin acquiring some basic communication skills. I do not have a facility for speaking languages other than English and it took me one whole month just to learn how to say "Zdravstvjutje" (How do you do, sir?).

ORDER OF THE PILGRIM

One interesting development during my winter layover in Anchorage was the publication in the *Anchorage Daily News*, of a three-full-page, plus front page, picture story on my way of life for the Thanksgiving edition on Thursday, November 26, 1992.[44] The photographer won the Gabriel Award for the best religious story photography in a secular newspaper in the United States in the year 1992, for these pictures. The title of the article, "Order of the Pilgrim," was suggested by a comment Bishop Bosco made in a telephone interview with the author Debra McKinney during the course of her research. She quoted him as saying, "George is his own religious order. A religious order of one." Ever since then, when people ask me "what order do you belong to?" I say, "the Order of Pilgrim."

SERVANT OF THE LORD

Speaking about this article leads me to introduce Lee Leinen (1941-2007), a tireless servant of the Lord whom He sent to me, and who subsequently became a tremendous help during and after the Russian pilgrimage. When she saw this article about me in the *Anchorage Daily News*, she felt that many of my friends would like a copy, so she took it upon herself to collect over forty copies for me to give away. To obtain that many issues she resorted to paper recycling bins, even at night, with a flashlight–with a friend to stand by her–as she climbed into the dumpsters and rummaged for those precious treasures.

Up until my mother died in 1999, Lee was the person who coordinated communication through mail, cassette tapes, and phone calls between me and my family and friends stateside. Lee came to mean so much to my mother, that she listed her in her funeral arrangements as one of her three "daughters-in-Christ." Lee, I believe, is among that multitude of unsung heroes who will never be officially canonized by the Church Militant, but who will shine as a bright star (Dn 12:3) in the Church Triumphant.

SPRUCE ISLAND

Among the many services Lee provided for me, one came in the form of an offer in the spring of 1993. She said to me one day, "Is there anything you would like to see or do in Alaska before you leave for Siberia in April?" Immediately the Lord brought to mind the thought about making a pilgrimage to the grave of the nineteenth-century Russian Orthodox missionary monk St. Herman of Alaska[45] who had lived on Spruce Island just 400 miles south of Anchorage. No sooner mentioned than executed.

Lee arranged and paid for my one-hour flight from Anchorage to Kodiak Island on Friday, March 26, and for my return trip on

Monday, March 29. The timing was precision perfect. A storm canceled all flights that weekend and mine was the last plane out on Friday and the first one back on Monday. The connection from Kodiak Island to Spruce Island by mail plane, plus personal escort to Monk's Lagoon on Spruce Island by Monk Joasaph, were just as arranged by Divine Providence. I returned with blessed soil from the grave of St. Herman that I was able to share with Russian Orthodox faithful on my way west across Siberia, reversing Herman's journey east exactly 200 years prior to that. Thank you St. Herman.

ENDNOTES

39. Father Boniface (Joseph) Luykx (1915-2004) held the rank of "archimandrite," a monastic superior in some Eastern churches roughly equivalent to that of an abbot in the West.

40. The Liturgy of the Presanctified Gifts is a combined Vespers-Communion service used in the Byzantine Christian tradition on Lenten Wednesdays, Fridays, and on the first three days of Holy Week. "Presanctified" refers to the Eucharistic Bread which was consecrated at a previous Divine Liturgy, beforehand.

41. Though dementia would eventually force Archimandrite Boniface to leave his post here and to retire back to his native Belgium, I kept up correspondence with him until near his end. His busy life was full of tragedy and bitter disappointment, from monasteries he founded burning to the ground, to his closest collaborators abandoning the faith for the world. Despite this, he kept his heart focused on his suffering Lord and showed dramatically the indomitable spirit of the Christian Faith. He has remained one of my lifetime heroes.

42. "Pilgrim Walks and Prays for All," *Houston Today,* July 15, 1992.

43. *Asian Journal* was published posthumously by New Direction Books in 1975. It was edited from his original notebooks. It seems to come from the pen of a completely different Merton than the one who was one of my spiritual mentors in the 1950s, when I read his *Seven Storey Mountain* (1948) and used his original *Seeds of Contemplation* (1949) from my high school days (1955) onward. I left Merton in the late 1950s, when his focus turned more deliberately toward pacifism and social action.

44. Debra McKinney, "Order of the Pilgrim," *Anchorage Daily News,* November 26, 1992. (Photos by Jim Lavrakas)

45. St. Herman of Alaska (1756-1837) was a Russian Orthodox monk who came with the first band of Christian missionaries from Russia to bring the knowledge of Jesus Christ to the Aleutian natives in 1795. Two miles from the larger Kodiak Island, he settled on tiny Spruce Island, where he lived a life of seclusion. But he was a true father to the natives of the area for forty years, establishing a chapel, a school, and an orphanage. His feast day is November 15.

PART TWO

MAGADAN TO IRKUTSK (1993)

ON TO MAGADAN, SIBERIA

How did the Lord get His pilgrim "across the pond" from Anchorage to Magadan? It was a 2,000-mile, four-hour plane ride, so I was in need of a plane ticket. A Lutheran man named Steve, from Amazing Grace Church in Anchorage–by the action of the Holy Spirit–came up to me one day and said, "I will take up a collection for you and buy you a ticket." And so he did. For $462. I was scheduled to leave at 10:00 p.m. on Wednesday, April 21, on the Russian airline, Aeroflot. On that day I walked with a group of friends to the airport from my *poustinia* in downtown Anchorage. As Archbishop Hurley wrote of me in his column, "He came with nothing...but a deep love of God... He left with nothing...(but) with the love of so many here."[46]

My landing in Russia was also perfectly orchestrated by the Lord. I had the names of several prominent members of the Catholic community in Magadan. This included Fr. Austin Mohrbacher, the American Roman Catholic pastor in residence and Alvina, a Russian/English translator, who had recently become Catholic through Madonna House. I had let them know that I intended to walk the 30 miles (50 kilometers) from the airport to Magadan.

Nevertheless, that did not stop Alvina and her friends from driving out to the airport to greet me with three, long stem, red roses as I disembarked and came through customs. They offered to give me a ride to Magadan, but I insisted on walking. And since it still got below freezing at night here, they were concerned about my sleeping outside in my tent. So the Lord provided a military officer, Sasha, at the terminal who invited me to stay with him, his wife, and his young daughter. It was on that first night already that I received my first taste of authentic Russian hospitality.

I ended up spending five days in Magadan, praying and sharing with the small Catholic community there as well as with the larger social groups making up this outpost of Russian culture in the post-Soviet era. It was obviously still a struggle for these hearty pioneer souls to make a go of it after the collapse of communism. They often found themselves short on electricity, water, and heat. Even though coal was mined in the area, when it got down to minus 40 degrees they could not get their buildings inside above 50 degrees. But these people were survivors–literally–and they knew how to help each other and were grateful for any sign of God's presence among them. I felt completely at ease entrusting myself into their hands.

ASIAN RUSSIA

The first stage of my pilgrimage through Asian Russia was from Magadan to Yakutsk, a distance of about 1,200 miles, and it took two months (May and June), to traverse it by foot. During this time I had to learn how to survive in a foreign country with few resources other than the kindness of strangers and unbounded faith in God's ability and desire to take care of me.

In May the weather was still cold, alternating between below freezing temperatures and bright warm days and between snow and rain. Sometimes I had to break the ice in a river to take a sponge bath. The second week of my walk my right ankle began acting up. One day I came to a complete stop, not able to take another step on it because of the pain. All I could do was stand still, pray, and trust the Lord would rescue me.

Very soon a man stopped and asked if I needed anything. When I explained my situation he took me up the road to a mining camp that had a nurse and sleeping facilities for workers. After bathing my ankle in hot water, I was able to stand on it without too much pain; after a good night's sleep indoors, I was able to continue on my journey alone. But for the next three weeks the pain kept returning, and I had to walk very slowly as well as to favor it over my other foot.

Once the temperatures rose into the nineties, in mid-June, it didn't give me any more problems the rest of the summer.

ROAD CONDITIONS

After the weather, the roads became my greatest challenge. They were mostly dirt, although parts of them were paved around the bigger cities. So, when the weather was dry they were essentially dust bowls; when it was wet, they were slippery mud. One day, the ankle-deep mud sucked one of my new rubber tire sandals right off of my foot, causing me to look for longer screws to put through the nylon straps that were attached to the sole of the sandal.

It was nothing to see potholes in the road the size of a car. In the villages they seemed to deliberately leave plenty of potholes in the road to slow down the truck traffic for the sake of safety. Outside the villages, road graders brought the dirt pushed by traffic onto the sides of the road, back to the middle of the road to form a crown, allowing the water to run off. If creeks crossed the road, vehicles just forded them. I would take off my socks and just walk in my sandals through the water (walking in wet socks is hard on the feet). The most heartrending thought for me at this point was of the dead whose bodies were under the road beneath me, on the average of one every 6 meters. During the horrors of the Soviet period, slave laborers from the camps who were building this road and who died on the job, were just buried right within the roadbed.

FOOD AND WATER

As for drinking water, my friend Lee in Anchorage had the foresight to purchase for me a mini-filter pump (a Katadyn microfilter made in Switzerland) with a $75 ceramic filter. The filter had a silver anode in it to prevent the growth of bacteria. With this I could take water (as long as it was optically clear) out of any puddle, pond, lake, river, or stream and after passing it though this pump, drink the water without boiling or adding iodine tablets. It took about ten minutes of pumping to filter eight ounces of drinking water. Of course, when people brought me food they often filled up my water jug–this being before the era of the now ubiquitous plastic bottles of springwater .

And food was brought in abundance. Although some days, only a handful of vehicles would pass me in one day, normally fifteen to twenty people would stop to offer help. Quite often I would have to say, "Thank you, but I cannot take any more food." Out on the road truck drivers would stop and make me a pot of tea by building a fire in the woods, using a coil, hot-wired to their engine, firing up a kerosene or gas stove or even just using a blowtorch.

One day a truck driver stopped and asked if I wanted a cooked meal. When I said yes, he pulled his truck off the road, built a fire, got a bucket of water from the creek, and put it on the fire. Then he added potatoes, carrots, cabbage, and canned meat. It was not uncommon for truck drivers to get out of their trucks, throw a few animal hides or blankets on the ground in the woods, spread out bread, salo (raw, cured pig fat), pickled vegetables, fresh tomatoes, cucumbers, hard-boiled eggs, jam, and little meat pies and invite me to join them for a meal.

HOSPITALITY

My whole two months on the Kolyma Highway, from Magadan to Yakutsk, my heaven-sent angel in Magadan, Alvina, sent care packages up the road for me by way of trucks and buses. She would go to the depot in Magadan and say to the drivers, "Here, when you see the Pilgrim on the highway, give him this." And it worked (at least most of the time). In the package there would be letters and tapes for me from the States and from her, food and drink plus addresses of people along the way where I might find hospitality. Of course she could not vouch for all of these addresses. People would just come up to her in Magadan and say, "Here, your pilgrim-friend can stay with this person I know in this town along the way." Usually it worked out wonderfully, but one time I knocked on the door of a man who, when he opened up and saw who it was, said, "Oh. You cannot stay here; I am a Communist." But he did find a room for me in a hotel and paid for it himself.

TURNING THE BEND

After arriving at the city of Khandiga on June 16, I enjoyed the hospitality of a man named Valeri. The next morning he took me to the "jet boat" which not only crossed the mighty Aldan River, but took its passengers 100 miles down the river to access a more passable road to the provincial capital of Yakutsk. Then, after ten more days of walking, I arrived at Yakutsk on June 27. There, two men–Ivan and Sergie–were waiting and provided for me over the next three nights. While there, they took me to the visa office in order to extend my stay in Russia for another three months. The following day I was taken to the fax office where it took them five minutes to scan a letter to my mother and father. (They did not charge me for the service; normally it would cost about $25.) On the other end in faraway Glenshaw, another one of my "angels," Stanley, had offered to receive communications from me by fax at his business office so my parents could stay in touch with their pilgrim-son. The Lord was providing this thinnest modicum of contact with those I had left behind to witness to Jesus in this place the Russians call a "bear's corner" ("УГОЛ МЕДВЕДЯ" the Russian phrase for a remote part of the world).

When I left Yakutsk on Wednesday, June 30, I was now heading due south. My next destination was Chita, 1,200 miles distant. This included a 300-mile piece of the Taiga, which everyone was telling me was not passable in the summer. I was told that people who set out to drive the 9,000 miles across Russia from Moscow in the west to Vladivostok in the east, put their cars on flatbed rail cars at this point to get them across those 300 miles. Maybe I could walk the railroad tracks. I had to see for myself and let the Lord direct me.

MORE OF THE SAME

The whole month of July went fairly well, although there were some very hot days and I sweat–a lot. The mosquitoes and black flies got pretty bad and I often walked with my head netting on. At night in my tent in the thick woods, the mosquitoes hummed all night long as they massed on the outside of the protecting screen of my tent. There was still lots of rain–three days straight at one point. Each day a primary task was drying out my tent and rainfly if at all possible. Otherwise I risked the growth of mold and eventual separation of the fabric and destruction of the waterproofing.

There continued to be an abundance of food and, again, I had to refuse many generous offers along the way. Because of the long days and hot temperatures, fresh vegetables were already coming into season and being harvested. So I was receiving tomatoes, carrots, potatoes, apples, and watermelon, plus the canned staples of corned beef and sweet condensed milk. Several times I was given "Siberian sok" to drink; it was maple sap just as it comes from the tree (not boiled down). People continued to give me souvenirs of their areas, usually small pins or flags, apparently left over from Soviet days. In return I would give them an image of Mary the Mother of God under her title of "Our Lady of Combermere."

EXPERIENCING THE TAIGA

On August 4, the going began getting rough. I had almost reached the border with Mongolia, at Solovyevsk, and turned west toward Chita. But the road was giving out and I was forced to follow the train track. Because spurs were constantly splitting off, I could not always determine which was the main track. I had to keep asking people and they often had to lead me back to the right track.

Now I began to experience what Taiga was–thawed permafrost. I was ankle-deep in water all the time. I knew that I could board the train and get through this area more easily, but I deliberately chose to take this harder path and to offer it up for the intention of World Youth Day, meeting in Denver this year. It was being held on the Feast of the Assumption of Mary into heaven, on August 15. Finally on August 16, after sloshing through mud for 4 kilometers, I came to a big river without a bridge. There was no way I could ford it on foot. What was I to do?

THE SIBERIAN RAILROAD

Off to my right I saw a train crossing the river on a high trestle and felt the Lord's prompting, telling me I could climb up there and walk across to the other side. I knew trains came by every ten minutes or so but I felt there was enough space off to the side of the track so that I could get out of their way. At the same time, I had to hope no one on the train would decide to flush a toilet just as they passed me, since the refuse exited right onto the tracks. An additional problem was that these trestles were high security points and the military guarded them from terrorists. Thankfully the guard on this one was at the other end and he only started shouting at me and gesticulating that I was not allowed to walk over the trestle, after I was halfway across. So I continued walking on, hoping for the best. After making it safely across and explaining to the lone guard who I was, I asked him where I could board the train and get out of the Taiga to a place where the road continued to Chita. He pointed me toward a gravel road to Amazar, only 4 kilometers away, and thanking the Lord I had not been arrested for trespassing or something, I headed in that direction.

When I arrived at the train station at 2:30 p.m., I asked how far I would have to travel on the train until I could find a road that I could walk west to Chita. They told me I would have to go all the way to Chernovesk–an eight-hour train ride of approximately 500 kilometers. When the ticket agent told me how much the fare was, I could not figure out if I had enough rubles. (The American Express travelers' checks I had been given in Anchorage would have been of little use in this out-of-the-way place.) This was the first time I had to buy anything in Russia and I did not know the conversion rates.

Also, because of the high inflation rate of the ruble at this time, the amounts sounded astronomical. Completely confused, I just dumped out all the rubles I had on the counter–hoping there were enough to cover the cost of the ticket–and indicated to the clerk to just take what she needed. Thankfully she was an honest clerk. She selected a few bills and pushed the rest back to me. Weeks later when I finally began to get a handle on the ruble system, I realized my eight-hour train ride cost the equivalent of about 65 cents (around 1,200 rubles at the going rate). This was amazing, in light of the fact that at one time the ruble was one for one with the U.S. dollar!

A CHILD OF GOD

When I got off the train in Chernovesk at 11:00 p.m., I only had a twelve-day walk to get to Chita. An incident occurred on this stretch of road that I have shared dozens of times since then. It teaches a very important lesson about not judging people. On Monday,

August 23, I was approaching a little village when a man stopped on his motorcycle. He did not speak a word of English but I understood he wanted me to come to his home in the village. So I said I would follow him on foot as he walked his motorcycle to his house.

Once there he introduced me to his wife and six children and invited me to join them for a meal. As we ate he shared with me that he was "the village atheist." (His neighbors for the most part were Orthodox Christians.) But who was the one who showed me hospitality? Who was the one with six children (most Russians think one or two children is enough)? He did not know who God or Jesus were, yet he was a child of God. That is why Jesus said, "Not everyone who says to me 'Lord, Lord' will enter the Kingdom of heaven, but only the one who does the will of my Father in heaven (Mt 7:21)." What is the will of the Father but that we love (Mt 22:36-39)? Just going to church, singing hymns, reciting the creed, and claiming to be Christian does not necessarily mean that one is growing in love. And just because one does *not* do all these things (undoubtedly good in themselves) does not mean one is not pleasing to the Father. So I learned once again the lesson not to judge people on what they call themselves or how others label them. The Lord said it already to Samuel in the Old Testament, "Not as man does God see because man sees the appearance but the Lord looks into the heart (1 Sm 16:7)."

GOAL IN SIGHT

I was very happy when, on August 30, I saw a sign, Irkutsk 999 Kilometers" (620 miles). My winter goal was in sight! By walking 21 miles (35 kilometers) a day, I should have arrived in Irkutsk the beginning of October. And that would be none too early; by the second week of September, the temperature dropped, the leaves started changing colors, and I had to get out my gloves and keep up my hood while walking during the day. Now ice appeared on my tent at night. On September 26, when I got up in the morning, I saw four inches of snow on the ground.

I was getting wonderful views of Lake Baikal, the "Pearl of Siberia." It was hard to comprehend the statistics. Baikal was the largest fresh water lake in the world (400 miles long), containing one-fifth of all the fresh water in the world, more water than all five Great Lakes combined. It was the deepest (over 1 mile deep in parts), the clearest, and the oldest in the world as far as geologists could tell. It froze over in the winter and the fish at the bottom had no eyes because no light penetrates that far below. On September 27, I met Karim, an artisan, who took me to his house to meet his wife and two young children and to eat with them. He told me when the lake freezes he takes a chain saw and cuts huge blocks of ice and constructs giant ice sculptures (he showed me some pictures of them).

ST. MARY OF THE ASSUMPTION

On October 1, I entered the largest city in south central Siberia, Irkutsk, and found St. Mary of the Assumption Catholic Church in the center of town. I felt like my heavenly mother was waiting to welcome me with open arms, as if I was coming to my home parish, St. Mary of the Assumption in Glenshaw. It was the Feast of St. Therese the Little Flower and she had more than a rose prepared for me. The local Catholic community of priests, religious sisters, and laity were all gathered at the church for prayer. I got there for adoration of the Blessed Sacrament, the Rosary, the Holy Sacrifice of the Mass, and Holy Communion. After five months in the wilderness without the Sacraments, it was like a spiritual banquet.

After the services I introduced myself to the pastor, Fr. Ignatius Pawlus, a Salvatorian priest from Poland. When I told him I was looking for a place for my winter *poustinia* he said, "You may be an answer to our prayers. We have a diocesan priest from Poland on sabbatical 130 kilometers from here and he is all by himself. Maybe you could live there with him and assist him for the winter. As a matter-of-fact he is in town these days and we can introduce you to him–his name is Fr. Voytek." And so I came to meet the priest who would be my companion for the next seven months. We took the bus from Irkutsk the very next day to the village of Vershina, founded by Polish settlers in 1910. It was the end of the bus line, and the end of my summer walk.

VERSHINA

Vershina was like one big farm. About a 150 log cabins lined the main street, which consisted of a dirt road. It was an open range for cows, horses, pigs, and chickens. Their only industry was a saw and planing mill that produced tongue and groove spruce boards. For five years now they had electricity, but still no running water or sewers; each one had an outhouse in their backyard. Every family was self-sufficient; each had a well with a balance beam in their yards for water. They also had cows for milk and cheese and chickens for eggs. They grew potatoes, cabbage, and carrots. The only thing they needed to buy in the city was coffee and sugar. There was very little cash flow in the village. The collection at Mass each Sunday totaled less than $2. But like past ages in the history of God's People, the faithful brought gifts of food in lieu of money.

When we first arrived in Vershina, Fr. Vojtek took me into St. Stanislaus's Church in the center of the village. It was a tiny log structure originally built in 1910, and now just completely refurbished. It could accommodate about seventy-five people on simple plank benches, arranged in two rows. There were small rooms off of each side of the sanctuary, one for the sacristy and the other for storage—and each had two floor to ceiling windows that provided lots of light.

I asked Fr. Voytek if I could use the storeroom for my *poustinia* and he agreed. I cleared it out, moved in a small desk and chair, built a bunk to sleep in, over the top of the desk, with a ladder to climb up to it. My icon corner had three shelves, each representing one of the three kinds of honor given to heavenly beings: *dulia, hyper-dulia,* and *latria* (veneration, exalted veneration, and worship). I added an extra, wall-mounted, electric heating element from the church, but even with that, when the outside temperature dropped to minus 40 degrees in January, it only went up to 50 degrees in my room. And if the water in the cruets at Mass was not previously heated, it froze when poured into the metalic chalice.

Fr. Voytek lived in the school building, although another building nearby destined to be the future rectory was almost complete. So I would join him in the school for meals as there was a wood stove there for cooking and for heating. I did not speak Polish and he did not speak English, so he said Mass every day in Latin, as that was our best common language. Each day we would take an hour and walk together through the village praying the Rosary, saying alternate decades in Polish and in English. It was a perfect arrangement from the Lord for both of us.

BUSINESS IN IRKUTSK

After a week in Vershina, I returned to Irkutsk by bus for twelve days to extend my visa for another six months. This was an all-day project as I was shuffled from one office and building to another, getting a form here, a signature there, a photo here, and a stamp there. It gave a lot of people jobs, even if it seemed in the view of some to be mere "busywork" or unnecessary bureaucracy. But while I was in the city, a TV interview and a talk to students in a local college were arranged for me. This also enabled me to have more fellowship with the two priests and two sisters of St. Charles Borromeo from Poland, and with the lay Roman Catholic community in Irkutsk. I found this little Polish enclave to be a poor, devout, and therefore joyful portion of the Body of Christ.

Little did I know then that in two more years, the Lord would give me a whole seven months in the country of Poland, itself.

A SEEKING SOUL

Back in Vershina, I settled into a daily rhythm of solitude, silence, and prayer. It would be quite a different kind of winter layover than that which I had the previous year in Anchorage. There I was in the midst of a city full of people who spoke English and where it was possible to have quite a few conversations. Here only an occasional visitor came in from outside the village to interrupt my solitude.

Early in January a young Russian woman by the name of Margarita came to Vershina asking me to give her a two-week private, directed retreat. She had met me briefly along the road on September 21, ten days before I got to Irkutsk. At the time of our first meeting, she had been with two American missionaries working in her home town of Krasnoyarsk. What drew her attention to me, she explained, was the fact that I was carrying a Bible in my left hand as I walked along. It seems that the Scriptures meant a lot to her.

Though she said she had been baptized by an Orthodox priest as an infant, she had very little religious instruction growing up under communism. Then, in 1991, a group of evangelical American missionaries came to preach the Gospel in her city. Now she had a weekly Bible Study in her apartment and was eager to seek the Lord's specific will for her life. She also expressed her desire to make this directed retreat during her holiday off work; she was a pharmacist in Krasnoyarsk.

CALL TO RELIGIOUS LIFE

We put her up in the almost completed but, as yet unoccupied, future parish house. I provided her with a dozen topics for reflection with a dozen or more Scriptures for each theme. By the end of her stay there was one Scripture which spoke to her heart above all others, "Everyone of you who does not renounce all his possessions cannot be my disciple" (Lk 14:33). She certainly wanted to be the Lord's disciple, but how could she follow these words of the Lord?

After returning to her job and to her faith community, along with continued months of prayer, she discerned that the Lord was possibly calling her to the vowed religious life in its active form as she saw it being lived out by the Sisters of St. Charles Borromeo from Poland. Margarita eventually went to the sister's novitiate house in Trzebnica, in southwestern Poland for her novitiate. She pronounced her first vows there on March 20, 1997, and in God's amazing Providence, I was able to attend. She was eventually stationed back in Siberia, now using her medical background to serve in the hospice work that her sisters did in the name of the Lord.

This story has a wonderful footnote that also shows the amazing way of the Lord. It involves Margarita's younger sister Irina.

THROUGH MARY TO JESUS

Irina heard about her sister's visit to Vershina and decided that she, too, wanted to come visit the Pilgrim. I agreed to the request and Irina came for a week retreat. Irina, however, did not know much English, and about all I knew in Russian were the prayers of the Rosary. So I began by teaching her the Hail Mary, the Our Father, and the Glory be, in Russian. Irina went back home and began praying the Rosary every day. Soon she started going to the local Catholic Church and taking instructions. She was baptized at the Easter vigil on April 1, and I was there as her godfather. Irina did not become a vowed religious but went on to marry, to have two daughters, and to raise her family in a village just east of Lake Baikal. "Thank you, Mary, for leading your devoted daughter to your Son, Jesus." It was one fruit of my walk the Lord allowed me to see mature very quickly.

A KNOCK IN THE NIGHT

The date, January 21, 1994, was a typical winter night in Siberia: the temperature was minus 20 degrees and by 8:30 p.m. it was pitch-black outside. I was sitting at my desk with the light on in my *poustinia*, writing a letter to my niece. Then I heard it. First, a knock and then a jiggling of the handle on the side door of the church. Then it happened again at the back door of the church. I figured it was probably one of the local drunks making their nightly rounds, so I did not bother to investigate; I went on writing and prayed for whomever was the originator of the noise.

Then a few minutes later I just about jumped out of my chair as I heard someone knocking on the widow behind me. The bottom of this window is seven feet off the ground outside. Whoever did that had to either have climbed or jumped up to reach it. At the same time a voice called out in broken English:

"I have clothes and letters from America."

"Really?" I thought. "How is that possible. No one told me to expect anything like that."

MONGOLIAN EXPRESS

So going to the side door of the church, I opened it onto that cold and frigid night and found a young man standing there with an eager smile, around thirty years of age, with black hair, Mongolian features, and a large, green camouflage duffel bag slung over his shoulder. (A Mongolian Santa Claus who had lost his way, perhaps?) In his right hand he gripped a copy of the pencil sketch I had done of St. Stanislaus Catholic Church a few months before and which I had sent to the States. He blurted out, "My name is Batzorig. I brought this to you from Lee Leinen in Alaska."

Then, right there on the floor, inside the door, having undone the chain and padlock on the bag, he took out two large cardboard boxes weighing twenty-five pounds each. He slit open the sealing tape and emptied out all of the contents. They had a total of forty-two items in them, ranging from an expensive pair of winter boots to a deck of playing cards, along with all kinds of foodstuffs and thirty-three personal letters from friends in Pennsylvania, California, and Alaska. I was overwhelmed by such an outpouring of love. The effort it took to get such a wonderful care package delivered right to my door was hard to fathom. "Lord, You sure just proved your love for me once again in a most amazing way."

MORE PILGRIMS

As we shared some tea, bread, salo, and jam, Batzorig told me he was from Mongolia, returning from a ten-month, walking pilgrimage from Ulaanbaatar to California and back. He and his two companions had met Lee in Anchorage and she had helped them raise the funds needed to fly back to Russia, by putting on a sellout martial arts performance in Anchorage. The agreement with her was that they in return for her help, would deliver these two boxes to the Pilgrim in Vershina on their way back home.

After flying from Anchorage to Khabarovsk, and waiting overnight at the train station there with the duffel bag chained to his body to prevent petty thieves from absconding with it, he left his two traveling companions in Ulan Ude to the south of Irkutsk and took the train alone to the city. From there he caught the bus to Vershina to bring me this bag of goodies (from St. Nicholas) having thus fulfilled his end of the bargain. Once Batzorig left Vershina the next morning, I was free to bask in the many signs of love from brothers and sisters who chose to share in my journey for the Lord. I was in for many a tearful moment in the coming weeks as I sifted through the many gifts in this treasure chest of blessings.

I should have realized that there were a great number of people who were praying for the safe arrival of this giant "Care Package." One witness to the truth of this came while writing up this present report in December 2017. A friend of mine from Anchorage, who introduced herself to me by mail back in 1994, as "the other Barbara" (another Barbara in Anchorage was a good friend of mine and hers) sent me a copy of her writings and poetry. It included a story, "The Dove."[47] This story recounted how Lee had asked a woman who had multiple ailments, to pray that the package would get to me safely. The woman agreed to "throw holy water" toward Russia and say, "God bless Pilgrim George." She told Lee that as she was saying this prayer one day, a white dove with a brownish circle around its neck flew in front of her window, circled three times, and then perched across the way but continued to stare at her through the glass. She felt it was a sign that she was to pray the Rosary. As soon as she finished the Rosary, the dove flew away, mission accomplished. How true that the Lord sometimes reveals His will to us in unusual and amazing ways.

BISHOP REVISITED

Among the many gifts in these two packages was a book from a dear friend from Glenshaw. It was a book by Bishop (later Cardinal) Wright entitled *Resonare Christum*.[48] It was a selection of sermons, addresses, interviews, and papers by Cardinal Wright during his years as Bishop of Pittsburgh–when I was a seminarian studying for the Diocese. Number XXVI in the collection was entitled, "Reflections on Conscience and Authority." It was given at the Thomas More Association on February 9, 1964, in Chicago, as the 1964 McGeary Foundation Lecture. The following sentences seemed to speak to me in a special way:

> The pursuit of vocation, whether clerical or lay, always presupposes dictates of conscience and sooner or later brings

one into collision with one or another form of authority. Sometimes it is the authority of God, impelling one to the vocation of the needed but unattractive work that one fears or resists. Sometimes it is the authority of parents, resisting a vocation to priesthood, to marriage or to one of those harebrained ventures which so frequently turn out to the good name of the family and the glory of God.[49]

Since these words were written in 1964, three years before the bishop and I sat down together to agree to put my ordination to the priesthood on hold, he could not have had me in mind. But since it shows his awareness of the tension between the charismatic and the institutional–in his terms, between conscience and authority–I could not help but see his reference to "harebrained ventures" as perhaps the basis of his understanding of my pilgrimage on foot to Jerusalem in 1970-71 and, at the same time, his warm welcome to me in Rome in 1971. Although a "Prince of the Church" and servant of the institutional authority, he clearly acknowledged the reality of the existence of individual conscience and freedom of the Holy Spirit to blow where He willed. I took it as his implicit affirmation–at least on an intellectual and theoretical level–of my vocation as a pilgrim/*poustinik*.

A BELL FOR VERSHINA

The Lord also used me here as a catalyst for one more amazing project that unfolded beyond my sight and out of my control. This was the provision of a bell for the recently rebuilt bell tower of St. Stanislaus Church in Vershina. When I arrived in October of 1993, I noticed that the bell tower was empty and no provisions were being made yet to remedy the situation. So, with the permission of Fr. Paulus, I wrote to my father back in Pennsylvania asking if he thought St. Mary's Church in Glenshaw would like to take on the project of providing a bell. I measured the space where it had to fit and sent him the dimensions.

My father began asking around at St. Mary's, and getting a favorable response, he set out to spearhead the project that ended up taking a full six months to complete. After three weeks he had located a new cast steel "Country Church Bell" at the Verdin Bell Company in Cincinnati, that might fit the bill. It weighed 235 pounds and with the used iron stand that came with it, the total weight was 519 pounds. He had it shipped to Glenshaw and first brought it to his workshop to bring it up to his standard of workmanship.

The following Sunday he took the bell to St. Mary's in the back of his pickup truck and parked it outside the back entrance to the church. There people could see it, ring it, and make a donation toward the project if they wished. Eventually, 120 people donated anywhere from 25 cents to $100, which covered the $800 cost of the bell. One parishioner paid to have it packed up and flown by Aeroflot first to Florida and then to Moscow where it arrived on February 8. However, the bell was placed in a Moscow warehouse and forgotten, due to the cancelation of Irkutsk-bound planes that would have been large enough to handle such a heavy piece of freight, along with union troubles at the Moscow airport.

PULLING STRINGS

When my father learned that the bell had not arrived in Irkutsk by the projected date in February, he began the task of trying to move the bell to its intended destination. It ended up taking him six weeks of frustrating efforts, $350 in phone bills, plus involving over fifty people including airline personnel, bishops, ambassadors, governors, and concerned individuals, in Russia, Alaska, Florida, and Pennsylvania, to finally get the bell put on the Trans-Siberian Railroad in Moscow on March 31. Upon arrival in Irkutsk it sat another two weeks because no one could get in touch with Fr. Ignatius who was the only one who could claim the bell.

That was how the situation stood when I left Irkutsk for my next summer walk to Alma Ata Kazakhstan, on April 25. Before I left, I handed over to Fr. Ignatius the papers my father had sent to me that would prove that the bearer had the right to claim the bell. Russian agents thoroughly examined all of the contents of the box. Assuring themselves that it contained no contraband, they allowed Fr. Ignatius to obtain a truck and to haul the bell to Vershina.

It was installed in the bell tower with a hand-operated winch with ratchet used to pull heavy objects my father had included in the package and on Sunday, May 8, the Feast of St. Stanislaus, it was christened "George." Amazingly this may have fulfilled a vision Fr. Gus had for me in prayer eighteen years before on March 25, 1976, in McKees Rocks, Pennsylvania. At that time, he told me that he saw "a cord with Franciscan knots hanging from a bell" (the bell in Vershina was rung from the floor of the church by a rope my father had included with the bell). So my namesake "George," coming from 17,000 miles away in Glenshaw, Pennsylvania, now calls the faithful in the remote village of Vershina to worship the Lord in the deep, black forests of Siberia.

TWO HEALTH ISSUES

There were two medical issues with which I needed the Lord's help at this time; I had developed an ingrown toenail on my left big toe that would not heal, and an open sore on my head that would scab over and fall off. The head sore would resist treatment for another year and a half until I found a dermatologist in Islamabad, Pakistan, in June of 1995. The toenail was cured by a doctor taking a rusty file (all that was available in the poorly equipped clinic) and scoring the nail halfway down so it would die and fall off, causing a new nail to grow out as it should. I was at the mercy of the Lord and His chosen instruments no matter what I thought about their procedures.

LOOKING AHEAD

Come spring of 1994, in my winter *poustinia* in Vershina, I began to plan for "Pilgrimage 1994." A priest-friend in Kerala, India, wrote to me inviting me to visit his retreat-center, Tabor Nagar, and to set up my *poustinia* there for as long as I wanted. As I prayed about it, the Lord gave me peace about taking up his suggestion. So, I could walk for another summer in Russia and in its former satellites in 1994, and then head for India in 1995.

One thing that took place in Vershina, though, before I set out on foot was that Fr. Voytek made a ten-minute video of me entitled, *How to Get to Jerusalem.*[50] He was a well-known video journalist in Poland and this documentary won a prize in the regional film festival there that same year. He filmed me in Vershina walking through a white birch forest, in my *poustinia,* repairing my sandals, reading my Bible, and sewing my robe, as well as sharing a meal with him in the schoolhouse. His most creative invention was a balance beam, with the video camera mounted on one end, and the operator on the other end. This made it possible to film someone walking in a circle at the end of the beam and talking into the camera, making it look as if the subject were walking along a straight road, with the cameraperson right next to them. He filmed me praying the Hail Mary in Russian, Polish, and English, because these were the languages used in the final three editions of the documentary. I was thankful to the Lord that He found a way to use my pilgrimage for a wider audience.

ENDNOTES

46. Catholic Commentary, *Anchorage Daily News,* April 30, 1993.

47. *The Dove.* Barbara A. Johnson, *Flowers from a Desert Garden* privately published, Anchorage, Alaska, 2017), 63.

48. *Resonare Christum.* Cardinal John J. Wright, *Resonare Christum,* vol. 2, *1959-1969 – The Pittsburgh Years,* prepared and edited by R. Stephen Almagno, OFM (San Francisco: Ignatius Press, 1988), 579. (The title *Resonare Christum* means "to echo Christ" and was taken from Cardinal Wright's coat of arms.)

49. Ibid., 333-34.

50. *Videojournal: The Catholic Church in Siberia,* Number One: "How to Get to Jerusalem," by Fr. Wojciech Drozdowicz, CKT (Siberian Catholic Television), October 4, 1994.

PART THREE

CENTRAL ASIA (1994-95)

PILGRIMAGE 1994

On Monday, April 18, I set out from Vershina to begin "Pilgrimage 1994." Eighteen people from the village attended the 8:00 a.m. Mass of the Holy Spirit in St. Stanislaus Church and then walked with me the first mile to the edge of their village, singing and praying the Rosary. It was a warm sunny day with temperatures in the high fifties. My intention was to head for Krasnoyarsk by way of Irkutsk, and then to continue on to Novosibirsk. This city, in addition to being the unofficial capital of Siberia and seat of the Catholic Bishop, was also the third largest city in the country, following Moscow and St. Petersburg. From there, I planned to go south through Kazakhstan, toward Afghanistan. It was a bit ambitious and I ended up stopping short of my final goal and rerouting my journey to India through China. Nevertheless, it was a summer of wonderful witnessing to the power and presence of the Lord Jesus in the Asian part of "Holy Mother" Russia.

It took me eight days to get to Irkutsk and then thirty-five more days to get to Krasnoyarsk. There was still some freezing rain, snow flurries, and thunderstorms these days, so I often walked with gloves on and the hood on my robe up all day. It was Orthodox Easter on May 1, so I was getting many greetings of "Christos voskrese!" (Christ is risen!), plus hard-boiled eggs and Pascha bread.

KRASNOYARSK AND FR. CISZEK

The Lord gave me four wonderful days in Krasnoyarsk. It was the time of the year when the cherry blossoms were in full bloom along the streets. It was like a white carpet of flower petals laid out upon my arrival.

I was especially interested in touching base with the memory of Fr. Walter Ciszek, SJ[51]. Fr. Ciszek was an important brother-in-Christ for me, first of all because he was born and raised in Pennsylvania, but most of all because of the spiritual wisdom he gained through his painful years in Russia. What impressed me most, was that he went to Russia intending to do great things for the Lord as a missionary. Ultimately, however, the Lord showed him how much work needed to be done on his heart before becoming a truly useful instrument in His hands. I appreciated being able to benefit from his wonderful spirit that was available through reading his two books.

BACK ON THE ROAD

When I left Krasnoyarsk on June 2, I was headed to Novosibirsk. It was a distance of about 500 miles and it would take me twenty-five days to walk. Now the weather turned hot; by the second week of June it was in the nineties and that would last until the middle of August, when I would again be wearing gloves, a hooded sweatshirt under my robe, and would keep the hood on my robe up. But the evening of June 12, ten days out of Krasnoyarsk, stays in my mind to the present day.

By hindsight, I see that I pitched my tent too close to a village. I was discovered about 11:00 p.m. by a group of young people who were high on drugs and who tried to get me to come and party with them. They built a big bonfire just a few feet from my tent, unzipped my tent screen, and reached in to see what they could steal. When I pushed one of them away, I got a fist right in my mouth. I thought my journey might end right here. But after that they gave up, put out the fire, and left. Word must have spread through the village about what happened, for on the next morning I was greeted by some older men with warm milk, brought as "a peace offering." The main damage I had experienced was a hole that had been burned in my tent screen from a lit cigarette–and a swollen lip from the punch. I thanked the Lord that I had not lost some front teeth or been handed something even worse. Still, I rejoiced to be able to suffer in the name of the Lord (Mt 5:11-12).

DELAYED IN NOVOSIBIRSK

On June 27, I arrived in the large city of Novosibirsk and was directed to the German Franciscans at Immaculate Conception of the Virgin Mary Catholic Church, on the west side of the Ob River. That became my home base for the next seventeen days, as the Lord stopped me here for that length of time. The main reason for such a long stay was to get treatment for the sore on my head, plus a four-day delay at the passport office. I stayed in a hospital and was under the care of the head of the clinical Lymphology Department. Dr. Wadim scraped the sore and packed it with black crystals every day. He also ordered urine, blood, and stool tests and X-rays. The tests all came back negative; the wound was actually reduced in size by the time I left. But in two weeks it was back to its ugly self. I would have to live with it for another year before the Lord would provide a final solution.

A FALSE RUMOR

Nevertheless, this affair turned out to be more trouble than it was worth.

While I was in Novosibirsk, a translator and I spent about an hour with Bishop Werth, the Roman Catholic Bishop of all Siberia at the time. It seems that later that summer the bishop traveled to Europe to meet with the organization, Aid to the Church in Need and gave a talk in which he happened to mention this pilgrim who had stopped to see him. He must have said something like this: "Pilgrim George has so much trust in God that even if he were to find out he had a brain tumor, he would not be disturbed but would continue to walk in faith." The secretary heard that and wrote in her notes on the meeting, "Msgr. Werth also told us that the doctors had found out that George Walter was suffering from a brain tumor and that it was rather serious."

A copy of these minutes were sent to friends of mine in Monterey, California, on November 23, 1994, and they passed these on to my mother. She, of course, was alarmed and so wrote to me asking if it was true. I had the lab reports in Russian from Dr. Wadim sent to friends for translation and for interpretation, and nothing alarming appeared in them. It was many months before this whole situation was cleared up. In the meantime, it showed how easily false rumors can start and spread–and one more area in which all had to trust in the Lord and to leave everything in His caring hands. At least it probably gained me greater prayer support.

VISA EXTENSION

Before leaving Novosibirsk, one of my final tasks was to have my Russian visa extended. The visa office had my passport for four days and finally returned it saying it could not be extended any longer. I would have to go back to Magadan and get a new one. Since that was out of the question, I would have to take my chances. The visa I had in hand was good until July 21. I would not get out of Russia into Kazakhstan until August 1. So it was possible that I would have overstayed my visa by ten days. The normal penalty for such an infraction is a fine of $50 a day. I had to trust the Lord in this matter, too.

When I arrived at the border of Kazakhstan I just walked through the gates and no one asked me any questions. Although Kazakhstan had been an independent republic for three years now, their infrastructure had not yet caught up. Thus, like the other Central Asian republics, they were not yet able to develop a diplomatic corps or to set up embassies in the main cities of the world. So when the police stopped me and asked for identification, I showed them my expired Russian visa and that was OK with them. When I got to Alma Ata, in a month or so, I could register with the police and get a new visa. I thanked the Lord for taking care of this little item for me.

REPUBLIC OF KAZAKHSTAN

Kazakhstan was a new country for me. Though officially and politically it became its own republic, entirely separated from Soviet Russia in 1991, those of us "on the ground" (like me), could hardly tell the difference. Russian was the language spoken and half of the population considered themselves ethnic Russians. I initially had no plans of remaining in Kazakhstan, but ultimately, the Lord showed me that I was to stay the winter in Alma Ata, then the capital of Kazakhstan.

One of the first places I discovered in Kazakhstan was the city of Semipalatinsk (since 2007, Semey). This was one of the "closed cities" (until 1990) in the Soviet era that no one could enter or leave without an official pass, and was not even shown on maps. It was also one of the Soviet's nuclear test sites, and continues to be highly contaminated causing many health problems (cancer, genetic defects, infertility, leukemia, depression, etc.) among the poor people who have no choice but to live here. During the months I was here (1994-95) Kazakhstan decided to be a nuclear free nation. It was working with the United States to remove all nuclear warheads and uranium-enriched material from the Polygon test site next to Semipalatinsk.

So, my prayers were going up for these poor people who had to suffer from the evil decisions of scientific, military, and political forces over which they had no control. It was one more example of how fallen humanity continually finds its way into destructive dead-ends. One more proof that without God's grace and love, we have no future.

A BANDIT IN DISGUISE

The road signs now were in three languages, Russian, Kazakh, and English. I began seeing the quaint Muslim cemeteries that looked like miniature walled cites with towers, domes, and pyramids as tombs.[52] The fruit and vegetable harvest was coming in so I was given many tomatoes, apples, and watermelons. For many days I had diarrhea. I thought maybe it was because I was eating so much unwashed or unpeeled fruits. Looking back at it now, however, I see my system may have been reacting to the radiation picked up in the region's agricultural fields.

The hospitality continued to be abundant, as was often the case on this pilgrimage, I had to refuse food offered me, as I had more than I needed. But on August 19, I accepted gifts of food and supplies from a young couple in a car who told me this most interesting story. Having driven past me they debated with each other about whether or not they should stop and offer help.

"Maybe he is a bandit and he will rob us of everything we have."

But they turned around and drove past me going the other way.

When they saw me this time they reflected, "A bandit would not be carrying a cross and a Bible. It is probably safe to stop," which they did, having turned around a second time. After they talked with me for a few minutes, they could not do enough for me. They rooted through everything in their car, giving me one thing after another. After they left I had to chuckle to myself, "I was a bandit to them; I took almost everything they had." But then Jesus was a "bandit," too; He who stole our hearts and gave them to the Father.

PROVISIONED IN ALMA ATA

On September 1, I walked into the large city of Alma Ata (now known as Almaty) tucked into the southeastern corner of Kazakhstan on the north side of the Tien Shan mountain range that bordered China. I had not originally planned to stop here, but intended to press on to Afghanistan. But after such a long delay in Novosibirsk and hearing of the political disturbances in Afghanistan, I began to wonder if the Lord was indicating that I should winter over here and then pick up the Trunk Road to India in Islamabad, Pakistan, in the spring, rather than in Kabul, Afghanistan. I had the address of the Catholic Church in Alma Ata, so I thought I should at least look it up. If God provided a place for me here for the winter, I would end "Pilgrimage 1994" a few weeks earlier than originally planned. But the Catholic Church was on a tiny obscure street and no one I asked seem to know where it was.

I was standing at a major intersection in the city center wondering what to do, when a young man by the name of Victor came up to me and said in good English, "Can I help you?" When I explained what I was looking for he said, "I do not know where the Catholic Church is or where this street address is, but I have an Orthodox friend who will know. Can you walk with me a few blocks to my bank building [which he owned] where I can call him on the telephone?" Of course I readily agreed.

Victor wrote out the directions for me and before I set out he said, "If they do not have a place for you to stay at the church, I can clear out a storeroom in my building here where you can set up your winter *poustinia*." I thanked him for his kind offer and set out to find Holy Trinity Catholic Church, on Esibulatova Street. After a two-hour walk I finally arrived and was pleasantly surprised to find out that one of the priests there was none other than Fr. Henry Howaniec, OFM.[53] He had been my contact person with Fr. Arcadius, the pilgrim Franciscan priest with whom I kept in touch by mail. He said they did not even have enough room for their own priests, so it looked like the Lord would have me stay at Victor's bank on Seyfullin Street in central Alma Ata.

GETTING INTO THE CHURCH

It became clear as the weeks and months of my winter stay unfolded, that this was no accident or merely an unfortunate development, but was rather part of the Lord's overall plan. Victor, his circle of friends, and six office employees soon all became interested in becoming more familiar with the Catholic Church. Since my Russian was so limited, I could not personally instruct them adequately in the mysteries of the faith. So ten of them decided to begin going to the Catholic Church and took instructions in the faith there. By Easter all of them had become Catholic. I thanked the Lord that, while Victor was able to show me how to get *to* the church, I was able to show him how to get *into* the church.

LOOKING TOWARD INDIA

Very quickly I set up my routine when in *poustinia* mode. Five days a week I walked the two hours to the church for morning Mass and breakfast, and then walked back to my *poustinia*. The other two days (Wednesday and Friday) I stayed in my *poustinia* for prayer and fasting. I also continued the practice of reading the whole Bible through from cover to cover in seven months by reading nine chapters of the Old Testament and two chapters of the New Testament each day. I also worked on laying out a walking route to India for the next summer by consulting maps and going to the embassies of India, Pakistan, and China to apply for visas. Eventually I was able to get a seven-day transit visa for China for $40. However, they warned me, "No evangelizing while there." A two-month visa for Pakistan for $22 was readily granted because, at that time, Pakistan loved the United States because we were giving them arms in their fight against India. The six-month visa for India was the most difficult to get and eventually took six months.

One thing puzzled me about the route I had laid out from Kazakhstan through Kyrgyzstan and a corner of China into Pakistan. As I studied the maps I found what seemed to be a road through the Tien Shan Mountains from Kyrgyzstan into China over what was called "The Torugart Pass." The only problem was that the details on my maps ended as they approached that fortieth degree of latitude, both from the north and from the south. It was as though this area was still uncharted. I would not find out why this was so until I arrived there in May of 1995.

WINTER BLESSINGS

One of the blessings I received this winter was meeting more American and English speakers who attended the Catholic Church in Alma Ata (the services in the church were in English).

Other special blessings during this winter layover included reading about John de Plano Carpini (1182-1253) and William of Rubruk (1220-93), two Franciscan missionaries in the thirteenth century who answered the call of Pope Innocent IV to evangelize the vast Mongol or Tartar Empire in 1245.[54] During that time, I also visited the hermitage and gravesite of two local Orthodox hermits-martyrs, Seraphim and Theognost. In 1921, they were shot in cold blood by Red Army soldiers in their remote hermitage in Aksai Gorge, outside of Alma Ata.[55]

And the final blessing was a visit from my dear friend Valeri from Anchorage, who was now in Russia as a lay helper at the Catholic Church in Vladivostok in the Russian Far East.[56] She had been inspired to come to Russia after listening to the tapes of my walk through Siberia. Valeri came to Alma Ata for Holy Week services and remained until Mercy Sunday when she and I carried a six-foot high banner of the Divine Mercy Image of Jesus through the streets of the city to the Holy Trinity Catholic Church. She also walked with me on April 25, the first day of "Pilgrimage 1995." We set out from the Catholic Church accompanied by three church members for the first 18 miles of my pilgrimage to India.

MANY UNKNOWNS

At this point in my journey I was really walking in "dark" faith. There were many unknowns ahead. First of all, my Kazakhstan visa would expire in five days; could I make the 90 miles to the border before then, or should I take one of the many rides offered? I chose to only walk the 18 miles a day needed and arrived at the border at noon on April 30. There was no customs station here, just a police car parked off the side of the road and he did not stop me; the first hurdle was passed.

Now I was in Kyrgyzstan without a visa. Officially, I was supposed to go to the capital city of Bishkek and to get a tourist visa, but that was four days out of the way and I had to use my seven-day China visa before the narrow window on that time frame closed. So, I decided I would show up at the Kyrgyzstan-China border with nothing but an expired Kazakhstan visa. At this point, my question was," Would they let me through or make me go back to Bishkek and get a proper visa?"

On my third day in Kyrgyzstan I received intimations of additional difficulties ahead. Around 3:00 p.m., a devout Russian Orthodox middle-aged couple offered me a ride to their home and something to eat. They said I was now walking toward some wild and desolate country; they were concerned as to the kind of reception I might receive.

PAYOFFS IN THE NIGHT

On my fourth day in Kyrgyzstan I was given a ride to the road that headed toward the border. But this road had no villages, houses, or even road signs on it. When a friendly group of visitors stopped and talked to me about my plans, they said I better get in and ride with them until we got to the next highway patrol check point. There they had the police fix me up with a ride in the cab of a truck that was part of a convoy of fifteen tractor trailers headed to China.

This was a godsend, for the last 140 miles to the Chinese border was an untamed, lawless, no-man's-land. All night long, as we bumped along on a narrow, dirt road, we were stopped by temporary roadblocks. When we stopped, men with rifles appeared at the windows of the cab, demanding to see our passports and that we explain what we were doing. The driver would reach for his roll of $100 bills, peel off a few, and hand them over to the leader of the gang. That would satisfy them and they would back off and remove the roadblock. I thanked the Lord for saving me from having to travel this area alone on foot.

BORDER STATION CLOSED

When we arrived at the border at 6:00 a.m. on Friday, May 5, we learned it was closed until Monday morning. This was a treeless, uninhabited part of God's creation. There were no stores, houses, or anything like civilization. Dozens of large trucks were all parked in the waiting line, but they had come prepared for such an eventuality. They all had brought along food, water, and extra cans of diesel fuel to keep their motors running. This allowed them to heat their cabs where they could sleep at night. I, myself, found a bit of bare ground free of snow and set up my tent. With my down sleeping bag I had a good sleep in spite of below freezing temperatures.

The next morning I walked up to the customs office to see if I could go through on foot. Thankfully, they did not insist I go back to Bishkek and get a visa for Kyrgyzstan, but put the exit stamp on the expired Kazakhstan visa, and let me through. After a 6-mile climb to the top of the mountain, I arrived at Chinese customs. Then, after a half hour wait, I was given a little piece of paper to surrender at the next checkpoint, 3 miles down the hill.

MANAGING IN CHINA

Now I was in a vast, new country about which I knew very little and whose language was totally foreign to me. I had seven days to cover the 300 miles that lay between me and the border with Pakistan, at the Kungerab Pass. I knew I had to go straight south to get to the first major city in China, Kashgar. There I could pick up the Karakoram Highway that I could take west into Pakistan. But all of the signs were in Chinese and I had no way of knowing which sign meant Kashgar. Therefore, on the second day of walking in China, I took one of the many rides offered and rode into the historic city of Kashgar, made famous during the days of Marco Polo and the Silk Road joining East and West.

Kashgar was a bustling, vibrant city, seemingly with more bicycles than cars. Steady streams of women in ankle length, flower print dresses, pedaled along the streets on simple bicycles. The markets were filled with all kinds of consumer goods from plastic washbasins to computers, and there seemed to be a goodly number of tourists mixing in with the locals. I had only one goal in mind: to inquire as to whether I could get a bus to Kungerab Pass, 200 miles to the west. I was directed to the Qiniwake Hotel where I was told that every morning a bus left from that hotel and I could purchase a ticket on it for $32. Also, I could sleep in a dormitory bed at the hotel for $2 a night. So everything was well arranged for me very quickly.

KUNGERAB PASS

The next day I boarded one of two buses headed for Pakistan. The highway we traveled, only opened in 1986, and snow kept it impassable until May 1 every year. Even at that, it was full of deep ruts from melting snow and we often had to get out and fill the holes with rocks so that the bus could continue on its way. It took us two days to go the 200 miles to Pakistan.

I tried unsuccessfully to get the driver to leave me off at the top of the pass (14,928 feet) so I could begin my walk. Security was tight in this area and the bus driver said he had to deliver all of his listed passengers to Sust, 6 miles into Pakistan. Nevertheless, since the Kungerab Pass was "the highest international crossing place in the world" and was called "The Roof of the World," I prayed the Divine Mercy Chaplet as we crossed over the pass in the bus and asked for God's mercy on the whole world stretched out beneath this magnificent natural roof.

ADJUSTING TO PAKISTAN

I was glad to be back on my feet and in walking mode again. But I had no idea what kind of reception I would receive as a Christian in this frontier province of "The Islamic Republic of Pakistan," as it said across the top of my two- month visa. The local language was Urdu, but because of the British having been here, most spoke English. Both men and women wore the traditional, two piece, *pajama* outfit and most of the women wore veils over their faces. It took three weeks before the first Pakistani woman (without a veil) broke Islamic law and spoke to me on her own initiative. I now had a journey of 400 miles ahead of me to make it to the capitol city of Islamabad in twenty-two days, allowing me to celebrate Pentecost with Catholic brothers and sisters. In these three weeks of traveling alone on foot, I had some of my closest calls with physical harm. Not only did the children–who did not go to school and who ran wild in street gangs–throw dust, stones, and sticks at me, they also tried to steal whatever they could get their hands on in my pack.

On May 24, the Vigil of Ascension Thursday, I thought it might be all over for me.

It was near midnight and I was in my tent camped in a grove of fruit trees. It was pitch- black (my flashlight had been stolen earlier in the day) and it had been raining hard for several hours. Then I heard these large stones raining down around my tent. Finally a gunshot rang out very close by. I grabbed my crucifix, Rosary, and holy water and said my Act of Contrition to prepare for the worst. Nevertheless, I was spared once again by the grace of God to continue lifting up Jesus in Asia.

TWO WEEKS IN ISLAMABAD

On June 1, I finally arrived in Islamabad after taking a few wrong roads due to poor directions. I had written ahead to the priest at Fatima Catholic Church, so he was expecting me. He greeted me with six pieces of mail and showed me to a private room where I could stay in the rectory. I hoped to be here only a few days, just long enough to pick up my visa for India and to consult with the dermatologist about the sore on my head. But I ended up staying two weeks and left without my visa. But the Lord used my time wonderfully to build up the local Catholic and Christian communities here.

Christians in Islamabad were segregated from the majority Muslim population and were compelled to live in ghettos; they were euphemistically called "colonies." These were always the poorest areas because Christians could only get the lowest-paying jobs like street sweeping and housecleaning. But they were the most joyful and devout people because they had a deep relationship with Jesus and knew how to worship Him freely in spirit and in truth. I prayed over dozens of people, gave teachings, and was received as an honored brother in Christ. The Catholic priest did not know what to make of me, but when I returned two weeks later I noticed he had a change of heart.

One of the many graces the Lord gave me in this city was the healing I sought for the sore on my head, which had been open now for four years. I had been unsuccessfully treated for it in the hospital in Novosibirsk, by acupuncture in Almaty, and by a vodka and honeycomb home remedy in Siberia. Now I was led to Dr. Hamid, who had trained in England, and who spoke perfect English. He sat behind his desk and described my sore as "a pinkish, slightly ulcerated lesion" popularly called a "Baghdad boil." He prescribed Efudex cream (used for basal cell carcinoma) which I was able to purchase for $12 at a local pharmacy. After six weeks of treatment, it was completely healed and never returned, although it did leave a permanently visible indentation in my scalp–perhaps reminiscent of the scars Jesus had on His hands and feet after His resurrection. Finally, with much prayer and treatment, the Lord decided to deliver me from this bothersome affliction.

THE GREAT TRUNK ROAD

I left Islamabad on June 15, and set out to make for Lahore, which was 180 miles away, in twenty days, in sweltering heat. After two days I made the turn onto the old east/west British Trunk Road that went 2,000 miles from Kabul to Kulkotta (Calcutta). It was 115-120 degrees during the whole month of June. I could only walk 6 miles and then I would collapse under a tree for the rest of the day. One day in Gujranwala an Orthodox priest (and formerly a Roman Catholic) took pity on me seeing that I looked awfully tired, actually near exhaustion, and he invited me into his home for a rest. I thanked the

Lord for putting us together briefly to share our faith journeys in this land of exile.

On June 22, I got to the large and historic city of Lahore, just 20 miles from the border with India. I made my way to the border to see if I could get a visa for India there, but Pakistan customs would not allow me to leave their country without a visa for India. There was no vehicular traffic between these two countries; only people on foot could pass through and security was very tight. I only had sixteen more days left on my Pakistan visa. The questions were, "Would my visa for India be approved before my visa for Pakistan ran out?" "Should I inquire about flying out of the country?" In prayer the Lord seemed to be saying, "Be still and wait" (Ex 14:13-14).

ST. THOMAS THE APOSTLE

In the meantime I made my way back to Lahore to contact the Catholic community there. I found St. Anthony Catholic Church and began praying to St. Anthony for his help. The pastor was a leader in the Charismatic Renewal in the area, and the people opened their hearts and homes to me immediately. For the next ten days I kept calling the Indian Embassy in Islamabad and kept getting the same answer: "No word yet from Delhi; call back in a few days."

Finally on July 2, on my twelfth call to the Indian Embassy, the customs official said, "Your visa has been approved; come tomorrow and pick it up." Some brothers in Christ put me on one of the mini-buses (they called them "wagons") and in six hours I was back in Islamabad. Arriving at 7:00 a.m. I entered the embassy at 9:00 a.m. After paying another $70 in fees I was finally granted a visa that would be good for six months. The date was July 3. It was the Feast of St. Thomas the Apostle to India and Pakistan. It proved that St. Thomas still loved the people of these lands and he wanted the Cross of Jesus lifted up among them today.

THE PUNJAB

After praying with Fr. Johnny's sister, he put me on the bus heading back to Lahore. It was dark when I arrived, but Joseph and Elizabeth were waiting up for me and ready again to bless me with their hospitality. The next day I was put on a shuttle bus to the border town of Batapur, and from there I walked to the border for the second time in ten days.

After an hour and a half wait, plus a thorough search by Indian customs, my passport received an entry stamp and I was let through. I was now on my way to Delhi 300 miles away. By walking the whole way, this part of the journey took me nearly a month. The first area I walked through was called "The Punjab."[57] Though still extremely hot it was a pilgrim's paradise, for this was flat land and it had a high water table (around 30 feet), so there were hand pumps for freshwater alongside the road every kilometer or two, which I could use for drinking, bathing, or for washing clothes, as needed.

In this area I encountered the Sikhs.[58] I found them to be among the most hospitable people I have met. They told me, "You can eat and sleep at any of our prayer houses free anytime you want. One generous Sikh man invited me to stay at his home two nights to answer questions about God, to give a talk at their prayer house, and to walk in an all-day procession.

NEW DELHI

On July 27, I arrived in Delhi and went straight to the post office to get mail sent to me there in care of general delivery. There were twenty-three pieces of mail waiting for me. I was given hospitality by Archbishop Alan at Sacred Heart Cathedral, so I stayed for three nights to get cleaned up and to get some rest.

When I set out from New Delhi on July 30, I was headed straight south toward Bombay (now Mumbai) 1,000 miles away. This was a completely different kind of terrain. Instead of rich agricultural land, it was a desert and mountainous area called "Rajasthan." Now the monsoon season started, so I was now usually soaking wet not only from sweat but also from the torrential rains.

ROAD TO BOMBAY

During my fifty-seven days of travel en route to Bombay, I had several interesting encounters. I enjoyed a three-day layover and beautiful hospitality from the staff of St. Thomas Seminary in Jaipur for the Feast of the Assumption of the Blessed Mother on August 15. During that time, I also rode for 250 miles in a new Japanese Cielo, driven by a Muslim man who told me he never picks up strangers, yet felt led by God to offer me this ride. I also received the heartfelt service rendered by a small Catholic school community in the village of Dhabhan on August 22, the Feast of the Queenship of Mary. I was most grateful for the many gifts of tea made from buffalo milk, instead of water, and sweetened with lots of sugar. It is served in small, thick clear glass beakers, slightly larger than shot glasses.

My arrival in the outskirts of Bombay on September 10, was, sadly, an experience of filth and poverty that was far beyond anything I had ever experienced in my life. People were living on the edge of the road in flimsily constructed shelters made of wood scraps, tin, and cardboard. The stench was horrendous. People urinated and defecated anywhere they could find a place to squat and left it uncovered–like a human barnyard. Garbage was everywhere. Huge rats that resembled large fat cats scurried here and there. Dead animals, even those as large as buffaloes, were left to rot where they had died, even if in the middle of the road.

I asked to sleep that night at a Free Will Methodist Church. For my protection against nocturnal rodent investigators, they sprayed some liquid repellent around my sleeping bag which I had laid out on the floor of a stage in their church hall.

BOMBAY TO GOA

A Muslim man picked me up the next day and took me to the Salesian School of Don Bosco in Mumbai (Bombay) where I stayed in seclusion for three days. (The rector did not want me to talk to anyone else in the school but him because he did not want me disturbing the routine of the school.) Then I was on the road to Goa. The first 30 miles I took a bus to get out of the Bombay suburbs and then covered the last 270 miles by foot and by rides. My goal in Goa was to pray at the coffin of the incorrupt body of St. Francis Xavier, SJ (1506-52), the sixteenth-century Spanish Jesuit missionary to South India and Japan.

On September 25, between Bombay and Goa, the Lord encouraged me in a most unusual way. I took a short ride with a man who said to me as we drove along, "I also passed you yesterday on this road. Who was that little child who was walking alongside of you?" I said to him that I was not aware of anyone walking with me. But later as I prayed and reflected on his question more, I began to wonder if maybe it was not the Christ Child Himself. Maybe this was His way of giving me a sign of His constant protection at all times. The Lord may have allowed this man to perceive for a minute the spiritual world in which we live all the time, but which is unavailable to our normal physical senses. No matter what it was, I felt very encouraged by the whole incident.

GOA TO COCHIN

The Lord arranged that I could stay one night at the Jesuit Residence in Old Goa, so I got to spend twenty-four hours in and around the Bom Jesus Church where St. Francis's body lay in state. After an overnight stay with the hospitable Missionaries of Charity the next day, I was now on my way to Cochin. My priest-friend Fr. Augustine Pallikunnen (1935-2011) had invited me to set up my *poustinia* at his retreat center Tabor Nagar,[59] near Cochin. As I had written to him that I hoped to arrive around November 1, I had 500 miles to make in twenty-eight days. With a few more rides from some of the many Catholics in this area–especially in Kerala which is said to be 30 percent Catholic–I was able to arrive a few days early, on October 27.

Now I felt more at home as I saw Catholic churches, outdoor shrines with life-size statues of the Saints (especially St. Sebastian, St. Anthony of Padua, and St. George) and lorries with scenes of Christ's life painted on the backboards against their cabs. I also began to meet the St. Thomas Christians who traced their origin back to AD 52, when tradition says the Apostle Thomas came to evangelize this part of India. Most importantly, I was now able to attend Mass, either in the Roman Rite or in the Syro-Malabar Rite; in most cases they were in the vernacular Malayalam, the language of the southwest Indian people.

While I now experienced the Catholic fellowship I had been missing in northern India, I physically and emotionally sensed the journey was taking its toll on me. At times I felt as though I was close to almost losing touch with reality. When I look at a photo taken of me at the retreat center in November, my eyes look glassy and distant. I think the Lord allowed me to come very close to the end of my rope on this journey to let me experience how weak and frail I really was on my own; without Him, the journey could not continue.

A FAMILIAR FACE

On the morning of October 27, five days before I was due at Tabor Retreat Center, I was still about eighteen 18 miles from my goal. Then about 9:30 a.m. a Jeep pulled up beside me and out of it came my priest-friend Fr. Augustine.

When all one sees day after day, month after month, are unfamiliar faces, it is an indescribable relief and joy to behold the face and live presence of a familiar brother or sister in Christ. Fr. Augustine and his brother, Emmanuel, had driven a 150 miles from a point further south where they had been attending a Marian conference. When a call came from friends back at the center that the Pilgrim was sighted nearby, they immediately got in their Jeep and drove north. He wanted to be home when I arrived.

I agreed to ride with him the last 10 miles to the retreat center, but I was able to get him to let me walk the last few hundred feet, so as to experience this new reality at a human pace. A welcoming committee of men and women who spent the whole day Friday interceding before the Lord, came out to meet me. A large banner had been painted and strung across the road at the entrance-way. It said:

Cordial Welcome to
Bro. George Walter
Pilgrim from America
To Tabor Nagar, Ezhumuttom
Praise the Lord!

What a blessing to be embraced by the love, and taken into the hearts, of so many brothers and sisters in Christ! After a tour of the various chapels, prayers of thanksgiving, a lei of fresh flowers, and colorfully dyed paper ceremonially draped around my neck and after many pictures taken, I was shown to the room that had been prepared for my *poustinia*. It had a bed, desk, chair, closet, sink, toilet, shower, running water, electricity, and ceiling fan. All of my physical needs would be amply provided for in the coming weeks. Thanks be to God!

END OF THE ROAD

Now the question was, how long would the Pilgrim stay here before he moved on toward Jerusalem? In the first talk I gave to the group of several hundred who gathered for prayer all day on Saturday, I said, "I do not know if the Lord will have me stay here two months or two years." It all depended on whether or not I could extend my visa for India, for my present visa ran out on January 3, 1996. For the next few weeks, Fr. Augustine tried every way possible to get my visa extended, but he was unable to do it. I would have to do what all other visitors to India had to do: leave India and apply for a new six-month visa from another country.

After much prayer I felt that the Lord did not want me to fly out and back, but rather to continue my journey on foot from another country. But which one? So I would have to approach the Holy Land from the west again. As an American I did not need a visa for Italy–my passport was enough. From there I could either go across North Africa or through the Balkans to Jerusalem. So Fr. Augustine got me a ticket for December 28, to fly out of Trivandrum to Sri Lanka and then on to Rome.

TWO-MONTH STAY

Still I had two whole months (November and December) to pray, rest, read, write, visit, and give talks to various groups. I found it fascinating to read about the history of the Catholic Church in this area from the time of the Apostles in the first century, through the Syrian influence in the fourth and fifth centuries, to the coming of the Portuguese and St. Francis Xavier in the sixteenth century. I also greatly appreciated the opportunity to more closely examine the Syro-Malabar rite of the Mass, which they called the "Holy Qurbana" (meaning offering, or sacrifice). It is a use of the Chaldean (or Assyrian) tradition, resembling other Eastern liturgies, like the Byzantine and Antiochian, rather than the Western Roman Mass.

As usual, when I am stopped for a period of time, I try to type up my daily log, as well as to catch up on correspondence. I not only wrote letters to the dozens of people who had written to me in India, I also wrote an article for the Catholic Charismatic renewal magazine in Poland, *List* (Dispatch). Their readers had been following my journey since Vershina, Siberia, in 1993-94. I also got to celebrate Christmas with my brothers and sisters in India and to note their particular traditions minus any thought of snow, seeing that it never got below 80 degrees in December here, 10 degrees above the equator.

During this pause, the Lord also refurbished my pilgrim robe and staff. Waiting for me when I arrived at the retreat center, was a new robe made of denim. My old one was literally falling apart at the seams from always being wet. I could not keep up with sewing new patches. I had sent the dimensions to my aunt Celine in the United States, as she was a good seamstress and had offered to make me a new robe. It was not made from patches like my old robe, but of a new, lightweight denim material. Fr. Augustine had his carpenter make me a new staff to replace the broken and patched one with which I arrived. It was made from teak wood with inlaid ivory crosses and had the three-lobed Syrian and St. Thomas Cross on the top, plus a dove. The Lord was reequipping me for the journey ahead.

And so my "Pilgrimage in Asia" was coming to a close and I prepared to seek the path on which the Lord was directing me next.[60]

THE PRAYER OF MY HEART

Lord, God, Father Almighty,

You have brought me this far

in my journey to the Jubilee 2000

celebration of Your Son's birth in Bethlehem.

Trusting in Your Holy Spirit,

I have experienced Your

care, protection and guidance,

in so many marvelous ways in these past three years.

I ask You to nourish the seeds

You planted along my walk of faith in Asia.

May each person touched by this journey

receive the grace to say yes

to Your will for their lives,

doing the next right thing that will

glorify You and further their salvation.

May we all one day meet again

in Your presence as promised to us by

Our Lord and Savior Jesus Christ.

Amen.

ENDNOTES

51. Servant of God Walter Ciszek, S.J. (1904-84) was a Polish-American Jesuit missionary priest to Russia, who spent twenty-three years in Soviet prisons and in labor camps, and was under house arrest in Siberia. In 1963, he was repatriated back to the United States. He wrote two books about his experiences in Russia: *With God in Russia* (New York: America Press, 1964); and *He Leadeth Me*, (New York: Doubleday Image Books, 1975). In 2016, *With God in America* (Chicago: Loyola Press, 2016), about his final twenty-one years in the United States, was published posthumously.

52. Kazakhs. The majority of the Kazakhs today are Muslim since their ancestors converted to Islam during the Arab conquest of Central Asia in the eighth and ninth centuries.

53. Fr. Henry Theophilus Howaniec, O.F.M., an American of Polish stock, was born in 1931. He was made the Apostolic Administrator for the Roman Catholic Church in Almaty, Kazakhstan, on July 7, 1999; he was consecrated a bishop November 26, 2000; and he was appointed a Bishop for the Roman Catholic Diocese of Most Holy Trinity in Almaty, Kazakhstan, when the administration was raised to the level of a diocese on May 17, 2003. He retired on March 5, 2011.

54. Franciscan missionaries. See John Laux, *Church History* (Milwaukee: Benzinger, 1930), 402-3.

55. See "documents" at <metropolia.kz.vu/info/svyt/1571-sf-moshi.html>.

56. For more information on Mary Mother of God Church in Vladivostok, see <vladmission.org>. Valerie eventually went to Poland to join The Sisters of Merciful Jesus founded by St. Faustina Kowalska's spiritual director, Fr. Sopocko. Becoming Sr. Mary Rose of the Pierced Heart of Jesus, ZSJM, she took her perpetual vows in Vilnius, in 2004.

57. The Punjab. See the appendix for a poem I wrote entitled, "The Punjab in July."

58. Sikhism, a monotheistic religion distinct from both Islam and Hinduism, was founded in this region around the year 1500. The Sikhs form up to 30 percent of the local population of the Punjab.

59. Tabor Nagar. See <www.taborretreatcentre.org>.

60. See Appendix for my reflections on my experience in India. It is called "India – as seen through the eyes of a Western observer."

1 "Hermitage of the Cross" in old pump house at St. Mary's, July 1974.

2 Tomb of St. Francis, Assisi, Italy, March 1975.

3 Embroidered jean cap, 1976.

4 With Fr. Augustine Pallikunnen at St. Mary's Prayer Group, March 1980.

5 Teen pilgrimage, August 1981.

1   Via Dolorosa, Jerusalem, Israel, 1982.

2   Walk with little mule (Unita) to Shrine of Our Lady of Guadalupe, Mexico, 1988

3   Walking in Mexico, 1989.

4   Crossroads Mall, Carmel, California, 1990.

5   "Clip Flashlight" lightweight backpacker's tent I was given in 1992.

1   With Lee Leinen at Anchorage airport for flight to Siberia, 1993.

2   Winter of 1994 in Vershinna, Siberia.

3   Tabor Nagar Prayer Group, Kerala, India, December, 1995.

4   Meeting Pope John Paul II, Rome Italy, January, 1996.

5   John Connelly and his daughter, Audree, outside Vatican, February, 1996.

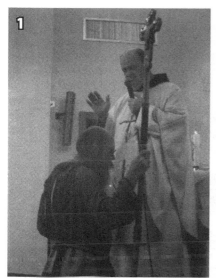

1   Fr. Philip Pavich, OFM, Medjugorje,
    Bosnia-Herzegovina, May 1996.

2   Jadwiga Dombrowska, Laski Institute for
    the Blind, Poland, 1996.

3   Jacob's Ladwder Stabbur, Ron, Norway,
    1997.

4   Motala, Sweden, 1998.

5   Ostra Brama/Divine Mercy, Vilnius,
    Lithuania, 1998.

1   Mount of Olives/Jerusalem, 1999.

2   Fr. Arcadius Smolinski, OFM, (1921-2005), pilgrim.

3   Latin altars on Calvary in the Church of the Holy Sepulcher in Jerusalem.

4   Star over the place where tradition says Jesus was born in Bethlehem.

5   Forty three-ring binders documenting my life from 1941 to present.

CHAPTER 5

PILGRIMAGE IN
EUROPE (1996-98)

EUROPE & THE NEAR EAST

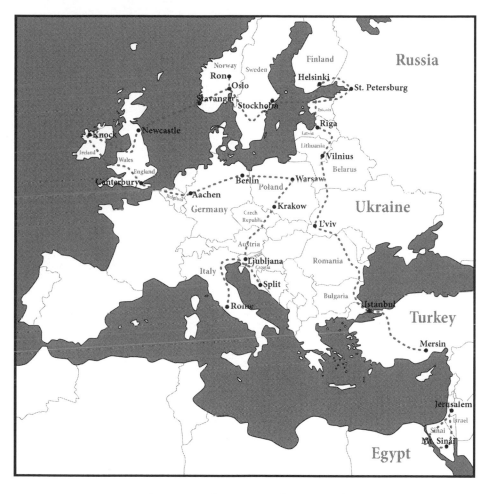

Rome, Italy to Jerusalem, Israel

December 29, 1995 to January 18. 2001

Six Years - 7,745 Miles

PART ONE

ROME TO WARSAW (1996)

PICKED UP

The first of January 1996, was fast approaching and I was nearing the end of my six-month visa for India. After prayer with Fr. Augustine on Wednesday, December 27, I was escorted by two brothers, first by Jeep to Thodupuzha, and then by all-night bus to Trivandrum. I would not be flying directly from India to Rome, but I flew south to the little island of Sri Lanka. On Friday, December 29, I went to the airport and amazingly received permission from the pilot to take my new teak wood staff on the plane.

From the airport in Columbo, Sri Lanka, I flew on Airlanka to Zurich and after a two-hour layover there, on to Rome's Fiumicino Airport, arriving at 10:00 p.m. I took a train into Rome and pitched my tent in the grassy "moat" of the San Angelo Castle. I knew it was not the safest place (later I heard the Mafia had murdered three Swiss campers there a few weeks before) but it was late and I did not want to be on the streets of Rome. St. Michael would have to protect me. Now at last I had my feet on the ground again on a new continent and was back to poverty mode, trusting in the Lord in a foreign land.

The next few days I began asking around about a place to stay. I checked hotels, monasteries, convents, seminaries, and colleges. I received the same answer Joseph and Mary received in Bethlehem–"No room." It was not until January 7, that some dear Franciscan sisters put up a bed for me in their parlor where I could sleep–if I got in before the gate locked each night at 6:00 p.m.

PLANING THE ROUTE

My main purpose in Rome was to seek the Lord's will concerning my journey to Bethlehem for the Jubilee Year 2000. I checked with the White Fathers who have missions in Africa but they said wars and political turmoil in Libya and Algeria would make that route across North Africa very difficult. So I began looking at a route around the Adriatic Sea by way of northern Italy, Croatia, Albania, and the Balkans into Turkey. The advantage of that route would allow me to visit Medjugorje where it was claimed the Mother of God had been appearing since 1981. That would certainly make a worthy destination for a pilgrim. So when should I leave Rome? Being that I had a three-month visa for Italy, I could stay six weeks in Rome, walk north, and be out of the country by the end of March. That would enable me to experience some of the holy sites in this historic city and country of my Catholic Faith.

MEETING THE POPE

I felt strongly that the Lord wanted me to meet Pope John Paul II and to let him know I had read his instructions on celebrating the Jubilee Year 2000, taking literally his suggestion to walk in the footsteps of the prophets and apostles of the Old and New Testaments. Those who lived in Rome said my chances were slim, as not even every bishop gets a chance to meet the Pope personally. Nevertheless, I wrote my letter, enclosed a copy of Bishop Bosco's letter to Canadian immigration in 1992, and sent it to the appropriate Vatican prefecture. Two weeks later word arrived that I had a spot with forty other people in the front row of the Paul VI Audience Hall during the general public audience on Wednesday, January 17, at 10:00 a.m. Each one of us in that row would get a chance after the audience, to go up one by one to speak with the Holy Father and to receive his blessing.

The security guards would not allow me to take my staff with me–it could be used as a lethal weapon–but they permitted me to take the San Damiano Cross off of it so I could hold it on my Bible to have it blessed by Pope John Paul II. I noticed there were two photographers, one on each side of the Pope, taking pictures of each person as they greeted John Paul II.

When it was my turn I knelt down on one knee and kissed John Paul II's ring. However, neither of the photographers who tried to sell me their photos later in the day, offered me any shot of that, but only of shaking his hand and receiving a blessing. I told him that I was walking to the Holy Land for the Jubilee Year 2000 and he said, "God bless you," raising his right hand and making the sign of the cross over me. That was all I needed. The grace of the Lord and the quiet assent of the Vicar of Christ on earth.

John Paul II had already written words that I could take as a guiding light: "On the way with Mary, to make the Gospel incarnate, along the roads of Europe." I would look for Marian shrines along the way, to direct my footsteps. The first after Rome would be Loretto (the Holy House of Nazareth) and then Medjugorje, Bosnia-Herzegovina. I decided to wait until after the Feast of Our Lady of Lourdes on February 11, and then set out from Rome after that.

PLACES OF PRAYER

During the remaining days in the Eternal City I set up a routine of prayer. First I would go to the 7:00 a.m. Mass in the crypt of St.

Peter's Basilica, beside the recently identified earthly remains of St. Peter, buried in the *scavi* (excavation site) under the main altar. The adoration chapel in the Basilica was open from 9:00 a.m. to 4:30 p.m. so I could spend time there. At 5:00 p.m. each day, the final Mass in the Basilica was celebrated before the Holy Spirit window, at the extreme far end from the entrance. When possible I tried to be present for this final prayer of the day, because then the Basilica was locked up for the night.

Then I would go out into the plaza alone and take up a position where I could see the basilica, the obelisk, and the icon of the Mother of God, while I prayed a Rosary. To me, this exemplified the three basic elements of my Catholic Faith: Jesus was represented by the relic of the true Cross on top of the obelisk; Mary was represented by the mosaic of Mary, Mother of the Church, lit up at night on the outside wall of the papal apartments; and St. Peter was represented by the basilica built over his tomb.

I did visit a few other places in and around the city including St. Susanna's, the English-speaking parish in the city; St. Callixtus's Catacomb where I served a Mass for a monsignor from New Orleans; Boys Town of Italy where I had lunch with the founder, Msgr. John Patrick Carroll-Abbing; the Church of St. Alphonsus Liguori which housed the original image of our Lady of Perpetual Help; and San Silvestro's which had a Charismatic prayer group meeting on Wednesday nights. And it was amazing how many people I ran into in Rome who knew me from other parts of the world: a priest from Pittsburgh; a priest from Mother Theresa's Seminary in Tijuana; a couple from Anchorage; staff members from Madonna House, Combermere; and even a businessman from my home parish of St. Mary's, Glenshaw. I also faced some difficulties while in Rome, which included being thrown out of St. Peter's for praying with two young fellows who came up to me; and being forbidden by the Swiss Guards from entering Vatican property. But I knew Jesus did not promise an easy path here on earth–just rest in heaven, so I accepted these trials as part of being one of His disciples.

"PILGRIMAGE 1996"

Come February 12, I left Rome and headed north toward Assisi. My plan was to walk to Croatia, visit Medjugorje on my way south to Albania, and then on to the Holy Land. Assisi was my favorite city in the whole world, so I felt that I should make at least a two-day stop there in honor of my hero, St. Francis. From Assisi I continued north toward Forli where I wanted to honor St. Pelligrino Laziosi (1265-1345) because his name *pelligrino* meant "pilgrim." I encountered rain, snow, and cold throughout February and March, especially crossing the Apennines. But the Lord got me through with a lot of help from the local people.

I was shown generous hospitality by a young Italian couple in Aquilea, a famous city from Roman times, legendarily evangelized by St. Mark and visited by St. Jerome. On St. Patrick's Day, I crossed briefly into Slovenia and then into Croatia, following the rugged coastal road[60] that gave me magnificent views of the Adriatic Sea. On the third day in Croatia a young priest invited me to speak at his high school, and I ended up sharing with six classes from 10:00 a.m. to 1:00 p.m. There was still evidence of the war all around, in bombed-out buildings and wrecked bridges.

My plan was to be in Split for the Paschal Triduum, which this year was April 4-6, Easter being April 7. By the grace of God I was able to arrive in Split on April 3. The following day, a young Croatian fellow found me a spare room near the Cathedral of St. Domnius where I could stay and even prepare meals. It worked out perfectly as I was handy to all the Holy Week services at the cathedral. This ancient church was built in the fourth century, originally as the personal mausoleum of the Roman emperor Diocletian, who so persecuted Christians. Talk about the Lord "turning the tables."

ON TO MEDJUGORJE

From Split it was just a six-day walk to St. James Church in Medjugorje. Many people stopped on this route to offer me help and to take pictures because a photo of me walking near Sibenik on Palm Sunday appeared in the *Free Dalmatia* newspaper on Wednesday, April 10. I ended up spending thirty-three days at the shrine, departing on May 16, Ascension Thursday. I participated in most of the services offered every day—Masses all morning in different languages and a three-hour prayer meeting with fifteen decade Rosary each evening from 6:00 p.m. to 9:00 p.m. During the afternoon, I would go to the Stations of the Cross on Mount Krizevac behind the church, go to confession, or pray at Apparition Hill. I came to the shrine believing completely in the apparitions, but before I left I came to seriously question their continuing authenticity. What changed my mind?

MANIPULATION

I noticed how the priests who staffed the shrine exercised control over the pilgrims, not allowing them to express their love and devotion in the spontaneous ways I observed at other Marian shrines around the world. For example, the priests had all the crosses placed by pilgrims on Apparition Hill collected and burned. The priests forbade pilgrims from leaving prayer lists or photographs at the cross on Krizevac Hill. Pilgrims were also not allowed to sing songs to Mary in church on their own after service times. While I did meet some wonderful people there from England, Poland, and the United States, with whom I formed ongoing friendships, it quickly became obvious to me that the Lord was not going to have me settle here for any protracted period of time.

There was one priest, however, Fr. Philip, who was assigned to the care of the English-speaking pilgrims who did value my witness and was a source of great encouragement for me. He celebrated the noon Mass in English on Ascension Thursday and he publicly prayed over me at the end of the Mass, to send me forth toward Jerusalem. A number of my good friends walked with me the first two hours and then returned to Medjugorje. One of those pilgrims would come up to me a year later in 1997 at the Marian Shrine in Knock, Ireland, saying: "Do you remember I walked with you the day you left Medjugorje?" The Lord does manage to connect the dots and occasionally gives us a view of the whole of what He is doing to show us we are on the right path.

CHANGE OF DIRECTION

When leaving Medjugorje my intention was to head for Dubrovnik, the ancient, picturesque, walled city on the coast of the Adriatic Sea, and then to go south toward Albania. As it turned out, I had only eight more days in Croatia and I had made a radical reorientation of my itinerary. I was no longer headed south but rather north, on a 3,000-mile detour of my journey to the Holy Land.

How did this happen? I arrived in Dubrovnik just fine and picked up seventeen pieces of mail waiting for me at the Atlas post office. But the next day on my way to the border of Monte Negro (which lay between Croatia and Albania) the police stopped me and said the border was closed due to political problems and military alerts. So I had to turn around and to go back to Dubrovnik. The police suggested I take a ferry from Dubrovnik to Albania.

NORTH TOWARD POLAND

With more prayer I felt perhaps the Lord was directing me to another route. Since I really still had three more years before the Jubilee Year 2000, I could visit more shrines in Europe and then head to the west coast of the Black Sea and enter Turkey that way. Besides, ever since Rome, the Lord had been putting on my heart the word "Czestochowa," and I did know people in Poland who had invited me to visit them. It looked like the Lord was directing my steps northward. So I got a bus in Dubrovnik that took me north to Rijeka, in northern Croatia. A man by the name of Andre who lived in Ljubljana, had given me his address and invited me to his home so I headed for the capitol of Slovenia as my next destination.

I arrived in Ljubljana on Monday, May 27, and reached Andre's apartment at 4:00 p.m. I was told there was a miraculous icon of Mary Help of Christians in Brezje just before the Austrian border that I should visit. So I was able to make that part of my way to the Jubilee Year 2000, with Mary. I was at this shrine just four hours but got to noon Mass, said the Rosary, and prayed a few hours before the image of Our Lady. The next day, May 31, I crossed into Austria with no problem at the border.

WALKING IN AUSTRIA

In Austria where flower boxes brightened the inhabited areas, I felt even more at home with the roots of my faith and family background. Here, German was the spoken language so I could use the little bit of that which I knew, and one day I was even able to pray the whole Rosary with a woman in German. Here, too, were displayed Saints who were very dear to me, like St. Christopher (patron of travelers on whose Feast Day, July 25, I was born), St. Roch (a popular pilgrim-Saint), and also St. Florian (patron of protection from fires), whose name I had for my middle name. I was in this country for Corpus Christi on June 6, this year and was able to participate in an outdoor procession as they blessed the fields and prayed at the outdoor temporary altars set up along the way.

On June 12, I came to the famous Marian Shrine of Mariazell. This shrine dated back to a monk's cell in 1157, and is said to be one of the most important pilgrimage destinations in Europe (currently drawing a million visitors a year). I was able to spend three hours in this basilica which was an interesting combination of Gothic and Baroque architecture. The statue of Mary with Jesus on her right hand, brought by the Benedictine hermit in 1157, although made of linden wood, is now very dark. All you can see are the faces of Mary and Jesus. The rest of their bodies are completely covered with rich robes. I noted the spot in the basilica where the brave, antifascist, anticommunist, Hungarian Joseph Cardinal Mindszenty's casket had rested from 1975 to 1991. And finally I took notice of a plaque on the wall indicating that another pilgrim, Pope John Paul II, had visited the shine in 1983. I felt very connected to Catholic Church history here.

THROUGH THE CZECH REPUBLIC

After Slovenia, my journey to Poland took me on an eleven-day walk through the Czech Republic. The ancient, historic city of Prague, with its hundreds of churches, was in the western end of the country, but I would only be passing through its eastern sector, going to Brno and Prerov. Still, the Lord arranged for several very personal encounters here.

The first occurred on a 10-mile detour I had to take on June 26. I was taking a rest stop sitting on a bench in front of a church in the little town of Brest, when this nearly bald man with white hair, came up to me with a pint of beer in his hand and said, "Welcome to Brest. Would you like to a have a glass of cold beer?"

"Sure."

"The mayor would like to invite you to her office just up the street. She can find someone who speaks English to translate for her."

So I ended up spending two hours sharing with Marie, the mayor, having a meal of pork, dumplings, and cabbage, visiting the church of St. James, and walking to the cemetery. I thought it was significant of their faith that they considered a visit to the cemetery–a remembrance of those who came before them–an important part of showing a visitor around their town.

The other personal encounter was also a total but most welcome surprise. On the second last day in the Czech Republic, coming out of Pribor, a man came up to me and exclaimed, "George. What are you doing walking in my home town?" I took a better look at him.

"Rudi!" I exclaimed, "I never expected to see you here. The last time I saw you was at a Sunday Mass at the Catholic Church in Alma Ata, Kazakhstan, the end of April a year ago."

"Yes. I was on business for a few months in Kazakhstan then. But this is where I live with my family. Come. I will introduce you to my wife and children."

So I ended up spending time with them catching them up on my walk. It was 3:00 p.m. the next day before I got back on the road, but I gladly accepted a break in my routine to enjoy fellowship with a brother in Christ.

ENTERING MARY'S LAND

On Monday, July 1, after a reporter and three crew members from the Cheski TV did an interview with me on the road, I was ready to enter into Poland. It turned out to be a place the Lord had prepared for me to experience a home away from home. The moment I stepped into the Polish border town of Cieszyn, I felt wrapped in the warm blanket of the arms of the Mother of God. The Lord allowed me to experience His Mother's presence here in an almost palpable way. Within my first two hours in Poland, a woman came up to me who recognized me from a video she had seen about me on TV and she took me to a convent of Franciscan Sisters who knew of me from their mission in Irkutsk, Siberia. From here on, for the next eleven months that I would be in Poland, I was literally passed from one brother and sister to another all along the way.

My first goal was to get to Cracow to meet my friend Robert whom I had met in Medjugorje and then proceed to meet Jan who lived in

Warsaw and who had written to me several times in Vershina inviting me to come visit him. On the way to Cracow I was in John Paul II territory, whom, after Our Lady, was the next most loved person in Poland. I not only was able to participate in my first Mass in Poland on July 4, in the Basilica in Wadowice, where St. John Paul II was born and grew up. I even ate mulberries off of trees that, no doubt, Karol Wojtyła enjoyed as a boy. On July 5, I spent several hours walking and praying on the vast grounds of Kalwaria Zebrzydowska where Karol loved to spend many hours of prayer all his life. I arrived at Cracow on July 6. I ended up spending nine days in Cracow visiting some of the historic sights like Wawel Castle and Main Market Square with Mariacka Basilica, that figured so prominently in Poland's history since the Middle Ages.

PILGRIMAGE TO CZĘSTOCHOWA

I joined a six-day pilgrimage group that was leaving from the Pauline Monastery. It was going to the main Marian shrine in Poland, our Lady of Częstochowa, Queen of Poland, and it was right on my way to Warsaw. So now I would get to experience real pilgrimage as was done in the old country with the Twentieth Cracow Skalka group of 280 walkers, led by the intrepid Fr. Zachariasz (who himself had already walked 7,000 kilometers on pilgrimage) of the Order of Pauline Hermits. These pilgrims were not youngsters walking the roads, either. They were veteran, middle-aged women (and some men) who endured a rugged 18 miles (30 kilometers) a day, carrying their own packs, and sleeping in barns at night. Throughout the journey they were occupied with singing hymns, praying the Rosary, and listening to teachings over the portable megaphones carried by the priests.

I came to consider them as among "the shock troops of the Catholic Church."

311

Arriving at the shrine in the Monastery of Jasna Gora ("Bright Hill") was amazing in itself. At the first sighting of the fortress-like monastery buildings in the distance (about 5 miles out), everyone prostrated themselves on the ground and put their arms out to form a human cross with their bodies, as a sign of repentance and thanksgiving. When we got to the actual chapel housing the image, one of the pilgrims took me by the hand and pulled me through the dense crowd of pilgrims right up to the front. There, as the pilgrims devoutly intoned a hymn to our Lady of Częstochowa, I watched a painted canvas slowly roll down out of the way, to reveal the famous ninth-century painting of our Lady and Jesus (in the *hodigitria*–Our Lady of the Way–style). Here was the image of their Queen. Here was their Heavenly Mother. Here was the one who succored the faith of these long-suffering followers of Jesus who had withstood the ravages of war, oppression, and tyranny over the centuries. I felt privileged to be part of such a valiant band of pilgrims bound for heaven.

WALK TO WARSAW

After two days at the Shrine of Our Lady of Częstochowa, I set out for the last leg of "Pilgrimage 1996." It was a fourteen-day walk to Warsaw and I arrived there on August 4. I was told this route was taken every year by 100,000 pilgrims on foot going to the Shrine for the Feast Day of Our Lady of Czestochowa on August 26. And they made up only one-fifth of the total of 500,000 pilgrims who walked to the shrine from all parts of Poland. Though there was quite a bit of rain these two weeks, here were nice patches of pine forests for camping at night. I was given shelter inside both at the parish house of St. Michael's in Inowłódz, and in the Capuchin novitiate in Nowe Miasto. On August 2 (the Franciscan feast of our Lady of the Angels), a priest stopped his car alongside the highway, got out, and came over to kiss the San Damiano cross on my staff. Many people had kissed the cross over the years, but this was the first time a Catholic priest had shown such devotion along the road. Thank you, St. Francis of Assisi.

Entering the city of Warsaw, the modern capital of Poland, I walked to the Church of the Holy Cross in the center of the city. There I attended two Masses and Benediction of the Blessed Sacrament to celebrate the completion of this year's pilgrimage. Jan, who had been writing to me over the past year, came in a taxi at 8:00 p.m. to pick me up and to take me to his apartment where I met his wife and their eight-year-old son, Paul. Although Jan had a good job as a professor at a local university, he, like most other Poles, did not have his own vehicle. Most people used public transportation. As a matter-of-fact, I often saw horse drawn wagons harvesting the crops on the farmlands I passed through on the way here.

CITY OF THE IMMACULATE

I explained to Jan that I was looking for a place to spend the winter in *poustinia*. So he set about checking out possibilities. Finally, after two weeks of asking around, the Franciscan Sisters, Servants of the Cross, who ran an institute for blind children called "Laski," just north of Warsaw, arranged for me to stay there until spring. The most memorable excursion for me was a whole day visit to Niepokalanów (City of the Immaculate) which St. Maximilan Kolbe, OFM Conv. (1894-1941) had founded in 1927, and which by the end of his life, housed 640 friars. We were shown around the friary complex by a spry, eighty-two-year-old Brother Felicissimus who had known the Saint personally in the last four years of his life, before he was arrested by the Nazis and put to death in Auschwitz in 1941.

I told the Brother and Jan that I felt a special connection with St. Maximilian Kolbe because I was baptized on August 10, 1941, when he was confined to the starvation bunker, four days before his execution by an injection of carbolic acid. When Brother Felicissimus took us to visit the cemetery, I noted another connection–the grave of Franciszek Gajowniczek (1901-95) whose life was spared because Fr. Kolbe volunteered to take his place in the bunker. I had actually met Franciszek ten years before at the St. Maximilian Kolbe Shrine in Footdale, Pennsylvania. The Lord continued to arrange the circumstances of my life as a way of writing His Word in my heart. Brother Felicissimus continued to give us the grand tour. At one point he stopped beneath the corner window on the second floor of an old building and said, "That is the room of Fr. Kolbe where he was when the Nazis came to arrest him in February of 1941." I felt like I was being led through the environs of Jerusalem by one of the original Apostles who pointed out the place in the Garden of Gethsemane where Jesus had been arrested. Jan and I left that day in a state of spiritual euphoria, overwhelmed by the goodness of the Lord and His arranging of such a blessed experience. It truly was a gift from Jesus, His Mother, and St. Maximilian, himself.

LIFE IN LASKI

Finally, the sisters had prepared a place for me on their large property where they cared for over 300 blind children. When I arrived, they gave me a tour of some of their sixty-five buildings, especially the all-wooden Our Lady of Angels log chapel and the dining hall. I also met a few of the people who would be a big part of my life here: Sr. Felixa, the superior; Sr. Anita who spoke English and arranged meetings for me; Jadwiga, my young blind translator; Bogdan, a building manager who spoke English; and Sophie, the ever efficient, dedicated secretary. Then they took me to a little trailer that had a bed, desk, chair, and lamp in it–a perfect *poustinia*. They said this would be my home until they could prepare another room in one of their buildings before winter set in; I would need more protection from the cold than this uninsulated tin trailer could provide. So I put down my pilgrim bags after six months of being on the road with them and thanked the Lord for providing for this winter's layover, until setting out again the following April.

So how did I spend the next eight months in *poustinia*? I had my daily routine: meals were at 8:00 a.m., noon, and 6:15 p.m.; Mass was at 6:30 a.m.; and Vespers at 7:00 p.m. I rose at 4:50 a.m. for personal prayer, meditation, and exercise. They asked me to do some gardening in the morning, which I was glad to. I took time to type up my pilgrimage notes and to catch up on correspondence. (During these winter months I averaged writing 400 letters, each with a dried wild flower or two that I had picked from alongside the road and pressed in the pages of my Bible.) I continued on with my reading of the whole Bible in one year, covering five chapters of the Old Testament and one chapter of the New Testament each day. One important rule I was given here though was not to go outside of my *poustinia* between 11:00 p.m. and 4:30 a.m., because guard dogs were let loose over the whole compound during those hours.

It was not long before people heard about my presence in Laski and I was asked to give talks and to do interviews. By the end of my stay in Poland I estimated that I had done thirty-three interviews for newspapers and magazines, radio, and TV. On Christmas Eve Fr. Vojtek (whom I knew from Vershina) hosted Jan and me at his mother's apartment in Warsaw. On January 16-20, my faithful pen pal, the widow Lodzia, invited me to her home town Katowice Ligota, to give talks at her Franciscan Church. That weekend I gave twenty-three talks and did a press conference for two dozen reporters. Everything was well arranged and the Lord made sure I did not get lonely or homesick and allowed me to get patched up during this layover.

ENDNOTES

60. Coastal road. See the appendix for my poem, "The Yugoslav Coast."

PART TWO

POLAND TO NORWAY (1997)

PILGRIMAGE 1997

All winter of course I prayed about "Pilgrimage 1997." I still was considering the possibility of going east from Poland into Ukraine and then south through the Balkans along the Black Sea to Turkey and on to the Holy Land. By looking at a map of Europe, however, I realized I still had enough time to visit another famous Marian Shrine in Ireland––Knock––and from that place in the far west of Europe, to walk to Bethlehem. I wrote to Erik, a retired Lutheran pastor and his wife Kirsten, friends in Norway who had invited me to spend a winter with them, if I was ever in their area. They lived on a private *tun* (arrangement of buildings around the central outdoor living space of the traditional Norwegian farm) 200 miles north of Oslo. Their *tun* included a chapel and a *stabbur* (small wooden building on stilts) where I could make my *poustinia*. So I set about laying out a route across northern Europe, the British Isles, and onto Norway. From April 21 to October 1, it would be a journey of 2,135 miles through seven countries. Now all I had to do was get a visa for Norway; for the other countries an American passport was sufficient to get me across the borders.

On Monday, April 21, I was ready to set out from Laski and to head due west toward the Polish border with Germany at the Oder River, 300 miles away. My Norway visa had not come through after two months of waiting, and the authorities in Poland said I could try again at the Norwegian Embassy in London. So I left without it. As is the custom in the Old Country, people walk with a pilgrim for the first few feet, or even first few miles. So I had my entourage; some walked to the edge of the property; others to the first bus stop and a few to the third bus stop. But for the next twenty-two days in Poland, I had visitors by phone and by car even up to three days before the border, when it meant a drive of 300 miles for three of my closest friends, who also had no guarantee they would find me. So attached to the Pilgrim had this family in the faith become, that they found it hard to let me go.

FINISHING OUT POLAND

My first stop for the day was the Missionary of Charity Sisters who had their novitiate house for Eastern Europe in Zaborow. There I was joyfully welcomed to pray, to eat, and to give a talk to the thirty novices and four novice mistresses. During my talk I could see their eyes were sparkling and it seemed that they were taking my every word deeply into their hearts. I knew when I left that I would remain in their hearts and be supported by their prayers for the months that lay ahead.

It was not long, however, before I realized I had put on a lot of weight, the bottom of my feet were tender, and my shoulders ached from carrying my packs (whose weight totaled about forty pounds). There was a lot of rain during this month but because I was so well-known through magazines, newspapers, and TV, I was offered shelter fifteen of the twenty-two nights I was in this part of Poland. Even Archbishop Mikarski of Gniezno, the Primate of Poland, put me up and fed me in his rectory on May 2. Not everyone of course was open to the Pilgrim and at the famous Marian Shrine in Lichen, on April 29, I was told they do not cater to individual pilgrims, only groups, and I was literally shown the door. Just one more opportunity to experience the privilege of the "perfect joy" of St. Francis of Assisi.

In a three-page letter I wrote to List on May 3, I reflected on my ten months in Poland. I said how I appreciated being able to experience a culture that had been formed by faith in Christ for 1,000 years and which continued to live that faith dynamically. I observed the deep love the Polish people had for the Mother of God whom they truly considered their Queen, not just at Czestochowa, but at more than 350 other places in Poland where miraculous images of Mary were venerated. And this love was brought home every night at 9:00 p.m. when–wherever one was–everyone joined in singing the Apel hymn to their Heavenly Mother. But I warned them that I saw Western secularization already making deep inroads into their country, especially among their youths who were being corrupted by Western music that rebelled against authority and that worshiped technology. Poland had endured many battles for its land and peoples over the centuries; now it would have to wage war for the hearts, minds, and souls of its people. Only through divine assistance and a deep personal trust in Jesus Christ, would they be able to survive this new struggle to the death. No wonder the gracious Lord had appeared to Sr. Faustina back in 1938, and equipped this people with a renewed experience of Divine Mercy.

NORTHERN GERMANY

On May 13, I crossed the Oder River, entering Germany through Frankfurt on the Oder. I now had ahead of me a thirty-three-day walk across northern Germany as I headed for Belgium and for the English Channel. My path lay through Berlin, Dusseldorf, and Aachen. Although this was Protestant territory (unlike southern Germany which was more Catholic) I was still able to find Catholic churches and fellowship. And while there were a few radio interviews and newspaper stories done on my walk, my pilgrimages were not as well-known here as in Poland, and in my month of walking I was invited to sleep inside only two times.

It was sad to see so many church buildings abandoned and falling into ruin, although the adjacent cemeteries were kept up immaculately. At. St. Hedwig's Cathedral in Berlin everyone sat on plush pews during the whole Mass and robustly sang eight hymns, accompanied by a full-throttled organ. Bells rang out from towers every fifteen minutes in most cities. I was glad to see the 1,000-year-old rose bush in Hildesheim blooming, but the church itself appeared to be mostly a museum. I was also disappointed to find notices on Catholic churches such as, Today the Service Is in the Local Lutheran Church. My pilgrim spirit rejoiced, however, to come across an ancient stone-carved fountain (not working) in the city of Soest on June 5, with the inscription, Santiago de Compostela-2,250 Kilometers. I was touching base with one of the medieval paths to my patron saint's shrine in Spain. I felt privileged to be able to walk into the towering octagonal cathedral in Aachen built by Charlemagne in AD 800, in imitation of the Holy of Holies in the Temple of Solomon. There I was able to venerate the miraculous image of the Madonna from the fourteenth century. And I was thankful to the Lord for the few personal encounters with individuals who took more than just a few minutes but a few hours and even over a night, to share their faith and lives with me on a deeper level.

CATHOLIC BELGIUM

My last full day in Germany was a Saturday (June 14) and as I was leaving Aachen, a professional photographer by the name of Kurt befriended me. He not only took my picture but called a reporter to do a story. The next day, Sunday, he took me to a church that first had an Evangelical (Lutheran) service, then a Catholic one, and I spoke briefly at both services. Afterward people handed me money as they greeted me on the way out. One of them said, "We have always read about pilgrims walking through our land, but it is nice to actually meet one in real life." From there, with a two-hour walk, I arrived in Belgium, which now in the European Union, had no check point at the border; actually it was hard to even tell where one country left off and the other began.

Belgium of course is a rather tiny country, just 175 miles across from east to west. So I was able to traverse it completely on foot in fourteen days. I was on the most direct path I could find to the city of Ostend on the coast, where I hoped to take the ferry across the English Chanel to England. Thankfully, my path lay through some of the major cities like Liege, Brussels, Ghent, and Bruges. How happy I was to discover that on the third day of my walk, before arriving in Liege, I would be passing through the little town of Banneux. I knew this name from a stained glass window in my home church of St. Mary's. Our Lady had appeared there eight times in 1933, to a twelve-year-old girl by the name of Mariette, as "Virgin of the Poor" and the apparitions were approved by Rome in 1949. I spent seven quiet hours at this simple shrine, yet I found it somewhat incongruous that although Our Lady specifically said the spring here was for the poor, there were signs everywhere saying, No Begging. (Who of us is not a beggar in need of God's grace?)

Occasionally, food was provided for me to eat in Belgium, but mostly I had to buy my own in grocery stores. In one store, however, an elderly woman in front of me at the checkout counter indicated to the clerk that she was paying for my purchases along with hers. On June 24, the Feast of St. John the Baptist, I was able to spend two hours at the Cathedral of St. Baaf in Ghent. I used most of my time there praying before the tabernacle in the front of the church. But I also took time at the back of the church, to carefully examine Van Eyck's famous "*Adoration of the Lamb*" polyptych, painted in 1432. Unfortunately, most of the many visitors to the cathedral were here as tourists, more interested in viewing and hearing detailed explanations of this historic art piece. They missed the Real Presence of the King of Kings and Sacrificed Lamb just a few feet away in the tabernacle at the front of the cathedral. Would we some day not be more impressed with the visible works of human hands than with the invisible, eternal truth of God's unselfish love present in the Eucharist?

MOTHER OF PEACE

Near the end of my short pilgrimage through Belgium, 6 kilometers outside of Bruges, where I had been able to attend a 9:00 a.m. Mass, two young men wearing crosses around their neck stopped their car, got out, and approached me. They explained that they were part of a small, new religious order called the "Mother of Peace Community." They were in the nearby village of Meetkerke and expressed their desire to have me for their guest. Always eager to share my faith with anyone who was open to it, I gladly accepted their offer.

I ended up spending two nights with this fervent group. They said they were inspired to form this group because of the messages coming out of Medjugorje. While I was there I was able to wash my clothes and to call the Norwegian embassy in London, to see if my visa for Norway had come through. They told me to call Oslo; Oslo said to call Warsaw; Warsaw said to call back the following day. When I called back they said they needed more information from my hosts in Norway. So there was no use for me to check at the Norwegian embassy in London. They instructed me to wait and to try their embassy in Dublin. I had to continue on in faith and trust in the Lord to work behind-the-scenes.

CROSSING THE CHANNEL

On Saturday, June 28, I left the friendly Meetkirke community at 11:30 a.m. and headed to the ferryboat on the coast. Just before I got to the harbor, a man came up to me and said, "I saw you on the TV newscast three days ago, and I would like to give you this donation." He handed me a 1,000 Belgian franc note–the ticket for the ferry was 800 francs (about $27 then). I thanked the Lord for His on-the-spot provision.

At 5:30 p.m. I was the last passenger to board the ferry and just as soon as I had taken my seat, the boat pulled out of the harbor. During the ride on smooth waters, I began to reflect on the significance of this passage. For the past four years I had been walking across the large continents of Asia and Europe. Now, I was about to step off of them, onto a group of small islands in the North Atlantic. When I stepped off the ferry onto dry land I was on one of the famous British Isles.

MERRIE ENGLAND

Now I was in "Merrie England," also known as "Mary's Dowry." This was a land I knew a good deal about from studying English literature in my college days, as well as from reading about its history, both secular and ecclesiastical. And this land of course was the origin of most of the early settlers in northeastern United States. One of its statesmen, William Penn, founded my home State of Pennsylvania in 1681. So how was I to lay out my walk? I now could put aside my thought of having to go into London, but I did have to stop in Canterbury to pick up any mail that might have arrived there for me at the American Express Office over the past month. After that, I could walk through southern England in two weeks and Wales in a week and get a ferry over to Ireland. After Ireland I could come back through northern Wales and northern England and sail to Norway from Newcastle on the northeastern coast of England. So my first goal was Canterbury, just 15 miles from the port at Ramsgate.

How well the Lord arranged my timing. Canterbury was the center of the evangelization of England in the sixth century. Pope St. Gregory I

(AD 540-604) had sent a man by the name of Augustine, who arrived here in AD 597, to begin the work of implanting the Gospel. This year, 1997, was the 1,400th anniversary of this key event and I was able to be a part of it. Canterbury was also famous for the martyrdom of St. Thomas A Becket in 1170, which made this a popular place of pilgrimage in the Middle Ages. Since Chaucer's famous *Canterbury Tales* was an account of one such group pilgrimage from London to Canterbury, I found a place to buy myself a copy so I could reread this classic of English literature. When I got to the American Express Office in Canterbury on June 30, the clerk exclaimed "Your mail bin is falling off the wall!" When I counted it up later I found there were 43 pieces of mail.

Indeed, I had not been forgotten.

ADJUSTING THE PACE

Now, I was heading west toward Wales. I soon realized, however, that I had miscalculated the distances, for I had consulted a map that was laid out in miles, but mistakenly took them to be kilometers. So I ended up walking only 200 of the total 430 miles in England and 90 of the 180 miles in Wales. It was a great adjustment for me to adapt to traffic driving on the left; more than once I almost stepped out into oncoming traffic because I looked the wrong way before stepping out into the road. Also, the ten-foot high hedgerows grew right up to the edge of the road and so I often had to walk right on the highway. Thankfully, I was never hit. I think perhaps because of the still active tradition of walking in England with its vast system of "footpaths and bridle ways" crisscrossing the whole country, drivers were used to being attentive to people on foot.

In my journey through southern England, I picked up the great Gothic cathedrals of Winchester, Salisbury, and Bath. Their size amazed me. They were like football fields. Winchester Cathedral's nave at 558 feet, was equivalent to one and half football fields. These magnificent houses of worship had walls of delicately carved stone and flying buttresses, holding massive stained glass windows, with a roof over them. I could not begin to imagine the cost of maintaining them today. These churches conducted tours and although still used for divine worship, they seemed hollow shells of their original selves. Still, they stood as a splendid testimony to the robust faith of an age gone by.

WALES AND BEYOND

I crossed into Wales at noon, July 12, and took one week to get to Pembroke, on the coast. In general I had a hard time finding secondary roads where I could walk. At one point the police stopped me and said motorists were calling them about my walking on their highway which they considered unsafe for pedestrians. So I allowed the police to transport me a few miles ahead to where it was not so busy. Having taken another ride, I absentmindedly left my large rope Rosary (one that I had made in 1992, and wore on my belt), on the floor by the back seat. I felt so disappointed to lose this faithful companion on which I prayed the fifteen mysteries of the Rosary every day for all these years. Thankfully, the driver found me the next day and returned it. I did have to ask the Lord for forgiveness for being so attached to a mere physical object that would eventually pass away anyway.

Finally, on July 18, I arrived at the harbor, purchased a ticket for the four-hour ferryboat ride across the St. George Channel, and sailed for Rosslare, in Ireland.

THE LAND OF ST. PATRICK

What a different scene I found in Ireland!

The pace of life here slowed down tremendously. There were fewer cars on the roads and people were on foot, on bicycles, and driving herds of sheep. It amazed me to see signs, even on four-lane divided highways that read, Cattle Crossing. Here, animals still had the right of way.

In order to savor some of the ancient monastic flavor of Irish Catholicism, I took the time to explore the ruins of Clonmacnoise, a famous monastic settlement that had been founded by St. Ciaran (Kieran) in AD 548. I took special note that its "Annals of the Four Masters" boasted the earliest record of pilgrimage in Ireland stating that "a pilgrim died here in AD 606." I viewed the remains of eight churches, two round towers, three intricately carved stone high crosses, and hundreds of early gravestones. When I read that fire burned the monastery thirteen times between 722 and 1205; that the Vikings plundered it eight times between AD 832 and AD 1163; that Irishmen attacked it twenty-seven times; and that the English had attacked it six times before reducing it to final ruin in 1552, I could see why there was not much left. I also reflected that the indomitable and imperishable Spirit of the Lord always rises from its ashes, even though the outer forms of religious life might change and pass away.

OUR LADY OF KNOCK

On Thursday, July 31, I arrived at the site of an apparition of the Mother of God and accompanying saints in the little village of Knock, in 1879. This was the high point of my whole summer's pilgrimage. At 10:00 a.m., I arrived at the apparition chapel and went to three Masses there. This chapel preserved the south gable end of the little village church of St. John the Baptist. Here, larger-than-life statues of pure white marble had been erected to depict the scene as it had been viewed by a group of fifteen people for two hours on that historic rainy night of August 21. The Blessed Mother stood facing them with her hands raised as if in prayer and her eyes looking up to heaven (interceding for God's children). Facing her, to her right, stood St. Joseph who was slightly bowed, his hands reverently folded.

To her left was St. John the Evangelist (with a miter on his head like a bishop) holding an open book in his left hand, as if he were preaching. And farther to her left, beyond St. John, was a plain altar with a small lamb standing on it (representing Jesus Christ) and a tall plain cross (representing Calvary) behind it. Around, the altar angels were hovering in adoration of the Sacrificed Lamb.

No words were spoken by the figures. But the symbolism seemed clear. By this tableaux the Lord was, as it were, taking away the veil from our eyes so that we could see the spiritual reality of heaven that surrounds us all the time–as He had done for John in the last book of the Bible, the Apocalypse. The Lord wanted to remind his Church that Jesus, the Lamb of God (Jn 1:29; I Cor 5:7; Rv 5:6), is still on His throne-altar, He still reigns supreme; He is still taking away the sins of the world. His heavenly court, the angels and the saints, continue to worship him day and night and intercede for us on earth. In the symbols of the Lamb, the altar, and the cross, representing the Holy Eucharist, the Lord was assuring His people that He is always with us, no matter what trials or tribulations we are facing.

IN THE FOOTSTEPS OF ST. PATRICK

After three wonderful days at the Shrine of Knock and truly experiencing it as "a window to heaven," as it was called, I set out for Dublin to see if my visa for Norway was finally approved. It took me eleven days to walk there, but it was a privilege to know this was where St. Patrick himself had walked and to know I could drink water from his own well. On that stretch I met a friendly Irish priest who stopped his car right on the road to engage me in a half hour of conversation. This encounter included his hearing my confession and giving me absolution. Also before arriving in Dublin, as I came out of St. Paul's Church in Mulligan on August 7, I was accosted by a man and a women who both accused me of stealing my staff and cross (which I had been carrying for two years) from their church. A little explanation on my part soon satisfied them that they had been mistaken.

When I arrived on the outskirts of Dublin on the morning of August 11, I called the Norwegian immigration office in Oslo and they said my permit to reside in Norway for nine months had been granted.[61] I could pick up my visa at their embassy in Dublin that afternoon. At 3:15 pm, I arrived at the Norwegian Embassy and received my visa papers without even having to pay a fee. I thanked the Lord for finally opening this door that had appeared to be stuck for so long.

A HOLY WELL

After a very busy last five hours in Dublin, taking a quick look at the Church of Ireland's Cathedral of St. Patrick,[62] personal evangelization of a group of youths at an outdoor café and engaging in a fifteen-minute public apologetics session with a zealous Protestant street preacher, I boarded the 9:45 p.m. ferry to Holyhead, Wales. Once in Wales I found a private wooded area at 3:00 a.m. to set up my tent and to catch two hours of sleep before packing up and getting back on the road through northern Wales.

I had a very dear friend in Rhyl, Wales, by the name of Tomasina, whom I had met in Medjugorje, who was eagerly expecting a visit from me. On August 13, she gladly welcomed me to her apartment and found friends to take us to Holywell, a famous shrine from the twelfth century associated with St. Winefride. Healings were still claimed by the faithful who drank from this local well. Here I also met a dynamic Charismatic prayer community, a Third Order Carmelite group, and a hermitess by the name of Sr. Seraphim, all of whom welcomed me as a brother-in-Christ. As a matter-of-fact, they ended up booking me a place on a boat that sailed from Newcastle, England, to Stavanger, Norway in just eleven days and paid the fare of about $100 (53 euros).

SNAKE PASS

My sights were now set on departing from England by August 27. Of the 250 miles I had to cover, I only walked 90 of them; the rest I rode by car. My walking days in England for all practical purposes came to an end on August 23, when I met Peter at St. Patrick's in Bradford and hooked up with the Charismatic community to which he belonged. But two days before that, on August 21, the Lord asked of me one more sacrifice for graces for this land.

I was walking through the Hope Forest District when about 1:00 p.m. it started to drizzle. About 3:00 p.m. I turned off the main road and headed up a steep, narrow, bendy, secondary road that was a shortcut over a mountain at a pass called "Snake Pass." I was wearing my rain poncho, but the wind picked up as I ascended and I was getting completely drenched. After two hours of wind and rain, I was soaked through. Then the fog set in and there was zero visibility.

I was looking desperately for a place to pull off and to set up my tent, but the guardrail and sheep fences, plus steep embankments on both sides of the road, prevented even a brief rest stop. Finally, about 500 meters from the top, I saw a little flat area with short cropped grass among some big boulders that would accommodate my tent. Battling rain and wind I somehow managed to get my tent set up without getting blown off the mountain, and got all of my gear inside, though most of it was soaking wet. Finally, I climbed in just as the last bits of daylight faded into night. About midnight the wind and rain stopped and I had some peaceful sleep until 5:00 a.m. The Lord had brought me safely through one more test. I offered it up for the conversion of hearts in this ancient land of the Christian faith.

When Peter found me on the streets of his home town, Bradford, I was just outside St. Patrick Church where he intended to go to noon Mass. I went to a Charismatic weekend retreat with the Ampleforth Renewal Community in Ilkley; after that I took a car ride to Thornaby, near Newcastle, where I would board a ferry to Stavanger, Norway.

Thus, my last six days in England were like being wrapped in the love of my brothers-and-sisters in Christ, before the last full month of walking on "Pilgrimage 1997."

LANDING IN NORWAY

But before walking in Norway, I had to cross the "pond"–the mighty North Sea. It was a twenty-hour ride on a luxury liner, only I was not going first class. I had asked for the cheapest ticket on the ferry and that was "a reclining chair" on the top deck. I did not realize until I got there that it was going to be at the furthest point forward on the ship. This is where the pitching is the most pronounced, so it was like being on the end of a seesaw. The North Sea was rather calm on this trip. (Thankfully, it was not at all like the previous week, when a ship just like ours was broken in half and everyone perished on a turbulent ocean.) I was glad to set foot once again on terra firma at 2:30 p.m. on Thursday, August 28.

I told my hosts in Ron that I planned to arrive at their home on October 1. This meant that I had twenty-five days to walk 470 miles, so I had to average about 14 miles a day. I first wanted to walk to Oslo to visit the Catholic bishop of the tiny Catholic community of Norway. On the way there, I decided to look up Holy Dormition Ukrainian Byzantine Monastery, a little Cisterian/Trappist skete in Telemark, where I had been invited by Fr. Robert, the American hermit who had found it years before. It was a two-week walk to the skete and it rained ten of those fourteen days.

Nevertheless, my journey was blessed in many ways. The very first day I was able to visit the twelfth-century Cathedral of St. Swithun, in Stavanger, and do an interview for the local newspaper. The scenery was stunning, with the mountains, lakes, fjords, and waterfalls. I also began to encounter the unique and historic *stavkirke,* all-wooden, tiny churches with steep cantilevered roofs of wood shingles and intricately carved entryways from the twelfth century that dotted the landscape and that riveted my attention. The Norwegians were a curious people, and before I arrived in Ron, I had done a dozen interviews with the media.

HOLY DORMITION SKETE

With the help of Fr. Robert's hand-drawn map that he had sent me, I made it back the 4 kilometers from the main road to Hylland Munkelyed ocisto (the name of the skete in Norwegian) on Saturday, September 13. So I was able to join them for Mass the following day. It was also one of my favorite feasts, the Exaltation of the Holy Cross. Amazingly, for the feast day, Fr. Robert solemnly enthroned on the *tetrapod* (table) in the center of the chapel, the San Damiano Cross from my staff which had been blessed in Rome by John Paul II (and touched to the original in Assisi) as well as carried publicly through nine European nations. When I mounted it on my staff four days later, I felt I had the prayers of this fervent community of four young men and Fr. Robert with me on the rest of my walk. I promised them I would return in February to spend all of Lent and Easter with them before beginning "Pilgrimage 1998."

FROM OSLO TO RON

From the skete I headed for Oslo to pay a brief visit to the Catholic bishop, so that he would have a personal knowledge of this pilgrim who was wintering over in his diocese. In the two weeks it took me to get to my hosts in Ron, the weather was beautiful and I only had two days of rain. In this two-week stretch, I did four interviews with newspaper and TV reporters, so people pretty much knew who I was when they saw me walking alongside the road. They connected me with their celebration of the 1,000th anniversary of the ancient Catholic pilgrimage site in Trondheim, far to the north. The night before I arrived in Oslo, I was invited to give my testimony at a large

Pentecostal prayer meeting. A collection they took up for me at that meeting eventually paid for three crowns I needed on my teeth.

The one sad note in this leg of my journey was the death of my father at the age of eighty back in Pennsylvania. He died of colon cancer on September 23, but I only received news of his death and burial when I arrived in Ron on October 1, as my mother had posted a letter to me there. But when I looked back at my log, I saw I was praying in the cathedral in Oslo when my father passed away after three days in hospice care. And during his funeral on September 26, the Lord got my attention through a falling leaf that gently descended right in front of me as I walked along. It caused this thought to go through my mind: "Mom just died." While it wasn't my mother, the connection was still there. I thought, "My father got to the heavenly Jerusalem before I made it to the earthly Jerusalem, but we were both heading for the same goal–union with the Lord." And as I concluded in a three-page reflection on his life that I sent him for Father's Day in 1991, "I love you, Dad, and look forward to being with you forever in heaven. I will be proud throughout eternity to always point you out to the saints and angels as 'there is my dad.'"

GREETED BY MY MOTHER

Finally, on October 1, the Feast of St. Therese of Lisieux, one of my favorite Saints, I arrived at a petrol station in Ron and called my host, Erik, to tell him I was on my way. The attendant in the station drew me a little map of my last 4 kilometers so that I could find Klvitsyn Kloster, the name of Erik's and Kirstin's *tun*. After an hour of climbing uphill in the light rain and fog, I heard ahead of me familiar voices of greeting, "Praise Jesus and Mary." Erik and Kirsten had walked down the hill to meet me and to personally escort me the last bit of the way to my winter *poustinia*. On the way up the hill Erik explained to me about how I was able to obtain a visa. The embassy in Oslo called him and said, "What does his answer on the application form mean when he says, 'God will provide for him?' We will grant him the visa if you agree to pay the first $5,000 of any hospital expense he might incur while here." Erik agreed to it, and so they granted me the visa.

As we entered their *tun* my hosts pointed out to me their wooden chapel called, "Noah's Ark" and then led me to their *stabbur* which they called "Jacob's Ladder." We climbed the steep, outside steps (which certainly *did* resemble a ladder) to the entrance of the attic apartment, which they had built as a guest room. They had prepared it for me as my *poustinia*. And who was inside to greet me? None other than our Lady herself. My hosts had been given a two-foot-high pilgrim statue of "Maria Rosa Mystica," and put it on the desk by the window where I would be reading and writing this winter. I was truly on the way to the Jubilee Year with Mary and she was now going to look over my shoulder these months of *poustinia*.

THE CATHOLIC COMMUNITY

I now settled in for a five-month *poustinia* at Jacob's Ladder *stabbur*. I had all of my physical needs taken care of, but was far away from a Catholic Church and the sacraments. There were only 30,000 Catholics in a population of four million Norwegians, so Catholics were less than 1 percent of the total population. And the bishop had only thirty Catholic churches that formed his little flock, scattered over this vast land. To get to the nearest Mass I had over a two-hour walk to the bus stop and then a two-hour bus ride to the nearest Catholic Church. So I only did this for Christmas as I had to stay over with the priest in his rectory.

And since I wanted to go to Mass more often during Lent and Holy Week, I left Ron at the end of February and went to the Hylland Skete where Fr. Robert had either Mass or Divine Liturgy every day. But I was kept quite busy in my Ron *poustinia* for four months answering letters, receiving visitors, and going out to see some of the historic stave churches in the area. I also had to make two trips by bus to the dentist near Oslo, to get crowns put on three of my teeth.

NEXT PILGRIMAGE ROUTE

During my winter layover I also began to pray about my route for "Pilgrimage 1998" so that I could continue to make my way toward the Holy Land. I saw that a five-month's walk of 1,800 miles could get me to Kiev in central Ukraine. From there, I projected my arrival in the Holy Land for the following year in time for the Jubilee Year 2000.

Providentially, there was a young monk from Ukraine at Hylland Skete who was interested in helping me get a visa for his country. He was from Lviv, in the far western part of Ukraine near Poland, but he said he would help me find a place for my winter *poustinia* in Lviv. So taking that as the Lord directing me, I obtained my letter of invitation to Ukraine and sent it by mail to the closest Ukrainian Embassy, which happened to be in Helsinki. I sent up many a prayer for the angels to look over my passport and breathed a prayer of thanksgiving when it finally came back to me safely through the mail.

ENDNOTES

61. Visa for Norway. They obviously were making an exception for me from the Schengen Agreement that says that visitors are only allowed three months in a participating European nation and then have to depart for three months.

62. St. Patrick's was a Catholic cathedral since around 1200. At the time of the English Reformation, all but two Irish bishops apostatized and around 1537, it became part of what today is the (Anglican) Church of Ireland.

PART THREE

NORWAY TO UKRAINE (1998)

"PILGRIMAGE 1998"

As it turned out, my original "Pilgrimage 1998" map that I handed out to people for prayer coverage, was the most corrected one I ever made. The Marian Shrine that I focused on for this pilgrimage was our Lady of Ostra Brama (the Eastern Gate) in Vilnius, Lithuania. I knew from being in Poland that this image rivaled Czestochowa in popularity as it did for John Paul II and for all Polish Catholics. But how I arrived in Vilnius was very different from what I had planned. Originally, I was to go from Oslo to Stockholm, then to Tallinn, Estonia, St. Petersburg, Moscow, Vilnius, and finally Kiev.

My first detour was on the Oslo to Stockholm stretch. A "professional pilgrim" (who made his living by organizing pilgrimages) by the name of Eivind Luthen said I definitely had to visit the famous shrine to St. Bridget (1303-73) in Vadstena, southwestern Sweden. When I looked at my map, I saw that it was only about 90 miles off of the direct route I had planned from Oslo to Stockholm. I felt the Lord wanted me to pray at this shrine, even though I did not previously have any special devotion to this twelfth-century woman-Saint. So, I made up the time and distance by leaving Oslo a few days early and walking an extra 5 kilometers a day. I am glad I did, for by taking it in, I was blessed to become more acquainted with this valiant woman who not only raised a holy family, but was also a great pilgrim in her own right and founded a religious order (the Bridgettines).

PASSING THROUGH SWEDEN

After only five days of walking in Norway, I crossed into Sweden. On May 15, the day before I arrived at the shrine in Vadstena, I was coming into the city of Motala, when a reporter stopped to ask if he could take some pictures. "You certainly have been making an impression on people by your walk in the last few days. Our newspaper office has received more than fifty telephone calls from passing motorists." I do not know if I was able to communicate to him on how exciting it was to follow Jesus or not, but at least the readers of his paper would have a photo of a modern-day pilgrim in their country, joyfully lifting up the Cross of Jesus as the sign of God's love for them.

Thankfully, I had friends in Stockholm who I had met in Poland with whom I could stay. My main goals in the capital were to obtain a visa for Russia, and a ferry for Tallinn, Estonia. My hope was to walk from Tallinn, along the south coast of the Gulf of Finland, to St. Petersburg, then on to Moscow and back to Vilnius. For that I needed a three-month visa for Russia. But the only letter of invitation from someone in Russia I could secure would only give me five weeks there. If I could not extend the visa inside the country, I would have to radically alter my route. When the Russian Embassy officials in Stockholm told me that a next day visa would cost $200, I was shocked. If I was willing to wait two weeks, it would only cost $35. Since the Lord had provided the finances, I felt He wanted me to be back on the road with the cross, rather than sitting around twiddling my thumbs for two weeks. I handed over the lump sum and received the visa the next day. Then I was on the boat for a fifteen-hour ride across the Baltic Sea to the capital of Estonia, Tallinn.

STUCK IN ST. PETERSBURG

In Tallinn I was met by my Ukrainian friend Igor. After an overnight stay with him, I was on my way to the border of Russia and on to St. Petersburg, 220 miles away. I saw that it would now be possible to arrive there for the Feast of St. Anthony, June 13. By walking 17 miles a day, I was able to make it in thirteen days. It was perfect timing, for St. Anthony the "miracleworker" was the patron of the friary and they celebrated with a big feast, including Mass with the Polish-born local Archbishop Kondrusevich and a hundred guests.

My intention was to spend just a few days in St. Petersburg, then to be on my way to Moscow. But that did not happen. It turned out that the visa office in St. Petersburg would not grant me an extension, and it took them three weeks to tell me that. By that time, I had only eight days left on my visa, so I headed for the border with Finland, which was only 110 miles away. However, when I arrived at the border, I was told that it was not for a walk across the border; it was only for cars, buses, and trucks.

But the Lord sent an angel in a Russian uniform to help me.

AN ANGEL IN A RUSSIAN UNIFORM

After I passed through the first check point and began walking the last few miles to the border, the officer who had let me through, came up in his military vehicle with his driver and said, "Get in. We will take you to the border." As we drove along, we came to more check points, barbed wire fences, plowed fields, burned down forests, and guard-dog areas. When the guards saw the official Jeep and their commander coming, the gate went up, the guards stood at attention and saluted, and we passed right through without even having to stop. (Leave it to the Lord to arrange VIP treatment for His poor Pilgrim.)

When we got to Russian customs, my "angel" took me personally to the main office and explained my situation. It took them an hour before they said I was free to go. They even flagged down a van going into Finland and asked the driver to take me along, for we still had to pass across a "no man's land." It took another hour at Finland customs, but there was no military present here at all. Finally, the officer came out and said, "Welcome to Finland," and handed me my passport back with a visa stamp in it. So after a four-hour ordeal of bureaucracy and security checks, I was free to now continue my walk in the peace of Christ. I gave a sigh of relief for having been delivered from any number of possible scenarios—fine, arrest, deportation, or having to go back to St. Petersburg and exit Russia at another border-point. We never know from how many enemies the Lord delivers us without our even being aware of it.

TEN DAYS IN FINLAND

Finland was a new country for me. But I am glad the Lord sent me here for ten days of walking, praying, and witnessing to Him. Although most of the people spoke either Finnish or Swedish, many knew enough English to communicate with me. I found it to be a prosperous, high-tech, secular society. People had money, were on the move, and had little sense of what a pilgrim was all about. When people stopped to talk or to offer help, they did not ask for a prayer or a blessing (as they did in Slavic countries), but wanted to take a picture or to give me money. I spoke with seven reporters in the ten days I was in Finland, so I had lots of publicity and people wanted to let me know they had seen me on TV or had read about me in the newspapers.

I was told there were only 5,000 Catholics in all of Finland; there was a Catholic bishop and a small cathedral in Helsinki. My best contact with the Catholic Faith here, was the American Carmelite Foundation in Espoo, where I spent three lovely days with nuns from California. Here, I was able to rest, get cleaned up, pray, and share with my sisters-in-Christ. The day I left the monastery was July 20, the Feast of Elijah, the zealous hermit-prophet of the Lord in the Old Testament with whom I greatly identified and who was the patronymic hero of the Carmelites, themselves.

TOWARD KIEV

My visit to Finland drawing to a close, I prayed about how the Lord wanted me to proceed toward Kiev. I obviously had to cross from Helsinki back to Tallinn in Estonia and head south. I figured I might as well head for Vilnius in Lithuania as I had originally intended, so I could visit Mary's Shrine in the East Gate. But instead of coming from Russia in the east, I would come from Tallinn in the north. Once I made it to Vilnius, I would figure out the route to Ukraine.

The Lord gave me a travel companion the first twenty-four hours of this leg of my journey, in the form of seventy-year-old French missionary priest, Fr. Guy, who spoke good English. He was the chaplain for the Carmelite Sisters in Espoo, and he agreed to escort me back to where he was based in Tallinn on Monday, July 20. So I did not have to figure out what road, bus, or ferry, to take; he knew all of these ropes and managed them smoothly. He not only heard my confession on the ferry, he bought my tickets and gave me a monetary donation to see me on my way.

THE BALTIC STATES

When I left Tallinn I had about 330 miles to walk to Vilnius, and I had to cross through the three Baltic states of Estonia, Latvia, and Lithuania. I found out there was an American Express Office in Riga, Latvia, so I notified my friends that they could write to me there if they could get a letter there by July 31, which was the date I planned to arrive in the city. That meant I should take the coastal road that went straight from Tallinn to Riga and I would have to keep up the stiff pace of 18 miles (30 kilometers) a day. That way, I could cover the 310 kilometers to Riga in ten days. From Riga I would have to decide whether to head due south to the famous Shrine of the Hill of Crosses, near Siauliai, or to go east to the Shrine of Our Lady of Aglona. Once I arrived in Riga, the Lord manifested His will in this matter in a very clear way.

Walking the coast route through Estonia and Latvia was quite pleasant. Though basically the weather was hot, the frequent rains kept it mercifully cool. As I neared the border of the two countries, I came so close to the Baltic Sea, I could hear the waves breaking on the beach at night, and once I even took a swim in the not too salty sea. For my fifty-seventh birthday on July 25, the Lord waited until the day after in Saulkrasti, Latvia, to celebrate it with a family who invited me in for warm fellowship. They took many pictures and sent a number of them to my parents back in the States. These people definitely exercised the ministry of hospitality.

CATHOLICS IN LATVIA

On July 27, I got to the end of Estonia and entered the tiny little country of Latvia, which I was told was 30 percent Catholic. Of the few weeks I spent in the country, I was with fellow Catholics most of the time, and so had access to Holy Communion. This was possible because when I arrived at the capital, Riga, on July 31, and was offered hospitality by the Missionaries of Charity, I was directed to join a group of forty-five pilgrims about to set out the very next day on a thirteen-day walk. It was the annual pilgrimage led by Fr. Augustine, a young Dominican priest, to their favorite Marian Shrine in Aglona, a tiny village in the southeastern part of the country.

This was a very blessed event, even though I was no longer free to follow my own schedule, but had to conform to that of the group. It did relieve me of the need to think about food or shelter, as these were provided (even though the food was often just snacks we carried and our bed was the floor of a barn covered with fresh straw). There were thirty young people and fifteen adults on this 180-mile pilgrimage, and each one carried their own gear as no "sag wagon" accompanied us. Fr. Augustine kept up a steady supply of prayers and teachings while walking and at Mass each evening. I was in charge of keeping a moderate pace for the group, as I had the cross on my staff and walked out front. It was a wonderful experience of the Body of Christ on earth on its way to the heavenly Jerusalem. I was still "on the way with Mary," this time under her title, "Our Lady of Aglona."

THE HOLY CITY OF VILNIUS

On August 16, I left my Latvian brothers and sisters, and headed directly south toward the Marian shrine that inspired my whole summer pilgrimage, Our Lady of Ostra Brama in Vilnius. It lay a little over 120 miles away. On the third day I crossed into Lithuania, and began to see many intricately carved, wooden crosses alongside the roads. This was mostly farmland and here horse-drawn wagons predominated, and water was being drawn from wells by buckets and ropes.

On Monday, August 24, I reached the city of Vilnius and made my first of several visits to the Shrine of Mary at the East Gate, also known as "Mother of Mercy." Then I walked another three hours to the home of a Polish woman Lucja, who was a kindergarten teacher, and whose name and address had been sent to me by my friend Jan. When I mentioned to Lucja that, if I got a visa for Belarus, I would go that way to Ukraine (rather than by way of Poland), she said it was all taken care of. It seems that a priest in Belarus who received a letter from my friend Sr. Immaculata, MC (whom I had met in Novosibirsk and St. Petersburg), asked him to write a letter of invitation to Belarus for me. He did so and he had sent it to me in care of Lucja, who–inspired by the Holy Spirit–opened the letter and took it upon herself to start the ball rolling. It took her seven visits to the embassy, a thick stack of paperwork, and making a photocopy of a photocopy of my passport picture. Now all she had to do was take my passport to the visa office the following evening, and I had a visa for Belarus in my passport. All I could do was give Lucja a big hug as the earthly representative (with her resourceful, determined, business savvy) of my caring heavenly Mother in this "city of mercy."

I ended up staying in her kindergarten classroom three nights, until I saw all of the sights I wanted to see in Vilnius; namely the original image of the Merciful Jesus by Kazimierski housed in Holy Spirit Church; Holy Trinity Church where St. Josaphat lived; the house where Sr. Faustina had the vision of the Merciful Jesus in 1935–sixty-five years before; and much more. I felt privileged to be walking in the footsteps of the Saints, on holy ground. As a matter-of-fact, when I think back now on all of the places where the Lord has taken me, I sensed the holiness of God in Vilnius more than in any other place, even Rome or Jerusalem. The sense of God's presence was almost tangible here. Even the beggars who sat in the street before the image of Our Lady of the East Gate, seemed to be aware of it, for they prayed the Rosary as they sat there begging, and they greeted passersby with, "God bless you." The Mother of God and her Son were indeed among the Father's children, literally, in this marketplace of the world.

BELARUS (WHITE RUSSIA)

When I left Vilnius on Thursday, August 27, I was halfway–20,000 miles–toward what would eventually total 40,000 miles of walking on pilgrimage. But only the Lord knew that at this time. Personally, I was not out to set any records or to achieve any such long-distance goals. I just tried to be faithful day by day, week by week, to walking and praying and trusting in the Lord, as He opened the doors, enlightened the path before me, and gave me the strength and the desire to go on. I had given Him my life and said, "Lord, I will walk until You come back again or until You take my life; whichever comes first."

I only had 43 kilometers from Vilnius to the border of Belarus, so I made it in two days of walking. When I crossed into this country, known in English until the end of the Soviet period as White Russia (the meaning of *belay-rues*), I thought I was back in Vershina in Siberia. Here, the peasants still lived close to the earth, hardly touched by technology or by secularization. Each had their own little garden for fresh vegetables, chickens, and eggs. So on Sunday, August 30, at the little village church in Zyrmuny, I was in for an experience of a lifetime, attending Mass with Polish Catholic peasants who knew how to worship the Lord with their whole being.

The church was decorated with long colorful streamers that went from ceiling, to wall, to pillars; images of the Saints were everywhere. The church was packed on this Sunday morning with devout worshipers. For receiving Holy Communion, those who went forward knelt in front of the Communion rail, five rows deep. When space was available in front, they would crawl forward on their knees to get closer. The priest distributing Communion was accompanied by four servers. One held the paten under the chin of the communicant. Two servers held lit candles, one on each side of the priest. A fourth server carried a large handbell, rung vigorously as the priest placed the sacred host upon the tongue of each recipient. What a visible testimony to the awesome reality of what was taking place in the Spirit here at this holy Sacrifice of the Mass, the Good Shepherd feeding His sheep on His very own Body and Blood. I felt privileged to be able to witness such reverence in my Slavic brothers and sisters.

MISSIONARIES IN BARANAVICHY

On the eighth day of walking in Belarus, I came into the large city of Baranavichy. I was totally unprepared for what the Lord had in store for me in this city. I thought I would just buy some bread and stamps, maybe fill up my water jug, and be on my way. However, as I walked along I saw this church building with the large letters, SVD on the side. I took them to stand for the Latin Societas Verbum Dei or Society of Divine Word Missionaries. If that was what it was, then this was a Catholic Church and if it was open, I could at least make a short visit to our Lord in the Blessed Sacrament.

But as soon as I stepped through the front door on the way to the chapel, I was met, not with the usual reserve and trepidation, but rather with a wave of love and hospitality, such as I rarely ever find. The receptionist asked me to wait right there until she could go and get the pastor to come and to meet me. Usually, pastors are trying to hide and to let the receptionist deal with anyone who does not have an appointment, but not here.

"HOW LONG CAN YOU STAY?"

When the pastor Fr. Vovek, appeared, his first words to me in English were, "Oh, I know you from videos and from reading articles about you. Come up to our recreation room and meet the other priests here. Make yourself at home. How long can you stay with us?" It seems I had stumbled upon the residence and headquarters of the Divine Word Missionaries for all of Eastern Europe. Of course, these were missionaries and they recognized a fellow missionary when they saw one, even if disguised as a pilgrim dressed in rags.

I ended up agreeing to spend two nights with them. So I was able not only to rest and to get cleaned up, but also to give several talks, to do some interviews, and to make a video. Even after I left them on Sunday afternoon and began walking again, one of the priests drove out twice to meet me, bringing different people for a blessing and to take pictures. On Friday a professional videographer by the name of Juri, along with his translator Sasha, met up with me to follow me for the next three days and to document my walk.[63]

This included a visit to the miraculous image of Our Lady of Polisia at the Polish parish in the village of Logishin, and a visit to the Cathedral of Our Lady of the Assumption in Pinsk where the Cardinal-Archbishop of the diocese resided. I got a firsthand account of the suffering of the Church under communism. I felt it a great grace to be touching base with the lives and places that for so long had stood behind The Iron Curtain. I could behold firsthand the triumph of the Immaculate Heart of Mary over the "Red Dragon" of communism and see the concrete results of all of the Rosaries prayed and first Saturdays observed in response to the request of Our Lady of Fatima.

ST. ANDREW BOBOLA

When I left the Cathedral of the Assumption in Pinsk on September 14, on the Feast of the Triumph of the Holy Cross, I only had about 45 miles to get to the border with Ukraine to the South. Since my visa for Ukraine did not begin until September 18, I had to slow down my pace. Providentially, the Lord arranged a two-day stopover at the little Catholic Church being reconstructed in Ivanovo. There I was shown the spot where St. Andrew Bobola, a nineteenth-century Jesuit missionary priest, had been martyred by some fanatical Orthodox believers. And during the day layover, I was able to spend six hours at a Latin alphabet typewriter typing up an eleven-page article I had written on my two-week pilgrimage to Aglona in Latvia. The Lord even provided a post office nearby so I could mail it off to my friend Lee in Anchorage.

CROSSING INTO UKRAINE

Early Friday morning I arrived at the border of Belarus and Ukraine. There was practically no traffic at this remote border station. The guards took me inside and sat me down, as they began copying information from my passport. After a half hour of more questions they let me go through.

After a 5-kilometer walk I came to the Ukrainian custom station. When I showed them my passport with the visa, they looked baffled. They started making telephone calls, and one went from one building to another with several forms in hand. Finally, after an hour, an official came to me and handed me my passport, duly stamped, and said, "Everything is fine—welcome to Ukraine."

SUFFERING PEOPLE

I now began to walk in the country I hoped to live in, to walk in, and to pray in, for the next seven months. Two years before this, in Rome in 1996, the Lord had already put it on my heart to pilgrimage in this "borderland" (the meaning of the word "Ukraine"). This was a land that had first accepted the faith in AD 988, with the conversion of the Grand Prince Vladimir the Great in Kiev, which began the baptism of the whole nation. This was the country that suffered so much under communism, especially in the Stalin era of the 1930s, when millions starved in what has been called "the Breadbasket of Russia" because it is such a rich agricultural land. And then there was the meltdown of the nuclear reactor in April of 1986, at Chernobyl, a tragedy which has caused untold suffering from radioactive fallout ever since.

These were some of the thoughts going through my mind as I walked through the light rain along a narrow dirt road full of potholes these first hours in Ukraine. Then I suddenly realized how much peace I was experiencing. It was as if Mary had placed her mantle of love and protection around me the moment I entered this historic land. It did not matter that I was in a strange country, did not know anyone, had little to eat, and that it was damp and cold. I was surrounded by love—the love of my Heavenly Mother, Mary. It reminded me of a similar sensation when I had crossed into Poland from the Czech Republic in July of 1996. It was as if I was experiencing the (Byzantine) Feast of the Protection of Mary on October 1, two weeks early. It seemed as if I had walked into the womb of the Mother of God, the place sanctified by the indwelling of the Word of God made flesh.

VLADIMIR VOLYNSKIJ

Now, indeed, my final goal for "Pilgrimage 1998" was in sight–the historic city of Lviv. It was195 miles directly south and it would take thirteen days to walk it. This part of my pilgrimage lay very close to the present eastern border with Poland. Actually, there were many Polish people living in this part of Ukraine, because this was part of Poland until after the Second World War when Stalin insisted the boundary of Ukraine be drawn this far west. My main reason for directing my steps this way was to visit St. Josaphat Kuntsevych's birth town, Vladimir Volynskij. I got there on Friday, September 25, but found everything locked up and could not find any way to enter the church where he received his call to the priesthood (through a crucifix that miraculously spoke to him). Nevertheless, just to be able to stand and to pray outside the church allowed me to be inspired by the bravery of this seventeenth-century Ukrainian Catholic monk who laid down his life for the unity of the one, holy, catholic, and apostolic Church of Rome.

Finally on Wednesday, September 30, I walked into the outskirts of the large city of Lviv, and began making my way to the city center. I thanked the Lord and especially the Holy Spirit, to whom this year 1998 was dedicated in preparation for the Jubilee Year 2000. His grace had brought me safely into port after a journey of 1,7000 miles on land, through nine countries. Only He could have managed it.

POUSTINIA IN LVIV

Now the Lord had to arrange for my winter *poustinia* as I took a break from pilgrimaging and went into a more contemplative time of resting in the Lord. I was taken over to the church I had seen on the way in, to meet the pastor Fr. Oleg, his wife, and three young children. (From ancient times to the present, as is the case with Byzantine [Greek] Catholic churches generally, most Byzantine Catholic priests in Ukraine are married and have families.) Fr. Oleg was very glad to see me and had everything ready for my arrival. He and twenty other pastors in Lviv were all building big new churches to hold the vast numbers of faithful flocking into the Catholic Church. Now that Ukraine had escaped the death-grip of communism, Ukrainian Catholics were given back their church buildings that had been confiscated by the Communists, and were again permitted to worship in public.

And on the construction site for the new church, they happened to have an empty work trailer on wheels that they had prepared for my *poustinia*. They had cleaned it out, put in a bed, a food prep area, and a chapel area with icons of Jesus and Mary. They added a couple of chairs for possible visitors. It was kept warm by electric heaters. I could also use the outhouse on the nearby construction site. The temporary building for Divine Liturgy and personal prayer before the Blessed Sacrament was just 100 feet away.

And so I established my daily routine of prayer five times a day and settled into my winter mode of *poustinia*. I caught up on my correspondence, typed up my journal notes, and received visitors who came for prayer or counseling. Being in the middle of a city, I was more available to people who could come on foot, by bus, or by car. I ended up with sixty scraps of paper with long lists of names to pray for while I was in *poustinia*. I also did some reading, as a Canadian woman living in Lviv supplied me with a steady stream of books by her favorite author, Henri Nouwen (1932-96). And, of course, people always brought some foodstuffs when they visited whether a few apples, a loaf of bread, a large jar of pickled vegetables, or homemade jam or preserves.

VIBRANT FAITH

One of the most precious gifts the Lord gave me during this winter *poustinia* was being able to attend Divine Liturgy each Sunday with the local faithful, and to pray over them afterward as they lined up for individual prayers. There were no pews or chairs in the temporary building they used for services, so the people stood or knelt on the floor. Packed tight together on a Sunday, the building could hold maybe 250 people. But there were that many also standing outside who could not get in – even in zero degree weather. I learned to get there an hour early so as to get a spot inside. But many others also came early. It was obvious that fifty years of persecution under communism (every Catholic Church had been closed or given to the Ukrainian Orthodox) had strengthened their faith and they now appreciated the ability to again worship publicly. And the seminaries and novitiate houses were bursting with vocations.

MOM IS CALLED HOME

As an example of this new life, I was invited to visit and to stay at a new Studite monastery just 90 miles to the east of Lviv in the village of Kolodiivka near Ternopyl that was bursting with young vocations. The founder, Fr. Gregory Planchak, sent me a letter inviting me to come and to pray with them. However, before I left for the monastery on February 14, I received the sad news that my mother had died on January 15, at the age of seventy-nine. Her death was not altogether unexpected, as she had been housebound with congestive heart failure, osteoarthritis, and shortness of breath for a few years, and was on oxygen twenty-four hours a day in the past year. My two brothers had tried to get in touch with me, but the fax they sent never got to me. The communication system in Ukraine at this time was still very unreliable. I only received word of her death and burial two weeks later when a letter came in the mail the end of January, with condolences from the Russian desk in Anchorage and from Archbishop Hurley.

But I had said goodbye to my mother and father ten years before, in May of 1988, when I left St. Mary's Glenshaw with my little mule, and began my walk to Jerusalem. It was then that I had answered Jesus' call to radical discipleship in Matthew, giving up "house, brothers, sisters, father, mother, children, and lands for His sake" (Mt 19:29). And they had accepted it. I believe God gave my mother special grace to accept my vocation as a pilgrim, just as He had given His mother, Mary, the special graces she needed to stand beneath the Cross and to suffer His death with Him. My mother once wrote to me saying, "People often ask me if I worry about you. I tell them, 'God can take better care of you than I can.'"

She truly had surrendered me into the hands of the Lord.

SEE YOU IN HEAVEN

After my father died in 1997, when I was in Norway, my mother wrote in one of her weekly letters to me that when people ask her, "Do you miss your son George?" she tells them, "I feel his presence with me always, because I know he is praying for me." In another letter she wrote, "Other people think you should come back; but I understand why you have to go on: it is better to do God's will than your own or other people's will." She was sustained spiritually by the Jesus Prayer, which she said continuously; she watched EWTN (the 24-hour Catholic television station) daily; and faithful friends brought her Holy Communion when she was confined to her home the last few years of her life. In her last letter to me, written in a stillstrong hand on January 5, ten days before her death in the nursing home, she concluded her four-page letter with, "See you in heaven someday. I love you, George."

So both my father and now my mother had gotten to the New Jerusalem before I to the earthly Jerusalem. Our prayers for each other would keep us connected, though now the earthly ties were sundered. They had passed on to me the Catholic Faith through their example of living for the Lord, and the best thing I could do in return now was to live out my calling as the Lord revealed it to me, step-by-step. I remembered St. Paul's words in Romans, "For I am convinced that neither death, nor life...nor any other creature will be able to separate us from the love of God in Christ Jesus our Lord" (Rom 8:38-39). God willing (and through my cooperating with His will) I would see them in the heavenly Kingdom.

BLESSED ENCOUNTERS

Before I left for the Studite monastery on February 14, the Lord gave me a few more faith-building experiences in Lviv. One was a meeting with His Beatitude, Lubomyr Husar, MSU (1933-2017) in the hospital, and sharing with him my pilgrim/*poustinik* vocation and getting his blessing. And a final, amazing experience was at a prison where more than 600 men were incarcerated, but who so valued my sharing with them, that they prayed for me by name for years afterward. One prisoner named Sergie wrote in July 2001, "The meeting was unforgettable and interesting. Frankly, I was envious of him, because there was so much brightness, love, and holiness shinning from him. This meeting added a lot of light to my dark life."[64]

ON TO THE MONASTERY

Because I had so many boxes of food to take to the monks in Kolodiivka, I accepted a ride there in a car. They welcomed me with open arms and gave me a private room in the guesthouse for my *poustinia*. There were forty-three members of the Community of the Monastery of St. Theodore the Studite in Kolodiivka, eight of whom were priests. And in the neighboring town of Birky, there was another monastic community, comprised of thirty-three young women. They were all young, joyful, enthusiastic monastics, excited about living their lives totally for the Lord. I was free to join in any of the monastic hours of prayer I wanted. Of course the Holy Week and Easter services were excellent celebrations and I felt privileged to share in this expression of the ancient Faith. One of the most memorable experiences was hearing the church bells rung continuously on Easter for twenty-four hours. Volunteers took turns pulling on the rope to ring the bell in the tower, and switched off every half hour. All of creation knew for certain that Christ had risen and was alive among us!

"PILGRIMAGE 1999"

During my stay at the monastery I laid out my tentative route to the Holy land through Romania, Bulgaria, and Turkey. I hoped to walk the entire distance, but that would have meant going through Syria or Lebanon to get to Israel. When a friend who worked in Army Intelligence saw my route, he checked with the American Embassy in Kiev and had Consular Information Sheets published by the U.S. Department of State sent to me. These bulletins, in fact, warned of dangers of travel in Syria and in Lebanon, particularly about possible terrorist attacks, the maintenance of very strict security, armed bodyguards, bombings, abductions, and live land mines. So I put aside any thought of taking that route, and planned to do what I did in 1971; walk through Turkey and after arriving in Mersin on the Mediterranean coast, fly to Cypress and take a boat to Haifa.

THE PRAYER OF MY HEART

Lord, God of heaven and earth:

I thank You for these years

of safe pilgrimaging in Europe,

where there are so many testimonies

to faith in Christ,

going back to the earliest centuries.

I ask Your blessing on Your children today
who are seeking to live faithfully
to Your plan for their lives.
I also enlist the protection of the Mother of God
on those who are devoted to You
under so many of her miraculous titles
proven effective over centuries of faith.

May those who saw the Cross of Jesus on my staff,
and who responded with love,
be strengthened in their resolve
to continue to follow Jesus
as their Lord and Savior.

All glory, praise and honor,
to the Father, Son and Holy Spirit,
now and forever. Amen.

ENDNOTES

63. Video. Yuri Goroulyov eventually published this material in a twenty-minute VHS videotape from "Studio 'Stopshot'" in Minsk, Belarus, in three languages: Russian, Polish, and English, under the title, "*Gospel of George-Profession Pilgrim.*"

64. Quote. *The Last Shall Be First,* Rev. Ihor Tsar, Papuga, Lviv, 2005, p. 208.

CHAPTER 6

PILGRIMAGE IN BIBLE LANDS

(1999-2001)

PART ONE

UKRAINE TO ISRAEL (1999)

PRAYERFUL SEND-OFF

To begin "Pilgrimage 1999" from Ukraine to Israel, I did not start from Kolodiivka where I had spent Lent and Easter, but I decided to return to Lviv. On Thursday, April 15, I attended, for the last time, Fr. Oleg's 8:00 a.m. morning Divine Liturgy. After Liturgy they all walked with me to the edge of the property for a final blessing. Then my friend Fr. Igor led us through the streets of Lviv to a cemetery at the edge of town where he conducted a *moleben* (prayer service) at the grave of the now Blessed Bishop Nicholas Charnetsky, CSsR (1884-1959). This holy bishop had been exiled to the labor camps by the Communists. Now he was working many miracles for those who sought his intercession. Fr. Igor made sure I had a little packet of dirt from this grave to share with others on my journey.

By 2:00 p.m., the last walkers who had been accompanying me left, and I was once again on my own to resume a more quiet life of solitude and silent contemplation. I had ahead of me a thirteen-day walk along the Carpathian Mountains in southwestern Ukraine to Chernivtsi, the border city leading into Romania. I had some ferocious winds, rain, snow, and ice to contend with in this stretch.

EAGER FAITHFUL

When I would come into a village, word would go out and everyone would come from their homes and kneel alongside the road for me to lay hands on them and to pray over them. One day in a town by the name of Kolomyia, the priest Fr. Ratislan, announced after the 9:00 a.m. Liturgy, that I would pray over people. They all came up and knelt by the Communion rail so I could go from one to another. However, I soon noticed that the Communion rail was never completely empty. After passing from one end of the rail to the other, I looked back, and instead of seeing an empty rail, I saw it was filled up again with new people. It seems that those who were prayed over were going home and telling their neighbors and friends, "If you want to get prayer, go over to the Catholic Church. There is a pilgrim praying over people there." At noontime I said to Father Ratislan, "We have to stop this or I will be here all day. I still have 25 kilometers to walk today."

But that was not the end of the crowds. Some days hundreds of people were coming. Factories released their workers; teachers released their students; buses and taxis came. Some stood in line in the rain for an hour as I (wrapped in my plastic poncho) prayed over each one of them.

Each person of course had to give me a few coins (*kopiyky*) or paper bills (*hryvnia*)–1 *kopiyka* equaled 3 cents; 1 *hryvnia* equaled 30 cents. Before I got to the border with Romania, I had over 1,000 (Ukrainian) *hryvnia* ($300) which I was able to give to a group of religious sisters so I did not have to carry all of those coins and stacks of paper bills. This experience helped me get a better sense of what Jesus must have felt when the crowds pressed around Him, giving Him no break for hours and even days on end (Mk 6:31). I had to trust that in the midst of all of these external demonstrations of faith, there was an authentic inner reality and true repentance. Emotionalism and superstition (at times found even in Christian regions) avail nothing for efficacious spiritual help. I did what I could and left the rest in the hands of the Lord.

HISTORIC ROMANIA

On April 27, after an examination by customs on the Ukraine side of the border, and on the Romanian side, I was now walking in a new country. It was predominantly Orthodox and with a small Roman Catholic minority and an even smaller Byzantine or "Greek" Catholic presence. I knew this country was founded as a Roman penal colony and that the poet Ovid had been exiled here in AD 8 for "corrupting" the youths in Rome with his poetry. Latin was the basis of the Romanian language, so I was able to figure out many of the words. The pronunciation, though, was another matter.

The greatest grace of my twenty-nine days in Romania was the fact that divine Providence arranged for another pilgrim, Pope John Paul II, to be in Romania at the same time as I. He was going to be in the capital of Bucharest May 7, while I would be walking near the coast. His visit was well publicized and when I showed people the photo of my meeting with him in Rome in 1996, people immediately understood who I was and accepted me. The simple poor always feel honored when a foreigner takes the time to come to their country and to visit with them. So I kind of rode on the coattails of the Vicar of Christ for these days in Romania.

FAITH AND SUPERSTITION

Nevertheless, there was one big difference between my pilgrimage and the Pope's: he was among the upper echelons of society; I was among those at the lowest rung of the social ladder. On May 10, a young man who belonged to a traditional, strict, old Orthodox Christian group (maybe even an "Old Believer") invited me to stay with his dirt poor family for a few days and I accepted. His extended family consisted of parents, grandparents, aunts, and uncles, all living in close proximity. Not one of them had a paying job. They lived off of what they could grow on their meager holdings. One day we took the horse and wagon out to the field to cut fresh grass to bring back to feed their livestock. The horse and wagon had been purchased with two-year's worth of earnings from hard physical labor in Israel. I counted it a true gift from the Lord to be able to share in the life of these simple folks who lived their faith far removed from the consumer society dominating the so-called developed nations of the world.

My next encounter with Romanians, however, was not so pleasant. As I got near the large city of Galati, I began to be "attacked" by Gypsies. Unlike the Gypsies who drove horses and wagons (or motor homes) in European countries, these Gypsies had money; they drove cars, owned palatial homes in the city (I was told), and were fanatical about their religious beliefs. They would approach me in groups of seven or eight, both men and women, shouting Parinte (Father) and performing *ceremonia* (kissing of the hand). Then they would tear out hair from my beard and rip off patches from the bottom of my robe to take home as "holy souvenirs." At night they unzipped my tent, reached in, and took whatever they wanted. Eventually I had to put away my icon, crucifix, Rosary, and all religious symbols so they would not have a reason to approach me. I was thankful to cross the Danube River in a few days and to be out of range of this troublesome, fanatical group of people. I could only pray for them to be enlightened to the truth of the Lord and what it meant to be His devoted followers.

TWO WEEKS IN BULGARIA

At noontime on May 26, I completed my 400 miles in Romania and passed through border customs into Bulgaria. Actually, I limped across the border because my right ankle was very sore, possibly from sleeping in the dampness near the Black Sea the night before. It took all morning to make just five 5 kilometers. But I had no problem at the border and was glad to be back in a Slavic country that used the Cyrillic alphabet and where many people spoke Russian, with which I was much more comfortable.

I only had 220 miles to walk in Bulgaria until I arrived at the border of Turkey. I was headed for Constantinople, hoping a Westernized Muslim country would let a Christian pilgrim walk through it for two months. The Bulgarian coast was not densely populated and the only two major cities were the port towns of Varna and Burgas. Otherwise, I was in rural areas with megafarms, walking up and down long hills all day with some great views of the Black Sea. This was also a tourist area because of the beaches and one day I took the time to swim in the sea, which I found to be optically clear but very polluted with tar.

In spite of the frequent rains and the fact that one day a man tried to steal my Bible when he thought I was not looking, and another day when I was almost hit by a passing car, my two weeks in Bulgaria went fairly smoothly. Enough people showed an interest in my pilgrimage. One *bubba* (elderly woman) even washed my robe for me the night I stayed in her house. But during these two weeks I was told several times I might not be allowed to carry the cross through Turkey or even walk through it while wearing my robe. One Franciscan friar had recently been required to take off his habit while he walked through Turkey. So I made a denim cover to put over my San Damiano Cross just in case it might be required. I decided that if I could not pass through ancient Asia Minor as I was, I would not walk without my denim-patched robe, but would instead head for Greece and walk to Athens to get to the Holy Land by boat.

"A PIECE OF CAKE"

When I made it to the border with Turkey on June 11, it was the Feast of the Sacred Heart of Jesus. I placed myself and the present situation completely in His hands. It turned out to be one of the easiest crossings I had ever made. As I stepped into the customs building an official came up to me and asked, "Do you have a visa?" When I told him I did not, he said: "Step right over here and I will sign you up." Then he said: "Take this over to the next window and they will stamp the date on it."

There was no line, no baggage check, no comment about the cross, no question about how much money I had, or what I was going to do. I breathed a sigh of relief as I walked away, thanking the Sacred Heart of Jesus for opening the door so easily and melting away all of my previous apprehensions.

Now I was in a country I had walked through in 1971, on my first pilgrimage to Jerusalem almost thirty years before. I wondered if it would still be as friendly as I had found it then. Indeed at first it was, especially the eleven days it took me to walk the 250 kilometers to Istanbul. After four and a half years, I was nearing the end of my pilgrimage on the European continent, for when I left Istanbul on June 25, and took the ferry across the Bosphorus, I would again be back on the Asian continent. But on this present 150-mile stretch of highway, there were still many Europeans, cyclists, and tourists, and I had plenty of visitors. A number engaged me in more prolonged conversation, like the young Turkish doctor Nuri, who stopped me several times the first day to ask me how Christians understand the meaning of the Trinity. Even as a Muslim he was struck by the thought that I shared with him, namely that a self-sufficient monad (a single Person, Allah) needed to be in relationship with another in order to love.

FOUR DAYS IN ISTANBUL

Another man who stopped to talk was Abi, an American/Turkish businessman who invited me to stay at his apartment with him in Istanbul. Providentially, he was a dealer in denim, so he gave me several large remnants of various weights of denim to take along and eventually to sew on my robe as patches. I knew that as a Muslim he was risking being ostracized by his friends for giving hospitality to a Christian, but I figured that a big city like Istanbul was probably more tolerant of such behavior and I prayed that the Lord would take care of him and reward him for his openness to the truth.

My main interest in Istanbul was to visit the American Express office to pick up my forty pieces of mail. My brother Tom had sent me a map showing in which Hilton Hotel in Istanbul the office was located. But I also made it a point to spend two hours in the seventh-century Hagia Sophia which was so central to Byzantine Christianity. Since it was no longer a functioning mosque but now a government-owned museum, the ancient mosaics on the walls were being uncovered and so once again they could inspire the faith of those who follow Christ. I also visited two Catholic churches, Holy Spirit Cathedral and St. Anthony's, staffed respectively, by the Salesians and the Franciscans. The Franciscans date their presence in the city back to St. Francis of Assisi himself, who came to the Holy Land in 1221. I was happy to once again be picking up the trail of one of my main patron Saints, especially as he himself had walked on pilgrimage in these lands of the Bible. Although the Catholic presence in Turkey is minuscule, I managed to make enough contact with them here, so as to receive the Hail Mary in Turkish, along with its pronunciation, and add it to my list of languages in which I prayed my daily Rosary. I even had my Muslim friend Abi, tape the proper pronunciation on my recorder so that I could memorize it from there.

INTO THE FIERY FURNACE

When I left Istanbul on June 25, I was headed for Mersin, a city on the Mediterranean Sea across from the island of Cyprus. My hope was to fly from Mersin, Turkey, to Nicosia, Cyprus, and to get a boat to Haifa, Israel, as I had done in 1971. Since this was a 600-mile trek,

I figured it would take me about forty-two days to walk it on the most direct route. But on the way, I wanted to pick up two cities that held special meaning for me, Iznik and Konya. Iznik because it was the ancient city of Nicea of conciliar fame, and Konya, because it was the New Testament Iconium which St. Paul evangelized. But these six weeks of pilgrimage were not going to be easy; the Lord decided it was time to take His willing Pilgrim through a few more trials.

The first test came on June 26, in the suburb called Pindle. Two young Muslim men pulled up beside me in their car.

"You better put that cross away or you will be arrested and put in jail."

I smiled at them, wished them God's blessing, and continued on my way. Five minutes later they came back, angry as hornets. They got out of their car and charged at me screaming, "This land belongs to Muhammad; the cross has no place here!"

One of them grabbed my staff, as the other swung and broke the top off of it. The San Damiano Cross fell off. But the beautiful, teak wood handcrafted staff made in India, that I had carried for four years throughout Europe, was not destined to serve the Lord in Asia. The other fellow wrenched the remaining piece of staff out of my hand, broke it in three pieces over his knee, and then tossed it over a high wall so I could not retrieve it.

Then the other fellow started jumping up in the air, headbutting me. He managed to knock off my glasses and raised a welt near my ear, but he missed his mark and I did not fall down dead. I took the scuffle out onto the busy highway so cars had to stop and then they could observe what was happening. Even though the young fundamentalist Muslims were haranguing the motorists, several of them quickly sized up the situation and came to my assistance by pulling their fellow Muslim citizens off of me, restraining them until I could pick up my San Damiano Cross from the roadway. I was not about to go to the police and file a complaint, but entrusted the radicals into God's hands and prayed for them. Thankfully, they did not follow me or make any more trouble and I was able to sleep peacefully in my tent that night and the following nights.

IN THE FOOTSTEPS OF ST PAUL

On June 29, I made a three-hour visit to Iznik (Nicea) and prayed by the Byzantine Hagia Sophia, where the Fathers of the First Council of Nicea had met in AD 325, to give us the Creed we still use. This is also where the Fathers at the Second Council of Nicea met in AD 787, to defend our use of religious icons, pictures, and statues. Then I was on my way to Iconium. And this is where the Lord put me through the next test. I was walking up and down hills through agricultural land; first with orchards of cherries, apricots, pears, and plums and then vast wheat fields on end. I began to feel weak and nauseated. At first I thought it might be from the heat and from eating too many fresh fruits. But when it kept up for weeks on end, I suspected that it was something worse.

At least there was plenty of good drinking water in this area. Every few kilometers underground springs had been tapped and the water was piped into concrete troughs alongside the road. One day a man even offered to kill one of his lambs and have dinner with me if I would accept his hospitality for a few days. I politely declined his offer, but it made me think of Abraham offering hospitality to the three angels in Genesis 18:1-5.

I was continuing to do a lot of sweating, felt weak, and developed diarrhea. So, on July 24 and 25, I got a hotel room in Karaman for $5 a night to try and rest up a bit. Being in a large city I was able to buy some cake and ice cream to celebrate my fifty-eighth birthday. (Eventually I came to realize that I was suffering from a severe cold and an ear infection.)

REACHING THE MEDITERRANEAN

Finally, on July 31, I reached the Mediterranean Sea at Silifke. Here I was pleased to be in the area of the famous St. Thecla, who tradition says was converted by St. Paul in Iconium and became a powerful evangelizer and healer. Eastern Christians call her "apostle and proto-martyr among women and equal to the apostles." I did not go to visit her tomb-cave and the Byzantine Church built over it, but I felt privileged to be so close to such an example of discipleship and holiness. I prayed for all the Theclas I had met over the years, especially those in Slavic countries, where her name is very common.

From Silifke I headed east along the coast toward Mersin, a four-day walk away. This area was all tourists and I took advantage of some of the beaches to take a dip in the Sea to cool off. But I still also used the abundant irrigation channels that ran alongside the highways in Turkey, for bathing. Now I was camping in olive groves. When I arrived at Mersin on August 4, and began looking for the Catholic Church, the Lord sent one of His angels, a Muslim woman by the name of Arzu, who befriended me on the street and who led me right to St. Anthony Cathedral. It seems she was being drawn toward the Catholic faith, and often came to this church to pray. The cathedral staff was super-hospitable and Fr. Anthony, a Franciscan, gave me a room in the guesthouse where I just crashed from exhaustion for four days.

THREE-THOUSAND MILE DETOUR

When I shared with them my desire to get to Israel, they told me that since the 1974 war between Turkey and Greece, no one can cross the Green Line in Cyprus. So I would have to fly to Haifa either direct from Adana or fly to Istanbul, then to Athens and get the boat to Haifa. I did not have peace about flying directly into Israel, so I chose the longer way around. For $246 I bought airplane tickets from Adana to Istanbul and from Istanbul to Athens. Since Adana was further east up the coast, I took a seventy-five minute train ride there for 75 cents and stayed overnight with Fr. Felice, a Salesian, who pastored a little church hidden away in the city. At least during this last week in Turkey I was able to receive the Sacraments and to also get some medicine for my cold and ear infection, so as to be fortified both spiritually and physically for my landing in Israel.

On the morning of Tuesday, August 10, I took a bus to Adana Airport and arrived in plenty of time for my 11:10 a.m. flight to Istanbul on Turkish Airlines. I passed through customs and security, and my three bags were checked through to Athens. From Adana to Istanbul by air my flight was roughly 600 miles. It had taken me two months to walk it; the trip by plane took about one hour. But I felt this was the Lord's will, so I had peace about it. After a five-hour layover in Istanbul, my fight to Athens took about an hour, covering a distance of about 745 miles. I arrived in Athens at 5:30 p.m. and began asking about the next ship to Haifa. The *Nissos Kypris*, a 900-passenger ship flying the flag of Cyprus, left in two days, on Thursday evening, from Port Piraeus, just 30 kilometers from the airport.

SAILING THE MEDITERRANEAN

I slept outside in my tent the first night in Athens and then took a room near the port Wednesday night. Guided by the Holy Spirit, I did not purchase a ticket for the ship at any of the many travel agent offices I saw along the streets, but sought out the main office of the Salamis Lines. Though they did not normally issue tickets to customers from there, they graciously made an exception for me. After purchasing my ticket for $110 (333,000 drachmas), the manager George, took a personal interest in my pilgrimage. He said to me, "Let me do something to help you on your way. When you board the ship tomorrow, go up to the reception desk and there you can pick up a free meal ticket so you can eat in the dining room during the three days you are on the boat." I thanked him, the Lord, and my patron St. George, for this generous gift. He became one more benefactor who received my daily intercessory prayers on this journey of faith.

I had booked the cheapest passage possible–a deck chair topside. But when I found the proper deck space, I noticed some reclining seats in an air-conditioned room inside and there were very few passengers in them. So I took a seat near the front so thankful to be in out of the 95 degrees outside. I spread my sleeping bag out on the floor between the rows of seats, and got a good night's sleep.

HISTORIC ISLANDS

Now I had two full days of sailing ahead of me (Friday and Saturday), as we were due to dock in Haifa on Sunday morning. We were scheduled to make brief stops at four islands along the way; Tinos, Patmos, Rhodes, and Cyprus. I did not get off the boat at the first two islands, but when we docked for two hours at the second, Patmos, I found a bench at the stern of the ship where I had a good view of the island. I gazed upon the island and especially upon the church and monastery that I could clearly make out high up in the mountains, and which I was told was built over the cave of the Apostle John. I pondered John's imprisonment here when he wrote his Apocalypse (Rv 1:9). I read from my Bible part of this vision/book and I thought how, from this tiny cave, on this little island in the first century, God revealed His perspective on the purpose of all of His creation–eternal unity through loving worship of the Most Holy Trinity, Father, Son, and Holy Spirit. And by His grace and by the preaching of the Gospel, I was privileged to share in that truth at this very moment. His revelation had come full circle. Thanks be to God for such a gift!

At the next two islands, Rhodes and Cyprus, I did get off the ship briefly. By this time I had met a priest and his youth group from California who were also on pilgrimage. They got off at each island to attend or to celebrate Mass if possible. I was thankful to be able to join them and to receive the Lord's Body and Blood in places where the Gospel had been planted in AD 44-45 and which flourished from the time of the Apostles (Acts 13:1-12).

UNDER MARY'S MANTLE

As our ship drew near our goal in Haifa, I realized that the Lord and His holy Mother had been orchestrating this part of my journey. When we docked in Haifa at 7:00 a.m. on Sunday morning, it would be August 15, the Feast of the Assumption of Mary into Heaven–the very title of the church honoring the Mother of God under which I had been baptized and where I grew up in Glenshaw, Pennsylvania. I was excited to realize that I might be able to get to Mass and Communion on this personally important feast at the Carmelite Monastery on the top of Mt. Carmel above the city of Haifa. There, our Lady's hermits had been carrying on the eremetical tradition of solitude and prayer in the spirit of Elijah, the fiery eighth-century Old Testament prophet, since Carmelite hermits first settled there in 1206. But before I could get to the holy mountain and the holy Mysteries, I had to make it through immigration and security at the port of Haifa. I expected difficulties, because I had been reading that Israel was having problems with religious fanatics traveling to Jerusalem to await the end of the world, at the beginning of the year 2000 in four more months.

PASSPORT CONTROL

Sure enough, when I disembarked in Haifa and approached the window where a young woman was stamping passports, she asked me, "Why are you here?" "How long do you intend to stay?" "What will be your address in Israel?" "How much money do you have?" After she satisfied herself with my answers–that I was probably not going to be a threat to the country–she half-heartedly stamped my passport and waved me through. Immediately, a young security guard walked up to me and told me to follow him to a special room off to the side. There he told me to empty out all of my bags and he carefully searched through everything. Then he told me to pack it all up and to step into a little cubicle and undress for a complete body search.

This new, poor little secular and military country was doing all it humanly could to insure its precarious survival as a thorn in the side of the hostile giant, the surrounding Muslim nations who were bent upon its expulsion. I could hardly blame Israel–except for their lack of faith in the God of Abraham, Isaac, and Jacob and in Jesus, their Messiah, who had shown them so much love. But I had to be thankful they at least left a Christian pilgrim come, lift up the Cross of Jesus here, and pay his respects to the places sanctified by His Master, Jesus Christ, for the coming Jubilee celebration of His 2,000th birthday on Christmas of the year 2000.

PART TWO

JUBILEE YEAR (2000)

PLAN FOR THE JUBILEE

My plan now was to spend the rest of the year 1999, and all of the year 2000, in the Holy Land. I especially wanted to be in Bethlehem where Jesus was born, for the next two Christmases. In 2001, I would leave the Holy Land for my next assignment from the Lord, wherever that might be. For the next seventeen months, I would travel in the footsteps of the Old Testament Prophets and the New Testament Apostles, in recognition of the great service they all performed for the Lord and for all of His chosen People.

Since the Lord deposited me in Haifa in the north of Israel–the Galilee area–I figured that He wanted me to start my Jubilee Pilgrimage in the Holy Land, by visiting Nazareth, Capernaum, and the Sea of Galilee, where Jesus grew up and did much of His public ministry. Then I could head south to Jerusalem and pray at the spots where He offered the final sacrifice of His life to the Father, on Calvary. There is no mention of Carmel in the New Testament, but it certainly played a key role in the life of Elijah in the Old Testament (see I Kg 17-21). So I was eager to experience all of the holy places here on this mountain, before moving on.

ELIJAH AND MOUNT CARMEL

I eventually came to understand that there were four important sites to visit on Mount Carmel (1) the large "Cave of the Prophets" at the base of the mountain; (2) the tiny cave of Elijah on the top of the mountain, now contained in the large Carmelite men's monastery called "Stella Maris" ("Star of the Sea"); (3) a women's international Carmelite monastery on the top of the mountain; and (4) Muhraqah, on the southeast tip of the Carmel Range where Elijah had the contest with the prophets of Baal (see 1 Kg 18:19).

I did not realize it until a few weeks later, but the Lord had one more place on Mount Carmel, the little Druze village of Isfiya, that would become key to my seventeen months in the Holy Land. My first goal was to climb the mountain and to go to Mass at Stella Maris Carmelite Men's Monastery in honor of the Assumption of the Mother of God. There I thanked Mary for the safe journey to the Holy Land and asked for grace to be open to all that the Lord wanted to do in and through me in the coming months of pilgrimaging in the Holy Land.

After attending the 11:00 a.m. Mass in Italian at Stella Maris Monastery, I headed down the side of the mountain to a shrine called "the Cave of Elijah." This was a rather large cave that could have been where Elijah had his "school" (of the Prophets) and where legend says the Holy Family camped one night on their return from Egypt to Nazareth. Now, the cave was mostly frequented by Jews and by Muslims, so I did not hang around long. I climbed halfway back up the mountain and found a private place to camp for the night. I also cut a scrub oak sapling to serve as a staff to hold the San Damiano Cross from my old staff. And that was my first day in the Holy Land.

WELCOMED IN ISFIYA

The next day I revisited Stella Maris Monastery and spent two hours at the Sisters' Carmel down the road. There I was captivated by the painting in the sanctuary which portrayed Elijah praying on Mt. Carmel and his servant seeing the cloud (symbolizing the incarnation) shaped like a human hand, arising over the water to bring the desperately needed rain (I Kg 18:44). Then I returned and camped in my same sleeping spot. On the following day, August 17, I again attended Mass at Stella Maris Monastery at 11:00 a.m. and set out for Muhraqah on the southern end of the mountain range, 18 miles away.

Still nursing a cold, sinus, and ear infection, I did not make it all the way to the monastery, but camped out in the National Forest along the way. The next morning I came into what was a village of destiny for me–Isfiya. It turned out to be the most friendly place I found in a month of walking in all of Israel. By 5:30 p.m. I arrived at Muhraqah, but the gates were locked, so I camped out on the hillside.

At 8:00 a.m. the next morning, Fr. Emmanuel, a Spanish Carmelite priest, opened the gates and warmly welcomed me to the site of Elijah's contest with the false prophets. Stavriani, a convert to Catholicism, came for the 5:30 p.m. Mass in English and then I went the next day with her to meet her elderly friend Julia and to see some property she owned in the National Forest where she said I could set up my *poustinia*. I promised her I would pray about it. But first I had to finish "Pilgrimage 1999" by walking though Galilee and then on to Jerusalem. We would see what the Lord had in mind after that.

WALKING IN GALILEE

So for the whole next month (August 21 to September 21), I followed the footsteps of Jesus and His Apostles as closely as I could. My first stop was Nazareth, where the Salesians, who staffed a large school for boys on top of the hill, gave me hospitality. The director there, Fr. John, gave me the Hail Mary in Hebrew and in Arabic (in print and in audio forms), which I then memorized and added to my daily Rosary. In Nazareth I visited the Church of the Annunciation, built over the remains of a fifth-century Byzantine Church where on one of the pillars were carved the first two words of the Hail Mary in Greek. I also visited the Little Sisters of Jesus who now cared for the convent where Charles de Foucauld (1858-1916), a twentieth-century French soldier, convert, hermit, and martyr-hero of mine, had found hospitality as a gardener for about a year.

From Nazareth I walked to Cana and visited both the Greek Orthodox and Roman Catholic churches, while groups of tourists stopped to renew their marriage vows in remembrance of how Jesus and His Apostles had once attended a wedding banquet in Cana (Jn 2:1ff). From Cana I walked to Tiberias, where I was in time for a 6:00 p.m. Mass at the Church of St. Peter, and from there continued on along the Sea of Galilee to Tabgha, which commemorates the multiplication of the loaves and fish (Mt 14:13-21), and which has fifth-century mosaics from an early Byzantine Church, one showing a basket of bread and two fish. From Tabgha I climbed the Mount of Beatitudes to pray in the eight-sided church, and then descended the hill to Capernaum down by the sea. There I spent three hours praying in the ruins of the first-century synagogue and in the reputed house of St. Peter.

AROUND THE SEA OF GALILEE

From Capernaum I headed east to walk around the Sea of Galilee and then toward Mt. Tabor back near Nazareth. During these days the temperature was in the nineties, and people were handing me bottles of frozen water; and I took advantage of the sea to take a few swims to cool off. In the little village of Yavneel, a man by the name of Dufny (he and his wife were Russian immigrants, but not religiously observant) invited me to his home and farm in Salona, to eat and to sleep the night. His wife washed my robe–which by this time was white with salt from sweating–in their washing machine, and hung it out in the hot sun to dry.

On September 1, I made the three-hour climb up the switchback road that takes one to the top of the isolated summit of Mount Tabor. Even though I had wonderful fellowship, prayer, and meals with the Franciscan friars and sisters who staffed the shrine, I counted it a privilege to be able to sleep two nights in my tent, on the spot where Peter had suggested, "Lord, let us build three tents here: one for You, one for Moses and one for Elijah (Mt 17:4)." Tent or no tent I thought it awesome to be on the spot where Jesus was transfigured in glory, and where Moses and Elijah showed up to give testimony to Him. I was thankful for the hours of quiet prayer I had before the Blessed Sacrament the two days I spent here. I was also able to identify with Jesus talking about His "exodus" in Jerusalem (Lk 9:31), for from here I, too, would set my face toward the Holy City (Lk 9:51) which lay about 75 miles directly south of here.

THROUGH SAMARIA

I followed a highway which goes from Nazareth to Jerusalem through, what in Jesus' day was called "The Hill Country of Samaria," and is now called by the Palestinains "West Bank." Just as it was hostile to Jesus then (Lk 9:52-53), so it can be a hostile place to Jews and Christians now. And though I could have taken one of two other routes to Jerusalem (through the Jordan Valley to the east or through the Shephelah to the west), I felt the Lord saying to walk this way which was probably traversed by Mary on her way to visit Elizabeth (Lk 1:39). The Israeli guards at the border told me to be careful but they let me pass, so I figured that whatever happened, it would be part of God's plan for me.

When I stepped into the West Bank on Saturday, September 4, at Jenin, it looked like I was in a garbage dump, with trash, paper, and plastic strewn everywhere. Though the youths walked around talking on their cell phones, there was no good drinking water available and the potholes in the road could have swallowed a bicycle. I learned later that a lot of money was coming into the West Bank from Europe (especially from Germany) but it was all going into the pockets of the local politicians whose big, new homes I could see being built on the outskirts of the towns.

I was only two days and one night in Palestinian controlled-territory proper, but even when in Israeli-controlled territory, I was still in ancient Samaria. On September 6, I came through Biblical Shechem (site of Jacob's well–[Jn 4:5-6]), where a reporter from Tel Aviv did an interview with me and on September 7, I passed around Ramallah. I refused an offer to sleep at a man's house there, preferring to sleep in olive groves, in my tent most of these nights.

ENTERING JERUSALEM

Finally on Thursday, September 9 (9/9/99), I caught my first view of the walls around the Old City of Jerusalem. I was approaching from the northeast and so I came through East Jerusalem which is mostly Muslim. Here, the young Arab children started throwing stones, sticks, bottles, whatever they could find, at me, shouting, "Masihi, Masihi" (Christian, Christian). It was only the first of many such encounters I would experience in Muslim areas in the coming year. But I found it an appropriate welcome to Jerusalem, as I was heading toward the east gate in the Old City walls, which is called "St. Stephen's Gate," because the deacon Stephen was stoned to death just outside this gate in AD 34 (Acts 7:57-59). For eleven years (1988-99) I had been walking toward this gate. And all along the way, each day, I had prayed in the words of Psalm 122, "and now our feet are standing within your gates, Jerusalem" (v. 2). After 24,000 miles of walking from Glenshaw to Jerusalem, my feet were passing through the gate Jesus had entered on that triumphant Palm Sunday before His Passion. He had traveled an immeasurable distance (from heaven to earth) to get here. I thanked Him for allowing me to join my tiny sacrifice to His great and infinite sacrifice (Ph 2:6-8).

Upon entering the Old City of Jerusalem, I found the Via Dolorosa, and retraced Jesus' ascent to Calvary from the chapel of the Flagellation. After a thorough check of my bags by police outside the Church of the Holy Sepulcher, I entered to pray the last five Stations of the Cross. I climbed the steps to Calvary, and venerated the spot where the Cross of Jesus was placed into the rock. I laid my staff, my Bible, and the list of 300 names of the people who had asked me to pray for them, on the metal star that covered the hole in the rock. From there I went to the chapel built over the tomb of Jesus, from which He rose after three days. I had completed my vow to walk to Jerusalem in honor of Jesus' 2000th birthday. Now I had to see what He wanted me to do for the next sixteen months in the Holy Land.

BACK TO MOUNT CARMEL

I ended up spending the next three nights just outside Jerusalem, camping on the Mount of Olives one night, and sleeping at the "Casa Abraham" guesthouse on the Mount of Offense, two nights. After being photographed by Debbie Hill (who worked for Catholic News Service) and doing a three-hour interview with Judith Sudilovsky for *Our Sunday Visitor*,[65] on September 12, I felt it was time to move on. The Lord had not opened any doors in this area for me to set up my *poustinia*. I figured that He was indicating that I should return to Isfiya on Mount Carmel, and take up the offer by Stavriani. But I also felt drawn to take in a couple more holy places on the way back north, specifically in Bethlehem, Ein Kerem, and Lod.

I walked the 6 miles from Jerusalem south to Bethlehem, and spent three days there venerating the cave honoring Jesus' birth and The Shepherds' Fields commemorating the angelic visitation to the shepherds (Lk 2:8-20). On my last day in Bethlehem, I noticed that it was September 14, the Feast of Triumph of the Holy Cross. Yes, I had brought the San Damiano Cross on my staff, blessed by Pope John Paul II in Rome in 1996, all the way to Bethlehem, over land and sea.

And appropriately, my friend Lee in Anchorage had sent me a set of twelve little jingle bells to hang on the cross to celebrate Jesus' victory over death and my arrival in the holy land. Yes, He was *born* that He might *die*, so that we–being born again–might *live*, forever. Glory to God in the highest!

From Bethlehem I made my way over to Ein Kerem, west of Jerusalem, and arrived there in the evening. I was able to pray at both churches, the one honoring the birthplace of John the Baptist, and the other commemorating the visiting of Mary with Elizabeth (Lk 1:39ff). Then I was off to Lod, near Tel Aviv on the coast, to pray at the tomb of my patron, St. George. An Orthodox nun opened the church for me so I could enter alone and pray at the tomb of the Great Military Martyr, George. But the silence was disrupted by the blaring of the Muslim call to prayer, amplified over the outdoor loudspeaker next door, which was aimed right at the church building. Again I laid my staff on the marble sarcophagus of St. George, to collect the blessing from this holy martyr, to take out into the world.

St George. Pray for us!

POUSTINIA IN THE FOREST

On Tuesday, September 21, I arrived back in Isfiya, that most friendly town in all of Israel. When I told Stavriani I was back, she was very pleased. She said she wanted to build some *poustinias* on her little parcel of property in the Carmel Forest, and wanted to put a fence all around it. I said that I would be willing to help her as much as I could, at least until the fence was up and she could move in, if I could camp there and use it as my *poustinia*. She agreed to the proposal and even managed to borrow a large canvas tent from some scouting friends, that I could temporarily use for my *poustina*.

So for the next four months, until Christmas, I lived on the site and worked digging a drainage ditch and helped the men she hired to do other work, like pouring concrete for a septic tank and foundations for the first two *poustinias,* as well as putting in posts for the chainlink fence. Eventually she got a metal container *poustinia* with running water, a sink, a shower, and a toilet in it. And I moved into it. In November, my three-month visa was going to expire, so I had to look into renewing it. Try as we could, even armed with Stavriani's sponsorship and a letter from the Maronite Archbishop of Haifa and the Holy Land, I was unable to extend my visa from inside Israel. I would have to leave the country and to get a new visa at the border coming back in.

FLIGHT INTO EGYPT

Although I could have gone into Jordan, I felt drawn to go into Egypt. That way, I could identify with the Holy Family who themselves had to flee into Egypt (Mt 2:13ff). So on November 15, I took a bus to Tel Aviv and on the seventeenth, another bus to Rafah, the border crossing to Egypt. Once in Egypt I decided to walk the 120 miles to Qantara on the west side of the Suez Canal. I surmised the Holy Family may have used this same coastal route (the Roman, Via Maris) on their flight from Herod. It was mostly unpopulated desert, but with many date palm trees along the way with their edible fruit just laying on the ground available for the gathering. In El Arish, a fair-size city on the coast, young boys hit me in the back of the left leg with a hefty-size rock and I limped along with a sore leg for a few days.

In Qantara I stopped at St. George Coptic Orthodox Church and Fr. George (how could a "George" go wrong here?) welcomed me and invited me in for the night. The next day I took a mini-bus back to El Arish, then on to the border, arriving there at 2:00 p.m. After about an hour, I received my new three-month visa for Israel and took two taxis and two buses to get back to Tel Aviv. There I stayed at the Immanuel House in Jaffa (old Joppa), an Anglican-sponsored fifty-bed hostel which welcomed travelers for only $10 a night. The next day I took a bus back to Haifa and then on to Isfiya, arriving at my *poustinia* at 2:15 pm–a thirteen-day, "Flight into Egypt" completed. I was good for another three months–until February 28, 2000.

CHRISTMAS IN BETHLEHEM

Now I was set for eighteen days in *poustinia,* and worked around Stavriani's property in the Carmel Forest. My next Holy Land pilgrimage would be a twelve-day walk December 15-27, on foot to Bethlehem for Christmas 1999. How could I be in the Holy Land and not be in Bethlehem for Christmas? My desire was to walk from Nazareth in the north (which was just over the hill from Carmel, literally) to Bethlehem, just south of Jerusalem, in honor of Jesus, Mary, and Joseph who had made that trip 2,000 years ago. Since I had already walked the route through the hill country of Samaria and Judea, I decided to take the Jordan Valley route.

This route would be very difficult in the summer when temperatures hover around 120 degrees. But in the winter it is a pleasant 70 degrees. The distance from Nazareth to Bethlehem, by way of Afula, Beit She'an, Jericho, and Jerusalem was about 100 miles and it took me eight days (December 16-24). When I arrived at Beit She'an on December 19, I met up with the highway that paralleled the Jordan River and which was all level walking–below sea level–through the Jordan Valley. Here I thought of John the Baptist who exercised his ministry of pointing out the Lamb of God (Jn 1:29), "where there was much water" (Jn 3:23). These sites, variously referred to as "Bethany beyond the Jordan" (Jn 1:28) and "Aenon near Salim" (Jn 3:23), could have been in the southern reaches of the Jordan or in the northern reaches. And John may have baptized in various places. Anyway, I asked him to intercede for me as I lifted up the very same Jesus in the very area where he walked two millennia ago.

There seemed to be TV crews everywhere, possibly because of Christmas coming. I was interviewed by TV crews from Dutch TV, Finnish TV, BBC, and freelance journalists.

CHRISTMAS 1999

Instead of going into Bethlehem proper, I set up my camp in Shepherds' Fields, in Beit Sahur, at 8:00 a.m. on December 24. I was busy most of the day sharing and praying with pilgrims from around the world, and doing interviews. But I did get to Confession, Mass, and Communion. As Christmas Eve approached, I walked up to Bethlehem with two reporters from BBC who were filming and interviewing me along the way. At midnight I watched Mass on the large TV screen set up in Manger Square outside of the Basilica of the Nativity until 3:00 a.m. Then I walked back to Shepherds' Fields and camped in an olive grove (like the shepherds might have done).

On Christmas Day I walked up to the Franciscan Church of St. Catherine in Bethlehem to attend Mass and to pray in the Blessed Sacrament Chapel most of the day. I also wrote twenty-five postcards and called my two brothers Paul and Tom in the States, to wish them a Merry Christmas from Bethlehem. Then I returned to my camping spot in Shepherds' Fields. Finally I got to meet my friend Fr. Arcadius, the pilgrim-priest with whom I had been corresponding for so many years. He also felt called to be in the Holy Land for the Jubilee Year 2000, and he was assigned to the Church of All Nations at the foot of the Mount of Olives, outside the Old City of Jerusalem. He made sure I had dinner and received permission to pitch my tent one night in the friary garden. Then the next day I took the bus back to Haifa and Isfiya, arriving at 4:30 p.m. in time to have dinner with Stavriani. Now I was set to be in *poustinia* until February.

JUBILEE YEAR 2000

On Christmas Eve, December 24, 1999, Pope John Paul II opened the Holy Door in St. Peter's in Rome to begin the Jubilee Year 2000. In his Apostolic Letter, Tertio Millennio Adveniente, he said, "The Jubilee celebration should confirm the Christians of today in their faith in God who has revealed Himself in Christ, sustain their hope which reaches out in expectation of eternal life, and rekindle their charity in active service to their brothers and sisters." In short, the Jubilee Year 2000 was to be an occasion to renew one's own life and to bear witness to one's faith to others. I was personally attempting to do that by my own pilgrimaging. He further said, "It would be very significant if in the year 2000, it were possible to visit the places on the road taken by the people of God of the Old Covenant, starting from the places associated with Abraham and Moses, through Egypt and Mount Sinai."

Because of political turmoil in Syria, I was not able to follow Abraham out of Ur of the Chaldeans (Gn 11:31) or of St. Paul in Damascus (Acts 9:3). But I found that it was possible for an American to travel in Egypt and in the Sinai. As I prayed about it, I felt the Lord was calling me to make this walk in the footsteps of the Jewish people out of Egypt (Ho 11:1) across the Red Sea to Sinai (Ex 3:12) and into the Promised Land. It further seemed that the perfect time to do this would be during the forty days of Lent, for this period of preparation for Easter was closely tied to the forty years the children of Israel wandered in the desert between Egypt and the Promised Land.

As it turned out, I had to leave Israel at the end of February to reenter on a new visa, and Egypt at the Rafah bordercrossing below the Gaza Strip proved to be the most convenient place for me to do so. The fact that I would be leaving from Mount Carmel to go to Mt. Sinai, also put me in the footsteps of the prophet Elijah, the fiery Old Testament prophet zealous for the glory and honor due to the Lord God of Hosts (I Kg 19:7-8).

ANOTHER PILGRIM

On February 21, I took a bus from Haifa to Tel Aviv, obtained a one-month visa for Egypt at the Egyptian Embassy, took the bus to the border at Rafah, and once in Egypt got a taxi to El Cantara and to the Coptic Orthodox Church there. The pastor of St. George's, the young Spirit-filled Father George, was prepared to welcome me once again. When I arrived at his church he said it was perfect timing, as the Orthodox Church was celebrating the three day pre-Lenten Jonah Fast and I could join in with them. A number of his parishioners came from far and near and a few were eager to meet with me for sharing and prayer.

When I left St. George's Church on February 24, I took the ferry across the Suez Canal and headed south for Ismaliya and Suez. This was the area called "the Land of Goshen" (Gn 47:1) in Bible times and this is where the Israelites settled during their 400 years in Egypt. I was now walking in the footsteps of Jacob and Joseph, as well as of Moses, Aaron, and Miriam. But there was one more pilgrim in this land whose presence I highly valued, and that was Pope John Paul II himself. He was in Cairo saying Mass on Friday, February 25, beginning a three-day visit in Egypt, that would eventually culminate in a visit to St. Catherine's Monastery at the foot of Mount Sinai. I did not go to Cairo, but the Lord arranged that I could see him on TV as a marvelous confirmation that I was exactly in His will.

At the very time the Holy Father was celebrating Mass in Cairo, I was in Ismaliya, buying some oranges and tangerines for 5 cents each at a roadside stand. While I was there a young Egyptian fellow in his early twenties speaking a little English, invited me to his makeshift shack just off the road. I noticed a large, brand-new TV sitting on a table; he went over to it and turned it on.

Who was on the screen but the Holy Father himself! He was saying Mass in Cairo and was at the Eucharistic Prayer. I watched in amazement as he drank from the chalice and received the Body and

Blood of Christ in the New Covenant, fulfilling the promise of the Old Covenant made in this very land. As much as I abhor televised Masses (as they make the holy Mass visible for scoffers and for nonbelievers), I thanked the Lord for this electronic hookup with the one event–the New Covenant in Jesus' Blood–that I was reenacting in a physical, historical way.

The Lord does find the most amazing ways to encourage His Pilgrim on his earthly journey home.

CROSSING THE RED SEA

When I left Ismaliya on Tuesday, February 26, I had approximately 60 miles to get to the tunnel just north of Suez, that went under the Red Sea and joined Egypt proper to the Sinai Peninsula. It took me three days to walk this distance in very mild temperatures with quite breezy winds and going down into the forties at night. When I arrived at the tunnel entrance I realized it was February 29, a leap year, a day set apart from all other days of the year. And I was about to experience a unique event on this day. I was disappointed that I could not walk through the tunnel (there was no walkway inside), in sync with Moses and with the people who followed him through the Red Sea on dry ground "with a wall of water to the right and wall of water to the left" (Ex 14:21-22). I would have to take a ride in a modern four-wheeled chariot; a pickup truck which the guards gladly flagged down and whose driver they asked to take me through the tunnel.

This event of deliverance from the slavery of Egypt by our ancestors, however, was so important to the Judeo-Christian world, that I wanted to get out and to shout to everyone, "People, stop! Consider what happened here some 3,000 years ago. The children of Israel experienced the love of God in a totally unique away here. He delivered them and set them free from oppression and slavery. This was the foundation stone of the Covenant He made with Moses on

Mount Sinai. And it looked forward to the New Covenant Jesus made for us on Calvary. Do you understand? God is Our Father; He loves us infinitely. He sent His only begotten Son, Jesus, to set us free from the guilt of our sins. Open your hearts and accept this saving love and know what it means to be children of God."

Of course, had I done such a foolish and prophetic thing I would have been ignored, laughed at, and maybe even escorted away by the police for being a nuisance. And so the truth continues to go unaccepted. Love continues to be unloved and God's children continue to choose the darkness over the light. All we can do is continue to weep for such hardness of heart.

"Lord, have mercy on us sinners."

THE SINAI DESERT

My ride left me off 30 miles south of the tunnel and I now had ahead of me a 160-mile walk to Mount Sinai. It would take me just twelve days to cover the distance it took Moses and the people almost two months to traverse. But the lay of the land must have been still very much like it was in Moses' day, especially after I left the tourist developments along the Red Sea shoreline, and headed inland. The desert was not highly populated and rather than a flat expanse of endless sand, it was all mountainous, rocky, and very dry. I was told they received, on the average, one inch of rain a year. The only place where people can live in the Sinai is near an occasional oasis that has springs and a few palm trees.

ST. CATHERINE'S MONASTERY

When I arrived at St. Catherine's Greek Orthodox Monastery at the foot of Mt. Sinai on Saturday, March 11, the Lord again provided an angel to take care of my needs. It was Fr. Justin, an American from Texas, and one of the monks living here. He was giving a group tour of the monastery and he invited me to come along. Our first stop was the Chapel of the Burning Bush, commemorating the spot where the Lord revealed to Moses His name, "I am who am" (Ex 3:13-14). The monastery closed at noon, but Father Justin invited me to join the monks for prayer the next morning, Sunday, at 4:30 a.m. in the basilica. It thanked him for the invitation, and said I would plan on being there.

From the monastery, I headed up the broad, switchback path that leads toward the top of Mount Sinai. I was disappointed how commercialized it had become since the Egyptians had taken it over from the Israelis (1979-82). Now Bedouins offered camel rides up the mountain and comfort stations and snack bars were built along the path. At the top an enterprising Arab was renting mats so that sunbathers and sun worshipers could lounge around and watch the beautiful sunrise. I would have nothing to do with it. I headed back down the mountain by way of the steep rocky "steps" that led directly back to the monastery, and found a place to camp for the night. From there I was able to make my way to the monastery for morning prayer and for Divine Liturgy the next morning.

Before I left St. Catherine's at 8:00 a.m. Sunday, March 12 (the First Sunday of Lent in the Latin Church), Fr. Justin packed me a lunch of homemade monastery bread, yogurt, and peanut butter with grape jelly that his mother had sent to him from the States. Then he took me to the Burning Bush behind the basilica, and with his tall height was able to reach up and pluck from the lowest branches, a three-leaf stem from the famous shrub. I let him place it in my Bible at Exodus 3:14, which describes Moses' meeting with God at this very spot. He said, "I tried to think of a souvenir for you that you could take from the holy mountain that would not weigh you down." It was greatly treasured, and eighteen years later, it still has a privileged place in my Bible. Many a Christian has felt blessed to see and even hold it in their hands, a present-day testimony to a key event in the history of our salvation.

GULF OF AQABA

From St. Catherine's I was now heading north, back to Israel in the hope of making it to Jerusalem for Holy Week and Easter. First I had a 70-mile walk straight east to Nuweiba on the Gulf of Aqaba, the eastern arm of the Red Sea. It was a desolate and uninhabited stretch with no towns and just a few Bedouin encampments. It took six days to walk it and gave me plenty of solitude and silence for prayer and for contemplation. My water was supplied by friendly taxi drivers or by tourist buses who would stop to talk and offer me water in plastic bottles. But my bread (half-baked) was supplied by two young teenage boys who volunteered to make me ten pitas from scratch. All they had was a sack of flour, water, a griddle and an open fire pit where they burned some cardboard, sticks, and bits of wood they scrounged from around the lean-to "cafeteria." Their final product left much to be desired, but I did not want to be a "grumbler in the desert" like the Israelites (Nm 11:4-9), so I gratefully received it from these young enterprising entrepreneurs and gave them 10 Egyptian pounds (about $3)–three times the normal cost. It got me through a couple of days until I got to the more civilized coast of the Gulf.

On the Feast of St. Patrick, March 17, I reached the large tourist city of Nuweiba on the Gulf of Aqaba. There I was able to fill up with food supplies and to take a hot shower in a campground where the manager generously allowed me to use his facilities. I had two more days of walking north now to get to Taba and to the border with Israel. Two days before I arrived at the border a young Sudanese man, speaking good English, invited me to stop at this beach resort for tea with his young Israeli wife. While we sat under a roof of palm fronds and drank our herbal tea, a young couple from the Czech Republic joined us. Although I could not place him, he said we had met in Alma Ata, Kazakhstan, in the winter of 1993-94. After years of traveling, such encounters no longer surprised me.

INTO THE NEGEV

After twenty-seven days of walking in Egypt, I arrived at the border of Israel at Taba, just 11 miles before the tourist and port city of Eilat at the top of the right arm of the Red Sea. The Israeli customs official would only give me a one-month visa which would expire on Holy Thursday. It looked like I might not be able to be in Jerusalem for the Triduum and Easter. How disappointing that would be after all the planning and expectation. I had to put it completely in the Lord's hands.

Now that I was in the Negev I thought I would try and visit my friends Yealit and Tzvika who had stopped me near Jericho on my walk to Bethlehem. It was a six-day walk to their kibbutz, Ein Yahav Moshav, and they gave me a warm welcome. I ended up staying two nights as they had to take me on a tour of their farm where they grew high-quality sweet peppers, tomatoes, and melons, under clear vinyl tents, as well as a tour of an archaeological site of a former caravansary on the ancient incense route from Arabia to Gaza. As only the Lord could arrange it, the day I arrived at the kibbutz, Pope John Paul II was in Jerusalem, on the last of his five-day pilgrimage in Israel.

When they turned on the TV we watched the Holy Father placing a folded piece of paper with his prayer intentions in the stones of the Western Wall. This gesture spoke deeply to the people of Israel, and as one of their commentators poetically put it, "When Pope John Paul II approached the Wall, the Wall seemed to reach out to him." The Raz family could not do enough for me. They let me send my first-ever email–with pictures– ....(which I found easy enough, with their assistance) to my brother Tom in New York. They wrote a letter of reference and recommendation in Hebrew that I could carry with me. I thanked the Lord for blessing me with such beautiful and open hearts.

BEERSHEBA

On March 29, I turned off the main north/south route, leaving the Wadi Arabah of the Rift Valley (1,292 feet below sea level), and climbed up to the Negev plateau in order to visit Beersheba, the city of Abraham (Gn 21:31) and Elijah (1 Kg 19:3). Before I arrived at this historic biblical city, I walked through Dimona where Israel has their cyclotron nuclear reactor (the Negev Nuclear Research Center) and was stopped three times, namely by the police, by the United Nations, and by the military. Thankfully, the Lord delivered me safely without too much hassle.

About 3:00 p.m. on Saturday, April 1, I arrived in Beersheba and began looking for St. Abraham Catholic Church where Mass was to be celebrated at 6:00 p.m. I had not attended Mass for over a month so I was very much looking forward to the graces of the Sacraments. It was very difficult to find the church on Ha Shalom Street because it was just a regular-looking house; no cross, no name, no sign of its being a church. Even inside there was no cross or statues; just two icons, an altar, and a tabernacle. Here I found out it was one of only four Hebrew Catholic churches in Israel and it had to maintain a very low profile to escape persecution by the State of Israel. (Remember that if a Jew becomes a Christian they are thrown out of their family and are, for all practical purposes, considered as having "died." Apostasy is a very serious sin in traditional Judaism.)

However, I soon learned that Mass today would not be in Hebrew, but in Romanian. It seems that once a month a priest from Romania came to celebrate Mass for the Catholic men who had come from Romania to work for a year or two in the construction industry in Israel, and then they returned home. When I saw the little chapel packed full with about seventy-five men, I could only imagine how many men from Romania must be in Israel, since all Catholics make up only about 6 percent of the population of Romania. But it was wonderful to be part of this service, for the men sang beautifully, putting their whole hearts and souls into their worship. It was obvious how much their faith meant to them in this, their voluntary, temporary exile.

HOSPITALITY IN BEIT JIMAL

Since there was no hospitality in Beersheba, I headed out-of-town after Mass for Hebron, which contained the famed "Tomb of the Patriarchs" (Gn 23:1-20). Since this shrine was now a Muslim mosque, I did not visit it but kept on toward Beit Jimal to venerate the tomb of the Palestinian Catholic layman known as Simon Srugi[66] whose cause for beatification was being promoted. But when I arrived in Beit Jimal on April 6, I found the Lord had a wonderful surprise for me—beautiful hospitality from the Salesian priests and from the Sisters of Bethlehem.

The first Salesian I met was ninety-year-old Fr. Dominico from Italy. When he opened the door to see who was ringing the bell, his face lit up with a big smile and he invited me to come in. It was as though I was his brother and he had been expecting me for a long time. The first thing he asked was, "Did you have breakfast?" When I said "no," he took me to the dining room and served me a bowl of warm milk and a plate full of chunks of bread. He told me about Simon Srugi, St. Stephen the First Martyr—whose grave was on the grounds—and about a new monastic community from France, "The Monastic Sisters of Bethlehem."[67] When the superior Fr. Anthony, who had joined us in the refectory by this time, mentioned there was a 5:00 p.m. Mass at the Sisters of Bethlehem monastery across the way, I said I was most interested in attending.

The sisters were just as hospitable as the Salesians. But it was the awesome 5:00 p.m. liturgy with about twenty-five nuns (mostly in their twenties, in full white monastic habit, with a large prayer rope hanging at their side) that blessed me the most. It turned out to be the most deliberate, reverent, contemplative, and prayerful Mass that

I have ever attended. At every mention of the Father, Son, and Holy Spirit, every sister prostrated herself flat out on the floor.

Since I spent two days with this fervent community of faith, I had the opportunity to hear more about these sisters, whose full title was "The Monastic Family of Bethlehem of the Assumption of the Virgin and of St. Bruno." The order was founded in France in 1951, by a Sr. Marie. Truly, the contemplative Cistersian spirit of St. Bruno, with its austere simplicity and profound silence, pervaded this monastic community to the core. It spoke deeply to my own life. I thanked the Lord for the gift of two days in which I could breathe in the spirit of this ancient, ascetical, self-sacrificing way of life which blossomed once again in the soil of our modern secular desert.

ON TO MOUNT ZION

When I left Beit Jimal on Saturday, I was on my way to Jerusalem. I arrived at Jaffa Gate on the east side of the Old City two days later, on the Monday before Palm Sunday. I headed for Mount Zion where Jesus celebrated the Last Supper in the Cenacle and where the Holy Spirit came upon the 120 disciples on Pentecost. I wanted to connect the two mountains (Sinai and Zion) by foot, thus joining the Old Covenant (Sinai) with the New Covenant (Zion). Although they were separated by more than 1,000 years in time and by 325 miles in distance, I had made it in twenty-eight days. Since the traditional site of the Cenacle was at this time in the hands of the Muslims, I went nextdoor to the Benedictine Monastery of the Dormition and went to the crypt to pray beside the life-size bronze image of the Mother of God in a reclining position, as if on her bier.

As I prayed here, the Lord had me turn to Hebrews 12:18-24, where the author compares Mt. Sinai where God revealed His transcendence, power, and unapproachability, to Mt. Zion where He revealed His immanence, humility, and availability in the Eucharist. Mt. Zion now stands for the earthly Jerusalem (Rv 14:1), the assembly of the firstborn. How fitting that the Mother of God, the first fruit of Jesus' death and resurrection in her Immaculate Conception, lived out her last days and "fell asleep" in this sacred place. She who was "full of grace" (Lk 1:28), the New Eve (Jn 19:26), the mother of all the living (Gn 3:20), was Our Lady of Mt. Zion, because "Zion was called mother of all God's children" (Ps 87:1-7) for all of the redeemed were born again here by Jesus' sacrificial offering. I felt uniquely privileged to be able to share in this great sweep of salvation history for "from Sinai the Lord entered His holy place (Zion–Ps 68:18)" and now dwells in a purified, holy nation, a priestly people (I Pt. 2:10), "Hallelujah. The Lord our God the Almighty reigns (Rv 19:6). Amen."

MAISON D'ABRAHAM

When I left Dormition Abbey on Mount Zion, I began to seek the Lord's will as to where He would have me stay. It was still thirteen days until Easter, and I hoped I could celebrate Palm Sunday and Holy Week in and around the Old City of Jerusalem. The Lord eventually led me back to the Mount of Offense and to the French hospice, Maison D'Abraham. They said I could stay there ten days if I worked three hours a day cleaning up the grounds and cutting grass and weeds. That suited me fine; I could work from 9:00 a.m. until noon and then be off to visit the holy sites in and around Jerusalem. Ten days would take me up to Good Friday; after that the Lord would provide something else.

During the rest of the week until Palm Sunday, I often went into Jerusalem, stopped at the Christian Information Center inside Jaffa Gate to get maps, Mass schedules, Holy week and Jubilee Year 2000 brochures, and visited with friends. I spent time with Fr. Arcadius at the Church of All Nations, with an American friar by the name of Joannes who was assigned to Jerusalem, and I also had occasion to share with Francis of the Heart of Mary, a pilgrim from Oregon who had walked through all lower forty-eight states in ten years. Likewise, I met various other pilgrims from Germany, Russia, Poland, and Korea. I also borrowed some books on Islam from the library in the Maison D'Abraham to better understand this unfamiliar religious group.

HOLY WEEK ARRIVES

Finally, Palm Sunday arrived and I went to Bethphage on the other side of the Mount of Olives to join the pilgrims who would walk the 2 miles that Jesus rode on the donkey as He made His way into Jerusalem that triumphant Sunday before His passion (Lk 19:29 ff). When I arrived there at 2:30 p.m. I found hundreds of mostly young people, dressed in uniforms like scout or school groups would wear. I was directed to join a group of pilgrims at the end of the procession. It turned out to be mainly a troop of lively Filipino Catholics who were already singing in English and dancing with guitars. With olive branches waving (cut from trees alongside the road and sold by enterprising young boys), we made our way over the top of the mountain, then down the other side toward Gethsemane and through St. Steven Gate to the Church of St. Anne inside the walls of the Old City. There we had a concluding prayer and I met other pilgrims from Poland and Medjugorje as well as Franciscan friars from the Holy Land Custody. It was good to be with so many brothers and sisters who publicly testified to their love of Jesus as their King and Savior. Now we just had to go through the suffering of the Cross to reach the glory of the resurrection.

When the sacred Triduum arrived on Holy Thursday, I was looking forward to being at each location where Jesus was for each event: the Cenacle on Mt. Zion for the Last Supper on Thursday night; Gethsemane at the foot of the Mount of Olives for Jesus' arrest early Friday morning; the Via Dolorosa to commemorate Jesus carrying His Cross to Calvary; and the Church of the Holy Sepulcher for

Jesus' death, burial, and resurrection on Easter Sunday. The Lord eventually got me to each of these places, but Satan tried to throw a monkey wrench into my plans very early, which almost prevented all of them from happening.

LOCKED IN

By Holy Thursday, my ten days were up at the Maison D'Abraham, so I packed up all of my things, cleaned my *poustinia,* and was preparing to set out, when two mischievous ten-year-old boys riding a donkey, locked me into my *poustinia* with my key on the outside and I had no way to get out. Unless someone came looking for me, I could be locked in there for hours or even days–there was no way (shouting, banging, telephone) for me to contact anyone. I wondered if maybe the Lord had His own plan for me this Holy week in Jerusalem, that was totally different from mine. All I could say was, "Lord, Your will be done."

Thankfully, after one hour, Joseph, the manager of the Maison D'Abraham and my boss, came looking for me. When I told him what had happened he could not believe it. Thanking him for the past ten days, I said goodbye to Joseph and with all of my packs I headed out to follow the Lord on His final earthly journey.

THE TRIDUUM

To celebrate Jesus' Last Supper with the Apostles on Thursday evening, I joined a Spanish- speaking group from Guatemala in the little chapel the Franciscans had built next to the Crusader Cenacle buildings on Mount Zion. From there I walked to Gethsemane, following the path Jesus and His Apostles possibly took through the City of David, beneath the temple platform walls, up the Kidron Valley, and into the Garden of Gethsemane. There in the Church of All Nations, I joined the Franciscans for their Holy Hour from 8:00

p.m. to 9:00 p.m. and then stayed to pray privately until 5:00 a.m. by the rock in the sanctuary venerated as the one on which Jesus prayed.

I rested for an hour in an olive orchard at the foot of the Mt. of Olives and then headed to the 8:00 a.m. Mass in the Church of the Holy Sepulcher. At noontime I walked the Via Dolorosa with the Franciscans who led a public Stations of the Cross. Then at 3:00 p.m. I went to a service in English at the Sisters of Zion Ecce Homo Convent. Here, we gathered in the basement chapel whose floor is a stone pavement from Roman times, which is believed to be the *Lithostrotos* (inlaid with stones) of John's Gospel (Jn 19:13), for there are markings in the stone, like a dice game soldiers might play to pass away the time.

Since I was feeling very tired, I decided to head for my camping spot on the Mount of Olives, the Paul VI Prayer Garden, where the gate was never locked and where I could set up my tent under an ancient olive tree. On Holy Saturday I spent most of the time in the Church of the Holy Sepulcher from 9:00 a.m. Saturday until 2:00 a.m. Sunday morning, breaking twice, first at noon to have lunch with my pilgrim friends from Poland, and then from 9:00 p.m. to 11:00 p.m. for the Easter Vigil in English in the Ecce Homo Convent. It was 3:00 a.m. before I got back to my camping spot on the Mount of Olives.

RESURRECTION DAY

On Easter Sunday I celebrated with the Franciscans in the Church of the Holy Sepulcher at a 7:30 a.m. Mass and then with my seminarian friends who had invited me to have dinner with them at noon in their Franciscan Monastery. Since it was April 23, the Feast of St. George the Martyr, I celebrated my patron Saint Day. On Easter Monday some Franciscan seminarians and I walked the 6 miles to one of the possible Emmaus sites as the two disciples had done (Lk 24:13). I had prepared a teaching on what Scriptures in the Old Testament Jesus might have shared with them which looked forward to His suffering, death, and resurrection (Lk 24:13). We could not get any closer to the first Easter than that.

NEW VISA

By Easter Tuesday I was ready to leave Jerusalem. I was already four days now in Israel with an expired visa. I had decided to chance not being fined $50 a day when I got to the border, based on a telephone conversation I had with a border guard. He had given the impression they offered some slide room: the question was, what did they consider an inconsequential "few days."

On April 25, I took a bus to Rafah, the border town with Egypt, and passed through without any questions. When I visited my Coptic Orthodox friends in El Qantara, I found they were in their Holy Week, so I stayed on to celebrate Easter a second time. Their Good Friday service was ten hours long. After a two-hour break, they then had an eight-hour Vigil Service. I thought to myself, "Here is a people who truly appreciate what Jesus has done to bring us salvation. They find it proper and fitting to give themselves over to long and enthusiastic chanting, processing, public reading of the Scriptures, and prayers. What a contrast to the normal anemic, abbreviated services offered the Western Christian in the twenty-first century." I thanked the Lord for this opportunity to experience such a pocket of fervor and devotion among His grateful people.

I took a bus back to Rafah on April 30, and received a new three-month visa for Israel, good until the end of July. Then, if I wanted to still be in Bethlehem for Christmas of 2000, I would have to return to Egypt for a new visa. That was still my goal and my vow to the Lord–to celebrate Jesus' 2,000th birthday in Bethlehem. So how would He have me spend the next eight months in Israel? Most of the time I would stay in my *poustinia* on Mt. Carmel–not at Stavriani's property (that door had closed the end of December), but at the Nursing Home in Isfiya named, "Maison de la Fraternite" run by the Sisters of Charity. They offered me one of their spare bedrooms during the rainy season (December to March) and then I used a storeroom in the social hall of the Greek Melkite Catholic Church next door. Thus I had my privacy for praying, reading, and writing, plus I could attend Divine Liturgy on Sunday right beside my *poustinia*. Also, I could store my few boxes of things there when I took a trip somewhere else.

LAVRA NETOFA

The first such excursion outside of my *poustinia* was from May 4 to May 17, to a fascinating, tiny monastic settlement on a hill above Nazareth called "Lavra Netofa."[68] There, five monks of the Melkite Church lived a primitive monastic life (without electricity or running water) in solidarity with the surrounding Palestinians and Israelis. They were founded in 1967, by two Trappist monks, one from Holland (Fr. Jacob Willebrands, 1918-2005), and one from the United States (Fr. Toma Farelly, 1927-2008). Their chapel was dug completely underground due to early building regulations which prohibited them from building anything aboveground. That regulation eventually was changed, so by the time I arrived there, they had constructed a number of normal dwellings and meeting places for the many international guests they attracted to this unique experiment in Gospel living.

I spent a very pleasant two weeks here helping around the grounds and sharing with the monks and guests. We had to be very sparing on our use of water, because their only source was cisterns that held the rainwater they gathered during the rainy season. I was encouraged to know of their existence and of their call to be a Christian monastic presence in the land that gave birth to our faith. I enjoyed reading in their *Typicon* on the topic of silence: "The monastic Fathers and Mothers who came before us did not seek in solitude an easy or tranquil life, but rather the most efficacious and rapid means to acquire purity of heart and continuity in prayer." I also copied out a quotation from N. Berdaev: "The Church cannot exist without bishops and priests, regardless of their human capabilities, but interiorly she lives and breathes by the holy ones, and the prophets, by the apostles and the monastic figures, by the martyrs and ascetics" (p. 25). This was the same spirit that powered my own life as a pilgrim/*poustinik*.

SUMMER TRIPS

The only other time I left my *poustinia* in Isfiya during these summer months, was from May 18 to May 23, to join my priest-friend from Medjugorge, Fr. Philip Pavich OFM. He was leading a group of pilgrims through the Holy Land, and he asked me to join them for a couple of days while they were in Galilee. I was glad to do so in order to renew our acquaintance, but the experience ended up giving me a new appreciation of the privileged way the Lord had me visiting the earthly sites of His ministry–free of the confinement that comes with being part of a tour group. This was brought home to me in a vivid way when I noted how the local tour guide gave our group only twenty minutes in Nazareth at the Church of the Annunciation (where the Word became flesh), and three hours at the Israeli diamond factory near Tiberias (where money could be made by selling diamonds to visiting tourists). I was glad that when I was on my own I could spend hours or days at one spot until I was able to receive the graces and blessings of that particular site, however long it took.

From August 2 to August 10, I went back to Egypt and then returned to Israel in order to renew my visa for another three months. I did not know it at the time, but this would be my last visit to Egypt (until 2016) to renew my visa. By the time the next three months were up, the "Second Intifada" had started (an Egyptian had shot and killed an Israeli border guard and Israel closed the border station at Rafa to all travelers indefinitely). By that time I was also seriously seeking the Lord's will as to what I was to do after the Jubilee Year ended in January of 2001.

ST. JOHN OF THE DESERT

Another wonderful excursion from my *poustinia* happened August 17-20. I was told about a fervent Greek Catholic Monastery called "St. John of the Desert," near Ein Kerem about 7 miles west of Jerusalem. It was named in honor of St. John the Baptist who it was said by tradition, spent his time "in the desert" (Lk 1:80) at this spot. There was a spring here that continued to pour out freshwater, held to have nourished St. John the Baptist during his years in this desert. This spring is still a very popular place of pilgrimage with both Christians and Muslims.

The buildings and land of St. John in the Desert actually belonged to the Latin Patriarchate of Jerusalem, but they had no one to staff it, so they rented it to the French Melkite monks in 1975.[69] It seemed to be flourishing with a dozen monks here plus two daughter houses in France, even though it was only founded in 1980. Though they were all French speaking, most of the monks here could speak English and they made me feel very welcome. I remember their dining hall especially as they had life-size icons of the desert fathers painted all around the four walls. They knew from whom to draw their inspiration. Each father held a scroll with a few words of wisdom. The one I remember best said, "The measure of love is love."[70]

JOURNEY TO BETHLEHEM

At the end of September, the Second Intifada had started. Suicide bombers were blowing themselves up on buses and in public places. Palestinians were throwing rocks at Israeli soldiers and Israeli soldiers were retaliating, sometimes with live bullets. Hundreds of Palestinians were dying in the uprising. It did not look good for the Christian celebration of the Jubilee Year 2000. As a matter-of-fact, most Christian pilgrimages to the Holy land were being canceled, as no one wanted to be caught in the crossfire. I, however, was determined to go ahead with my planned walk to Bethlehem for Christmas 2000. On December 13, I cleaned my *poustinia*, packed up my tent, and headed down the east side of Mt. Carmel toward Nazareth. This time I would approach Jerusalem and Bethlehem by way of the Shephelah between the coastal plain and the Judean Hills. This was the rainy season in Israel so I was grateful for my tent at night. Still there were some cold and damp days of walking.

MUSLIM HOSPITALITY

On Sunday, December 17, in Baja el-Gharbiya around noontime, a Muslim man by the name of Hamid approached me, speaking good English. He explained that he had spent several years in the States and in return for all of the hospitality he was shown there, he wanted to return the favor by offering me hospitality at his father's house in nearby Tulkarm. It was the month of Ramadan in the Muslim calendar, and his whole family would be gathering for a festive meal after sundown. He invited me to join them. I gladly assented. He said he would meet me there after work.

The only problem was, Tulkarm was inside Palestinian Territory. When I arrived at the border, the Isareli soldiers would not let me through. When I showed them the paper I had, they said they would call my hosts and they would have to come and pick me up at the border. And so they did. Hamid eventually arrived at his father's home after work and we had a nice meal sitting outside–men only, of course. The women were apparently gathered in the kitchen or in some other place inside the house.

After the meal, Hamid invited me to stay the night at his home in Israeli Territory. So I got in his car and we proceeded to drive back to Baqa el-Gharbiya. But as we talked in the car I could sense he was having second thoughts about hosting me overnight in his house.

His fellow Muslim neighbors might not take too kindly to his having a Christian sleeping in their neighborhood overnight. So I said, "Hamid, if my staying with you is going to cause you a problem, you can leave me off on the road and I will find a camping place. I thank you for your goodwill and generous hospitality." So that is what he did. After he was certain I had found a place to camp for the night, we parted company friends and he returned home alone. We do not live in an ideal world and often we have to make the best of situations we cannot change. I asked the Lord to bless him for his good heart.

NEARING JERUSALEM

All along this part of my route through the Shephelah, I observed Israeli construction of a brand-new four-lane divided highway running just west of the Palestinian Territories extending from north to south. They even had a movable roof so they could pour concrete in the rain. I wondered if it was a strategic military effort in order to move troops quickly enmass whenever necessary. The construction of the 20-foot-high concrete wall between Israel and Palestine had not yet begun, but this was already a sign of increasing hostility between the two groups.

On Wednesday, I arrived at The Catholic Community of the Beatitudes in Emmaus Nikopolis at 4:00 p.m., and enjoyed wonderful hospitality. This fervent group of Catholics was part of a movement that had been founded in 1973, out of the Charismatic Renewal in France. It now had hundreds of members (consecrated brothers, sisters, priests, and lay members) all over the world. Their website says their spirituality is both Eucharistic and Marian, but is also inspired by the Carmelite tradition of contemplation coupled with apostolic and missionary outreaches. I only stayed one night here, but I was thankful to be inside, out of the pouring rain all night. I was especially happy to be able to join them Thursday evening for a Holy Hour of adoration and Vespers and then on Friday morning for Mass. They pointed out the ruins of a fifth-century Byzantine basilica on their property, but in the pouring rain the next morning, I did not get much of a view of it. I thanked the Lord for the gift of my being able to experience such good spiritual fruits from this particular outpouring of His Holy Spirit.

ARRIVING IN BETHLEHEM

I arrived in Jerusalem on Saturday and contacted my Franciscan friar friends at St. Savior's. At the Information Center I obtained my ticket for midnight Mass at St. Catherine's in Bethlehem, and then went to visit Fr. Arcadius at the Church of All Nations. He and I made a little pilgrimage on foot up to the top of the Mount of Olives, where he had Mass in English for a group of orphans at the Home of Peace Orphanage, run by the Sisters of St. Elizabeth from Poland.

On the morning of Christmas Eve I walked back to St. Savior's Franciscan Basilica in the Old City of Jerusalem and at 10:00 a.m. boarded the private bus with the friars who were headed for Bethlehem. The friars told me that if I was with them, I might have a better chance of getting past the Israeli guards who had sealed off Bethlehem to all traffic trying to enter the city at this time. Our bus was allowed through and we drove right up to Manger Square. I found hospitality for two nights' lodging at the Pentecostal House, but I was back in Manger Square at 2:00 p.m. for the procession at St. Catherine's and at 4:00 p.m. for Vespers.

The mood was very somber. It was known that the Palestinian Muslims had warned the Christian authorities: "No lights, no marching bands, no festivities, no celebrations for Christmas. We are hurting too much." And the Christians had apparently listened. When I arrived in the rain at 10:00 p.m. in Manger Square for midnight Mass at St. Catherine's, I was just about the only foreign pilgrim in the plaza. It was full of military vehicles and police cars, along with foreign television, and radio and newspaper reporters.

One reporter asked me, "Are you disappointed there are not more pilgrims here?" I replied, "Bethlehem is in your heart," for I knew well that there were devout Christians all over the globe who were celebrating Christ's birth on this night. Obviously those who accept the Prince of Peace experience His peace. Those who reject Him have no peace. It is each person's choice.

THE GROTTO ITSELF

At 10:15 p.m. I arrived at St. Catherine's Roman Catholic Church and upon entering was surprised to find the two center aisles of the church already filled with local Palestinian Catholics who lived in the city of Bethlehem. So I began to make my way to one of the side aisles to find a seat. But as I did so, one of the Franciscan friars who was serving as an usher, came up to me and said, "Pilgrim George, do you want to go down to the Grotto to pray for a while?" I could not believe what I was hearing; it was beyond my every expectation. "Yes," I replied, and he said "Follow me."

The Grotto was the cave under the Basilica of the Nativity honored since the fourth century as the very place of Jesus' birth. It was now in the hands of the Greek Orthodox. Since they did not celebrate Christ's birth on December 25, the upper church was empty, and we made our way through it toward the entrance to the cave on the right side. I saw that on this night there was no long line of devout or curious people waiting to descend the long flight of steps that led to the Grotto as there usually was. Obviously, the Grotto was officially closed. Only by personal invitation and private escort, could one enter on this night.

And what met my eyes as I entered the darkened cave, lit only by the flickering oil lamps and votive candles? Just a room full of reverent and silent worshipers–most of them nuns and sisters in full habits–kneeling and sitting on the stone floor facing the Greek Orthodox altar which contained the vermilion star with the hole in the center and around it the Latin words:

HIC DE VIRGINE MARIA JESUS CHRISTUS NATUS EST
(Here Jesus Christ was born of the Virgin Mary.)

OVERWHELMING

I found a place to stand just a few feet from the venerated niche and, overcome with emotion, I began to thank the Lord for getting me here after eight years of walking 26,000 miles across North America, Asia, and Europe. To think of how He had gotten me past border guards and customs officials, over mountain passes and across deserts. In spite of being thrown on the ground by thieves, pelted with stones by Muslim children, stolen from and lied to, deliberately misled and refused service, ousted from churches and shrines, drenched by rain and baked by the sun, lost in strange cities, and cursed in a dozen languages, here I was standing on this holy night at this holy place to celebrate the Lord's 2000th birthday in Bethlehem. Was that a miracle in itself? The impact of it all was overwhelming.

It was only right I thought, that I should lift up here all those people who had been part of this pilgrimage; all those whose acts of kindness had helped me along the way; the unsolicited gifts of food and drink; the hospitality of kind strangers; the encouragement of friends who took the time to write to me; the many kind words, loving prayers, knowing smiles, warm hugs, waving hands, and tooting horns that had greeted me alongside the road; the patient listeners trying to understand a foreigner who did not speak their language; and the many generous people pointing me or even walking me in the right direction. For all of these, I gave thanks.

So, I felt like I had now fulfilled my vow to the Lord to be here on this night, and standing here on this spot was a sign that He accepted and confirmed my offering. I would have been content to be in the church above on this supreme night. But it was the Lord's unexpected and undeserved gift that I could be in the holy cave itself. Here Christ was being reborn in the hearts of a few of His faithful followers. It did not matter what was going on outside of this holy place–the weather, the war, the politics, the coldness of hearts. It was much the same way the first Christmas 2,000 years ago, when heaven slipped onto the earth and so few knew it. If the media outside had been in Bethlehem for the first Christmas, they would have been as unable to capture His birth then as they were now, for incarnation and rebirth are spiritual events that take place quietly and unobtrusively, with no big fanfare, in the hearts of those who are open. It always was and it always will be. Glory to God in the highest and peace on earth to men of goodwill.

FIGURING OUT THE NEXT STEP

On Tuesday, December 26, I left Bethlehem and took a bus to Tel Aviv. There I stayed at Beit Emmanuel in Joppa as usual, but I also met with Nachman and his wife Ofra. They were Jews who had accepted Christ as the Messiah and belonged to a small, Evangelical home church. When they heard of the predicament with my visa, they did all they could to help me. My visa for Israel was now almost two months expired. The border with Egypt was closed and the visa office in Tel Aviv was on strike. My friends had contacted everyone they thought might be able to help me, but without success.

I obviously had to leave Israel, and soon. The Jubilee Year was officially over on January 6. But where did the Lord want me to go next? Should I go to Poland? A Polish priest I met on the Mount of Olives said if I would come to Poland he would pay all of my expenses and set up a schedule of talks for me around his country. Should I leave Israel and come back? I was welcome at St. John of the Desert Melkite Monastery just outside of Jerusalem. Should I return to the States? As I prayed about it, I felt that the Lord wanted me to return to my point of origin. My own country needed to be evangelized. It needed the Cross of Jesus to be lifted up so that the Lord could draw more hearts to Himself (Jn 12:32).

At this time, I was in contact with a veteran airline stewardess by the name of Mary, from Florida. She flew on TWA Airlines every week from New York to Tel Aviv and back. She was a very devout Catholic and went to Mass at St. Anthony's Catholic Church in Joppa, when she was in Israel. I met her there through our mutual Franciscan priest-friend from the States, Fr. Petronius, who celebrated Mass in English there at 7:00 a.m. on weekdays. Mary said she could get me a one-way "e-ticket" to New York for under $200. Mary said her special rate ticket was for standby, economy class, but she gave me a list of flights in the next month that looked like a good possibility for a seat. I thanked her and said I would pray about it.

BACK TO GLENSHAW

So where should I go once I returned to the States? It only seemed right that I should return to the community from which I had been sent out on mission in 1988 (Acts 14:25) –twelve years before: St. Mary's, Glenshaw. Of course a few pastors had come and gone since I left and the new pastor, Fr. John, had never met me except by reputation. So one day I picked up the telephone and gave him a call. I briefly introduced myself and said to him, "I feel the Lord wants me to come back to St. Mary's. Is there any room for me there?"

I knew from friends that my old "pump house *poustinia*" in the woods was buried under twenty feet of backfill from a cemetery expansion, so that was no longer a possibility for me. But he generously responded, "Come back and we will provide for whatever you need."

So with that invitation, plus the possibility of an airplane ticket and funds to cover the cost, I felt that was the direction the Lord was leading me. I notified Mary that I had selected January 18, as the day I would fly back to the States. Since she was scheduled to work on that flight I thought that would be a good backup. Now all I had to do was somehow take care of my expired visa so that I would not show up at the airport customs with an overextended visa. Thankfully the workers at the visa office in Tel Aviv went off their strike, and Nachman took me to the Ministry of the Interior in Tel Aviv. Since I could show that I already had my ticket of departure in hand for January 18, they extended my visa to January 19, for the fee of 135 shekels ($35). Now I just had to hope I did not get bumped off the flight on the eighteenth.

PASSING SECURITY

I did some last minute shopping in Jerusalem (where one Arab shop owner told me I was his first customer in six weeks) for maps, slides, place mats, icons, and crosses. I packed up a box of things I wanted to keep and sent them to myself at St. Mary's, on January 14. I said goodbye to my many good friends in Isfiya, and on January 17, I headed down Mount Carmel to Haifa where I could catch the bus to Tel Aviv. On the way to the bus station I dropped off the portable manual typewriter I had purchased the year before, at the same secondhand store where I had bought it. Once in Tel Aviv I walked to Joppa and to the Beit Emmanuel Christian Messianic Hostel, where I could stay for $12 a night. Along the way I found a perfect-size cardboard box in which to put my six-foot-long staff so it could go through baggage at the airport. The next day Thursday, January 18, I took an airport bus from Tel Aviv and began the complicated vetting process for flying out of Israel.

First, our bus was stopped at the gate within the high fence that surrounded the whole airport. Everyone had to get out of the bus and all the luggage had to be pulled out from beneath for careful inspection. When our bus started on its way again, we drove through a "no-man's-land" that was patrolled by guard dogs and security vehicles. There were high lookout towers and barbed wire fences everywhere. I knew I should be three hours early before taking off and so I was ready for such delays. Sure enough, myself and another middle-aged man (who claimed dual U.S. and Palestinian citizenship), were called out of the line for special treatment. A security man told me to follow him to an examination room. There he said I should have a seat and enjoy a cup of coffee; this was going to take some time.

So for the next hour, four security men went over everything with the proverbial "fine- toothed comb." I had reduced my baggage down to two pieces–a sleeping bag/tent parcel and my shoulder bag with my personal items in it, probably about twenty-five pounds all told. Each of the four men worked assiduously the whole hour taking each piece, bending it, feeling it, smelling it, X-raying every tiny seam and stitch of everything I carried.

Finally they were satisfied that I was not a threat to anyone and told me I could pack everything up and get back in line. I thanked them for their service, because I remembered that no airplane leaving Ben Gurion International Airport in Tel Aviv had ever been hijacked or bombed, to date. So their rigorous security measures had paid off, so far.

BOARDING THE PLANE

Now I had to hope enough people had canceled their tickets for this flight so that we who held standby passes could all board. By the grace of God there was room for this pilgrim. So I climbed the ramp and entered the door to the plane. There waiting to greet me was my friend Mary. She whispered to me, "Do not take a seat just yet. If there is an empty First Class seat up here in the front, I will seat you there." So I stood aside to let the other passengers enter. Finally, after everyone was aboard, Mary ushered me into a roomy First Class seat, and I settled in for a twelve-hour flight to JFK Airport in New York.

So that was it. After seventeen months in the Holy Land, making nine pilgrimages in the footsteps of the prophets and Apostles, and walking a total of 1,326 miles in the Promised Land, the Lord was picking me up and transporting me back to the land of my birth. How had living in the Holy Places that had witnessed the mysteries of my faith, changed me? It would probably take me the rest of my life to fully unpack such rich experiences.

One thing that I could say for sure about the last seventeen months is that I am more sure, now than ever before, that God loves me, that He is my heavenly Father concerned for my good, and that He is able to take care of me in situations way beyond my control. And therefore the one thing necessary is that I continue to trust in Him alone, for my identity, peace, security, and everything else. The future might be unknown, but based on His love for me in the past, I knew it also had to be good.

THE PRAYER OF MY HEART

Father in heaven:

all glory be to You,

for revealing Your love,

through the sending of Your Son Jesus

to live among Your people

the thirty-three years of His life on this earth.

May His life, death and resurrection

continue to be my life blood,

and the life and hope of many others.

May His love not go unrequited.

I offer myself to continue

to live in thanksgiving

for having received so many graces

from Your loving hands.

I ask this

through the power of Your Holy Spirit,

and through the intercession

of Your All Holy Mother,

and of all the Saints.

Now and forever.

Amen.

ENDNOTES

65. Magazine article. Judith Sudilovsky, "A Pilgrim's Progress," *Our Sunday Visitor*, December 19, 1999.

66. The Venerable Simon Srugi (1877-1943) was born in Nazareth. He was a pupil at Holy Family orphanage in Bethlehem from 1888 to 1891, and a Salesian lay brother from 1896, until his death. He spent all the years of his religious life serving at the Salesian Agricultural School in Beit Jimal, working in the mill, the tailor shop, and the infirmary. At the dispensary he served both Christian and Muslim, young and old, at any time of the day or night, in a spirit of prayer, humility, and with supernatural graces.

67. The Monastic Family of Bethlehem. Presently the order has 600 nuns and 70 monks in fifteen nations. It also has lay associates, companions, and friends. In May of 1987, a foundation of their nuns was made in the United States, in the Catskill Mountains, near Livingston Manor, New York.

68. Lavra Netofa. This Melkite-Chritian hermitage continued on until the death of Fr. Jacob in 2005, when the property and buildings were handed over to the Monastic Family of Bethlehem, who continue to live there and make it available for retreats and for guests.

69. Melkite monks. This site, which tradition says is where Elizabeth hid her son John (the Baptist) from Herod's soldiers, was reclaimed by the Franciscan Custody of the Holy Land in 2001, and the Melkite monks were forced to leave.

70. This quote is attributed to a number of authors, including St. Augustine of Hippo and St. Bernard of Clairvaux.

WISDOM FROM THE ROAD

Originally, I planned to write my final chapter as a continuation of the previous one, covering the long-distance walks (mostly in the continental United States) between 2001 and 2013 (when I did my last walking pilgrimage). Yet in a real sense, anything occurring after the Jubilee Year 2000 pilgrimage would be somewhat anticlimactic, essentially repeating and reinforcing what went before. So, it seemed fitting to instead conclude with a chapter entitled, "Wisdom from the Road." This will serve as a type of summary of the lessons I learned from the Lord, in being faithful to His call to walk in faith, lifting up the Cross of Jesus on the highways and byways of the world.[71]

LIVING THE WORD

Most every Christian in our day has access to a copy of the Holy Bible, so we all share the same inspired words handed on to us from biblical times. However, not all of us are called to live out every one of these Scriptures in a radical and literal way (Mt 19:11). In this last chapter I would like to review the particular Scriptures that the Lord has highlighted in my life (how He taught me their absolute truth and power) followed by a list of points and lessons I learned "on the road."

The first such word of the Lord comes from Matthew 19:27-29. There we read:

> *Then Peter said to him in reply, "We have given up everything and followed you. What will there be for us?" Jesus said to them, "Amen I say to you that … everyone who has given up houses or brothers, or sisters or father or mother or children or lands for the sake of my name will receive a hundred times more, and will inherit eternal life."*[72] (New American Bible)

Whether boarding a freighter bound for Spain, setting out with a mule for Mexico, or touching down in a plane in Siberia, I lived out this Scripture passage very literally time after time. Leaving everything behind, I experienced the promised reward: "a hundredfold" (Matthew and Luke) and an "overabundance" (Mark) in the present age. Abandoning all of the normal securities of familiar family and friends, a place in which to rest, eat, and sleep, having a regular income with a job, bank account, and credit card, I threw myself completely into the providential hands of the Lord. In doing this, I found I had mothers and fathers, brothers and sisters, houses and lands–and persecution (Mk 10:30)–all over the world. They were not mine to own or to claim, but I had the use of them gratis, and all my physical, emotional, and spiritual needs were take care of.

Furthermore, I experienced the difference between knowing God's care and providence as a servant or slave, and knowing it as a disciple or son. The rich young man in the passage just before this (Mt 19:16-24) was told by Jesus he could receive eternal life as a reward for good conduct and hard work: as a servant or slave. But the disciple who sold everything and who followed the Lord, received eternal life as a free gift–as a beloved disciple or son. Both received the same gift of salvation, but what a world of difference because of the way in which it was received.

I will thank the Lord of Hosts for all eternity that He allowed me to experience the gift of His life as a disciple and as a son.

DIVINE PROVIDENCE

The next Scripture the Lord "worked into my bones" in a similar vein, comes from the Sermon on the Mount. In Matthew 6:25-34 Jesus says:

> *Do not worry about your life, what you will eat or drink or about your body, what you will wear....Your heavenly Father knows that you need them all. But seek first the Kingdom of God and his righteousness and all these things will be given you besides.* (New American Bible)

In all my forty-three years of walking for the Lord, there was never a day when I did not have something to eat–not three square meals, but certainly enough for the journey. In all those years I never once had to ask for food because I was hungry, although I did often ask for water. Otherwise, everything else was freely offered. And at times I had to say, "Thank you, but I cannot carry anymore food or water." Jesus can be taken at His word, literally, without rationalization or compromise.

When Jesus sent His disciples out, He told them to take nothing for the journey (Mt 10:9-10; Mk 6:7-9; Lk 9:13, 10:4): no money (or credit cards, being the modern equivalent), no sack of food or change of clothes. (Every summer when I set out on my four-month walks, I made sure that I did not have even a penny in any of my pockets.) What is the purpose of this directive? I think it is very profound and not usually understood. If a disciple goes forth in Jesus' name, in the power of the Holy Spirit, they do not depend upon all kinds of human aids such as financial backing, education, knowledge of language, culture, geography, advertising, programs, institutions, letters of recommendation, and hands full of gifts. Rather, they throw themselves completely upon the heavenly Father and trust He will supply everything as He sees fit. This act of trust in God, rather than in natural means of assistance, is itself the most powerful proclamation of the Gospel. It demonstrates concretely the truth that the disciple is conveying verbally: "God is your Father. He loves you and He will care for you, just as He is taking care of me (or us) now."

LIFT UP JESUS

Another key Scripture by which the Lord has called me to live is John 12:32: "When I am lifted up from the earth, I will draw everyone to myself." In other words, it is not the disciple's job to get others to accept Jesus as their Savior, or to join their church, or to think like they think.

Conversion of heart is the work of the Holy Spirit. The disciple's job is to "lift up Jesus" in word and deed, by the things they say and by the way they live. I "lifted up Jesus" by displaying the crucifix on my staff and by my way of life of trust in God. It was letting the light of Christ shine (Mt 5:14-16) out into the darkness to let Jesus draw others to Himself, not to myself or to my thoughts. We proclaim the Gospel best when we are faithful to what God calls us to do (Jn 21:20-22): for me that was "to walk and to pray and to trust in Him." That is when the Holy Spirit can work the best, touching, converting, delivering, and blessing others.

THE BODY OF CHRIST

Another important Scripture I frequently share with people is from St. Paul's epistle to the Corinthians on "The Body of Christ" (I Cor 12:12-30). There, St. Paul says the church is like a body with different members: the head, the eyes, and the ears. I am the foot: so I walk. Not everybody can be the foot, and the foot needs the other members of the body. If someone did not bake the bread and plant the potatoes, the pilgrim could not walk.

People often said to me: "I could never do what you do." And I would reply: "God probably does not want you to. Just be faithful to what He has called you to do." He gives us the grace and the faith necessary to do our part (Rm 12:3-8), not someone else's part. We should not envy or want to be some other member of the body that God has not made us to be. We should rejoice and be encouraged when we see another member of the body exercising their gifts, but not be intimidated or feel inferior when we behold them. We are all members of one body and when one member does their part well, the whole body benefits. It does not matter how small or hidden the part is. I like to take note of the internal organs like the liver, lungs, and heart, which I believe are exemplified by groups like cloistered religious and abandoned elderly in nursing homes. They too, have their part and are actually more essential to the overall health of the body, than the more visible, external active members. Praise the Lord.

GOD'S LOVE

Now I would like to move on to some of the spiritual principles I have learned through a lifetime as the Lord's pilgrim/*poustinik*. When reporters stopped me on the road to talk with me, often their last question was something like this: "What would you like to say to our readers (or listeners)?" I would say: "If you open your heart to God's love for you, you will have peace, joy, and happiness in this life and forever hereafter." That to me sums up the whole revelation of the Old and New Testament. Yet it is seldom taught that way. Usually Christian evangelists and teachers sum up Jesus' teaching by quoting the Two Great Commandments in Matthew 22:37-39: "love God and love your neighbor." And thereby they lay an unbearable burden upon their listeners. No human being, on their own, can fulfill those commands in the flesh.

Something has to happen before one can even begin to love God and others. Namely, they must first experience God's overwhelming, unconditional, all-sufficient, liberating, re-creating love for them.

This is exactly what happened in the Old Testament. Before God gave Moses and the people His commandments at Mt. Sinai, He first liberated them from their slavery in Egypt. Once they experienced individually, immediately, dramatically, unquestionably, in their bones, God's personal care for them, then they were ready to respond. Once one experiences being loved, then one says, "Your will is my command. Let me know your will so I can do it to show how appreciative I am for your choosing to love and care for me."

After this experience of being loved, the "command" to love is cast in a whole new light. Without the preliminary experience of being delivered, the commandments are little more than onerous, freedom-limiting, burdens. But after the experience of being loved, the commandments become so many welcome ways of expressing one's gratitude and joy for being saved. This to me is the secret of a meaningful Christian life. St. John says, "Perfect love casts out fear" (I Jn 4:18). Only God's love is perfect. But once we have experienced that, the life of a disciple of Jesus becomes a joy. (And all of the difficulties in our lives become no longer *problems* to be solved, but *opportunities* to trust–in our merciful Savior.)

THE HOLY SPIRIT

That brings me to the second spiritual principle I learned through forty-three years of walking for, and with, the Lord. And that is the necessity of the Holy Spirit in a Christian's life. The eminently popular St. Seraphim of Sarov, the nineteenth-century Russian hermit, once said: "Acquire interior peace, and multitudes will find salvation near you." (The Woman of Samaria who encountered Jesus at the well in John 4 is a powerful example of this.) By "interior peace," St. Seraphim meant the Holy Spirit. Jesus told His apostles at the Last Supper: "The Advocate, the Holy Spirit (of truth) that the Father will send in my name–He will teach you everything and remind you of all that I told you" (Jn 14:26). And Jesus, after His resurrection, ".... enjoined them not to depart from Jerusalem, but wait for the promise of the Father (the Holy Spirit) about which you have heard me speak" (Acts 1:4). This was the Holy Spirit who came upon those gathered in the Upper Room on Pentecost (Acts 2:1ff). Before the Holy Spirit came, the Apostles were huddled in fear behind locked doors: after He came, they went forth boldly proclaiming God's Kingdom, willing to suffer every kind of torture and even death.

And so it remains to this day. Without the manifest power of the Holy Spirit, the Body of Christ will be anemic, crippled, and ineffective. At best, without the Holy Spirit, the Church is not much more than a social club or a do-good, service agency. But empowered with the Holy Spirit, it produces disciples who are free from all fear and say: "Lord, I am totally Yours: do with me whatever You want. You can take me home to heaven any time, any way, any place You choose. Your will is my will." And they mean it and live by it at all times.

This is the solid rock upon which Jesus tells us to build our lives (Mt 7:24-27). The rock is the truth, "God loves me. He is my Father. He is more than able to care for me in every situation. I have nothing to fear." Everything else in life is shifting sand and will pass away. All of our possessions, friends, family members, will be swept away. The only thing that will never change is God's love for us. That will endure for all eternity. The disciple of Jesus builds His life on that solid rock.

THE ARMOR OF GOD

The next Scripture the Lord worked into my life was Ephesians 6:10-17, on the armor of God. We cannot go out into the world as God's missionaries without being equipped with spiritual armor and weapons (Lk 22:36). St. Paul lists six pieces of equipment: five defensive and one offensive. The five defensive pieces of armor are the belt, breastplate, sandals, shield, and helmet. The one offensive weapon is the sword of the Spirit (the Word of God). And that sword must be used in the power of the Holy Spirit. It is not to be used "to beat people over the head with" or to win an argument with, but to "penetrate between soul and spirit, joints and marrow, and able to discern the reflections and thoughts of the heart" (Heb 4:12). And this "Word of God" is not just the written text, but is primarily the Word incarnate (Jn 1:14), Jesus Himself, who is "the Way the Truth and the Life" (Jn 14:6). He, the Light of the world (Jn 8:12, 9:5) is the one who cuts through all of the fogginess of the world system of our cultural wasteland, as well as our own unruly desires and confused thoughts, and brings us to eternal life.

Once the pilgrim/*poustinik* is in the right relationship with the Holy Trinity, Father, Son, and Holy Spirit, then his whole focus is to constantly abide in the will of God. The disciple must be where God wants him, when He wants him there, and in the way He wants him to be there. Jesus constantly pointed out that He only did what the Father told Him (Jn 3:11; 4:34; 5:19, 32-33; 6:38, etc.). This is powerfully demonstrated by the scene of Jesus in the Garden of Gethsemane, where in great agony, He comes to the final resolution: "Father, not my will but your will" (Lk 22: 42). Knowing He was in the will of the Father, Jesus had great peace throughout His arrest, trial, passion, and death on the Cross. He had so much peace up to the end that it converted the Good Thief (Lk 23: 40-42). Being in the will of God gives the disciple so much peace, that no amount of misunderstanding, rejection, persecution, or opposition, can disturb him. He knows for certain that "nothing will be able to separate us from the love of God in Christ Jesus our Lord" (Rm 8: 38).

THE WILL OF GOD

People often ask me: "How do you know what is God's will?" The first thing one needs to realize, is that there is God's general will and His specific will. God's general will is "our sanctification" (I Tm 2:3-4). God's general will is made known in the Bible, as, for example, in the Ten Commandments, and these are pretty straightforward.

But God's specific will for us at a particular moment in unique circumstances, requires additional graces and help from the Holy Spirit. Here it becomes a matter of docility and teachability. I believe Psalm 37:3-7 can point the way for us.

> Trust in the Lord and do good that you may dwell in the land and live secure. Find your delight in the Lord who will give you your heart's desire. Commit your way to the Lord: trust that God will act .... Be still before the Lord; wait for God.

All of our efforts should be to "rejoice in the Lord," "to wait upon Him." That is, trust completely in Him; surrender everything into His hands and be like wet clay in the hands of the potter. Then, "He will give you the desires of your heart."

That does not mean He gives us what we think we want and what we think will make us happy. It means He will put His desires (His will) into our hearts: His thoughts will replace our thoughts and what we might at first think will make us happy. In other words, we must learn to pray always (Lk 18:1; I Th 5: 16-17; Eph 6: 18). This is walking in the power of the Holy Spirit. We keep our hearts humbly submitted to Him as Lord and Savior, saying with the Publican, "Lord Jesus Christ, Son of the living God, have mercy on me a sinner" (Lk 18:13). In other words, the Jesus Prayer becomes our life, our very breath, and our heartbeat. It says simply who God is (everything) and who we are (nothing), as lived in the life of St. Francis of Assisi, and so succinctly spoken by the Apostle Thomas after Jesus' resurrection– "My Lord and my God" (Jn 20:28).

And we need to accompany this prayer with fasting. Prayer without fasting and without deep repentance is mere wishful thinking. Fasting opens our hearts to God's will like nothing else can. It shows our bodies we are serious about seeking the will of the Lord, and that we are ready to invest our whole selves in this project. Otherwise, our prayers are just empty words. Jesus told His disciples we would fast when we are serious about seeking His presence and guidance (Lk 5:35).

CONFIRMATIONS

If in prayer we have peace in our heart when we think about a certain decision, that is probably a confirmation that it is God's will. And we should begin moving in that direction and say, "Lord, I am depending on You to steer me every inch of the way." We do not want to end up trying to do God's will "in the flesh," or in our own limited human power. And if in the process we encounter what appears to be a closed door, do not jump to the conclusion it is not God's will we go through that door: it might just be stuck and it requires a stronger push (Lk 18:5-7).

We need to be on the lookout for "confirmations" that a particular decision is God's will. These can come from Scripture, from a book, from a friend, or from the most unexpected directions, like a totally secular or unrelated source. Likewise, we should be open to the possibility that while we are pursuing a particular goal we believe is God's will, God Himself might have something else in mind for us. Learning how to hear the voice of the Good Shepherd (Jn 10:3), and being docile to the inspirations of the Holy Spirit, is a lifetime task. This side of heaven, most of us will never get it perfectly right. But at least we are trying, and that is what pleases the Lord.

JUDGING

The next bit of wisdom I would like to share has to do with making judgments in the sense of discernment. Jesus said: "Do not judge by appearances" (Jn 8:15; see also 1 Sm. 16:7). But we must constantly be making decisions about right and wrong, and about good and evil. The pilgrim out in the desert of the world and on the highway, has to sum up situations quickly: friend or foe, life-sustaining, or death-dealing. I have come to realize that one cannot trust completely in what words people say. Thus the man in Siberia who identified himself as an atheist, turned out to be a child of God who showed hospitality to a stranger. And the man in Pakistan who said, "You are my best friend," proceeded to signal three thugs to attack me and to wrestle me to the ground.

The same thing can be illustrated by the situation of asking for directions in a foreign country. One learns not to phrase a question so that it can be answered with a yes or no, because many people do not like to say no. Thus, you do not say: "Is this the way to?..." You ask, "How do I get to?..." Of course they can still say anything just to get rid of you. So one learns to ask three or four people the same question, and then to find the commonality in their answers. Thankfully, many times people will go out of their way and say, "Come follow me. I will show you the way."

HOSPITALITY

People often comment to me: "You must often receive hospitality from churches and monasteries." But this is not true. I have come to not expect hospitality from religious people or groups. Churches, schools, and rectories have insurance policies in place that trump hospitality. Thus priests say, "If I let you sleep on our property I could lose my insurance, because you might start a fire and burn the place down or break or steal something." Nor could I expect an offer of help from a small group of daily Mass goers with whom I have just prayed, exchanged the greeting of peace, and been united with in Holy Communion. After Mass all just walk out with not so much as: "Oh, welcome. Who are you? Would you like a drink of water?"

Actually, as a poor pilgrim on foot I got most of my hospitality from unchurched people. These were the people who invited me into their homes (with their wives and children present) and offered me food, water, a shower, a place to sleep, and then said: "I do not go to church." (Obviously going to church does not automatically make one a more loving person. And not going to church does not mean one has not learned how to love.) But those who showed hospitality had learned that life is about loving and service and about looking out for the stranger. It just proved the truth of Jesus' saying: "Not everyone who says to me 'Lord, Lord,' will enter the Kingdom of heaven, but only the one who does the will of my Father in heaven" (Mt 7:21).

And more times than I can count, young mothers with children in car seats in the back, stopped to offer me a ride. (I was not hitchhiking or soliciting rides.) That goes against every natural and human instinct or concern for safety (and often their husbands' specific directions). How could that be? Because love and God's command wins out over human wisdom and authority. People who have learned how to walk in the Holy Spirit and to listen to the Lord, know when it is safe to go ahead with what is naturally foolish. Praised be to God!

And one final note on hospitality. Generally the poorer countries were the most hospitable: they were not preoccupied with riches (Lk 6:24) because they did not have any. For them, family and people were most important, not what one had or what one did. What was in one's heart is what defined you and is what interested them. They looked with the eyes of the Lord and the Holy Spirit.

LEADING

Several times over the years I have had the experience of walking on pilgrimages with a group of pilgrims. On these occasions I learned some valuable lessons about leading people. The first one is: "You cannot lead people to where they do not want to go." That is, people will not follow a leader if they feel unsafe or threatened. In that case, the leader will have to choose another path to reach the same goal, even if it takes longer and is not as direct.

Also, I have observed that no two people naturally walk at the same pace. On a group pilgrimage you always have your slow walkers and your fast walkers. Some are always dashing ahead: others are always lagging behind.

HAPPINESS

Perhaps I could best sum up all that I have learned on the road this way. In all of my travels, I have found that there are basically only two kinds of people in the world: happy people and unhappy people. Those who know that God loves them are happy; those who do not know that God loves them are unhappy. It does not matter if one is rich or poor, black or white, young or old. True, God loves everyone: but not everyone opens their hearts to that love. Those who do so are fundamentally happy. Those who resist God's love and close their hearts to it are not happy. So though the secret of happiness is very simple, it is not easy. It is the most difficult thing in the world. Why? Because it presupposes death to self (Jn 12:24); it requires humility and a childlike spirit (Mt 18:3).

I have imagined my life as a pilgrim like this. I have a loaf of bread in my two hands and I am holding it out, offering it to whoever passes by or whoever meets me. But still, some come right up to me (or pass by) and they are shouting (usually not literally), "I am hungry. I am starving." But they refuse to take the bread I am offering. Why? Are they blind? Do they have a hard heart? Are they afraid? The reason they do not take the bread, I believe, is because true life can only be received on one's knees. One must be broken of all pride and self-will. And this goes against the grain of fallen men and women and all that the world values and teaches. This requires grace. And so in the end, it is a gift. Truly, "all is grace."

A FINAL NOTE

I hope, dear reader, that you have enjoyed traveling this road with me. I have tried to offer you what I have felt the Lord urging me to share with you. I offer this autobiography as a way of glorifying the Lord for what He has been able to do through my willingness to take up the cross and to follow Him (Lk 9:23) over the years and over the miles. In light of where Western society and contemporary

Catholicism is today, such a life is hard to understand. So much effort today is focused on building this earth (which is passing away), and keeping one's eyes focused on the transcendent and ultimate end of life (heaven), is most difficult. The pilgrim /*poustinik* is truly "an eschatological sign." He seems, literally and otherwise, to be walking to the beat of a different drummer.

Is this "extreme living?" Is this something to be admired but not imitated? But it is true that Jesus invites us to extreme living when He says, "For whoever wishes to save his life will lose it, but whoever loses his life for my sake will find it" (Mt 16:25). The Sermon on the Mount (Mt 5 -7) is full of extreme statements. Jesus hanging on the Cross is pretty extreme. Are not the Saints' lives full of examples of throwing caution to the wind; examples like caring for plague victims, selling oneself into slavery to rescue captives, and leaving one's country for mission fields? Look at Jesus on the Cross, my brothers and sisters. "See what love the Father has given us (I Jn 3:1). The "measure of love is love without measure."[73]

THE PRAYER OF MY HEART

Lord Jesus Christ,

Son of the living God.

You have gone ahead of us

and become for us the way to heaven.

Help us to open our hearts

to the love the Father has given us.

Let Your Holy Spirit breathe afresh

upon our cold hearts,

so that we might become

Your true disciples,

sons and daughters of Your heavenly Father.

We thank You and praise You

Most Holy Trinity, One God,

for creating and redeeming us

Your hopeful children.

All glory, honor and praise be to You,

Three and One,

Now and forever.

Amen.

Be at peace, all.

I love you and bless you always,

In Jesus, Mary and Joseph,

Pilgrim George

ENDNOTES

71. By adding 29,000 miles walked up until the year 2001, and the 11,000 miles walked in the final thirteen years (between 2001 and 2013) one can arrive at the 40,000 miles given in the title of this book.

72. This same Scripture is found in parallel passages in Luke 18:28-30 and in Mark 10:28-30.

73. See footnote 70.

FORTY-THOUSAND MILES WALKED

(Only walks of over 200 miles are included here, since among hikers world wide, walks under 200 miles do not qualify as long distance walks.)

Year	Destination	Miles
1970-71	Jerusalem	1,400
1981	Midland, Ontario	1,300
1988	Mexico City	2,500
1989	Monterey, California	2,500
1992	Anchorage, Alaska	3,200
1993	Irkutsk, Siberia	2,700
1994	Alma Ata, Kazakhstan	2,100
1995	Cochin, India	3,400
1996	Warsaw, Poland	1,600
1997	Ron, Norway	2,135
1998	Lviv, Ukraine	1,800
1999	Jerusalem, Israel	1,640
2000	Mount Sinai, Egypt	570
2001	Midland, Ontario	1,200
2002	Toronto, Ontario	820
2003	Stockbridge, Massachusetts	1,400
2004	Chicago, Illinois	1,378
2005	British Isles	1,461
2006	Washington, D.C.	991
2007	Auriesville, New York	744
2008	St. Meinrad, Indiana	751
2009	Hanceville, Alabama	669
2010	Santa Fe, New Mexico	528
2011	Scranton, Pennsylvania	435
2012	Montreal, Quebec	370
2013	Carey, Ohio	244

Total miles walked: **40,436**

PHOTOS SINCE 2001

1   Walking south on Route 119 near Connellsville, PA.

2   Resting at picnic grove on Connellsville Road, Uniontown, PA.

3   Sewing patch on robe at St. Kateri Catholic Church in Penns Valley, PA.

4   Praying over a little pilgrim at Mt. St. Macrina, Uniontown, PA.

1   Receiving prayer while wearing "Chains of St. George" Cairo, Egypt.

2   Greeting Archbishop Damianos at St. Catherine Monastery, Sinai, Egypt, December, 2016.

3   Receiving figs from monks of St. Paul Monastery, Eastern Desert, by the Red Sea, Egypt.

1 "In the Silence" - Rock face of Mount Galala beside the cave of St. Anthony near the Red Sea, Egypt.

1   Examining one of the forty three ring binders documenting my whole life.

2   Cutting wood on table saw in workshop.

3   At my pridieu in the icon room.

4   Sandals made from rubber tires in Anchorage in 1993 have 30,000 miles on them by the end of Pilgrimage 2013.

APPENDIX A

A LETTER FROM PARIS

The following letter was written in Paris, in August 1970. The Pilgrim intended it to be sent to his seminary classmates for distribution, but it was never mailed. It is reprinted as it appeared in <u>A Pilgrim Finds the Way.</u>

As one most concerned about "the glory of God and the salvation of men," I am writing to you who have been chosen to be leaders of the People of God. I hope I will not be imposing on your time by merely adding to the flood of words with which you are already daily saturated. I write in the spirit of praising God for His mercy and faithfulness to me.

The theme of these reflections will be my personal search for, and discovery of, PEACE. Beginning several years ago, when my life was mostly in turmoil, I hope that I will be able to trace the basic process and identify the contributing factors that have brought me to this peace. Possibly in this way I will be able to kindle a small light for you.

Three years ago, when I left St. Vincent Seminary with the graduating class of 1967, I did not take the path of ordination to the priesthood and service in parish ministry. After years of seminary training, I found myself not only NOT ready and NOT willing to take up the originally planned ministry, but found myself instead involved in a deep questioning of that ministry as well as of all life. Certain changes had been made throughout the Church in general, and more specifically in the seminary itself, which had led me to a state of basic confusion and uncertainty.

The first 22 years of my life, up to and including my last years in college, I had been formed by all the religious structures available for Christian education as they existed before Vatican Council II – the Mass and Sacraments, a good Catholic home and neighborhood, Catholic grade school and minor seminary. Within this world I had grown up to believe that the most important thing in life was to BE SUBMISSIVE to my superiors who would direct me how to think and act. By following their counsel I would be led to a meaningful and happy life. It was simply a matter of learning what they expected of me and of my carrying out their suggestions. I trusted them and at all times cheerfully obeyed. I was comfortable, well taken care of and happy. Possibilities outside this religious world did not much interest me.

Then with Vatican II and its new perspective of dialogue with the secular world and less rigid control of its faithful, I began to hear a different message. My superiors were now less willing to regulate every detail of my life. I was encouraged to assume more responsibility for my own life. Now I began to believe that the most important thing in life was to think and act on my own. So I eagerly set about exploring new and diverse ideas, trying out new forms of behavior, questioning old forms and suggesting new ones.

As I became more and more involved in these new trends, I began to realize just how much I had been taking my life for granted up to that time, especially my life of faith. It had been a given: it was never questioned, challenged, or threatened in any serious way. Nor did it much depend upon my own personal effort. It was just there: always had been and always would be as far as I knew.

Now, however, in an effort to better understand this faith as well as to be better able eventually to communicate it to others, I began to think and raise questions about it. I was brought up against other possibilities, other ways of thinking, other ways of living. At the same time as my thinking was changing, there were changes being made in various other forms of Christian life. New patterns of thinking, speaking and acting all combined to give the Christian in general, and the seminarian in particular, a new image.

Of course throughout all these changes, it was said again and again that the *substance* of the faith was remaining the same: that just its "forms" were changing. But as time went on, I more and more began to get the feeling that we really were going beyond just the forms and were making basic changes in our identity. I, for one, no longer felt like the person I used to be. As I looked around at my fellow Christians, they no longer looked or acted or thought as they had before. If we had changed our thinking as well as our acting, how could we claim to be the same as before?

In general, it seemed like we no longer considered ourselves "a pilgrim people, passing through a vale of tears, primarily on our way to another land." You might say we were "hanging up our rough pilgrim garb" and "putting on the stylish clothes of the new city." We were learning their language, customs and manner of living. It was as though we had arrived at the land to which we as a people had been journeying for so long and now our primary goal was to "settle down," and build comfortable homes here and become citizens of this new city.

During my last years in the seminary, I eagerly participated in all of these changes, for I was finding the old unattractive, embarrassingly out-of-date, and lacking in meaning. The new looked much more attractive, exciting and relevant. And as long as I remained within the secure world of ideas and the academic community, this questioning and theorizing was interesting, challenging and fun. When, however, the time came for me to undertake the serious work of leading the people of God, I found I was not ready for such responsibility.

For I was still out exploring, searching and testing the new world that had been opened up to me, and I had not yet settled this question of our identity. Had we changed that much or hadn't we? If we had changed our purpose and goal as a people, then my main task as leader would be to help the people adjust to the new life of the city by getting them to think and act on their own and encouraging them to get involved in the world around them. But this was not a significant enough task in my mind. Besides, I was not that well equipped to do this and the "new city" was itself accomplishing this task much more efficiently and rapidly than I could ever hope to as a priest.

But if we had not changed our identity, then my job would be the same as that of priests in all ages past - to lead the People of God on their pilgrimage to another life beyond their present one in the city of man. However, I was unwilling to assume this task, for I did not feel I had a strong enough awareness of that "other life." I did not have a sufficient "sense of direction" myself to attempt to lead a whole people.

One would have thought that after all my seminary training that I would have had an excellent "sense of direction." With my study of theology I should have been able to give a very detailed account of where we as a people came from and where we were going. And in words, I could. But this was not a sufficient knowledge for me. I needed to KNOW it in a much deeper way - with my whole heart and body, as well as with my mind. I had to experience it in a TOTAL, LIVING WAY.

And I was unwilling to go into the pastoral ministry without this deeper sense of identity, for though I did not see it too clearly then, I really wanted to make a PERMANENT commitment and to give myself COMPLETELY. But I had to have a sufficiently clear idea of the goal before I would give my life to working on a project, and if it were going to be a "life-long commitment" this goal must be UNCHANGEABLE and beyond the reach of doubt. So far nothing in my life met these requirements, for I had opened up everything first to questioning and eventually to doubt.

Nor would I take the normal path of settling for a TEMPORARY commitment to limited and changing goals. I would not go the way of trying out different roles, within the ecclesiastical society or the secular society, with the idea that in time I would come to a clearer sense of this identity. These roles assumed certain principles as true and expected certain patterns of behavior. They were not open to the kind of questioning I was doing, for I was striking at the very root of all human activity. To throw myself into some "work" would mean I would either have to put aside my search, or live with the contradiction of acting as though I no longer doubted, while continuing to internally doubt.

Neither alternative was acceptable to me. My search was my primary goal and working in the "straight" way would too seriously cramp my style. My style would be to set out on my own, staying loose and unattached, looking, observing and testing from a position independent of the structures whose validity I questioned and whose meaning I sought. This would mean "dropping out" of all the major institutions of present-day society as far as this was possible.

Granted, this was a rather drastic step, and those very close to me who did not have the same need to assure themselves of the solidity of the foundation of their lives, were anxious and fearful for me. For they sensed, and accurately so, that by cutting myself off from the supporting structures of society, I was going into a "wilderness," as it were, and exposing myself to exceedingly great dangers. But as one driven by some powerful force, I was determined to explore these deeper regions of the presumed, forgotten and unknown, in spite of its many risks.

My search first took me west to California, which still seemed to be a frontier where everything "newest" was happening first. Once there, I was soon attracted to a group of "dropouts" and seekers, who were called hippies. These people seemed to be living witnesses of many of the new ideas of love, freedom, authenticity, creativity, etc., which had come to me from my reading and thinking. They too, were looking for new meanings, questioning and refusing to accept the roles handed them by their parents' societies, and at times were even raising questions about the ultimate meaning of life.

Eventually, however, I came to see that most of them were satisfied that the meaning of life lay in enjoying oneself, in "turning on," and that there was no more distant or ultimate goal in life than that. This, however, could not be the ultimate solid basis of the identity I sought. For the pleasures they offered were too temporary and fragile, even in the intensity and variety of forms they found possible in today's society.

So I began hitchhiking from place to place on my own, looking, observing, testing. But no person, no place, no project, was strong enough to elicit my total dedication. All the numberless roles and jobs to which other men dedicated themselves and which satisfied their search for meaning in life, failed to satisfy me. I wanted to know more. I sought to go deeper. I had an uncommonly strong desire to prove to myself that there was an ultimate solid basis underlying all these other various meanings.

Everyone, to my mind, was acting as though an ultimate basis did exist - even the "modern man" who denied an ultimate future and admitted only temporary goals - for all continued to find it worthwhile to support life by their daily activities. Few, however, ever seemed to give this ultimate basis much thought. Most people seemed to operate best on short range goals. But for me, to find it worth living for even a short range future, implied there was an ultimately worthwhile future. I could not find, however, even a single person who could talk to me convincingly about an ultimate future. Most of all, what I sought was someone whose LIFESTYLE was a witness to a CONSTANT AWARENESS of this ultimate and unchanging reality.

Unable to find such, I proceeded to attempt to live completely in the present: to do what those modern men claimed to be doing but actually denied by their living for even a limited future–to live as though all were relative, temporary and passing. In practical terms this meant that I make no plans, set no goals and just let happen what may. I refused to take on any responsibilities or obligations. I just did what was necessary to basically stay alive, and my only reason for doing this was to continue my search.

During this period of my life, many looked upon me as a symbol of total freedom. They envied my not having any ties, responsibilities, and worries like those with which they felt themselves burdened. But in a way, I envied their ability to be satisfied that life did have an ultimate basis to the extent that they were able to take on tasks which supported life. But I had a burden too. I had the final responsibility of searching out what others either accepted on an intuition, on the authority of others, or just plain took for granted: namely, the solid and enduring basis which ultimately made life worth living.

So I continued alone in my search. I refused to dedicate myself to building the earth if I could not find a more solid and permanent goal than either pleasure or work. If this were all that there was to life, I did not find it worth my effort. In Chardinian [sic] terms, I was threatening "to call a strike (to stop work) in the noosphere."

And then in the Summer of 1968, while camping alone in the Rocky Mountains of Colorado, with nothing on my mind and little to occupy my body, surrounded by rivers and mountains, sun and sky, moon and stars, wind and clouds, trees and grass, birds and wild animals, I caught a glimpse of God again in the world and experienced an awareness of His relationship with me. Here, where the hand of man had scarcely touched, I desired to thank someone for such a beautiful masterpiece. And since no single man and no group of men could take the credit, there was no one else to turn to but the Father and Creator of all life.

Here among all these natural elements which so faithfully and harmoniously lived the life given to them, I became very aware of the life given to me. The first question and answer of the Baltimore Catechism hit me with all its concise truthfulness: Who made me? God made me. Why, that's where I came from! It was that simple. In such a context it was not a catechism lesson to memorize, an abstract thesis to analyze, or a hard truth to preach. It was just a clear statement of what was. And how wonderful that it should be so. The light of this first truth in its simple grandeur was dazzling.

This then was the deep solid bedrock of all reality. This was that ULTIMATE basis which I had so desperately been seeking. Knowing the Father to be the origin of my life, I also knew Him to be the goal and end of my life - the second question and answer of the Catechism. Here was that which remained constant from the beginning to the end of my life and to which I could attach all the changing realities of daily existence. Here was the One to whom I could make a total and permanent commitment of my life without fear of change or deception.

Having discovered a solid basis upon which I could build my life, I felt I was now able to emerge from the wilderness and return to the societies which I had left. For I now knew that my life did not really depend upon the structures of these societies for its ultimate meaning. These structures were secondary, temporary supports to man's life on earth. They could not ultimately account for its origin, nor were they the final goal of life, as I had once feared. Realizing this, I felt I was now ready to assume a part in the society of man and give witness to my life as a Christian.

Still having the order of Diaconate, I decided to attempt once again to live this in some official way. I thought that possibly here I would be able to put together again, now around this new awareness of my relationship to God, all the pieces of my Christian faith. Now that I knew "union with God" to be the ultimate goal of my commitment and all other activities and forms of service to be secondary, I thought I would be able to work out a form of witness and service consonant with both the old and new thinking and structures of the church.

Such, however, was not to be the case. For one thing the pastoral ministry expected busy, active forms of service and I was still mainly listening to the Word of God speaking in His Scriptures and through His people. Also I did not yet have a strong enough awareness of Christ as being the way to the Father and needed to grow closer to Him before I was ready to speak His word to others. The hierarchy grew impatient with my silence and slowness, so I had to withdraw for the moment from the pastoral division of the Church.

I thought I should continue my listening to the Word of God from some small corner of the "secular society" and from there possibly I could build an appropriate form of witness to God's holiness. So I chose an apartment in Uptown Pittsburgh, Pennsylvania, and got a part-time job as an orderly in a nearby hospital. I also set up a regular prayer schedule and spent time each day visiting with the people living in the neighborhood.

But after seven months, nothing concrete had developed out of this. I was close now to the man-made world of the city with its noise and air pollution, brick and asphalt, crowded and impersonal surroundings, but I still did not have a strong enough sense of my Christian identity to undertake with confidence what I could label as authentic action in the inner city. I still lacked a vital awareness of the Biblical faith and so I was still unwilling to assume more than a "part- time" responsibility for working in the city of man.

Finding myself, however, still determined to pursue this "Christian thing" until it rendered up its meaning, and unable to come to a satisfactory experience of it through reading and study, through the power of my imagination or with all the ecclesiastical and secular institutions at my disposal, I conceived yet another effort. This time I would attempt a physical relocation of myself into the land of Israel - where our faith had been born and was nurtured for centuries. It would be a kind of "physical realignment," a "bodily configuration," a "total environmental experience": the kind of thing the Church tried to give its members through symbols, liturgies and rituals (though all of these in their present forms had failed to speak to me).

And since I desired this to be a total experience, this relocation must not take place by a quick easy flight on a jet plane. It must be a real JOURNEY: one which cost me much effort: one which involved every resource of mind and heart and body. I would go on foot and by boat. I would be as dependent upon my immediate environment as possible so that I could be close to the source of each action which supported my journey - the goodwill of people who gave me rides, food, housing, etc.

Once I got to Spain I also came to see the importance of WALKING rather than taking rides and of SLEEPING OUTSIDE rather than taking rooms. Walking gave me an experience of space and time similar to that of all men up to the present: that is, measuring them in terms of one's own bodily capacities. Sleeping outside gave me a deeper sense of the earth and the natural forces of the environment. Living with the farmers and shepherds of Spain I came to realize better how they felt the rhythm of life and how they could believe that all depended upon an eternal law which guided the movements of the heavens and earth. With such an experience of life subject to powers beyond the creation and control of man, it was a much shorter step to belief in, and prayer to, the Lord of the universe.

Now, too, as never before, the imagery of the Psalms came alive as I daily experienced the warmth and heat of the sun, the cool and damp of the night, the vastness and infinity of the stars, the majesty of the clouds and snow-capped mountains, the refreshment of cool springwater, good fresh bread, and pure natural wine. With this new awareness of the heavens and earth, I came to a new appreciation of the God who made the heavens and the earth.

I came also to understand better the primitive distinction between good and evil. Living close to the earth and the forces of nature, things fell much more easily into one of two categories - yes or no - than when living in a city where basic survival is taken for granted and it is possible to make all kinds of fine distinctions. In a country environment, and even more in a wilderness, things are judged as either supporting life or threatening to life. When meeting another person, an immediate judgment must be made: friend or enemy. There is much less possibility of just ignoring each other and passing on, as there is in a city. Man is in a life and death contest with forces beyond his control. He needs to have trustworthy friends and has to know his enemies.

This kind of experience also made me much more appreciative of my own life. It was no longer so easy to take it for granted. It required effort and often depended totally on the goodwill of one or two people who were immediately and physically present to me. I understood better the Biblical sense of supernatural powers of good and evil and the psalmist's feelings of helplessness and cries for divine assistance. If one takes away all the life-supporting structures of the city of man, he comes face to face with some pretty terrifying, as well as awe-inspiring, powers of life.

In this context I slowly pondered the words of the evangelists, and as I did so, they, too, became more and more real. As I came close to physically living in the kind of world they and Christ knew, their witness to His life and teachings no longer seemed so distant and strange. All the words and pictures that had been given to me over the years in an attempt to help me understand His message, failed to even come close to re-creating the reality as I now understood it. It was really very simple: too simple, perhaps, for one born and raised in the complicated world of modern man.

But this is the way I have been led back, first to a vital experience of the Father as the source and origin of all life and then to Christ as the way back to the Father. This has been my passage from uncertainty, confusion and ignorance, to certainty, peace and understanding. Nothing new was really added: it was just that what was there was arranged in its proper order and enlightened by the grace of truth. This, in turn, has led me to dedicate my life in a new way to growing closer to Christ every moment of my day through the mediation of His Word in all its sacramental forms.

As a result of this experience, my perspective has now become radically eschatological. It is only with this perspective that I have finally been able to find something that gives me as a Christian, an identity distinct from that of a citizen of the new city. I am convinced that only to the extent that one looks beyond the goals and projects of the city of man, and places his hopes in the one Lord and God of the universe who sent His only Son to transform this city and lead it back to the Father, can one authentically claim to be Christian. That is, we still are a pilgrim people, because our primary goal does lie beyond this present city.

In day-to-day living, of course, most Christians are intimately involved with building this new city. Their lives may not appear much different from those of the citizens of the city of man and there may even be a great similarity of thinking and reasoning between the two. But there must be a radical difference of perspective. Insofar as one dedicates himself completely to the building of this city, whether it be to his work, his family or his community, to that extent does he cease to be a full Christian. And if his work in this city becomes of ultimate importance, he has ceased to serve God at all and has chosen to serve "mammon."

I know this is a hard saying for those who have been shaped by the modern world and who have little experience of going very deeply into remote origins or carefully pondering long term implications—of ultimate questions—and whose lives are filled with a seemingly infinite variety of changing realities. To them such an eschatological perspective will look like a self-centered cop-out from society and a failure to take seriously the commandment to love our neighbor and cooperate in the building of the earth.

But what I am saying is that I found the incarnational perspective led me to limit my vision to the point where I was no longer able to see beyond the second commandment and came to forget there ever was a first commandment. Thus my service-to-man theology depended more on a lack of awareness of the holiness of God, than on a dedication to that holiness. In my eagerness to think of all men as belonging to the People of God, I forgot I was supposed to lead them to a deeper appreciation of God and not just leave them where they were.

Maybe others have been able to find God mainly by considering His closeness to man and man's work in the new city. But I was not. All I saw there was man and the objects of his creation. My vision stopped at the people, places and events themselves. It seemed that the city of man was the origin of life, its total support and final goal. It was not a symbol of another reality to me. I failed to discern the presence of God shining through it.

It has only been with an awareness of God's distance from and inability to be contained by man and man's work in the new city, that I have been able to come to an awareness of Him. From this perspective, man's projects and activities look tiny and insignificant, temporary and passing, superficial and vain. Only with an experience of God's otherness did I come to know what is meant by sacrifice, detachment, penance, sin, judgment, and death. In the process, erotic pleasure has been replaced by reverential love: wild excitement by a tranquil joy; surface calm by a deep inner peace; and superficial brotherhood by a union of hearts. I have gone from knowing, depending upon and fearing man and the structures of his civilization, to knowing, depending upon and fearing only God.

Thus I have become determined to make union with God the all-consuming goal of each moment of my life. So far I depend mainly upon meditation on His Word in the Scriptures to aid this union. Possibly some day I will receive a call to leave this wilderness and come back to the city to live some kind of communal witness to the transcendence of God or to put into practice my belief that only with an eschatological perspective can one engage in incarnational activity. For now I will continue to meditate upon the Word of God in the desert—keeping alive, at least in my own heart, this awareness of His holiness.

To those of you who may experience a need to go this far out into the desert, I send you these words as some reassurance for your darkest and most bleak moments. To all of you I send back this witness to God's continuing goodness and mercy to those who seek Him with all their strength of mind and body. I trust all of you will continue to labor for Christ, always seeking to be ever more faithful to His Word, remembering that He said not a dot of the law shall be changed or unfulfilled, and that anyone who teaches any differently will be called least in the Kingdom of heaven. Amen.

APPENDIX B

POEMS AND PRAYERS

The Yugoslav Coast
by Pilgrim George
[Easter, 1996]

the setting sun
      skipping sunbeams
            across the mirrored sea

rocky slopes
      leaching minerals
            from age old hills

crevice clinging grasses
      gathering moisture
            from the morning mists

unattended stone walls
      tumbling
            into abandoned pasturage

mountain goats
      climbing deftly
            nibbling tufts of greenery

wild hyacinths
　　　lifting purple clusters
　　　　　proclaiming life

sea gulls airborne
　　　on unseen currents
　　　　　free of earth's bonds

elaborate outdoor spits
　　　grilling meat
　　　　　for hungry appetites

ocean-going ships
　　　silently plying
　　　　　the inner channel

gathered olive branches
　　　prepared for the blessing
　　　　　the Sunday before Easter

food baskets filled
　　　the fast is over
　　　　　Christ is risen–Alleluia!

The Punjab in July

by Pilgrim George

[India, 1995]

Sun-baked streets; Temples and Prayer Houses;
Dirt and mud; Hindu and Sikh;
Open drains; Pilgrims and devotees;
Road side vendors. Hospitality and prayer.

Ox carts and motorbikes; Fields of wheat;
Bicycles and buffaloes; Rice-paddies and corn;
Pungent odors; Hand pumps and sweet water;
Ripening fruit and donkey dung. A pilgrim's delight.

Loaded lorries; Summer in the Punjab;
Blaring horns; Fans and flies;
Crowded buses; Life in the open;
Jam-packed vans. Fruitful and free.

Bearded men wearing turbans;
Schoolchildren in full uniforms;
Women in flowing robes;
Balancing heavy loads.

Folded hands;
Bowing heads;
"May I be
Of any service to you?"

A cup of water;
Then hot sweet tea;
Fresh baked chapati;
Made on a griddle.

Houses small;
Shoes off;
Blanket on the floor;
Sit cross-legged to eat.

India (as Seen Through the Eyes of a Western Observer)
by Pilgrim George
[Kerala State, India; October 1995]

INDIA – where animals, men, and machines mix
in unorganized, scarcely rigid forms of association.

INDIA–Where life is uncluttered by gadgets
and the electricity can go off for hours or days
without interrupting the flow of life.

INDIA–where animals have the right of way on the road,
and traffic respectfully proceeds around them.

INDIA–where the smell of decaying animals and human excrement
alternate with whiffs of fragrant burning incense.

INDIA–where during the daylight hours of summer,
man competes with flies for the goods of the earth.

INDIA–where vehicles drive on the left,
and the drivers of trucks and buses use their horns liberally.

INDIA–where dimmer lights are called "dippers"
and replacement parts are called "spares."

INDIA–where truck drivers slide open or take off their doors while riding
for more air or to get a better view.

INDIA–where safety is not a consideration
and helmets are rarely seen on cyclists.

INDIA–where luggage racks on top of buses
are as much for people as they are for baggage.

INDIA–where bicycles are peddled so slowly they flop from side to side,
and they are pushed up the slightest grade.

INDIA–where usually there are no doors or windows in buildings–
just open spaces to let in and out
air, light, people, animals, birds, and insects.

INDIA–where water is drawn from hand pumps
and meals are cooked on open fires.

INDIA–where tea is made with milk, not water
and cows are not butchered for food.

INDIA–where prepackaged foods are a rarity,
and Western ways are embraced by few.

INDIA–where the Westernized life of Asians portrayed on TV commercials,
scarcely resembles the actual life of the masses.

INDIA–where women carry loads on their heads
and men can sit all day and watch their animals graze.

INDIA–Where bare feet and thongs
are more popular than shoes and socks.

INDIA–where men wear their shirttails out
rather than tucked in.

INDIA–where bows replace handshakes
and smiles and hugs are rare.

INDIA–where the polite forms "Excuse me" or Hello, how are you?"
when entering one's presence are seldom heard.

INDIA–where staring is not considered impolite,
and childlike curiosity is not lost with age.

INDIA–where men and women keep segregated
at home, on the bus, and in the church.

INDIA–where a boy and girl or a man and woman
are never seen in public holding hands,
but two boys or two men are often so seen.

INDIA–where parents select the spouses for their children
and a large dowry is required of the bride.

INDIA–where the medium of exchange is the rupee,
and thirty of them make a dollar.

INDIA–where temples and shrines dot the landscape,
and Hinduism is part of the national heritage.

INDIA–the land
of free-flowing lifestyles
of little exertion
and of deep despair.
INDIA–It's not "tucked in."
INDIA–God's children wandering in darkness.

St. Thomas, pray for us.
St. Francis Xavier, pray for us.
Blessed Mother of God, hear our prayer.

The Breastplate of St. Patrick
(said every morning upon waking)

I arise TODAY,
through a mighty strength;
through the invocation of the Holy Trinity;
through a belief in the Threeness,
through a confession of the Oneness
of the Creator of creation.

I arise today,
through the strength of Christ's Birth and His Baptism;
through the strength of His Crucifixion and Burial;
through the strength of His Resurrection and Ascension;
through the strength of His Descent for the Judgment of Doom.

I arise today,
in the strength of the love of Cherubim;
in obedience of Angels;
in the service of Archangels;
in the hope of the Resurrection to meet with reward;
in the prayers of Patriarchs;
in the prediction of Prophets;
in the preaching of Apostles;
in the faith of Confessors;
in the innocence of Holy Virgins;
in the deeds of Righteous Men.

I arise today,
through the
strength of Heaven;
light of the Sun;
radiance of the Moon,
splendor of Fire,
speed of Lightning;

swiftness of the Wind;
depth of the Sea;
stability of the Earth;
firmness of Rock.

I arise today,
through
God's strength to pilot me;
God's might to uphold me;
God's wisdom to guide me;
God's eye to look before me;
Gods' ear to hear me;
God's word to speak for me;
God's hand to guard me;
God's way to lay before me;
God's shield to protect me;
God's hosts to secure me:
against the snares of devils;
against the temptation of vices;
against the inclinations of nature;
against everyone who desires me ill;
afar and a-near;
alone and in a multitude.

I summon today all these powers:
Angels;
Saints;
The Holy Family;
The Three Divine Persons,
between me and these evils:
against every cruel and merciless power
that may oppose my body and my soul.
against the incantations of false prophets;
against the black laws of pagandom;
against the false laws of heretics;

against the craft of idolatry;
against the spells of witches;
against every knowledge that endangers
man's body and soul.

Christ, shield me today,
against poison;
against burning;
against drowning;
against wounding;
so that reward may come to me in abundance.

Christ with me;
Christ before me;
Christ behind me;
Christ in me;
Christ beneath me;
Christ above me;
Christ on my right;
Christ on my left;
Christ where I lie;
Christ where I sit;
Christ where I arise;
Christ in the heart of every man who thinks of me;
Christ in the mouth of every man who speaks of me;
Christ in every eye that sees me;
Christ in every ear that hears me.

I arise today,
through a mighty strength;
through the invocation of the Holy Trinity;
through a belief in the Threeness;
through a confession of the Oneness
of the Creator of creation.

Salvation is of the Lord;
Salvation is of the Lord;
Salvation is of Christ.

May Thy salvation, O Lord,
be ever with us.

St. Patrick,
Pray for us.

SELECTED BIBLIOGRAPHY

Ciszek, Walter J.,S.J. *He Leadeth Me: An Extraordinary Testament of Faith*. New York: Image Books, 1975.

_____. *With God in America: The Spiritual Legacy of an Unlikely Jesuit*. Chicago: Loyola Press, 2016.

Ciszek, Walter J., S.J., and Daniel L. Flaherty, S.J. *With God in Russia*. New York: McGraw-Hill, 1964.

De Hueck Doherty, Catherine. *Poustinia: Christian Spirituality of the East for Western Man*. Notre Dame, Indiana: Ave Maria Press, 1975.

_____. *Sobornost: Eastern Unity of Mind and Heart for Western Man*. Notre Dame, Indiana: Ave Maria Press, 1977.

_____. *Strannik: The Call to Pilgrimage for Western Man*. Notre Dame, Indiana: Ave Maria Press, 1978.

_____. *Urodovoi: Fools for God*. New York: Crossroad, 1983.

De la Gorce, Agnes. *St. Benedict Joseph Labre*. Translated by Rosemary Sheed. New York: Sheed and Ward, 1952.

The Philokalia: On Prayer of the Heart. Translated by E. Kadloubovsky and G. E. H. Palmer. London: Faber and Faber, 1951.

The Way of the Pilgrim and the Pilgrim Continues His Way. Translated by R. M. French. New York: Crossroad, 1965.

Thomas a Kempis. *My Imitation of Christ*. New York: Confraternity of the Precious Blood, 1954.

Walter, George Florian. *A Pilgrim Finds the Way*. Pittsburgh: Typecraft Press, 1988.

WA